SHORT & SKINNY

Little, Brown and Company
Hachette Book Group
1290 Avenue of the Americas, New York, NY 10104
Visit us at LBYR.com

First Edition: October 2018

Little, Brown and Company is a division of Hachette Book Group, Inc.
The Little, Brown name and logo are trademarks of Hachette Book Group, Inc.

ISBNs: 978-0-316-44049-3 (hardcover), 978-0-316-44051-6 (pbk.), 978-0-316-
56317-8 (ebook), 978-0-316-44050-9 (ebook), 978-0-316-56351-2 (ebook)

Printed in China

APS

10 9 8 7 6 5 4 3 2 1

SHORT & SKINNY

MARK TATULLI

LB

Little, Brown and Company
New York   Boston

Memorial Jr. High School
Newspaper Club, 1977

Me,
staff cartoonist

TO MY BROTHER, DEAN, SISTER, TERRI, FATHER,
MOTHER, AND TO MY FRIENDS AND FAMILY WHO
SHARED THIS TIME—I MAY NOT HAVE GOTTEN
IT ALL PERFECTLY RIGHT, BUT THANK YOU
FOR YOUR PART IN SHAPING ME.

TO MY TEACHERS MR. MATTA, MRS. CHARVAT,
MR. FISHER, MR. EDGAR, MRS. MASTERS,
MR. GILLIS, MR. BASNER, MRS. BRUMFIELD,
MR. DRESH, AND MRS. DENSLER...WHO INSPIRED
ME AND ALWAYS ENCOURAGED MY WEIRDNESS.

AND OF COURSE, THE WONDERFUL FOX THEATRE
AND SUPER 130 DRIVE-IN.

CHAPTER 1

may 1977

A SUMMER PLAN

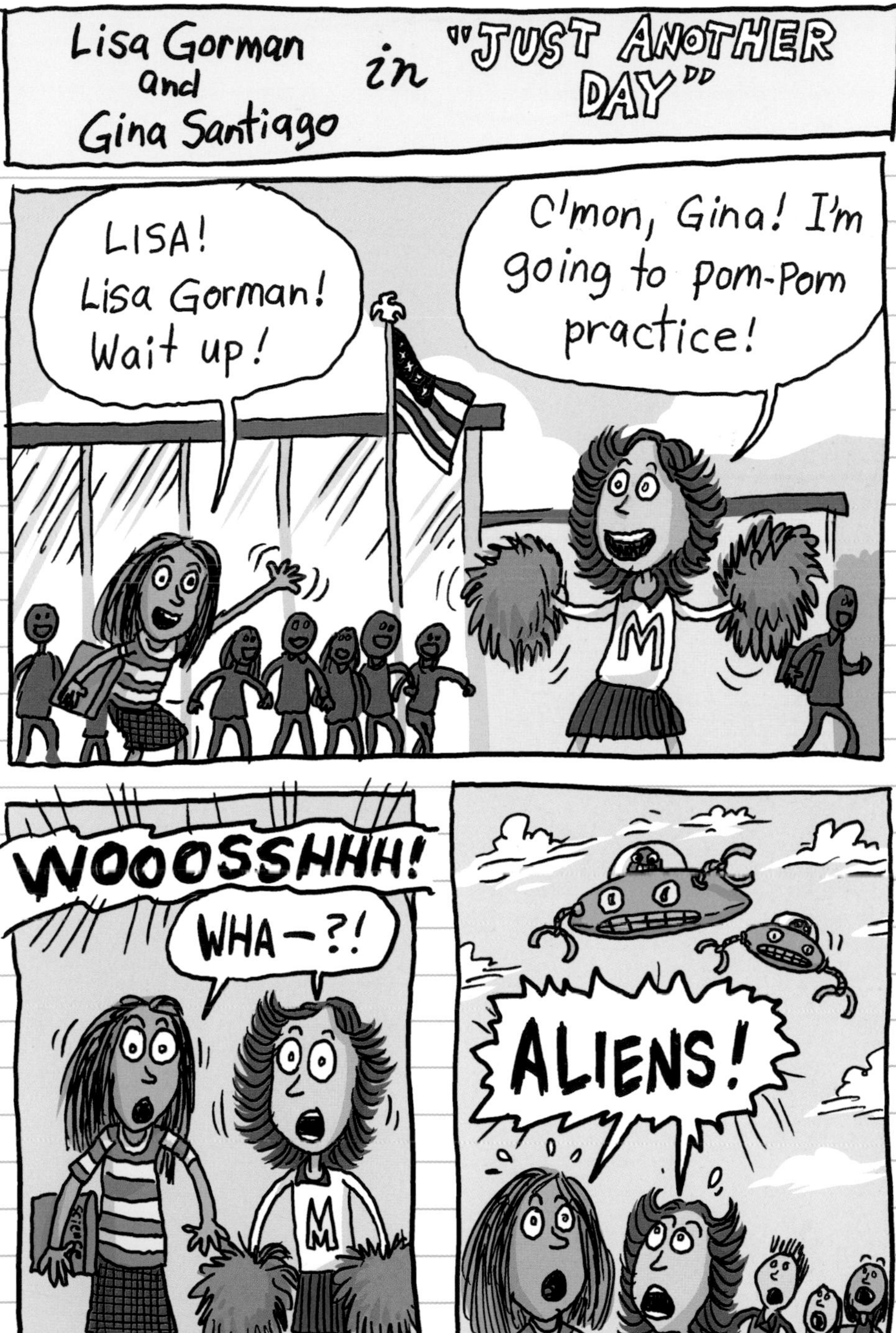
Lisa Gorman
and
Gina Santiago
in
"JUST ANOTHER DAY"
LISA! Lisa Gorman! Wait up!
C'mon, Gina! I'm going to pom-pom practice!
WOOOSSHHH!
WHA—?!
ALIENS!

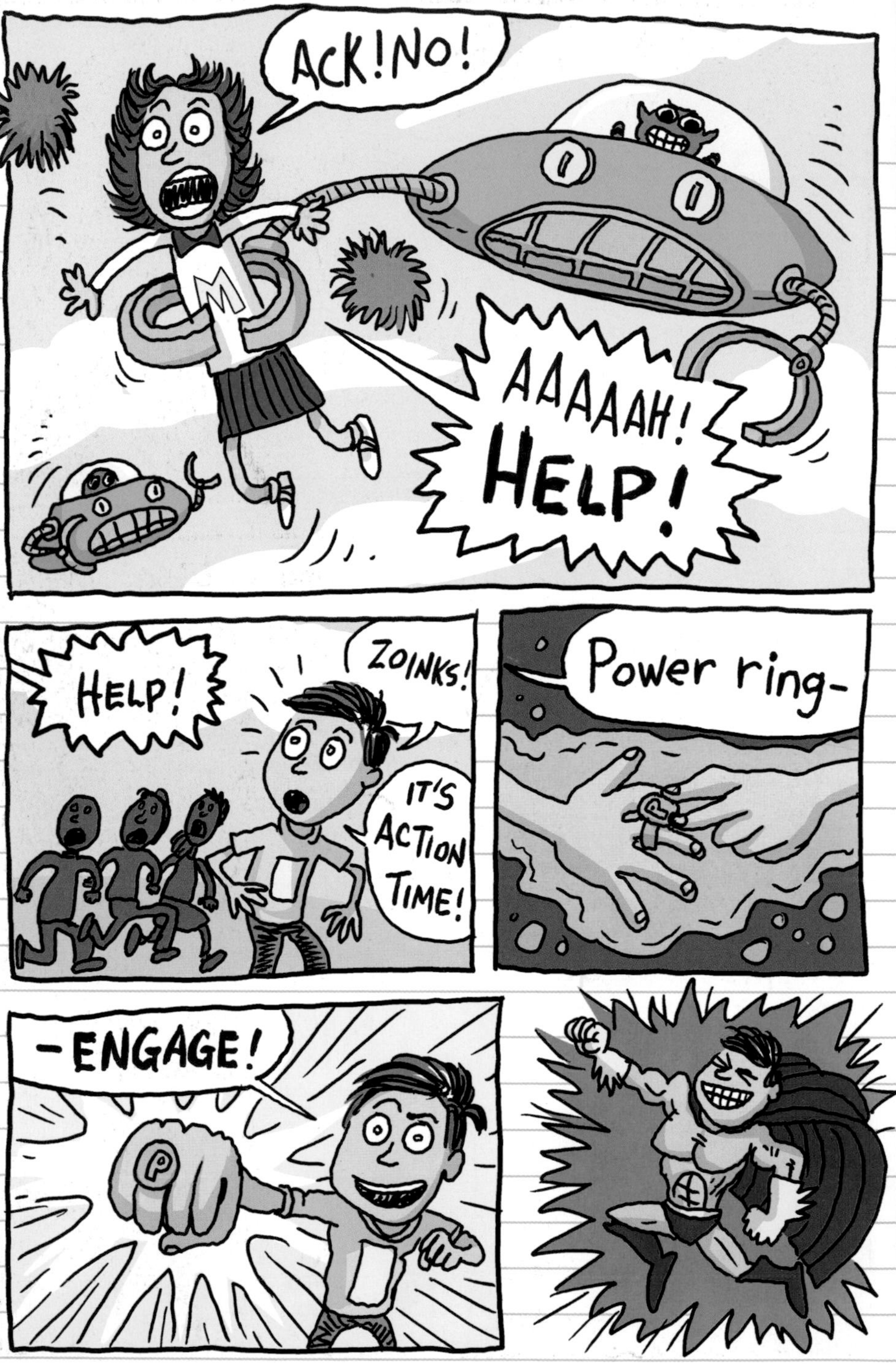
ACK! NO!
AAAAAH! HELP!
HELP!
ZOINKS!
IT'S ACTION TIME!
Power ring-
-ENGAGE!

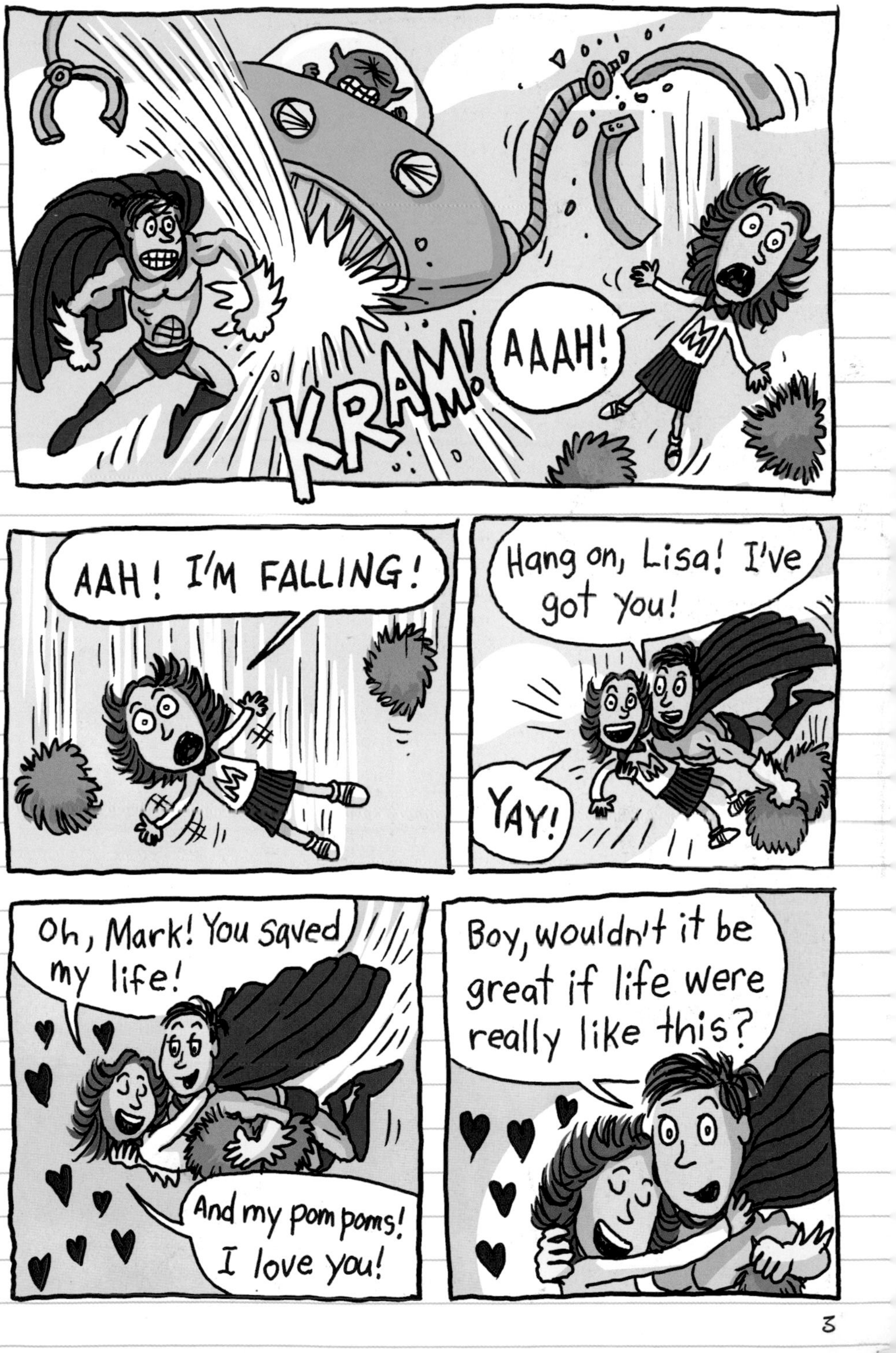
KRAM!
AAAH!
AAH! I'M FALLING!
Hang on, Lisa! I've got you!
YAY!
Oh, Mark! You saved my life!
And my pom poms! I love you!
Boy, wouldn't it be great if life were really like this?

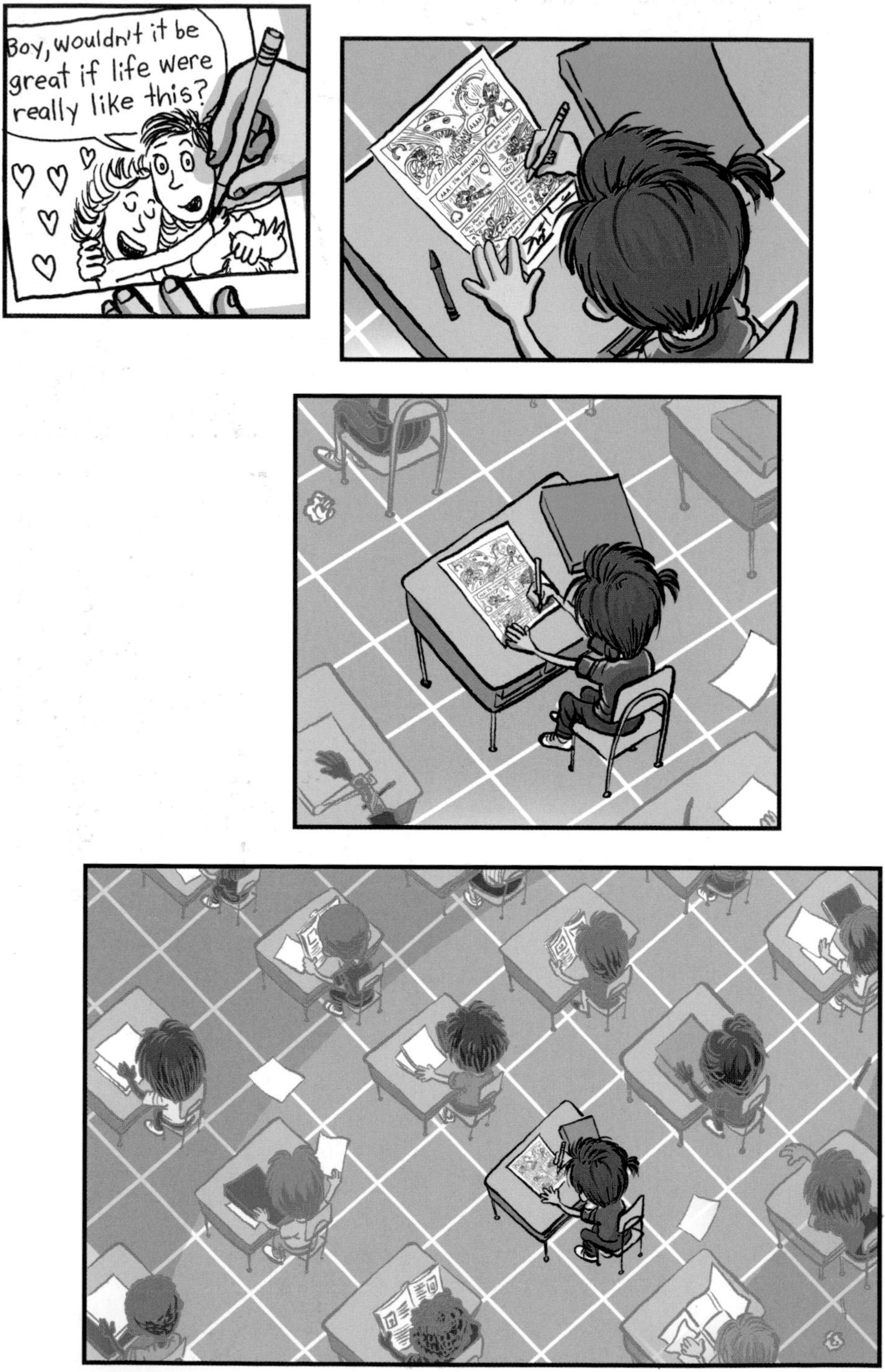
Boy, wouldn't it be great if life were really like this?

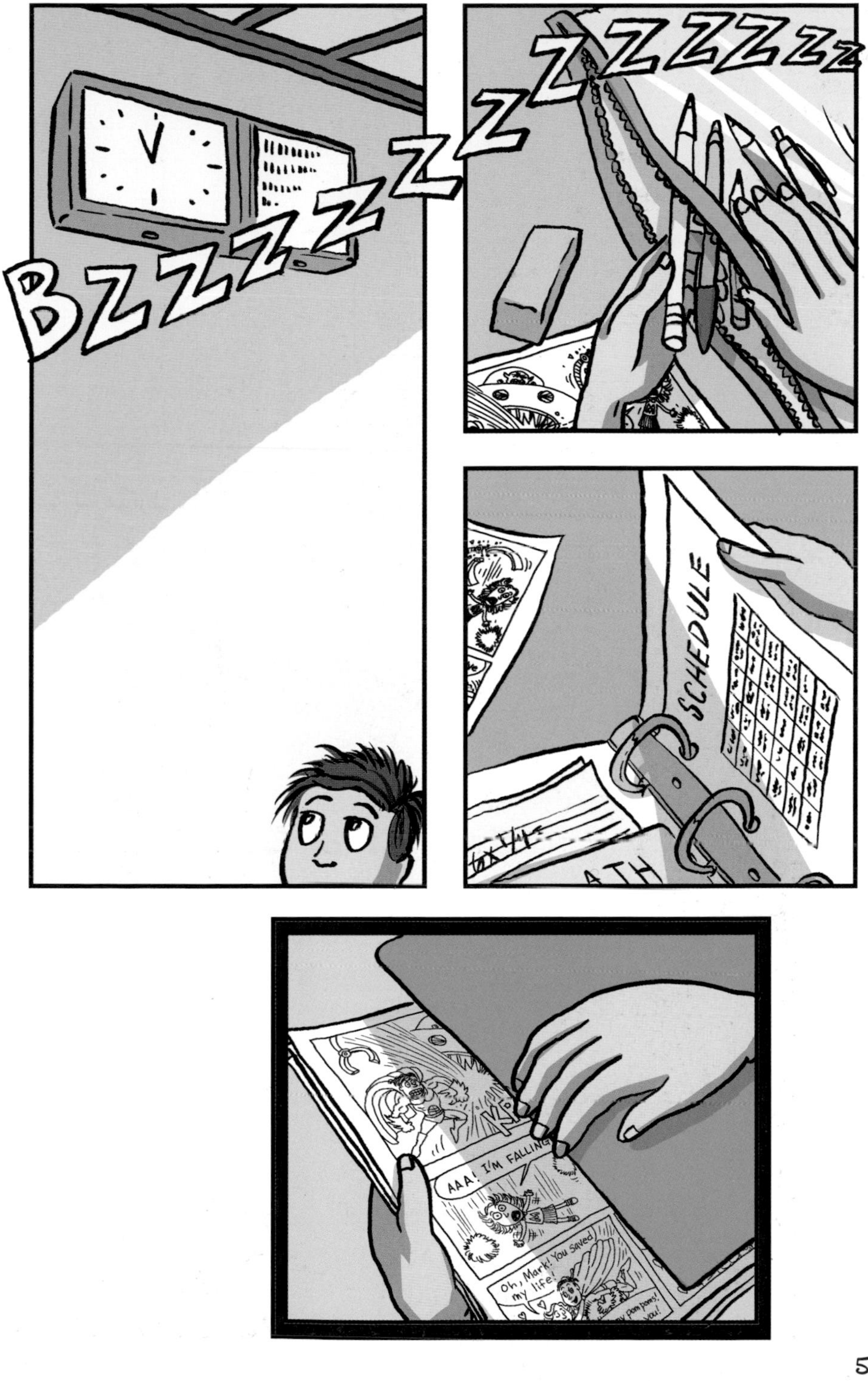
BZZZZZZZZZZZZZZZ
SCHEDULE
AAA! I'M FALLING
Oh, Mark! You saved my life!

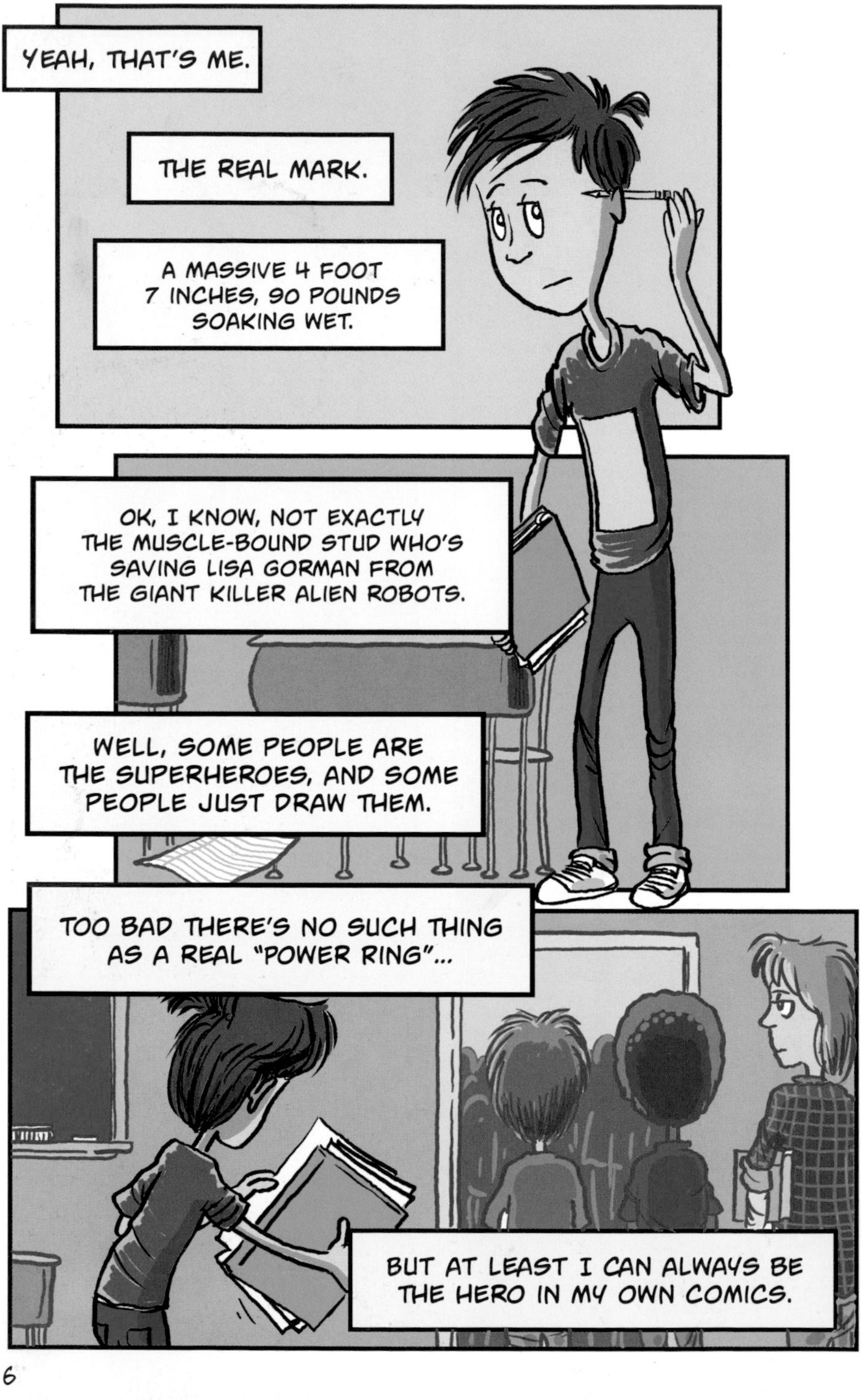
YEAH, THAT'S ME.
THE REAL MARK.
A MASSIVE 4 FOOT 7 INCHES, 90 POUNDS SOAKING WET.
OK, I KNOW, NOT EXACTLY THE MUSCLE-BOUND STUD WHO'S SAVING LISA GORMAN FROM THE GIANT KILLER ALIEN ROBOTS.
WELL, SOME PEOPLE ARE THE SUPERHEROES, AND SOME PEOPLE JUST DRAW THEM.
TOO BAD THERE'S NO SUCH THING AS A REAL "POWER RING"...
BUT AT LEAST I CAN ALWAYS BE THE HERO IN MY OWN COMICS.

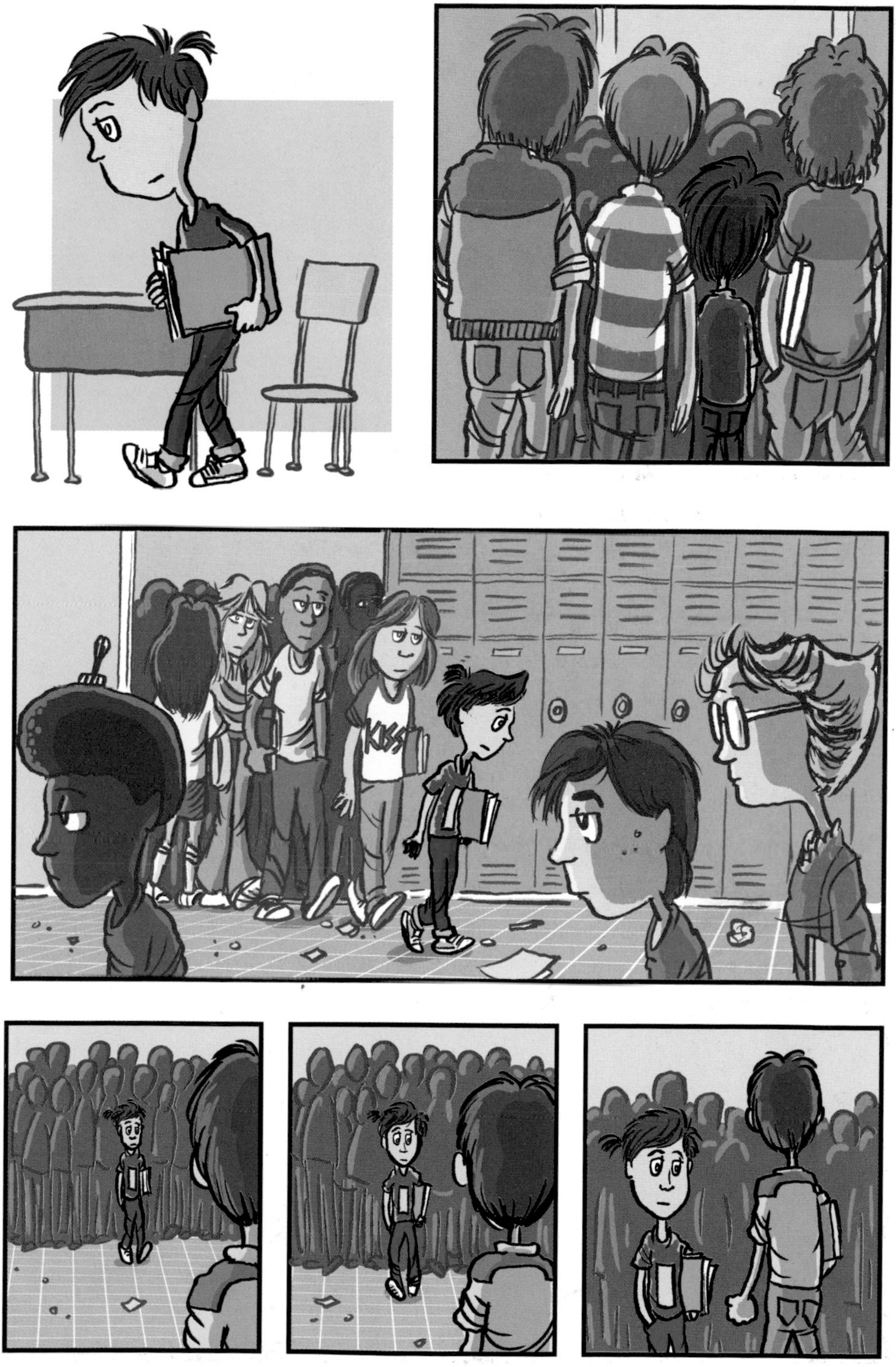
KISS

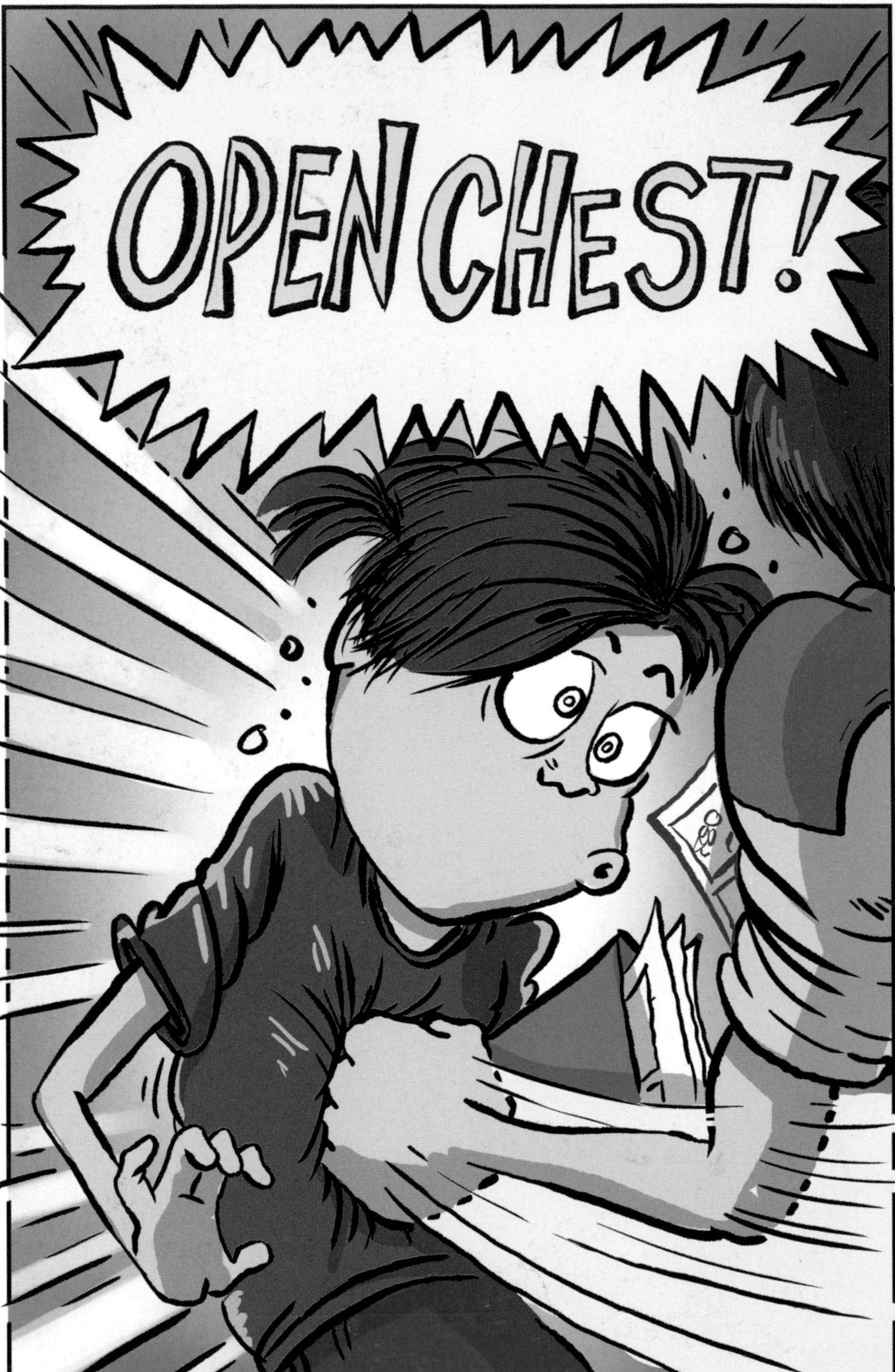
OPEN CHEST!

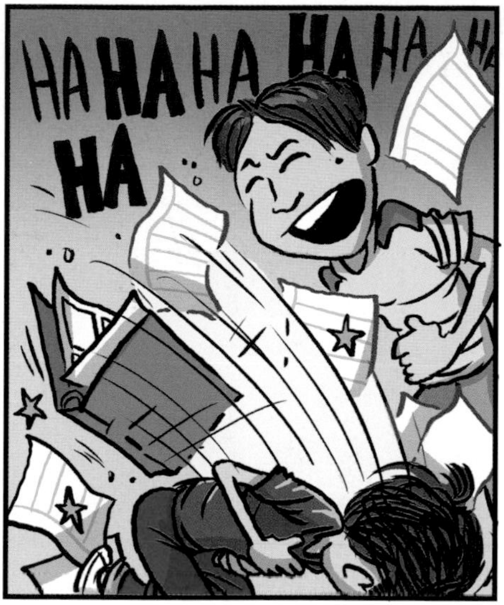
HA HA HA HA HA HA
HA

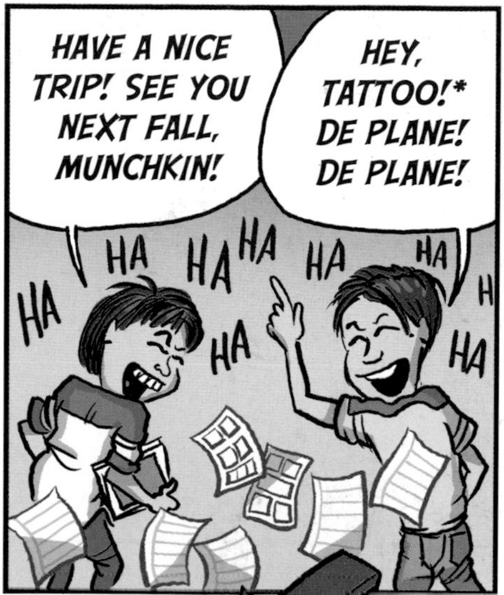
HAVE A NICE TRIP! SEE YOU NEXT FALL, MUNCHKIN!
HEY, TATTOO!* DE PLANE! DE PLANE!
HA HA HA HA HA HA HA HA HA

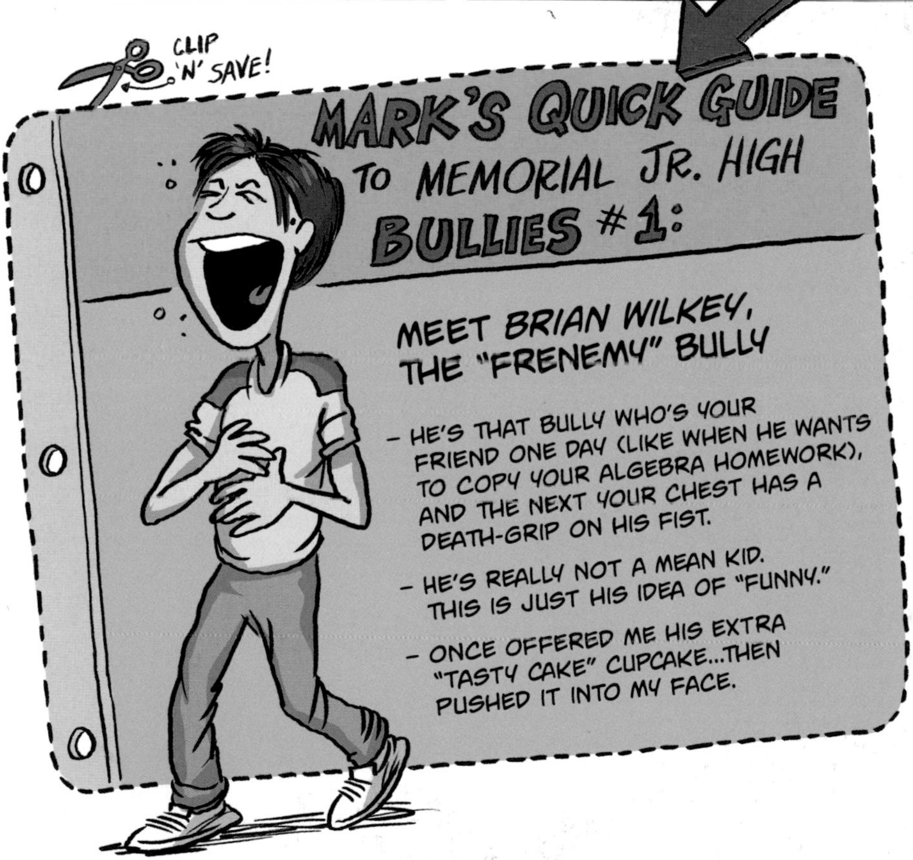
CLIP 'N' SAVE!
MARK'S QUICK GUIDE TO MEMORIAL JR. HIGH BULLIES #1:
MEET BRIAN WILKEY, THE "FRENEMY" BULLY
- HE'S THAT BULLY WHO'S YOUR FRIEND ONE DAY (LIKE WHEN HE WANTS TO COPY YOUR ALGEBRA HOMEWORK), AND THE NEXT YOUR CHEST HAS A DEATH-GRIP ON HIS FIST.
- HE'S REALLY NOT A MEAN KID. THIS IS JUST HIS IDEA OF "FUNNY."
- ONCE OFFERED ME HIS EXTRA "TASTY CAKE" CUPCAKE...THEN PUSHED IT INTO MY FACE.

*SEE "TATTOO," PAGE 18!

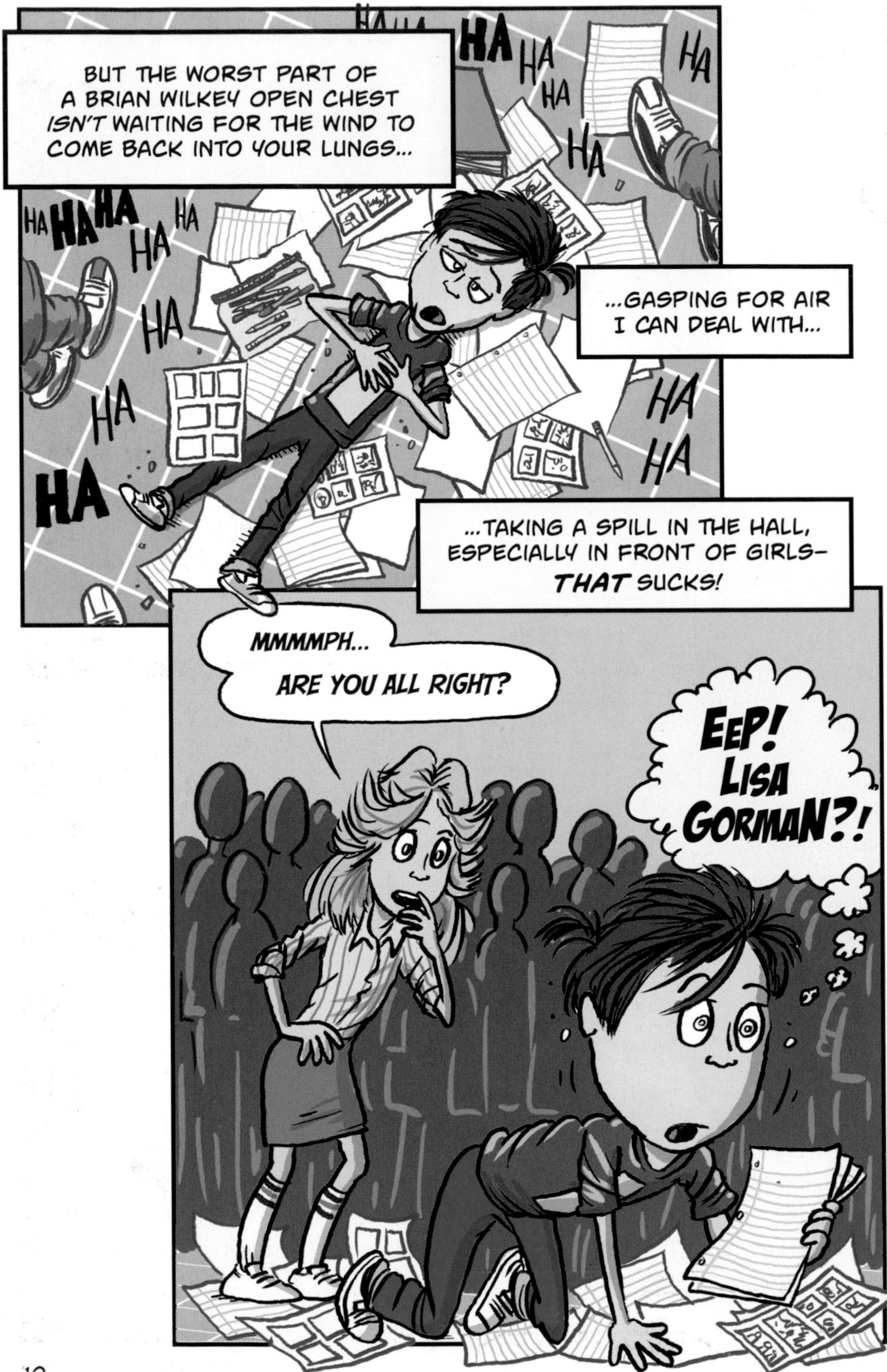
BUT THE WORST PART OF A BRIAN WILKEY OPEN CHEST *ISN'T* WAITING FOR THE WIND TO COME BACK INTO YOUR LUNGS...
HA HA HA HA HA HA HA HA HA HA HA HA HA HA HA HA
...GASPING FOR AIR I CAN DEAL WITH...
...TAKING A SPILL IN THE HALL, ESPECIALLY IN FRONT OF GIRLS– *THAT* SUCKS!
MMMMPH...
ARE YOU ALL RIGHT?
EEP! LISA GORMAN?!

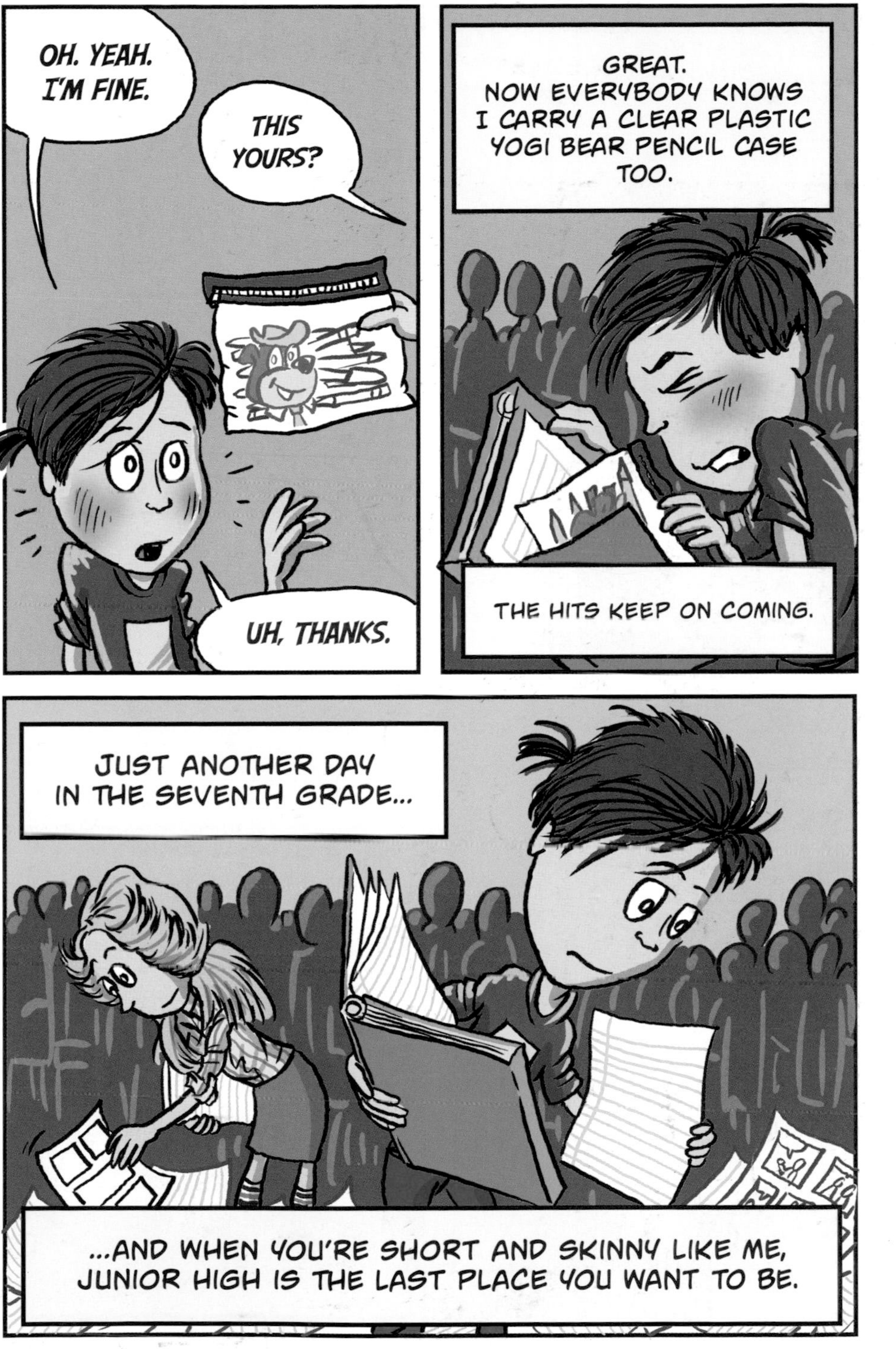
OH. YEAH. I'M FINE.
THIS YOURS?
UH, THANKS.
GREAT. NOW EVERYBODY KNOWS I CARRY A CLEAR PLASTIC YOGI BEAR PENCIL CASE TOO.
THE HITS KEEP ON COMING.
JUST ANOTHER DAY IN THE SEVENTH GRADE...
...AND WHEN YOU'RE SHORT AND SKINNY LIKE ME, JUNIOR HIGH IS THE LAST PLACE YOU WANT TO BE.

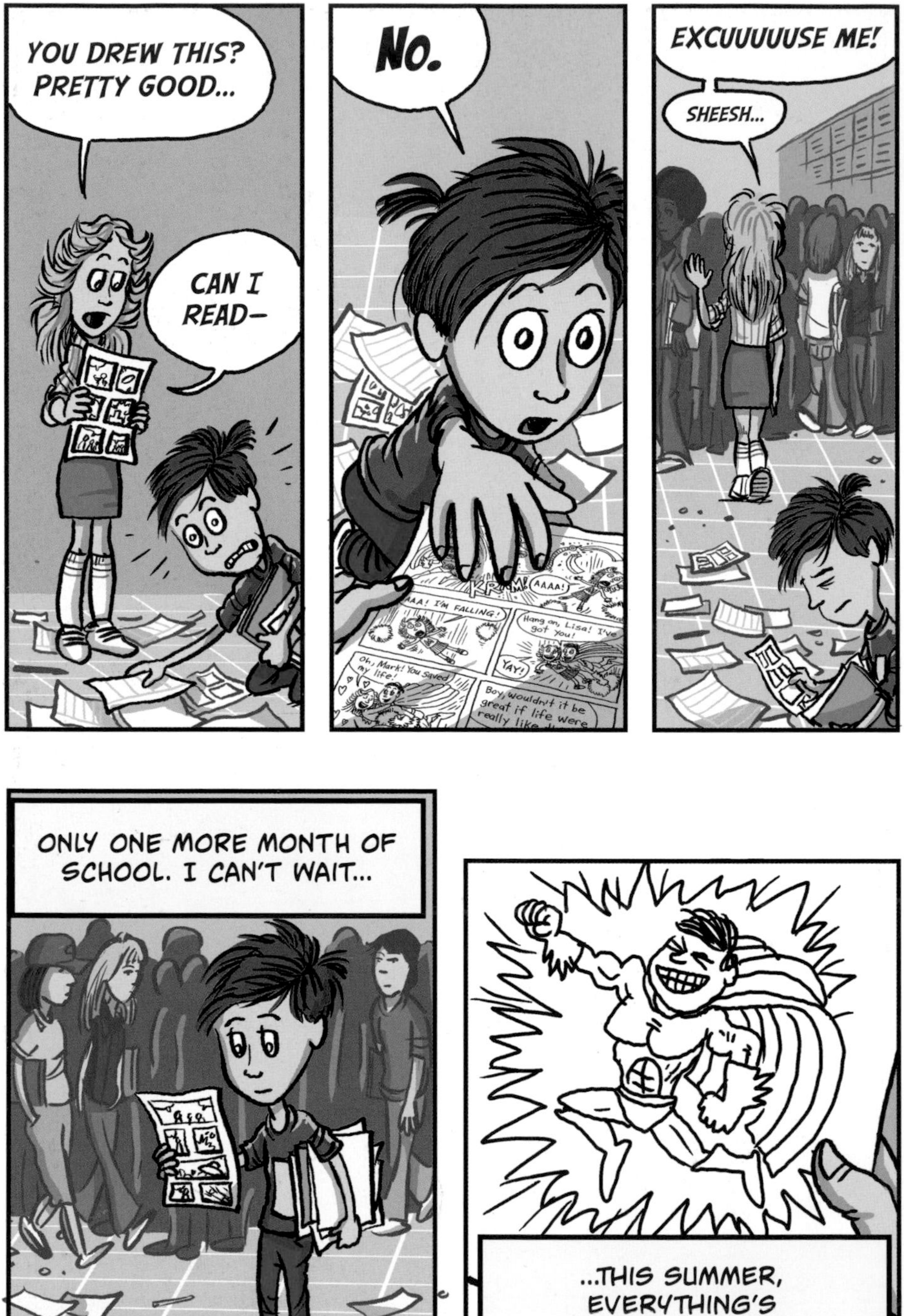
YOU DREW THIS? PRETTY GOOD...
CAN I READ—
NO.
AAAA!
I'M FALLING!
Hang on, Lisa! I've got You!
YAY!
Oh, Mark! You saved my life!
Boy, wouldn't it be great if life were
EXCUUUUUSE ME!
SHEESH...
ONLY ONE MORE MONTH OF SCHOOL. I CAN'T WAIT...
...THIS SUMMER, EVERYTHING'S GONNA CHANGE.

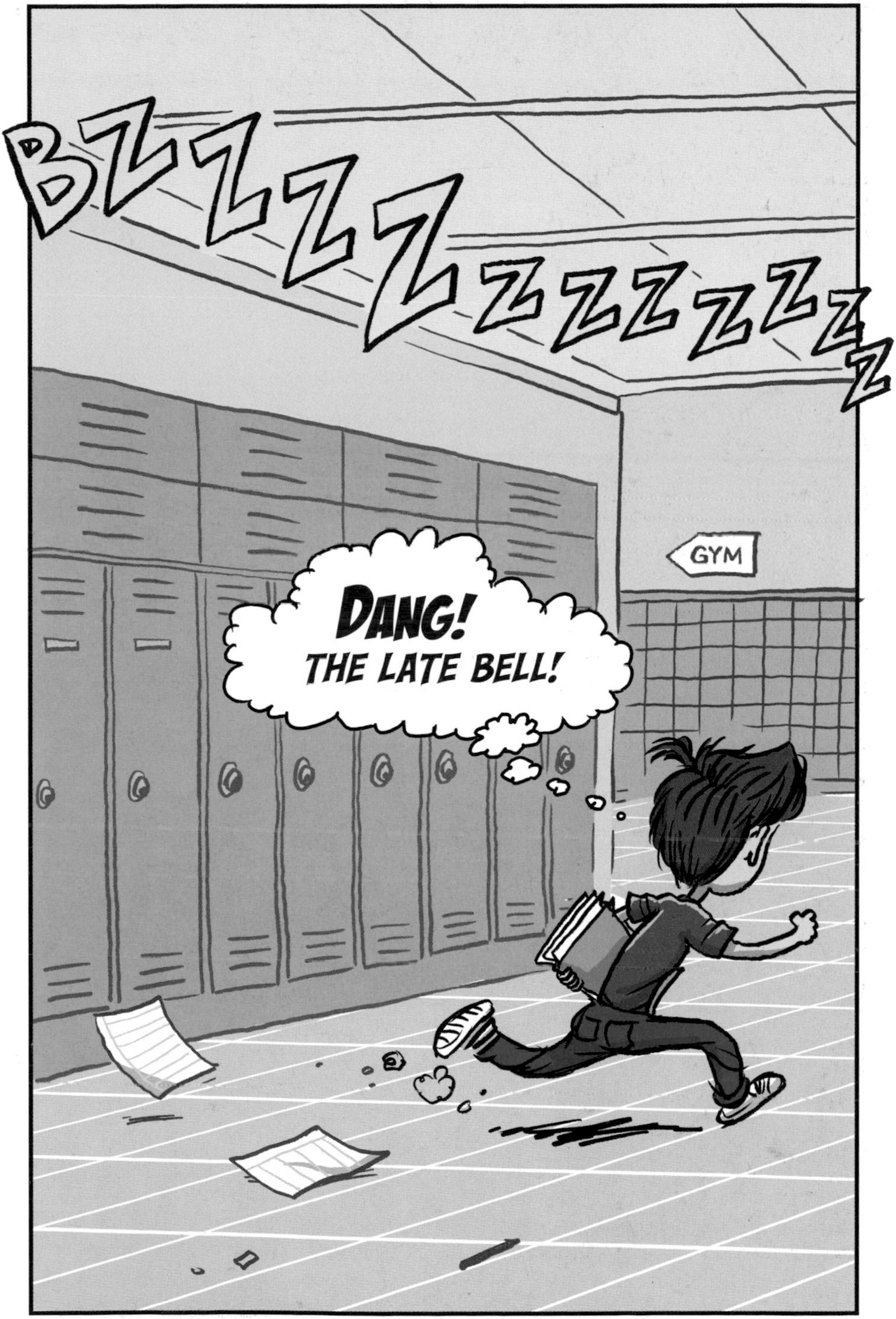
BZZZZZZZZZZZZ
DANG!
THE LATE BELL!
GYM

CHAPTER 2

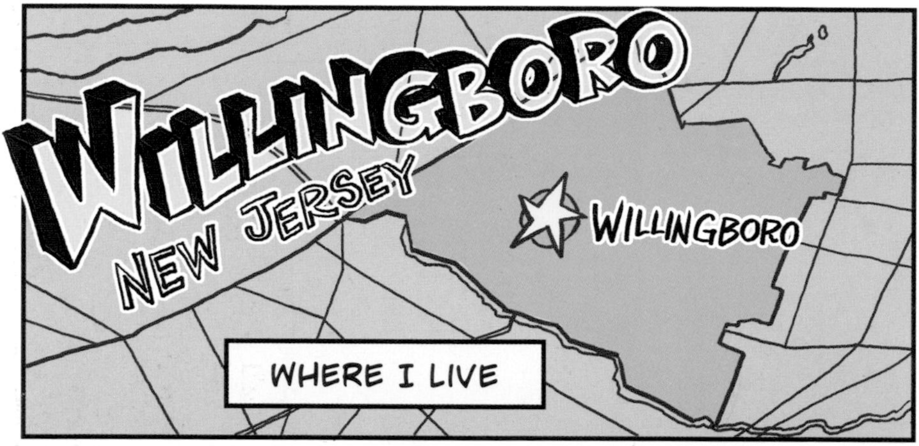
WILLINGBORO
NEW JERSEY
WILLINGBORO
WHERE I LIVE

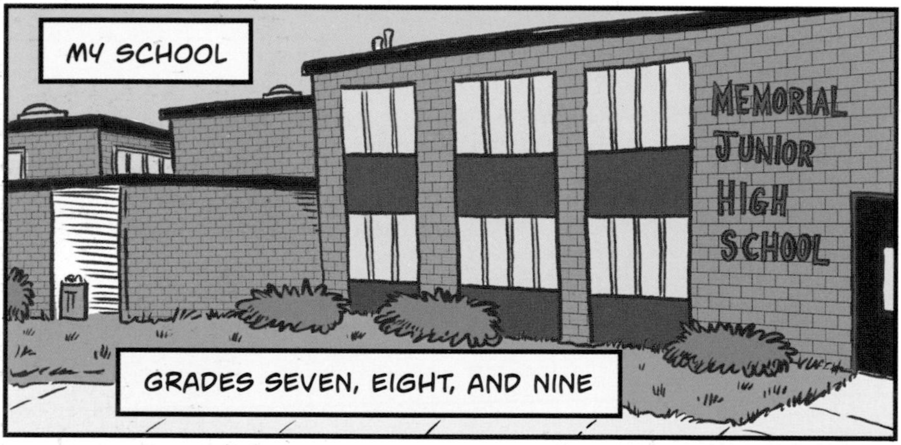
MY SCHOOL
MEMORIAL JUNIOR HIGH SCHOOL
GRADES SEVEN, EIGHT, AND NINE

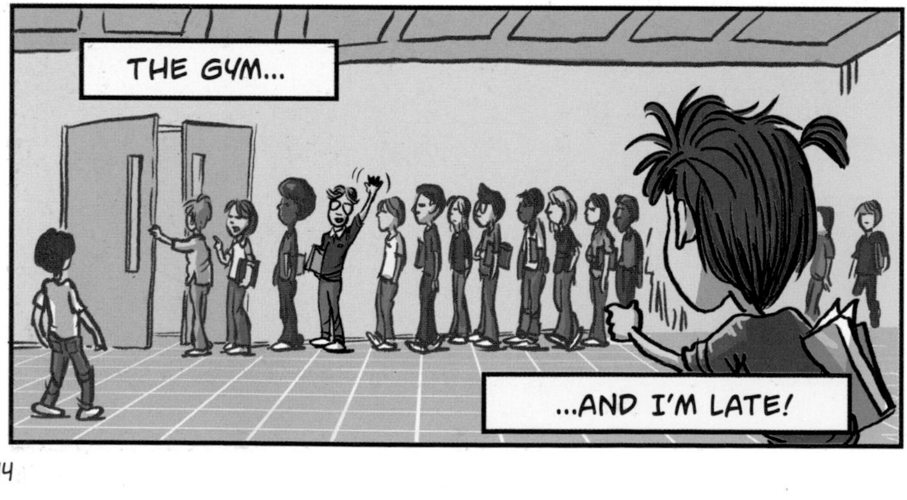
THE GYM...
...AND I'M LATE!

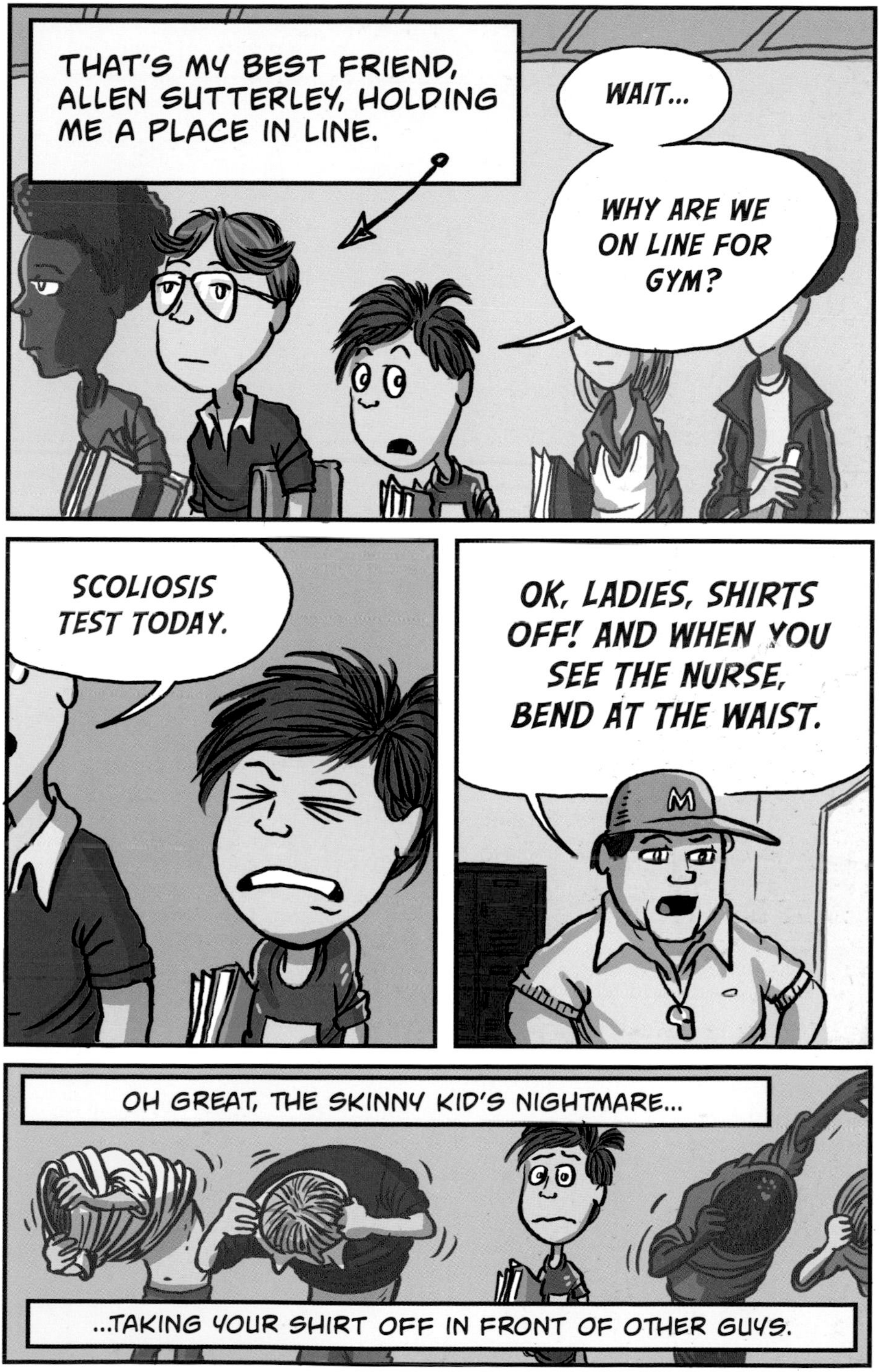
THAT'S MY BEST FRIEND, ALLEN SUTTERLEY, HOLDING ME A PLACE IN LINE.
WAIT...
WHY ARE WE ON LINE FOR GYM?
SCOLIOSIS TEST TODAY.
OK, LADIES, SHIRTS OFF! AND WHEN YOU SEE THE NURSE, BEND AT THE WAIST.
M
OH GREAT, THE SKINNY KID'S NIGHTMARE...
...TAKING YOUR SHIRT OFF IN FRONT OF OTHER GUYS.

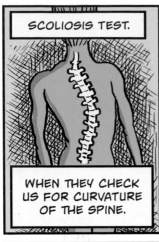

SCOLIOSIS TEST.

WHEN THEY CHECK US FOR CURVATURE OF THE SPINE.

EVERYBODY IS WORRIED THEY'LL WIND UP WITH HARDWARE LIKE JEFF BLAIR.

IT'S NOT SO BAD! REALLY!

ME? I'M JUST WAITING FOR THE "SHIRTS OFF" PART TO END...

...EVERY GUY IS SO MUCH BIGGER...

...AND I FEEL LIKE THEY'RE ALL STARING AT MY BONY BODY...

...EVEN THE GYM TEACHER.

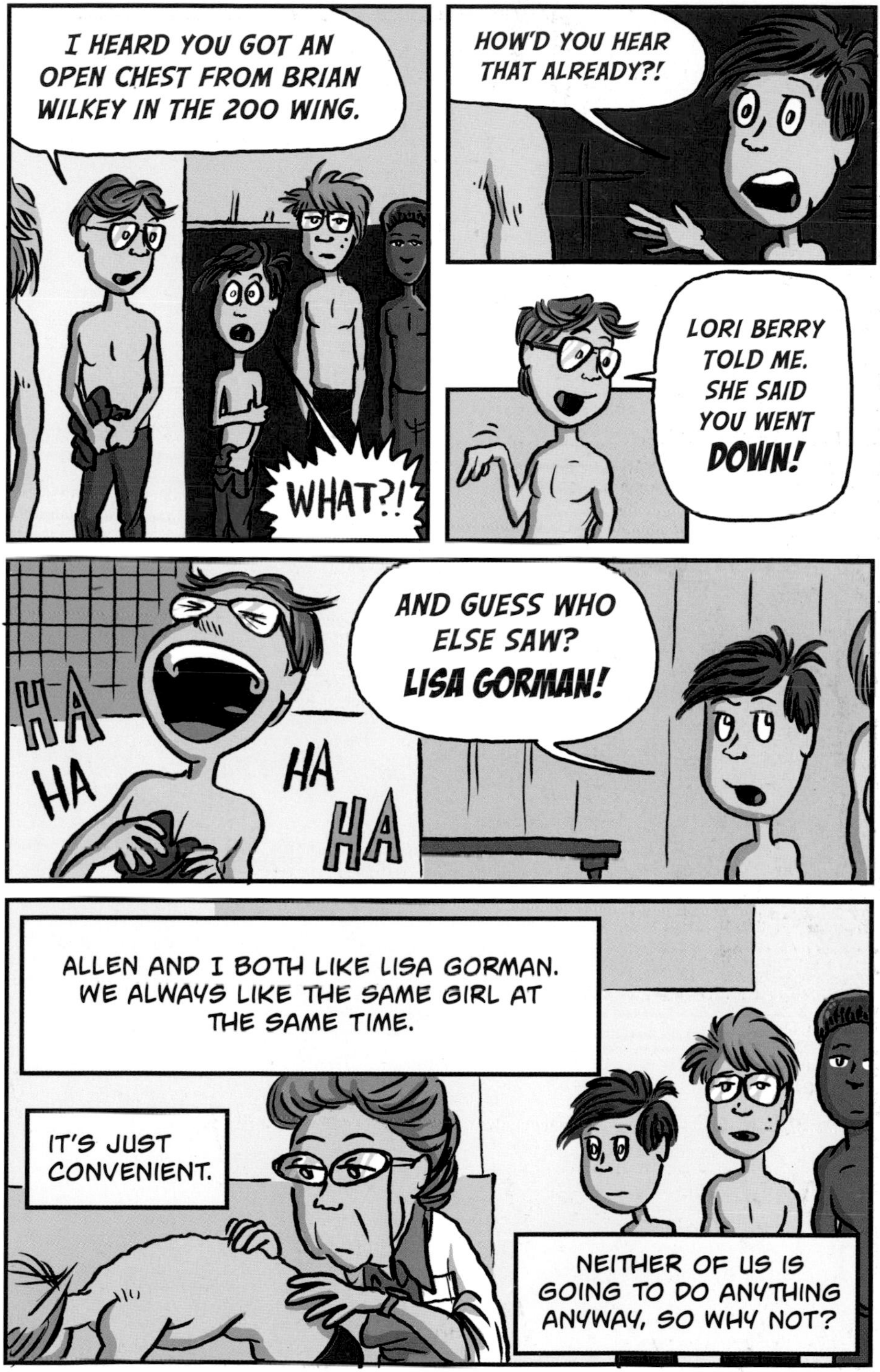
I HEARD YOU GOT AN OPEN CHEST FROM BRIAN WILKEY IN THE 200 WING.
WHAT?!
HOW'D YOU HEAR THAT ALREADY?!
LORI BERRY TOLD ME. SHE SAID YOU WENT DOWN!
AND GUESS WHO ELSE SAW? LISA GORMAN!
HA HA HA HA
ALLEN AND I BOTH LIKE LISA GORMAN. WE ALWAYS LIKE THE SAME GIRL AT THE SAME TIME.
IT'S JUST CONVENIENT.
NEITHER OF US IS GOING TO DO ANYTHING ANYWAY, SO WHY NOT?

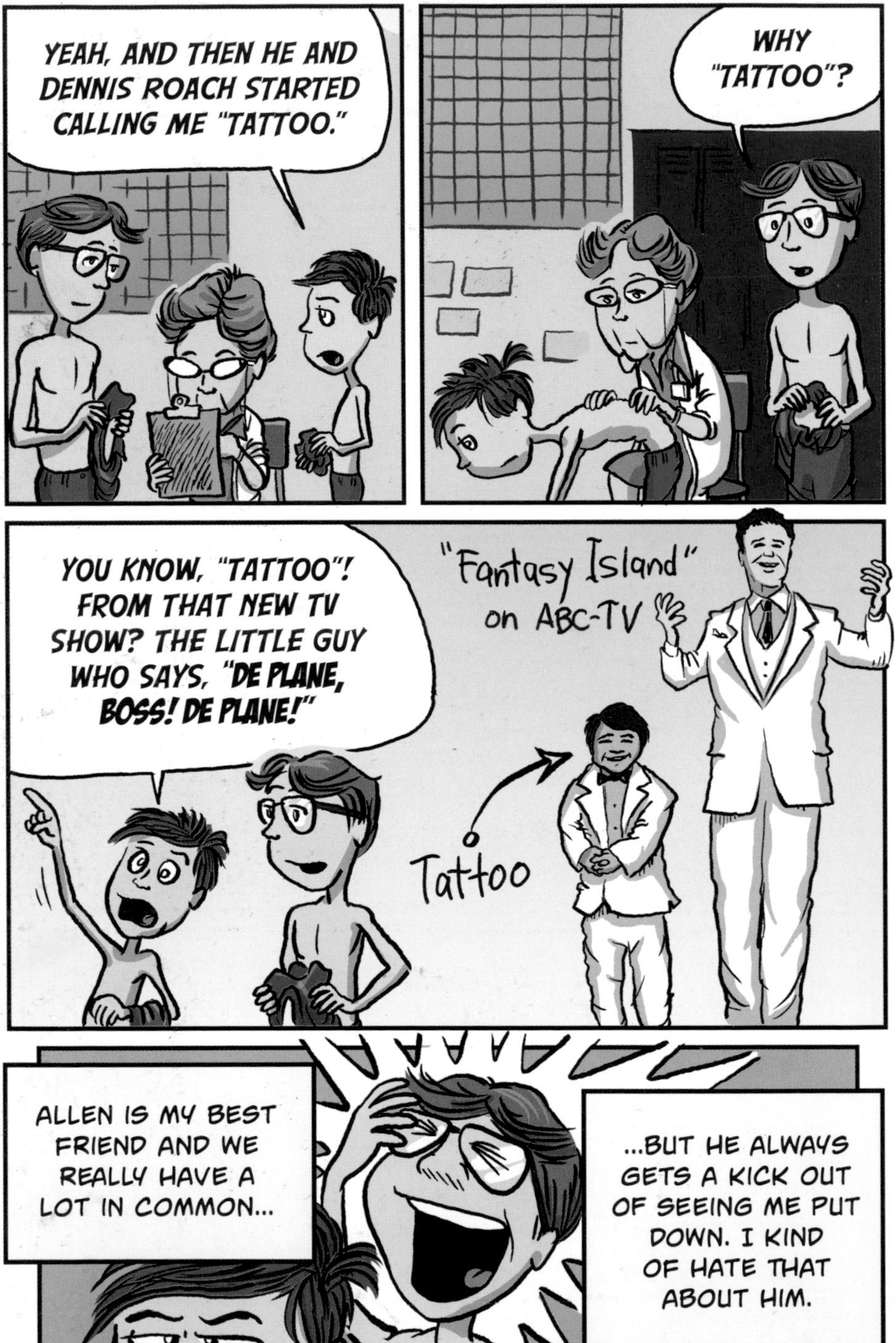
YEAH, AND THEN HE AND DENNIS ROACH STARTED CALLING ME "TATTOO."
WHY "TATTOO"?
YOU KNOW, "TATTOO"! FROM THAT NEW TV SHOW? THE LITTLE GUY WHO SAYS, "DE PLANE, BOSS! DE PLANE!"
"Fantasy Island" on ABC-TV
Tattoo
ALLEN IS MY BEST FRIEND AND WE REALLY HAVE A LOT IN COMMON...
...BUT HE ALWAYS GETS A KICK OUT OF SEEING ME PUT DOWN. I KIND OF HATE THAT ABOUT HIM.

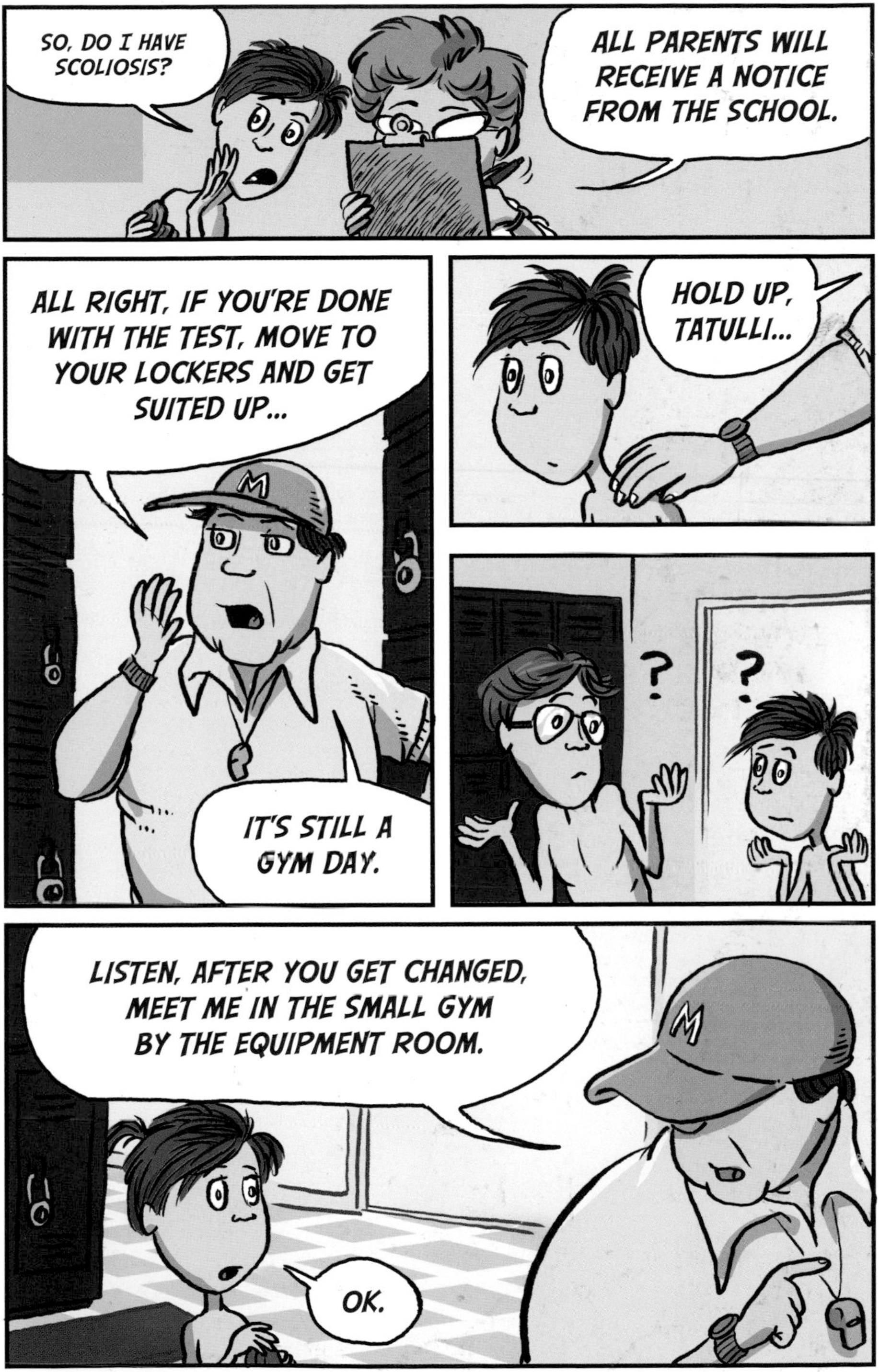
SO, DO I HAVE SCOLIOSIS?
ALL PARENTS WILL RECEIVE A NOTICE FROM THE SCHOOL.
ALL RIGHT, IF YOU'RE DONE WITH THE TEST, MOVE TO YOUR LOCKERS AND GET SUITED UP...
IT'S STILL A GYM DAY.
HOLD UP, TATULLI...
?
?
LISTEN, AFTER YOU GET CHANGED, MEET ME IN THE SMALL GYM BY THE EQUIPMENT ROOM.
OK.

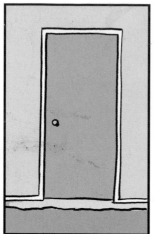
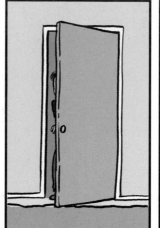

HELLO?

I'VE NEVER BEEN IN HERE BEFORE...

...THIS IS WHERE THE FOOTBALL PLAYERS WORK OUT...

AND IS THAT—

—NICHOLAS MESSER?

...IT IS!

AND *TODD JAMERSON?*

JEFF BLAIR.

THE GERMAN EXCHANGE STUDENT *MARCUS SHUEMOCHER.*

AND *ADAM CHO.* THE ONLY KID IN SCHOOL SMALLER THAN ME. HE HAS TO HEAR THE "ADAM ANT" JOKES CONSTANTLY.

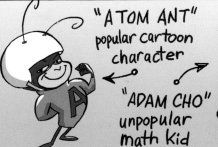

"A TOM ANT" popular cartoon character

"ADAM CHO" unpopular math kid

IT'S LIKE A WHO'S WHO OF ACADEMIC EXCELLENCE.

21

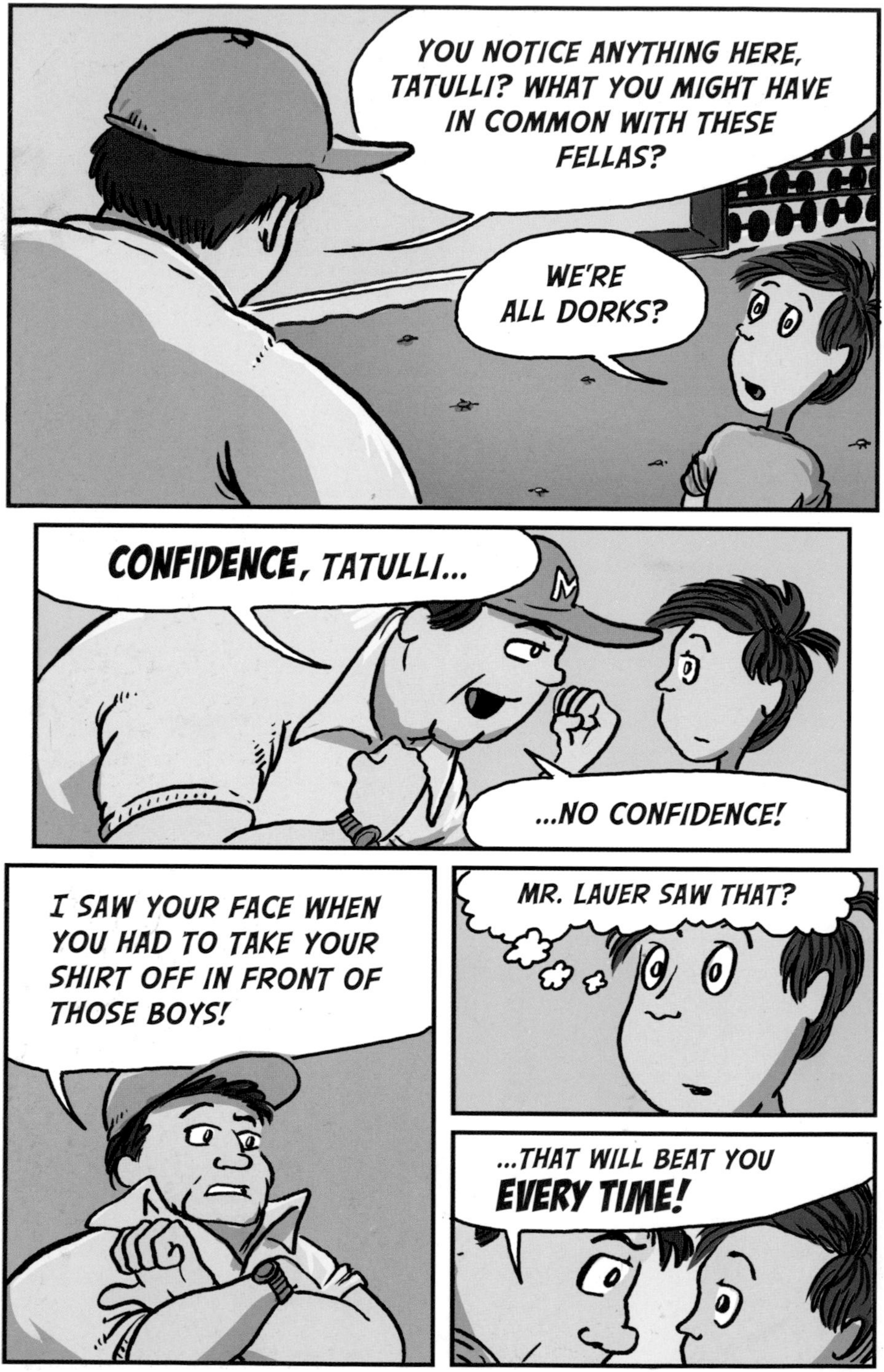
YOU NOTICE ANYTHING HERE, TATULLI? WHAT YOU MIGHT HAVE IN COMMON WITH THESE FELLAS?
WE'RE ALL DORKS?
CONFIDENCE, TATULLI...
...NO CONFIDENCE!
I SAW YOUR FACE WHEN YOU HAD TO TAKE YOUR SHIRT OFF IN FRONT OF THOSE BOYS!
MR. LAUER SAW THAT?
...THAT WILL BEAT YOU EVERY TIME!

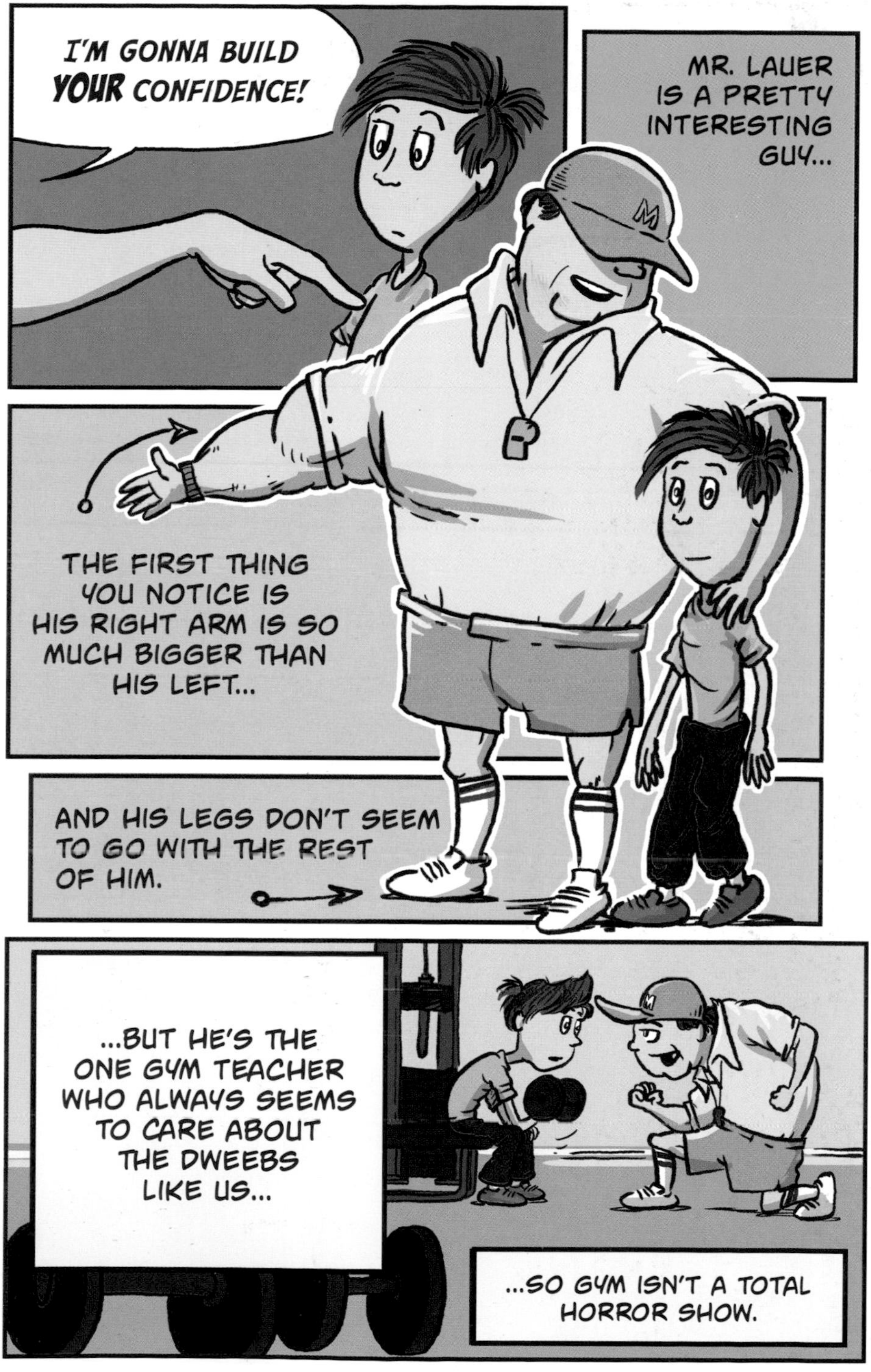
I'M GONNA BUILD YOUR CONFIDENCE!
MR. LAUER IS A PRETTY INTERESTING GUY...
THE FIRST THING YOU NOTICE IS HIS RIGHT ARM IS SO MUCH BIGGER THAN HIS LEFT...
AND HIS LEGS DON'T SEEM TO GO WITH THE REST OF HIM.
...BUT HE'S THE ONE GYM TEACHER WHO ALWAYS SEEMS TO CARE ABOUT THE DWEEBS LIKE US...
...SO GYM ISN'T A TOTAL HORROR SHOW.

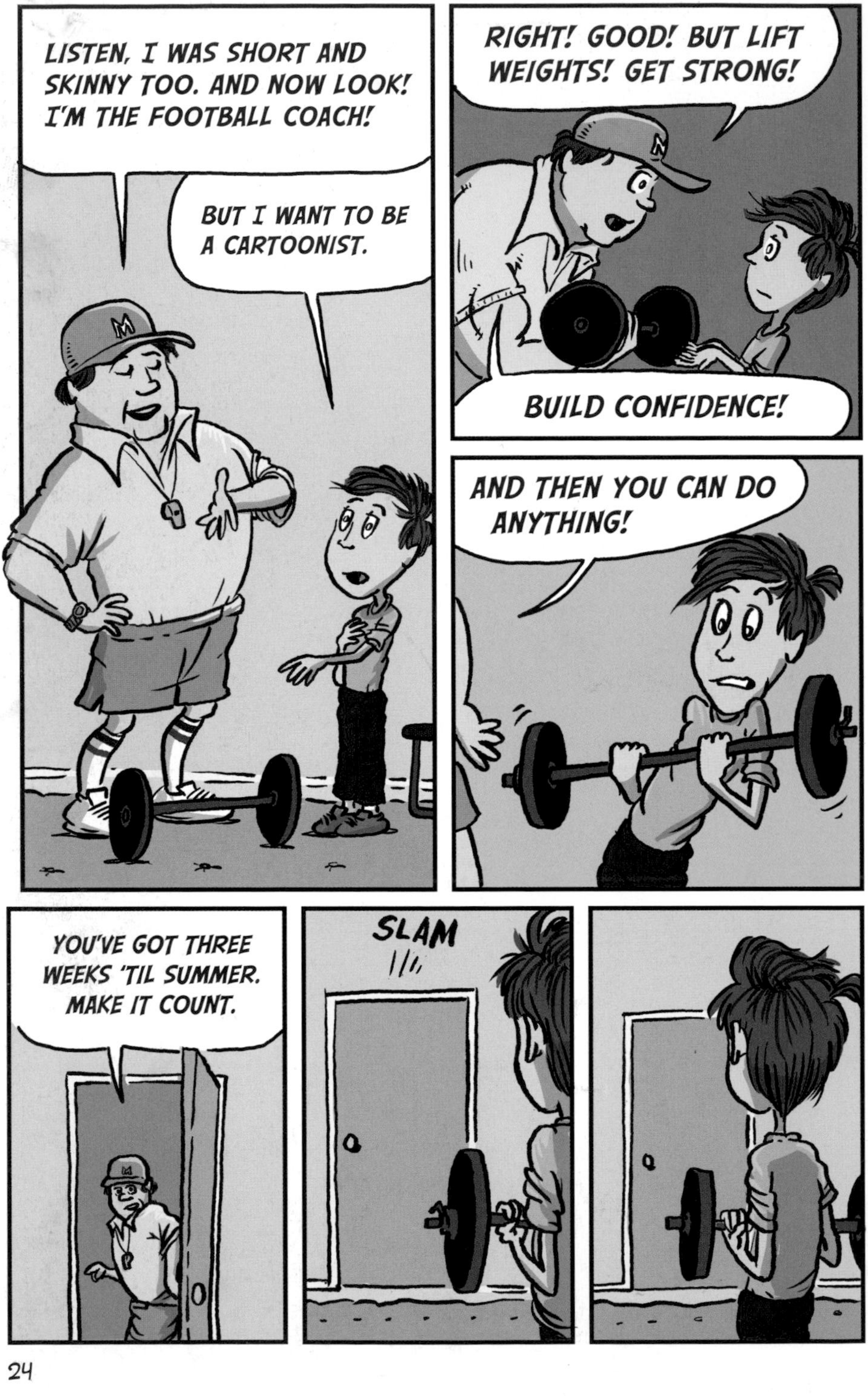
LISTEN, I WAS SHORT AND SKINNY TOO. AND NOW LOOK! I'M THE FOOTBALL COACH!
BUT I WANT TO BE A CARTOONIST.
RIGHT! GOOD! BUT LIFT WEIGHTS! GET STRONG!
BUILD CONFIDENCE!
AND THEN YOU CAN DO ANYTHING!
YOU'VE GOT THREE WEEKS 'TIL SUMMER. MAKE IT COUNT.
SLAM

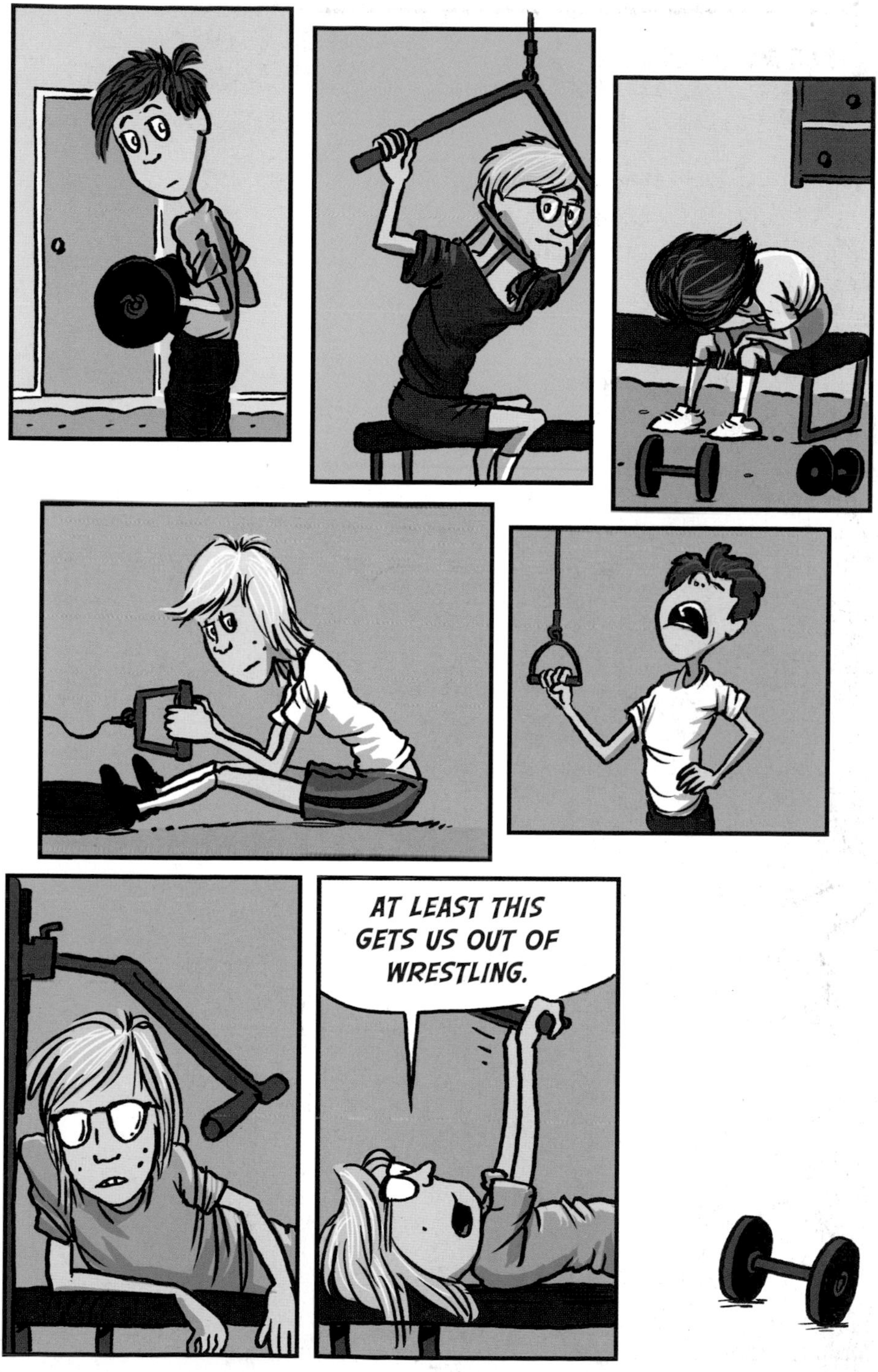
AT LEAST THIS GETS US OUT OF WRESTLING.

CHAPTER 3

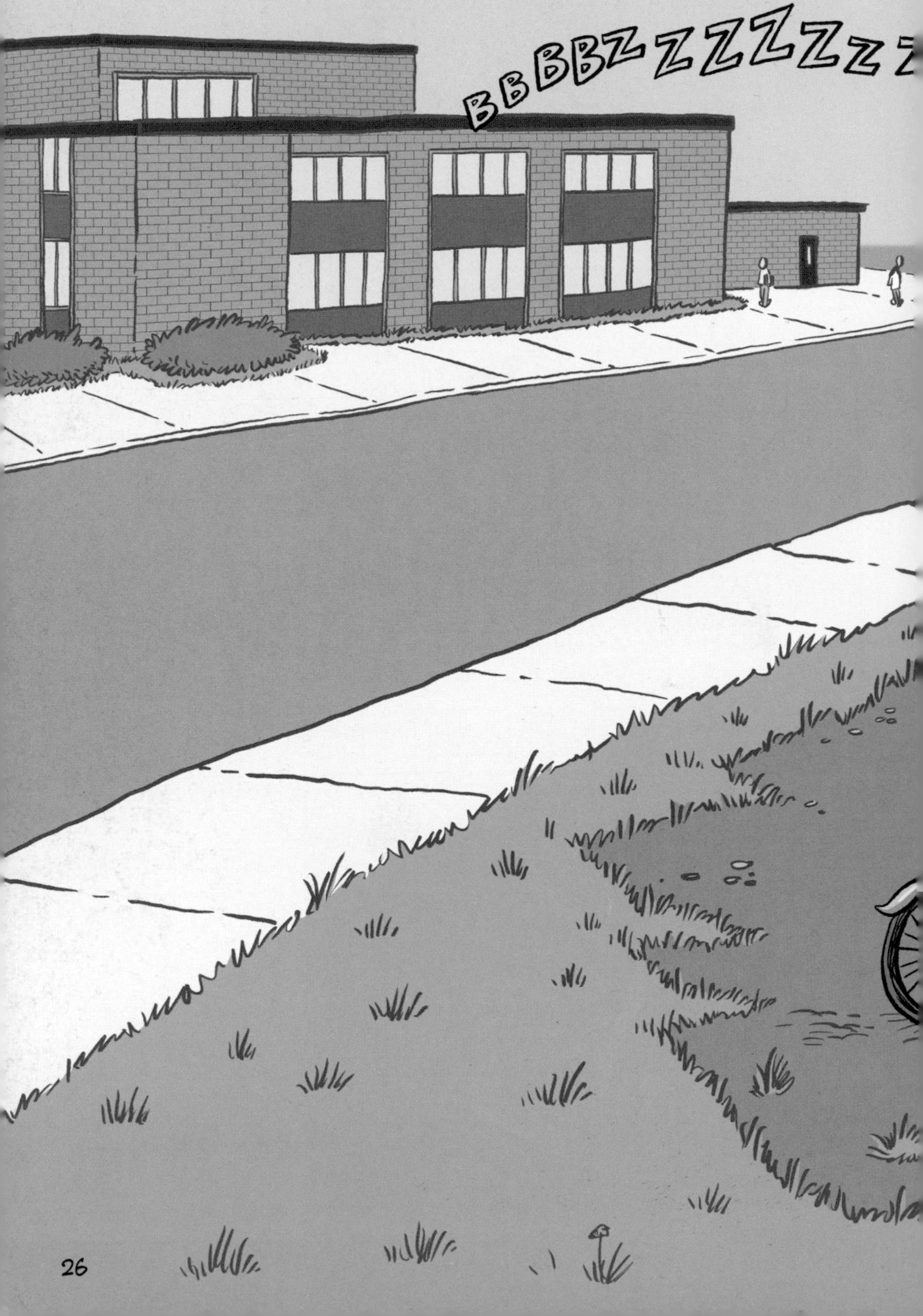
BBBBZZZZZZzz

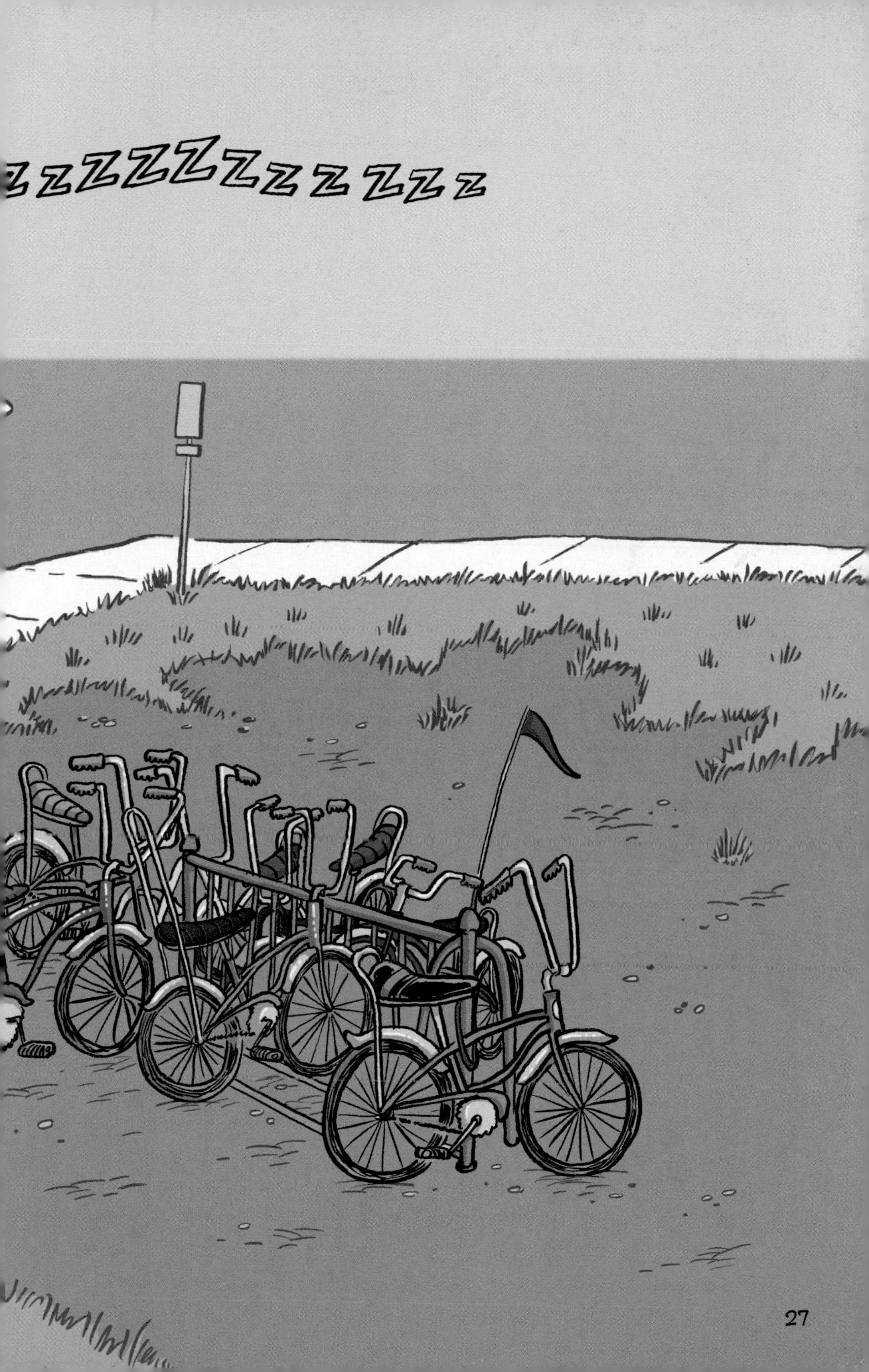
zzzZZZZzzzzZzz

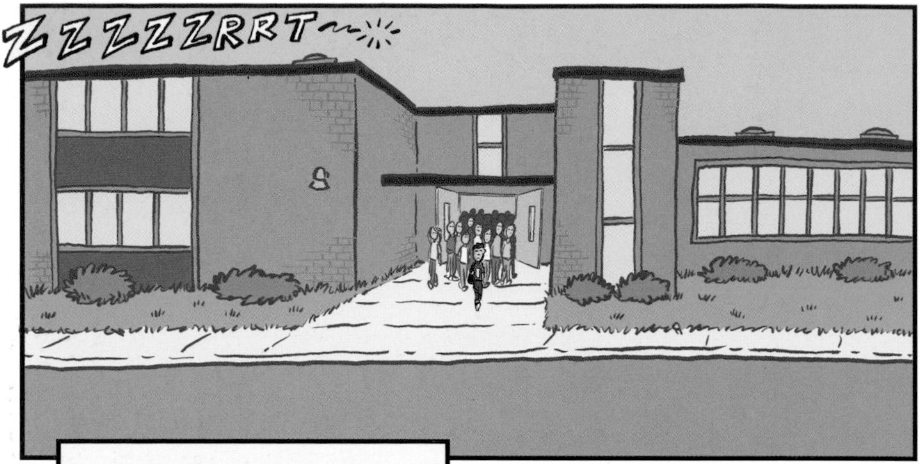
ZZZZZRRRT

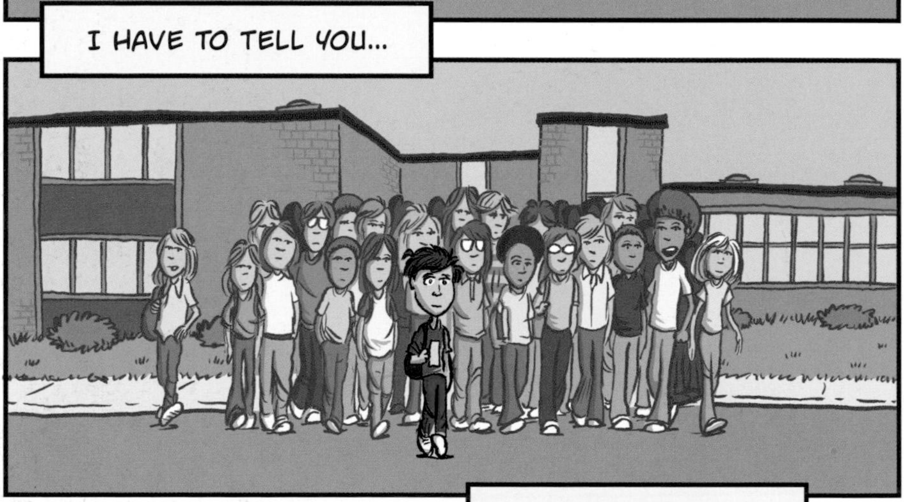
I HAVE TO TELL YOU...

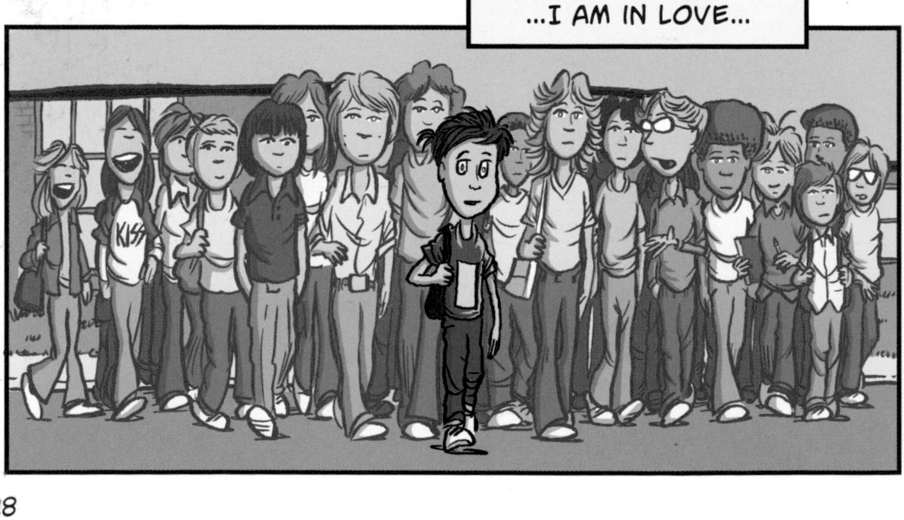
...I AM IN LOVE...
KISS

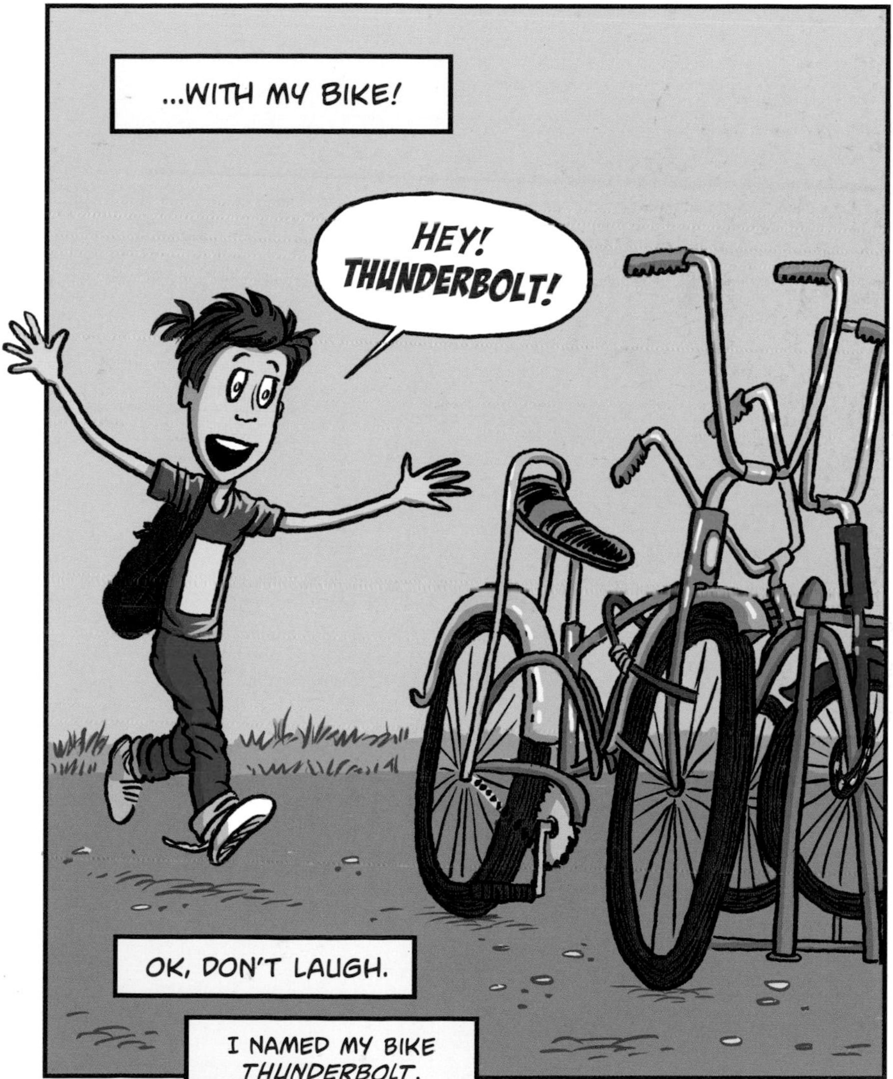
...WITH MY BIKE!
HEY! THUNDERBOLT!
OK, DON'T LAUGH.
I NAMED MY BIKE *THUNDERBOLT*.

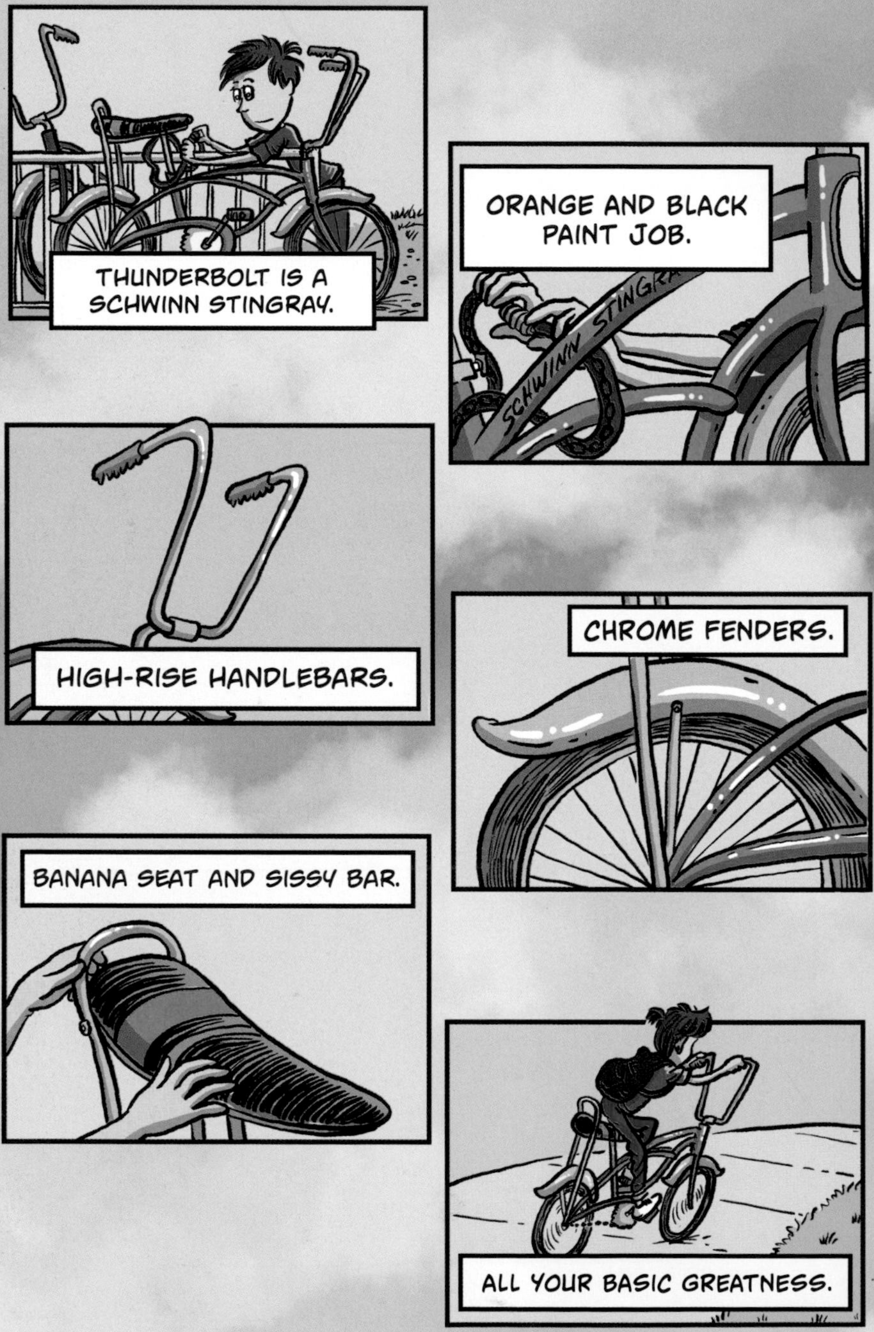
THUNDERBOLT IS A SCHWINN STINGRAY.
ORANGE AND BLACK PAINT JOB.
SCHWINN STINGRA
HIGH-RISE HANDLEBARS.
CHROME FENDERS.
BANANA SEAT AND SISSY BAR.
ALL YOUR BASIC GREATNESS.

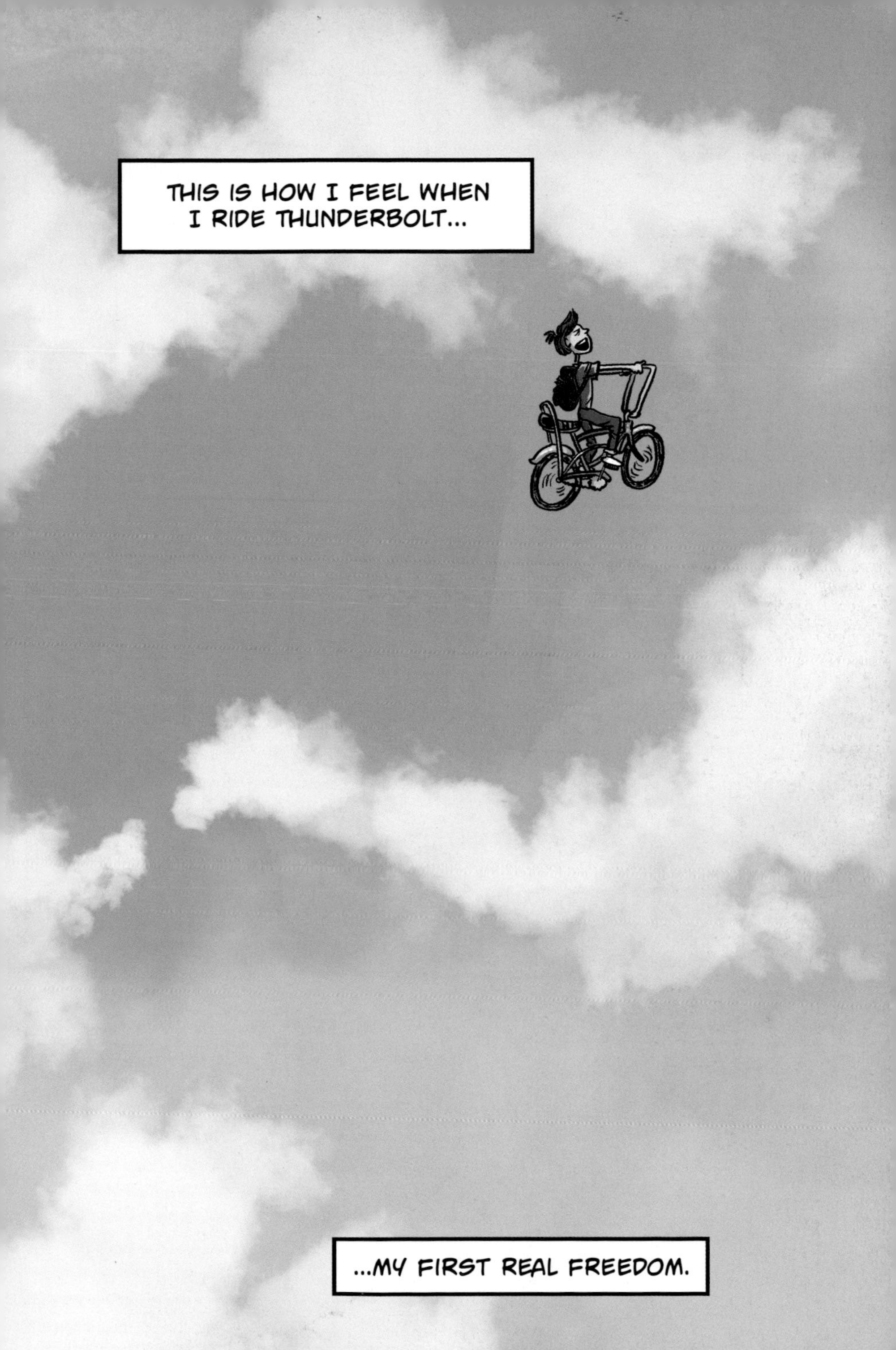
THIS IS HOW I FEEL WHEN I RIDE THUNDERBOLT...
...MY FIRST REAL FREEDOM.

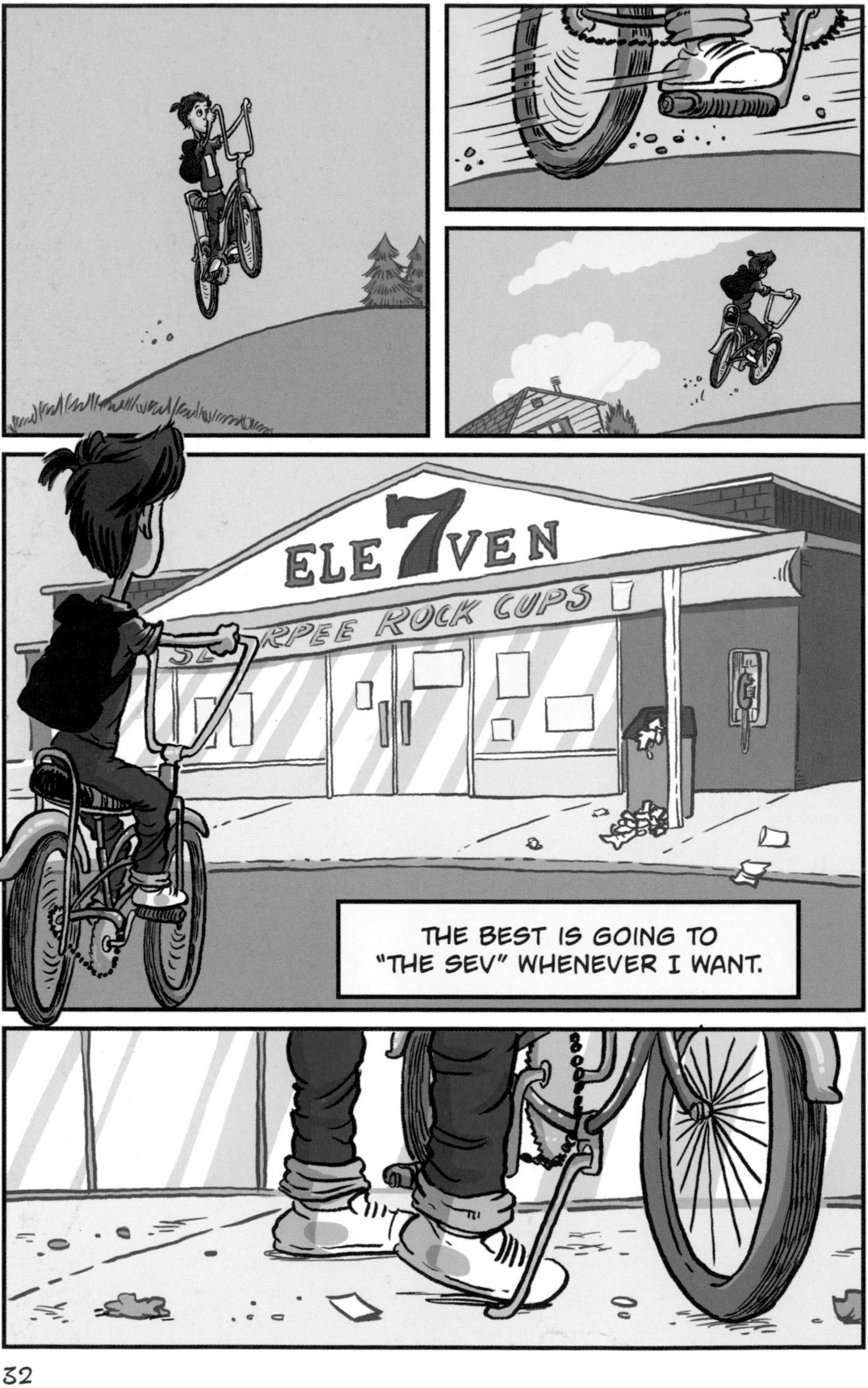
ELE7VEN
RPEE ROCK CUPS
THE BEST IS GOING TO "THE SEV" WHENEVER I WANT.

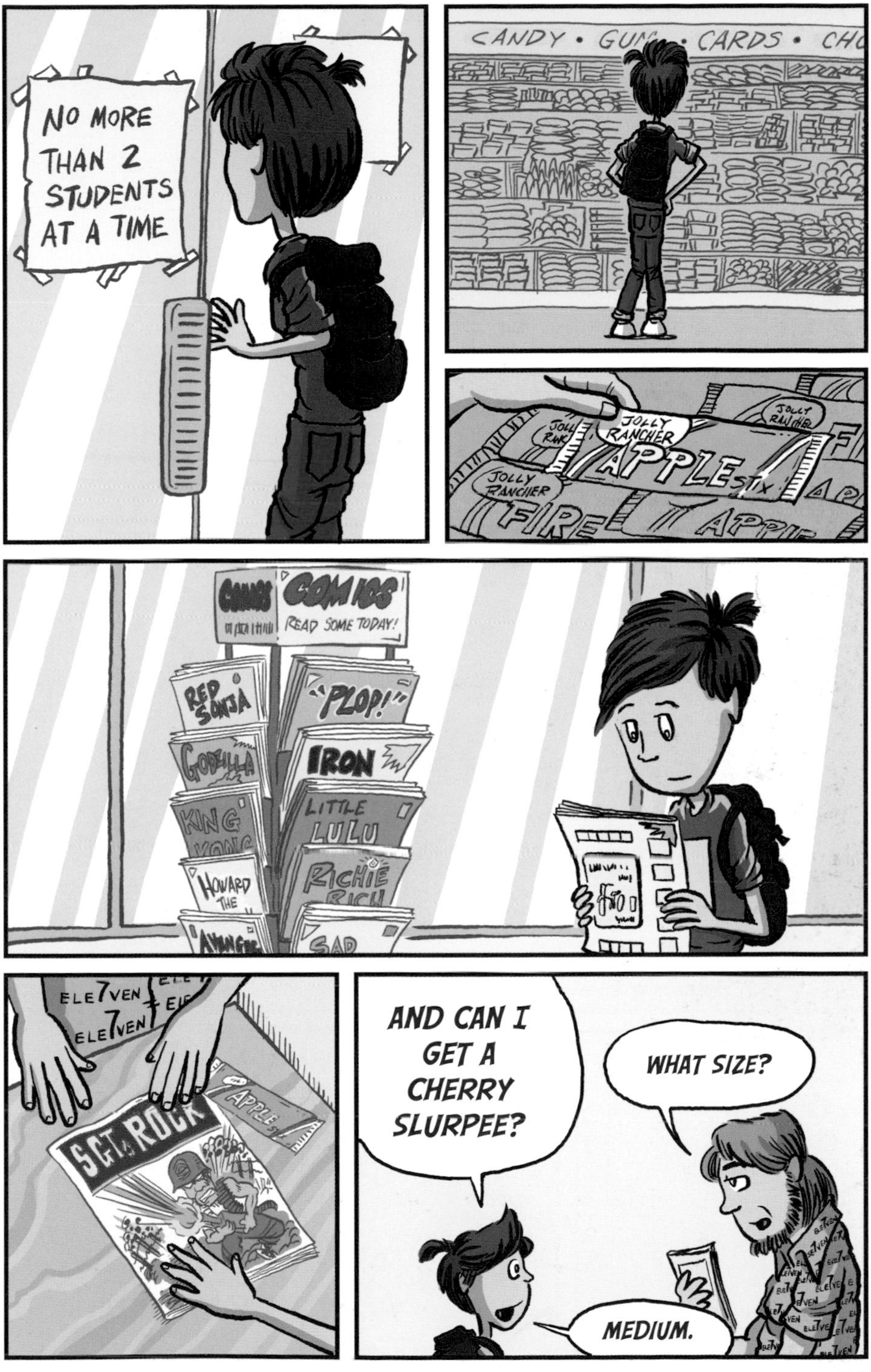
NO MORE THAN 2 STUDENTS AT A TIME
CANDY • GUM • CARDS •
JOLLY RANCHER APPLE STIX
COMICS
READ SOME TODAY!
RED SONJA
GODZILLA
KING KONG
HOWARD THE
"PLOP!"
IRON
LITTLE LULU
RICHIE RICH
SGT. ROCK
APPLE
AND CAN I GET A CHERRY SLURPEE?
WHAT SIZE?
MEDIUM.

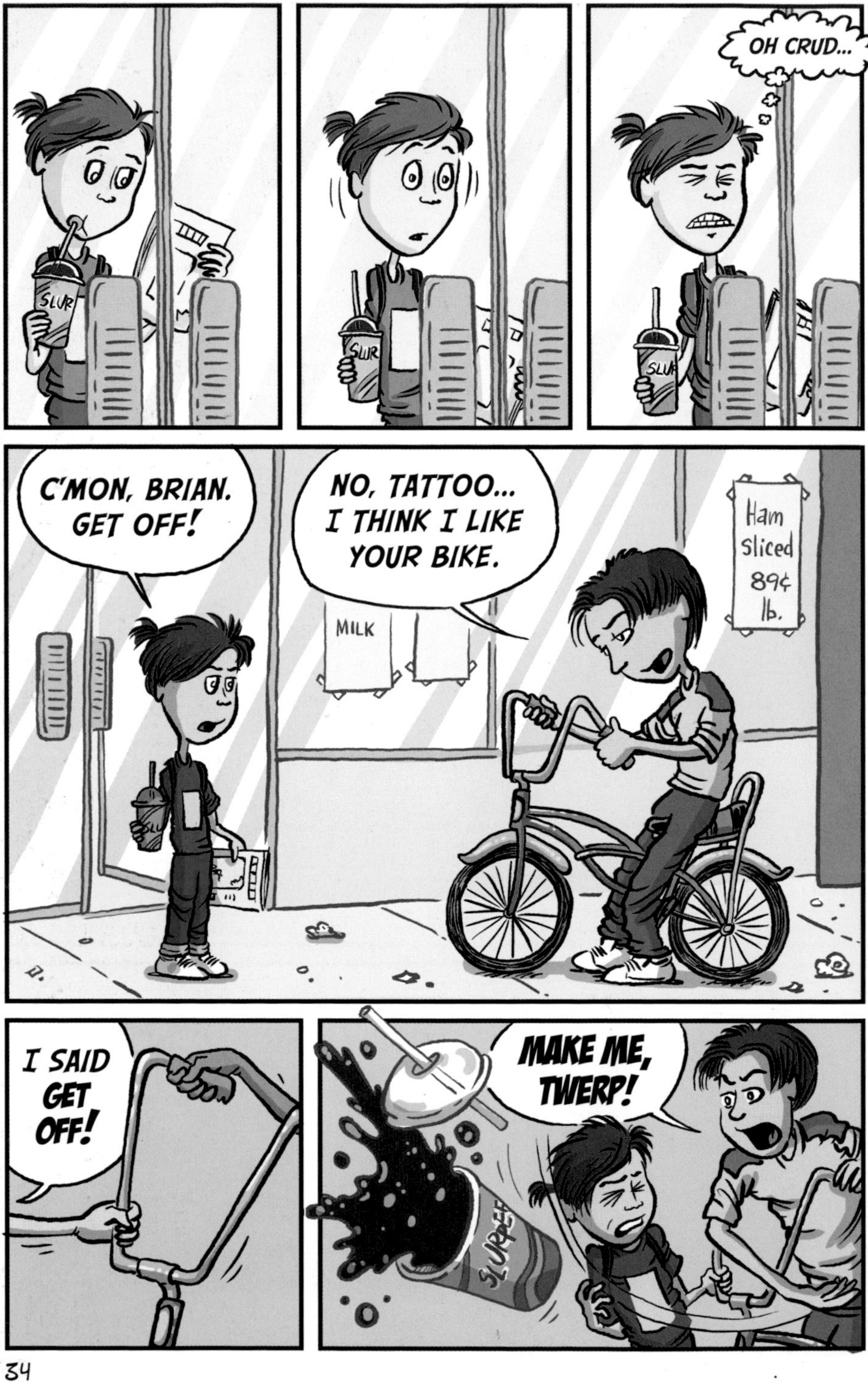
SLUR
SLUR
SLUR
OH CRUD...
C'MON, BRIAN. GET OFF!
NO, TATTOO... I THINK I LIKE YOUR BIKE.
MILK
Ham sliced 89¢ lb.
I SAID GET OFF!
MAKE ME, TWERP!
SLURPEE

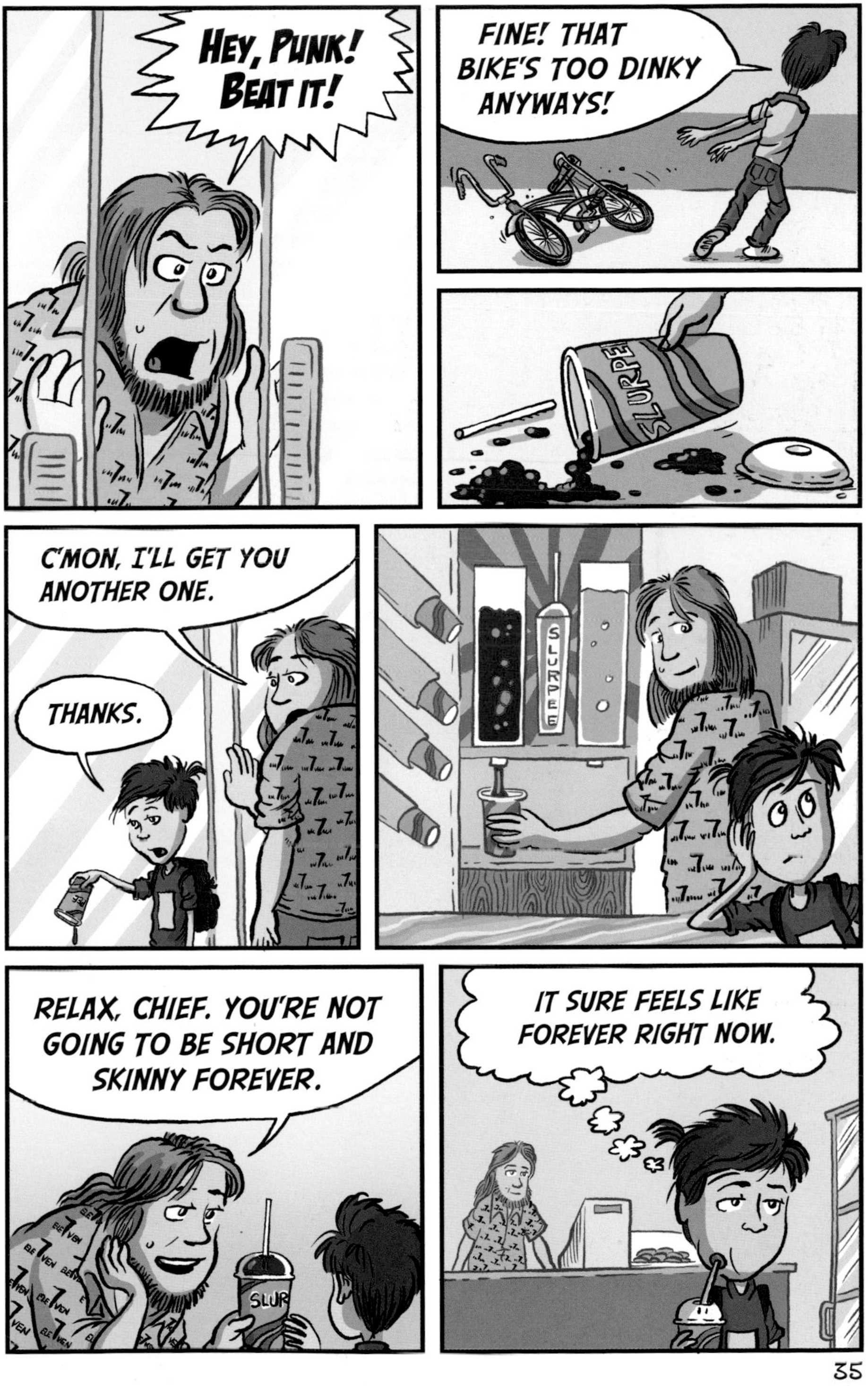
HEY, PUNK! BEAT IT!
FINE! THAT BIKE'S TOO DINKY ANYWAYS!
SLURPEE
C'MON, I'LL GET YOU ANOTHER ONE.
THANKS.
SLURPEE
RELAX, CHIEF. YOU'RE NOT GOING TO BE SHORT AND SKINNY FOREVER.
SLUR
IT SURE FEELS LIKE FOREVER RIGHT NOW.

CHAPTER 4

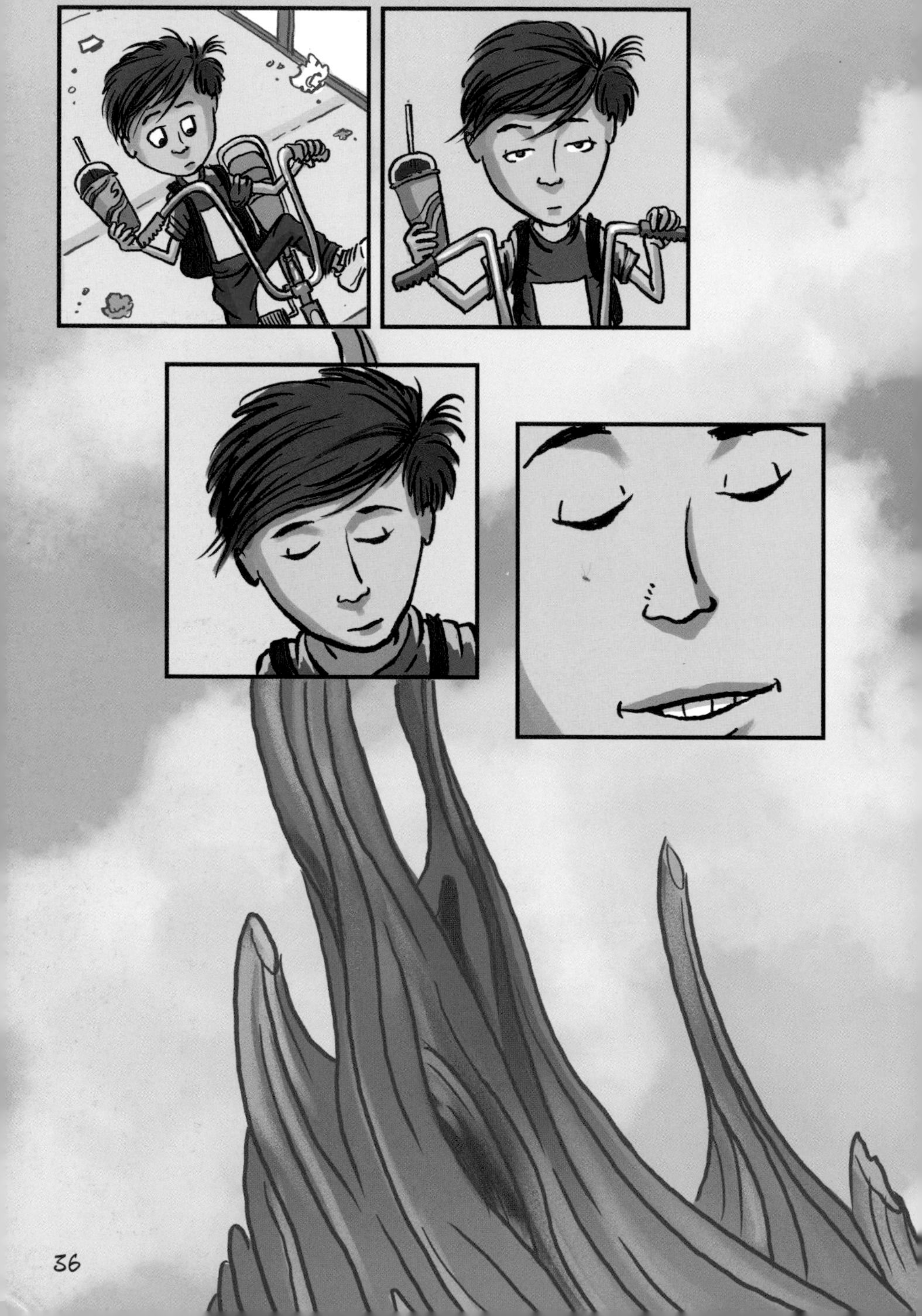

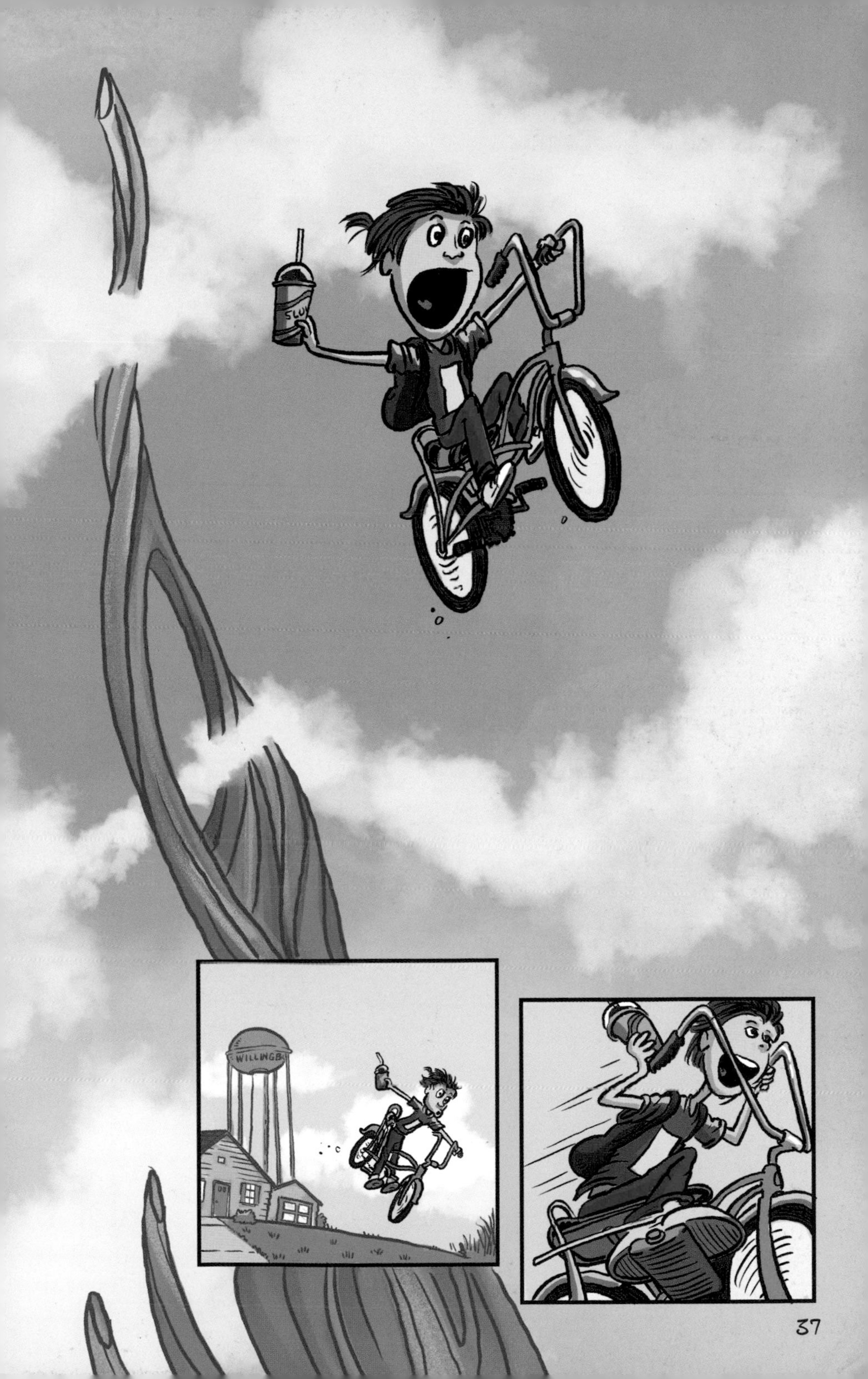

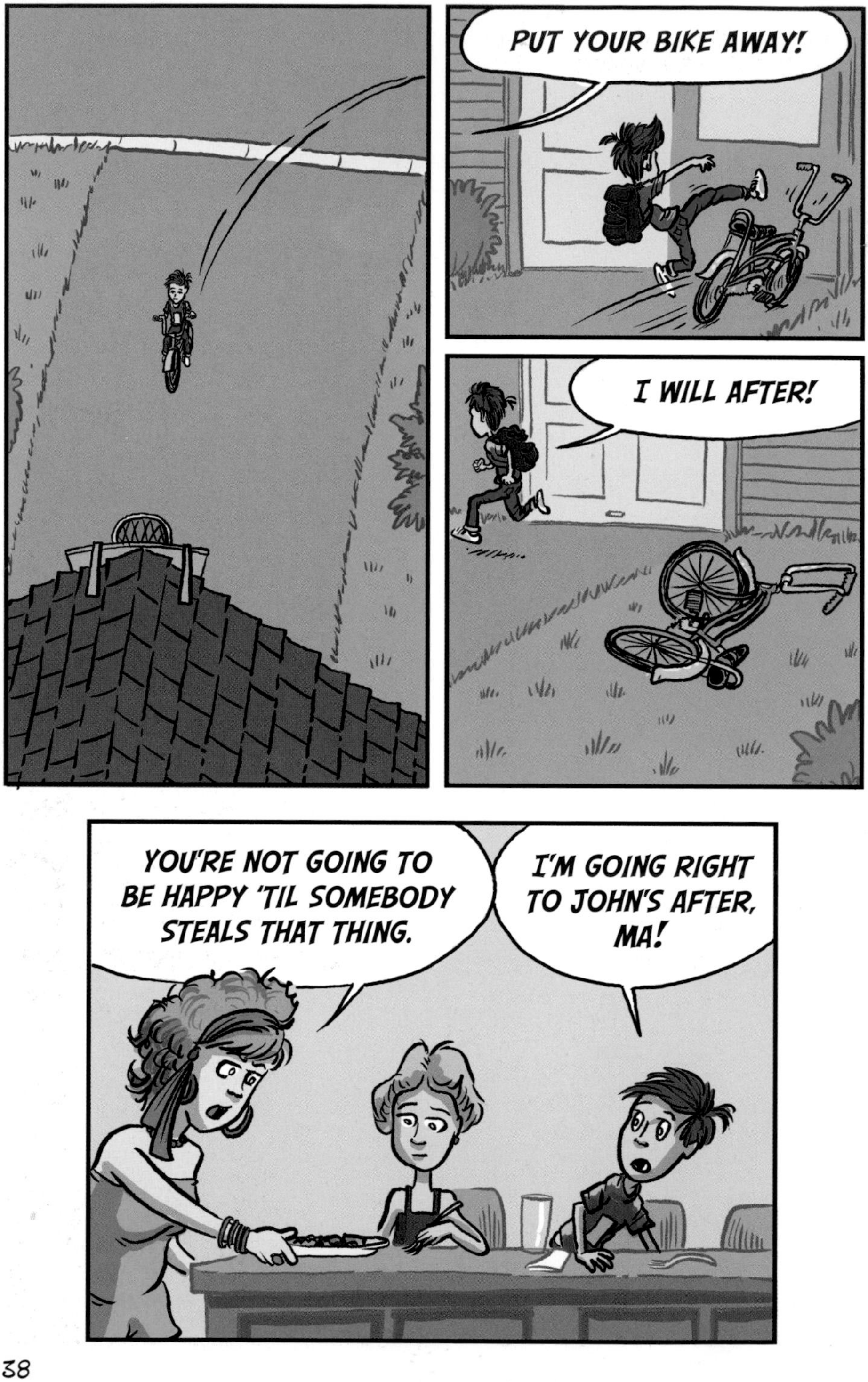
PUT YOUR BIKE AWAY!
I WILL AFTER!
YOU'RE NOT GOING TO BE HAPPY 'TIL SOMEBODY STEALS THAT THING.
I'M GOING RIGHT TO JOHN'S AFTER, MA!

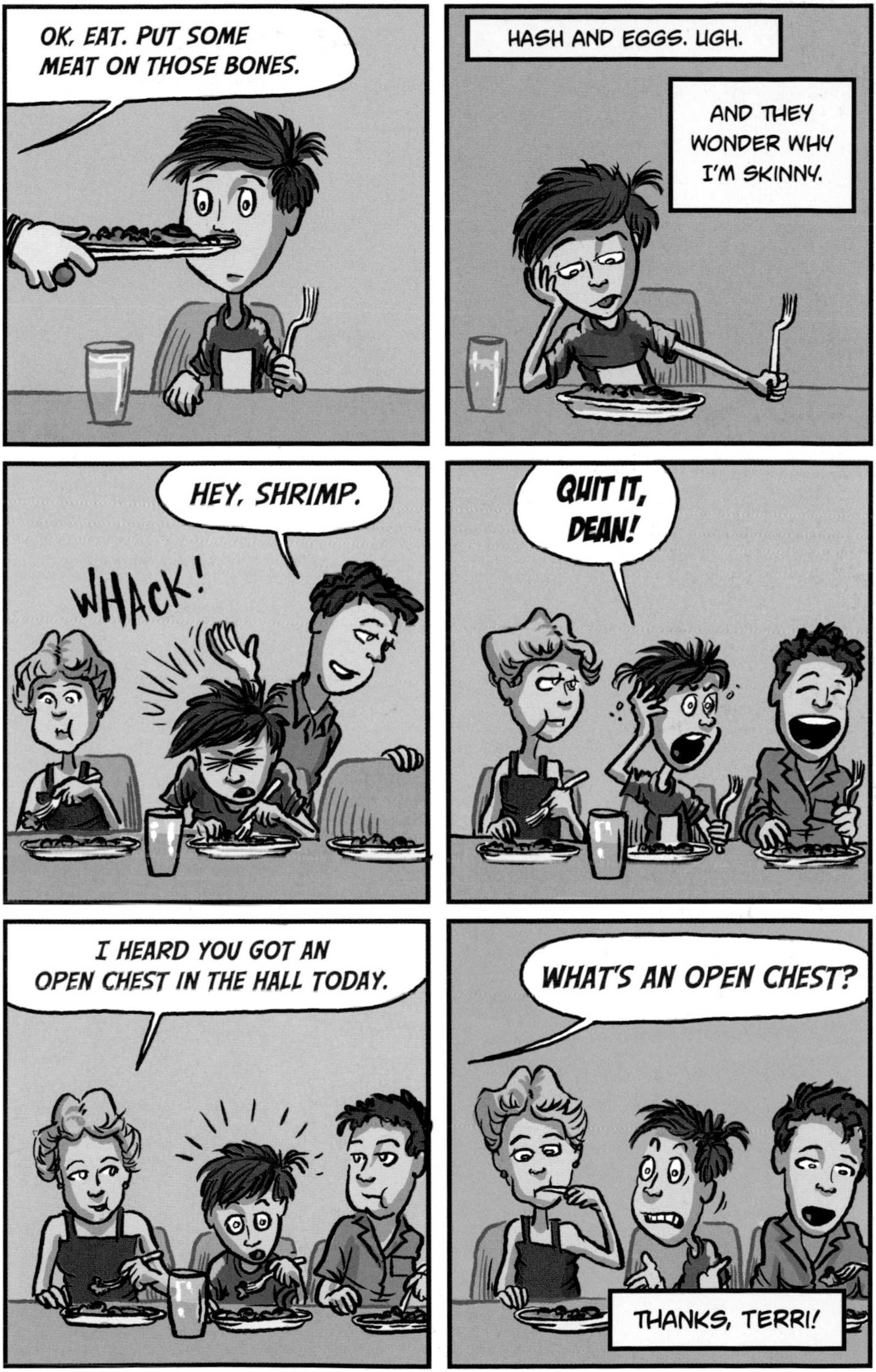
OK, EAT. PUT SOME MEAT ON THOSE BONES.
HASH AND EGGS. UGH.
AND THEY WONDER WHY I'M SKINNY.
HEY, SHRIMP.
WHACK!
QUIT IT, DEAN!
I HEARD YOU GOT AN OPEN CHEST IN THE HALL TODAY.
WHAT'S AN OPEN CHEST?
THANKS, TERRI!

WHAT'S AN OPEN CHEST?!
NOTHING, MOM.
IT'S WHEN YOU'RE JUST WALKING ALONG AND SOMEBODY SLAMS YOU IN THE CHEST.
OOOF!
SLAMS?! YOU MEAN "HIT"? SOMEBODY HIT YOU IN THE CHEST?
IT'S NOTHING, MAA!
YOU KNOW WHO DID IT?
NO, I DON'T KNOW THE KID. IT WAS FAST.
I HEARD IT WAS BRIAN WILKEY.
YEAH, SO THIS IS MY SISTER, TERRI, AND MY BROTHER, DEAN...

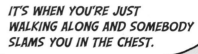

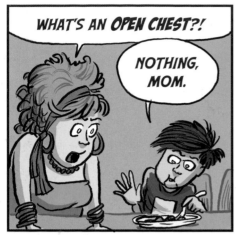

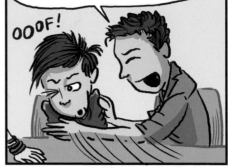

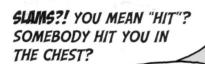

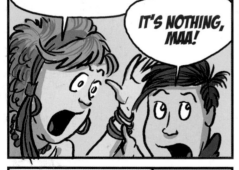

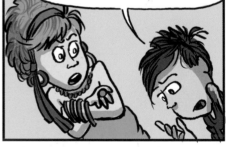

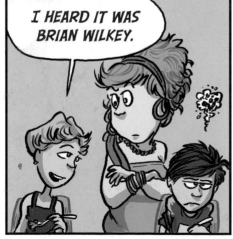

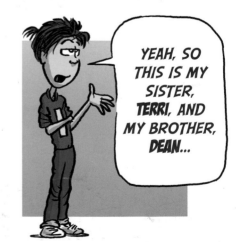

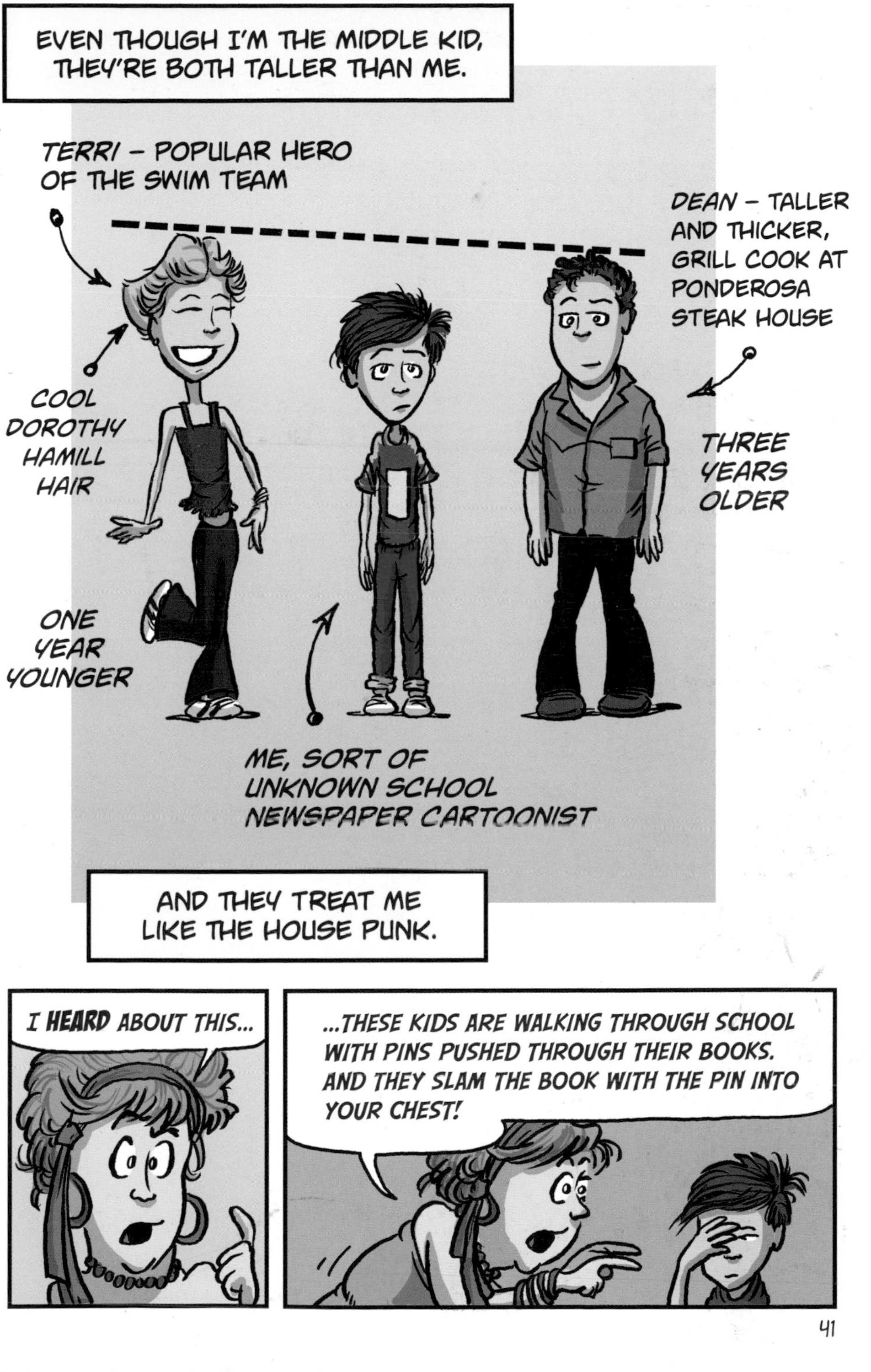
EVEN THOUGH I'M THE MIDDLE KID, THEY'RE BOTH TALLER THAN ME.
TERRI – POPULAR HERO OF THE SWIM TEAM
COOL DOROTHY HAMILL HAIR
ONE YEAR YOUNGER
DEAN – TALLER AND THICKER, GRILL COOK AT PONDEROSA STEAK HOUSE
THREE YEARS OLDER
ME, SORT OF UNKNOWN SCHOOL NEWSPAPER CARTOONIST
AND THEY TREAT ME LIKE THE HOUSE PUNK.
I HEARD ABOUT THIS...
...THESE KIDS ARE WALKING THROUGH SCHOOL WITH PINS PUSHED THROUGH THEIR BOOKS. AND THEY SLAM THE BOOK WITH THE PIN INTO YOUR CHEST!

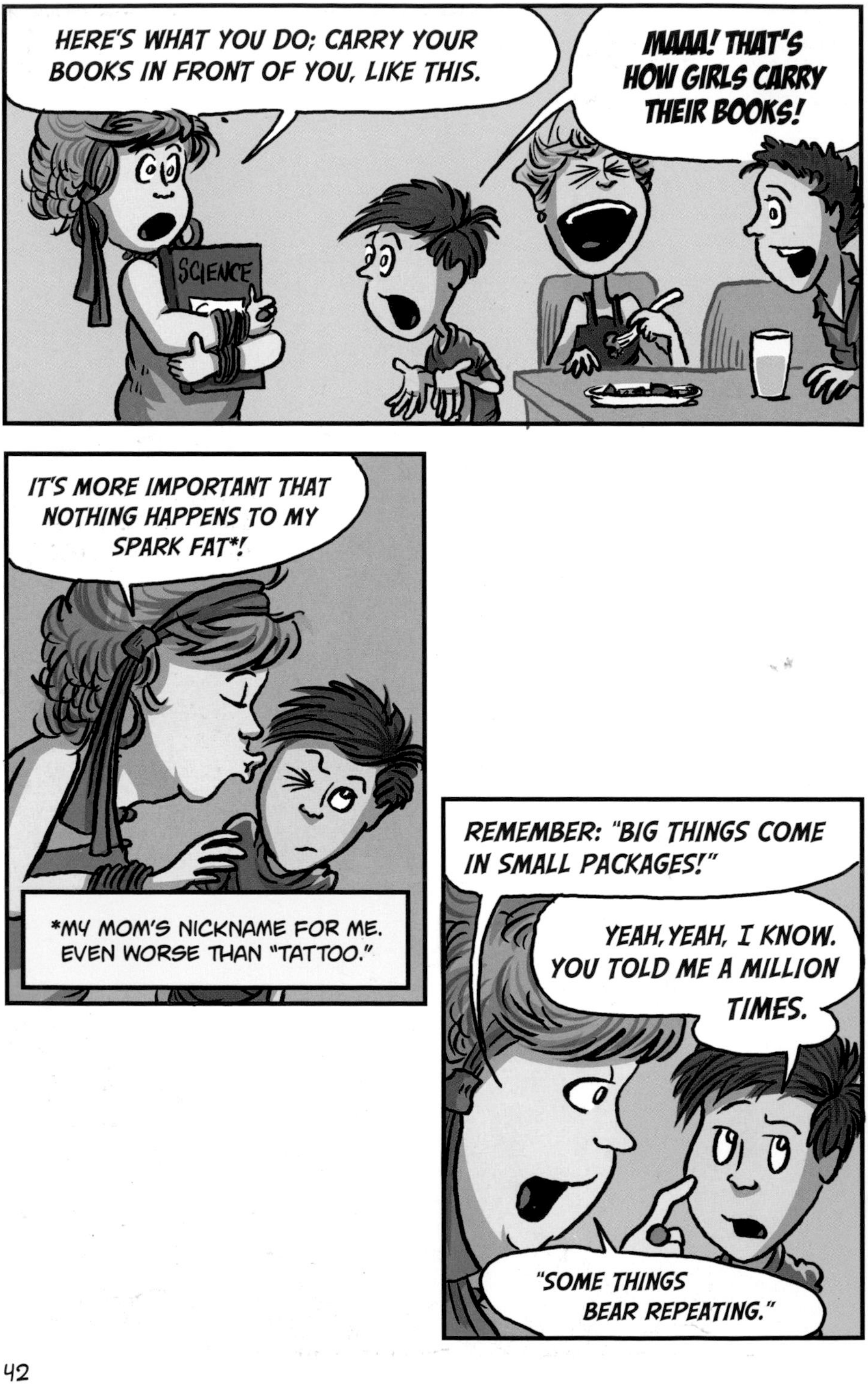
HERE'S WHAT YOU DO; CARRY YOUR BOOKS IN FRONT OF YOU, LIKE THIS.
SCIENCE
MAAA! THAT'S HOW GIRLS CARRY THEIR BOOKS!
IT'S MORE IMPORTANT THAT NOTHING HAPPENS TO MY SPARK FAT*!
*MY MOM'S NICKNAME FOR ME. EVEN WORSE THAN "TATTOO."
REMEMBER: "BIG THINGS COME IN SMALL PACKAGES!"
YEAH, YEAH, I KNOW. YOU TOLD ME A MILLION TIMES.
"SOME THINGS BEAR REPEATING."

plat·i·tude ← I JUST GOT THIS AS A VOCAB WORD IN ENGLISH...

/ˈpladeˌt(y)o͞od/

noun

a remark or statement, especially one with a moral content, that has been used too often to be interesting or thoughtful.

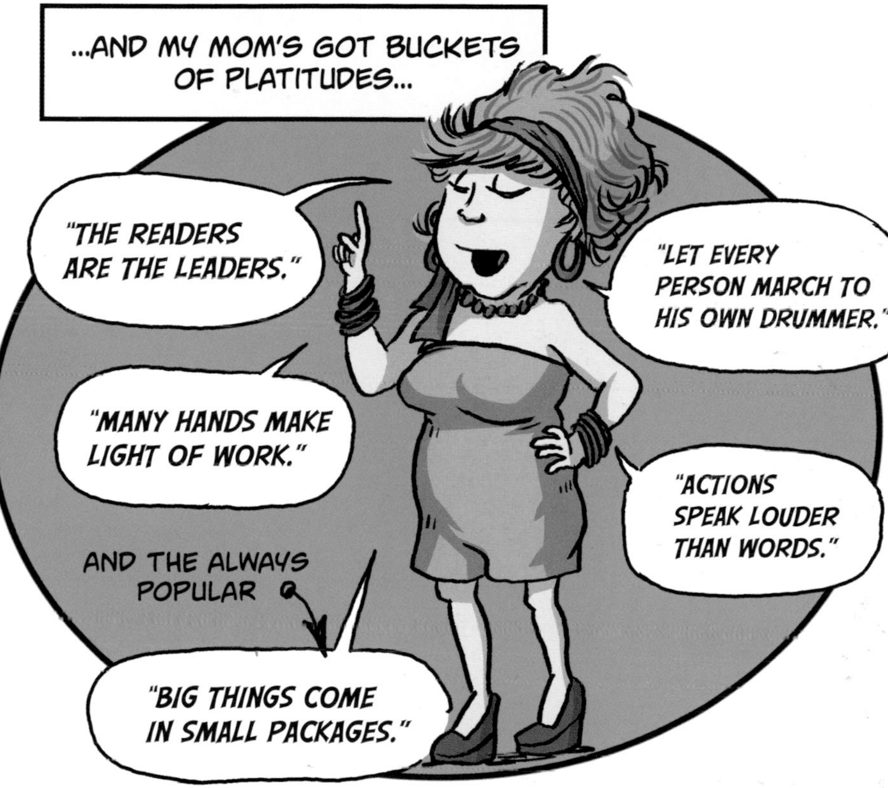
...AND MY MOM'S GOT BUCKETS OF PLATITUDES...
"THE READERS ARE THE LEADERS."
"LET EVERY PERSON MARCH TO HIS OWN DRUMMER."
"MANY HANDS MAKE LIGHT OF WORK."
"ACTIONS SPEAK LOUDER THAN WORDS."
AND THE ALWAYS POPULAR
"BIG THINGS COME IN SMALL PACKAGES."

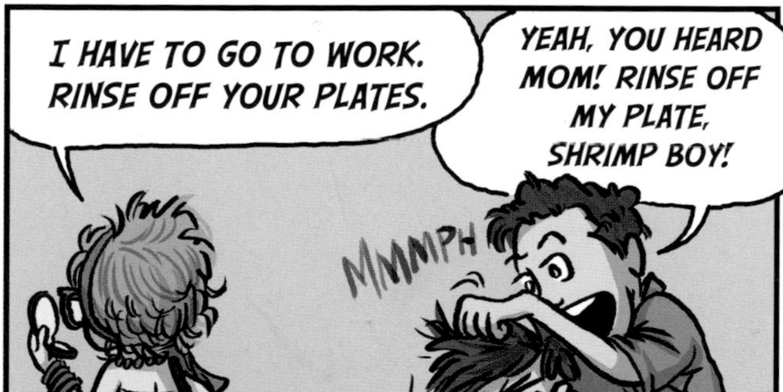
I HAVE TO GO TO WORK. RINSE OFF YOUR PLATES.
YEAH, YOU HEARD MOM! RINSE OFF MY PLATE, SHRIMP BOY!
MMMPH

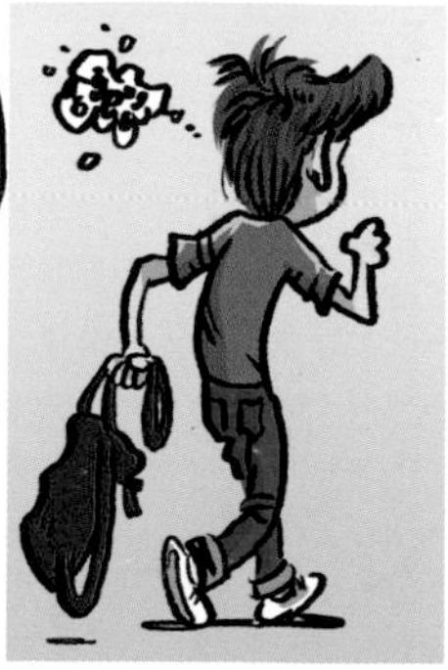

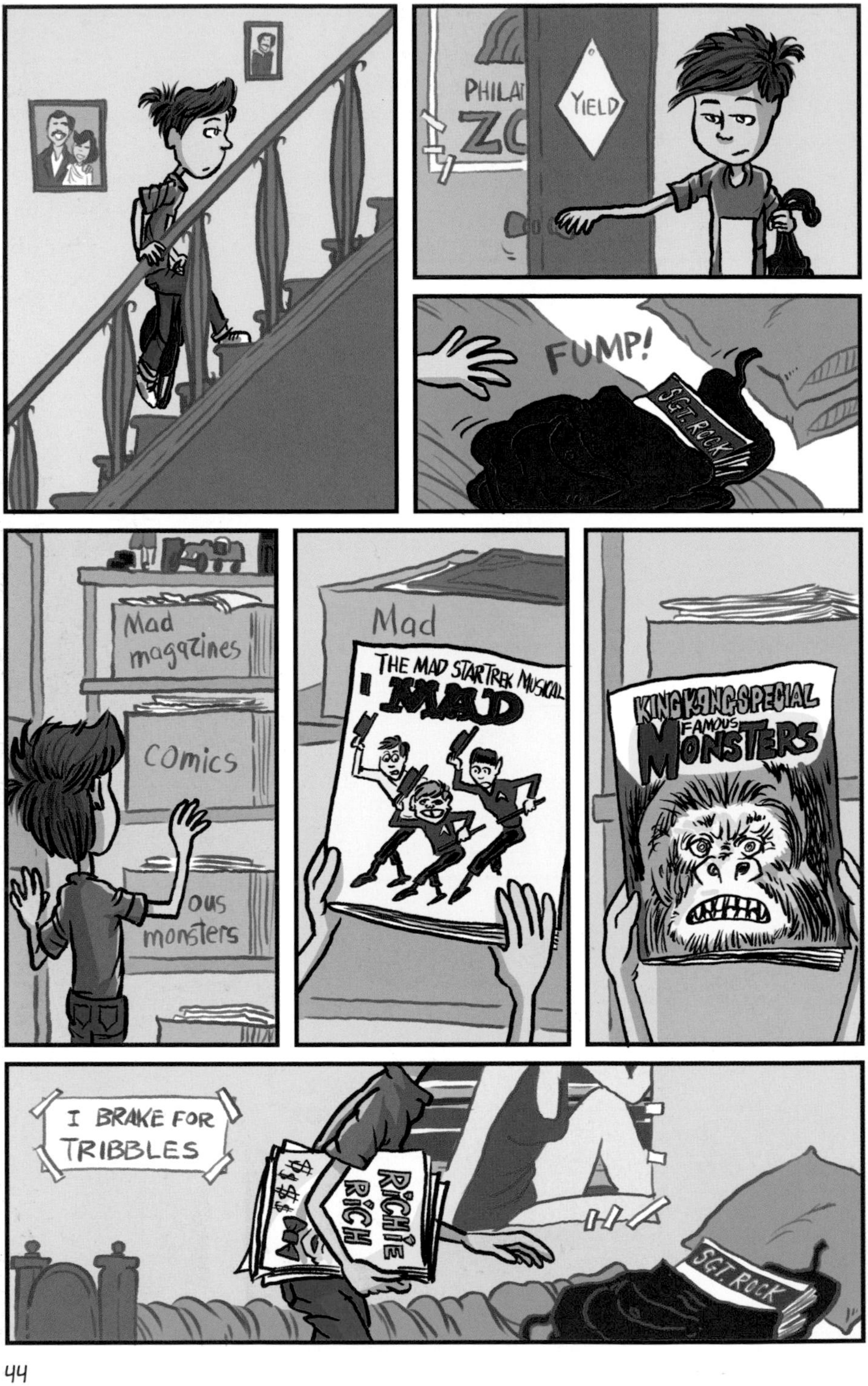
PHILA
ZO
YIELD
FUMP!
SGT. ROCK
Mad magazines
comics
ous monsters
Mad
THE MAD STAR TREK MUSICAL
MAD
KING KONG SPECIAL
FAMOUS MONSTERS
I BRAKE FOR TRIBBLES
RICHIE RICH
SGT. ROCK

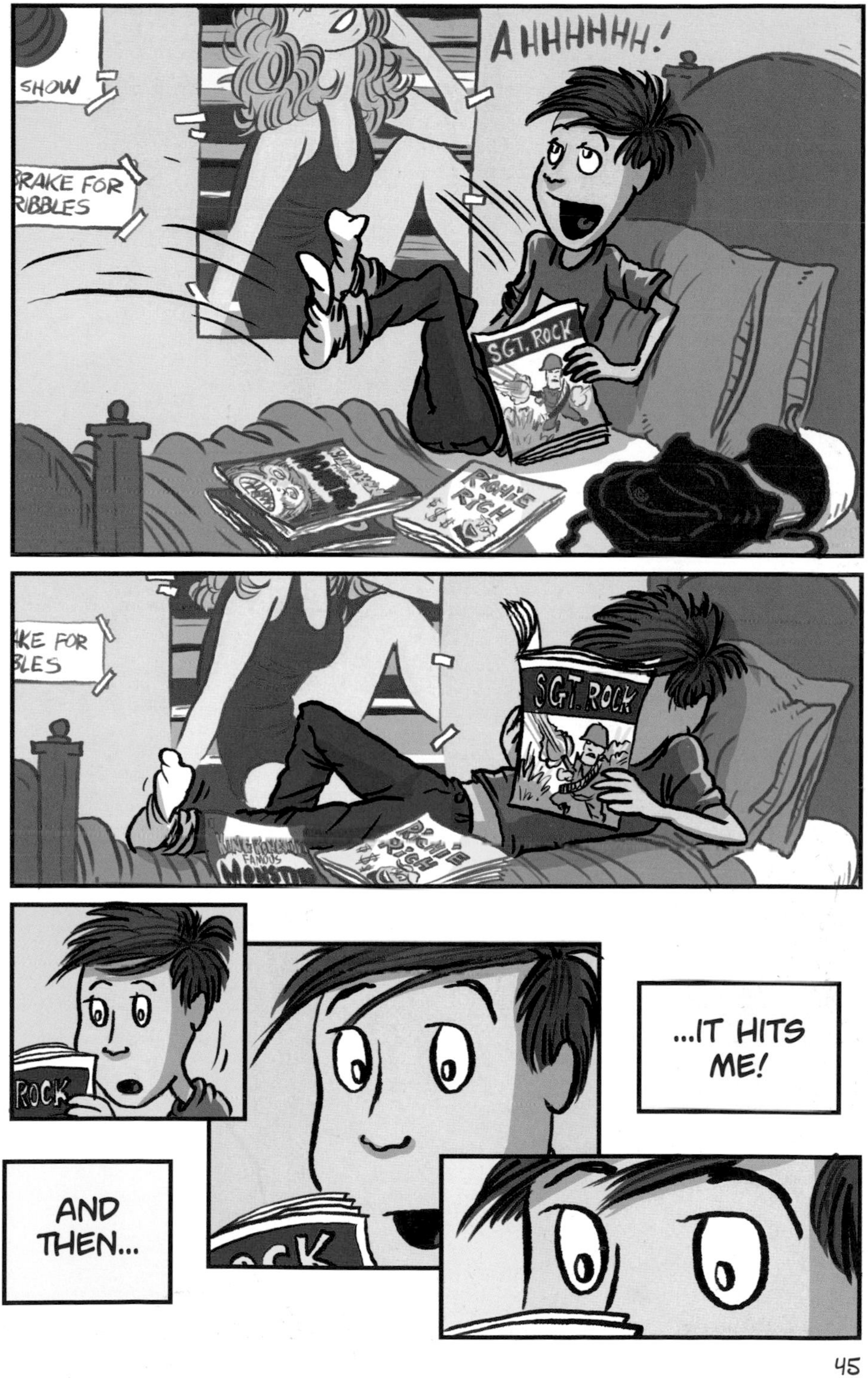

SHOW
BRAKE FOR
RIBBLES
AHHHHHH!
SGT. ROCK
RICHIE RICH
AKE FOR
BLES
SGT. ROCK
FAMOUS
RICHIE RICH
ROCK
...IT HITS ME!
AND THEN...

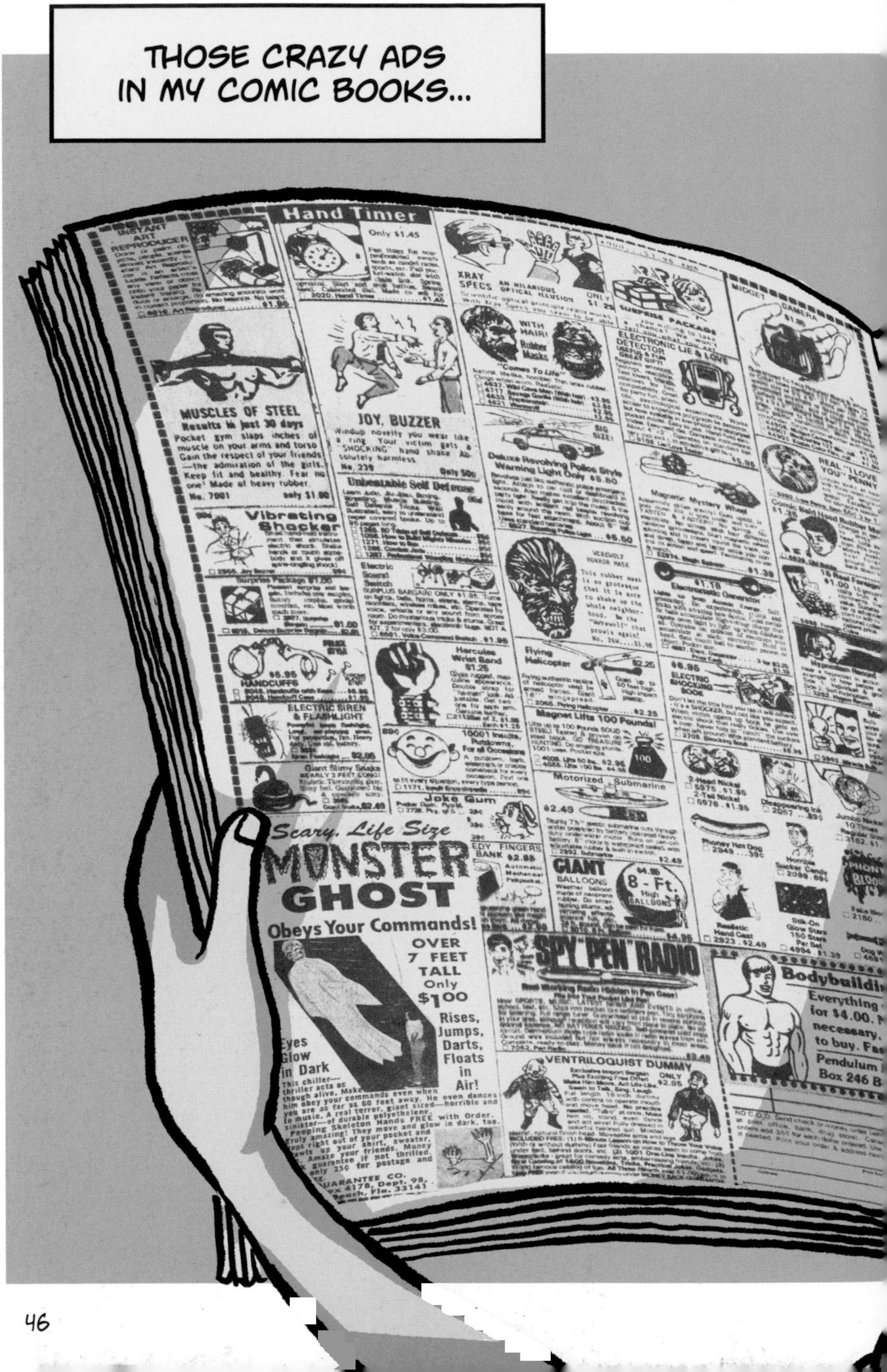
THOSE CRAZY ADS IN MY COMIC BOOKS...
Hand Timer
XRAY SPECS
MUSCLES OF STEEL
JOY BUZZER
Vibrating Shocker
WEREWOLF HORROR MASK
Magnetic Mystery Wheel
Electrostatic Generator
ELECTRIC SHOCKING BOOK
Hercules Wrist Band
Flying Helicopter
Magnet Lifts 100 Pounds!
Motorized Submarine
Joke Gum
Scary, Life Size
MONSTER GHOST
Obeys Your Commands!
OVER 7 FEET TALL Only $1.00
Rises, Jumps, Darts, Floats in Air!
Eyes Glow in Dark
GIANT BALLOONS
8-Ft. High BALLOONS
SPY "PEN" RADIO
VENTRILOQUIST DUMMY
Bodybuilding
Phoney Hot Dog
Disappearing Ink

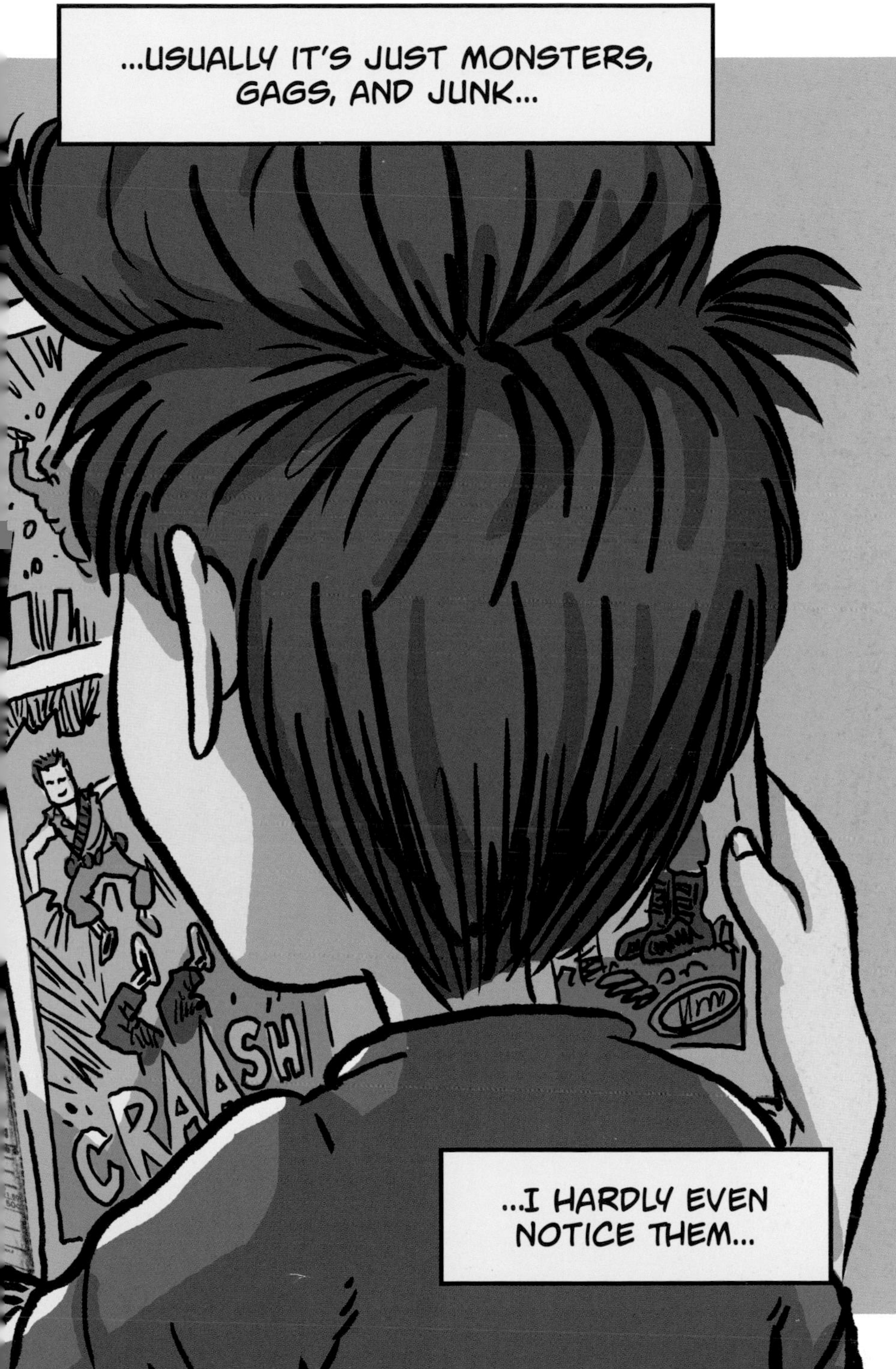
...USUALLY IT'S JUST MONSTERS, GAGS, AND JUNK...
CRAASH
...I HARDLY EVEN NOTICE THEM...

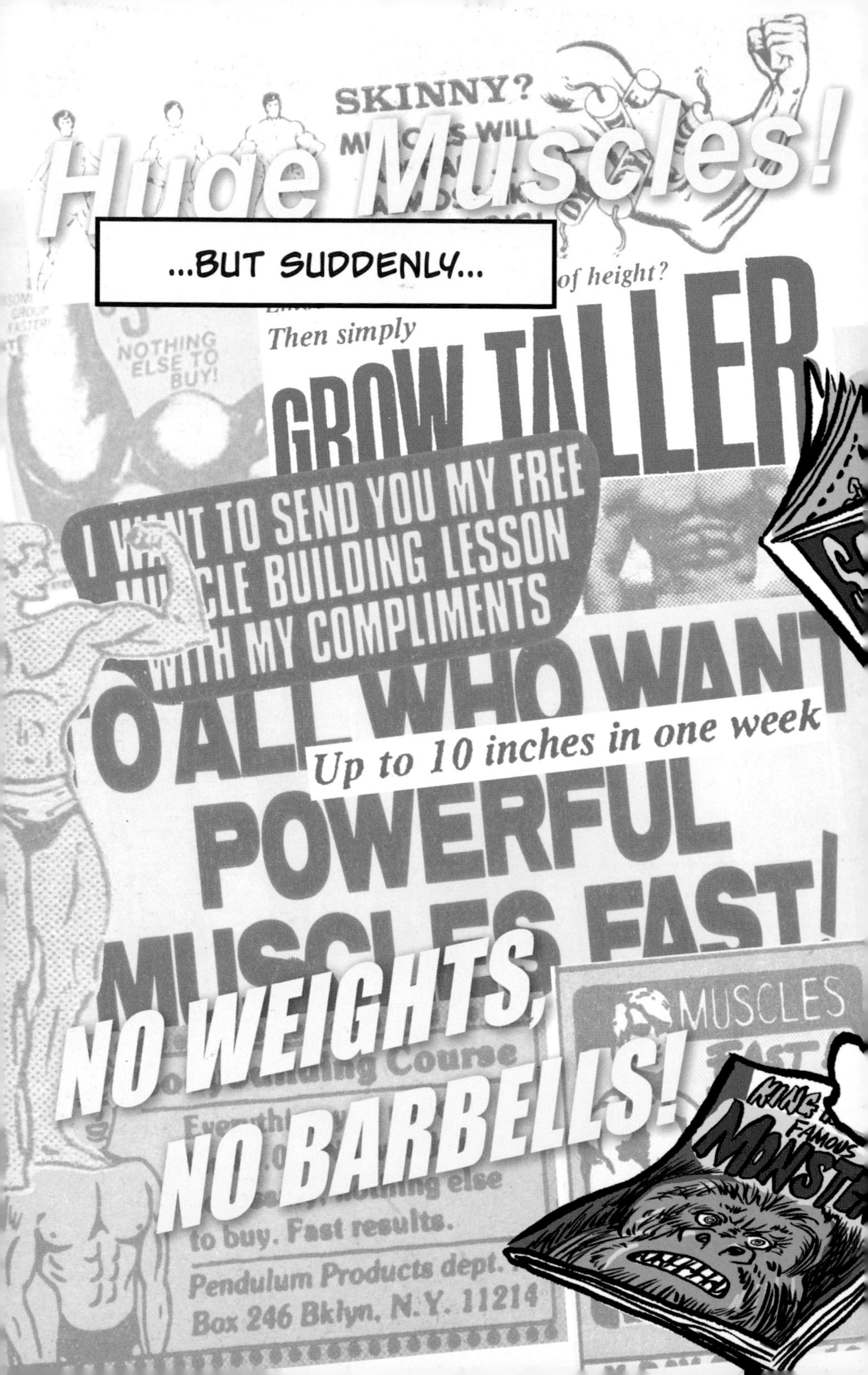

SKINNY?
Huge Muscles!
...BUT SUDDENLY...
of height?
Then simply
GROW TALLER
NOTHING ELSE TO BUY!
I WANT TO SEND YOU MY FREE MUSCLE BUILDING LESSON WITH MY COMPLIMENTS
Up to 10 inches in one week
POWERFUL
NO WEIGHTS, NO BARBELLS!
MUSCLES
to buy. Fast results.
Pendulum Products dept.
Box 246 Bklyn, N.Y. 11214
FAMOUS

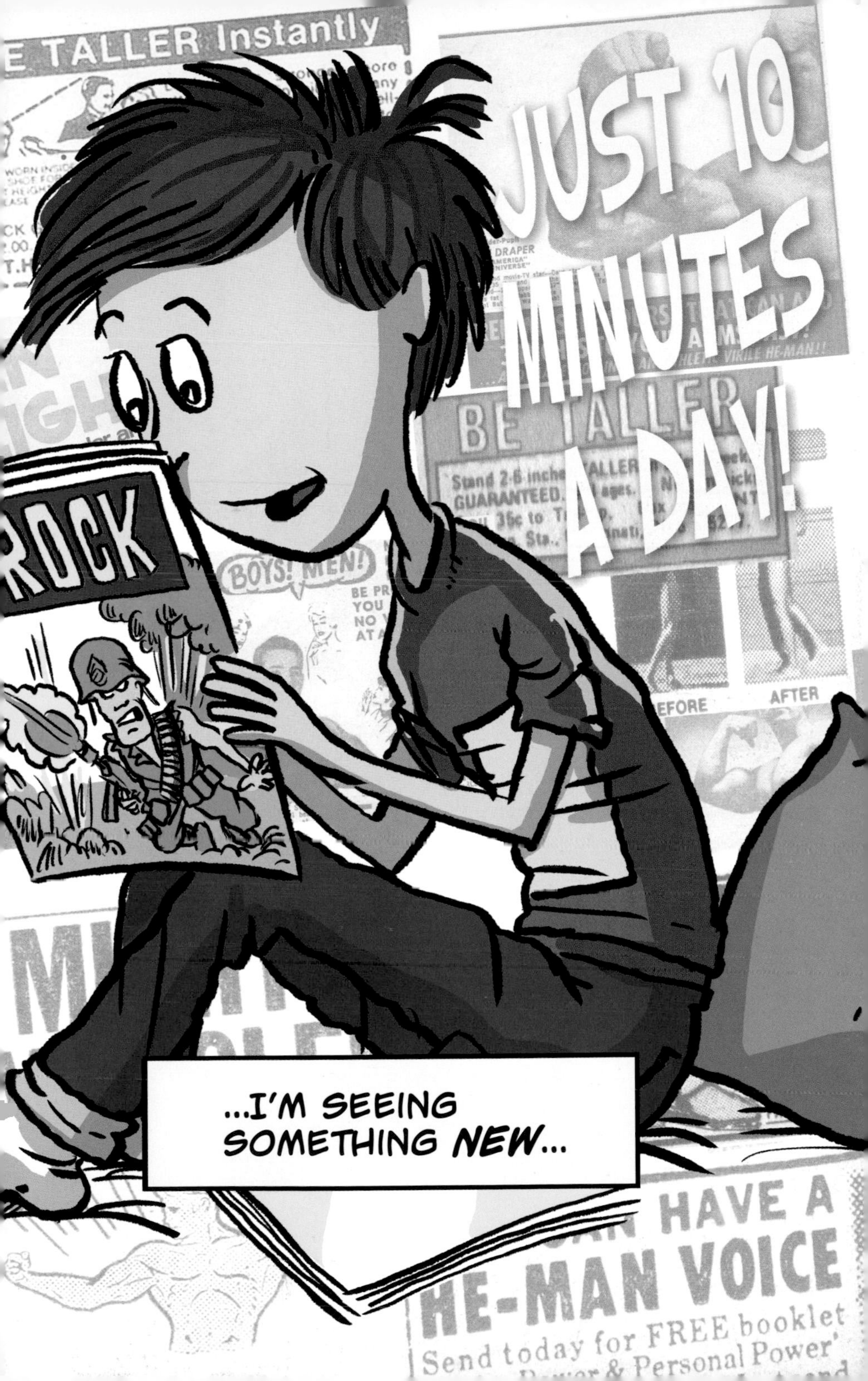

BE TALLER Instantly
JUST 10 MINUTES A DAY!
BE TALLER
GUARANTEED.
ROCK
BOYS! MEN!
BEFORE
AFTER
...I'M SEEING SOMETHING *NEW*...
HAVE A HE-MAN VOICE
Send today for FREE booklet

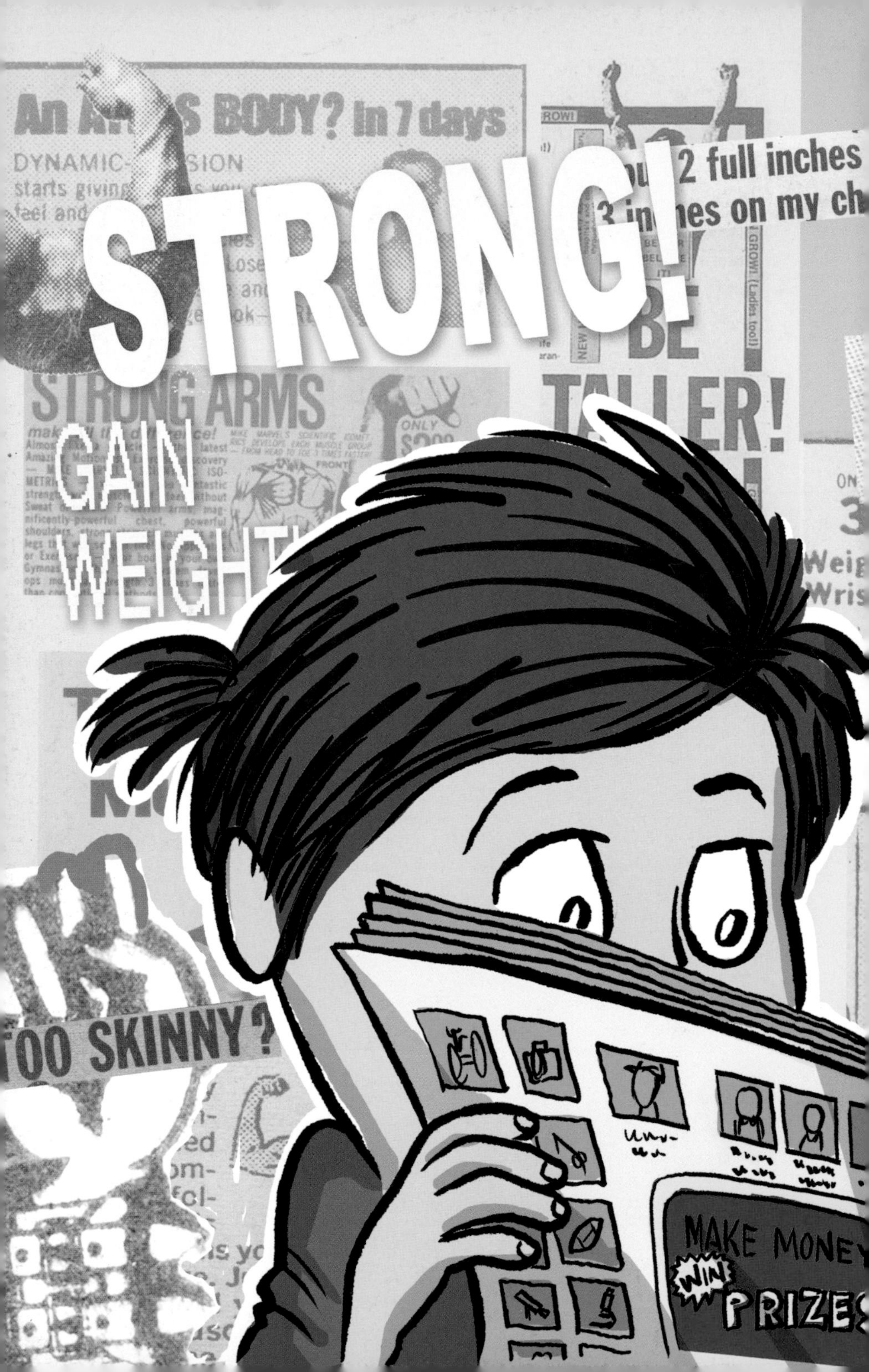
STRONG!
GAIN WEIGHT!
STRONG ARMS
BE TALLER!
TOO SKINNY?
2 full inches
MAKE MONEY
WIN
PRIZES

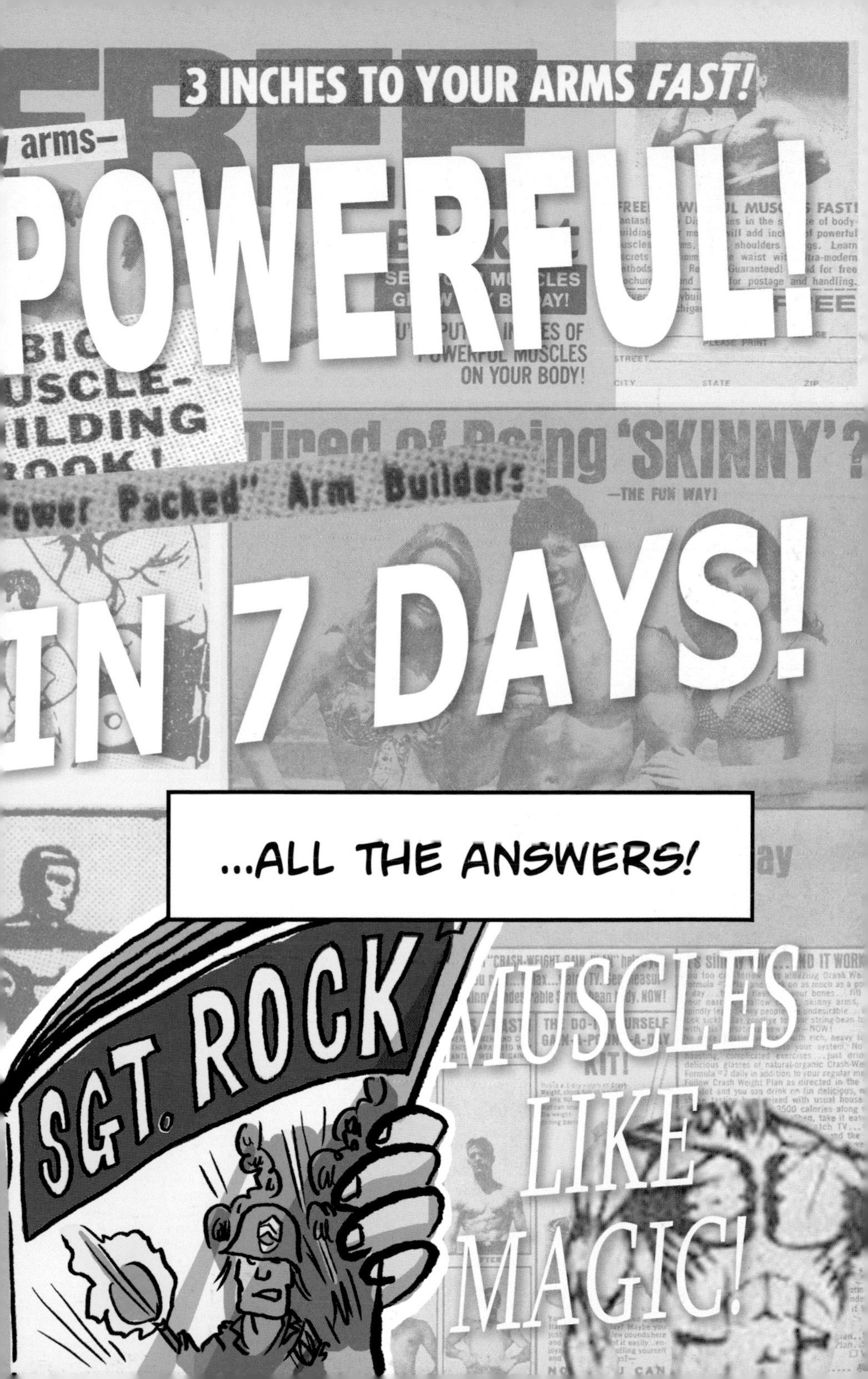
3 INCHES TO YOUR ARMS FAST!
arms—
POWERFUL!
POWERFUL MUSCLES
ON YOUR BODY!
Tired of Being 'SKINNY'?
—THE FUN WAY!
"Power Packed" Arm Builders
IN 7 DAYS!
...ALL THE ANSWERS!
SGT. ROCK
MUSCLES
LIKE
MAGIC!

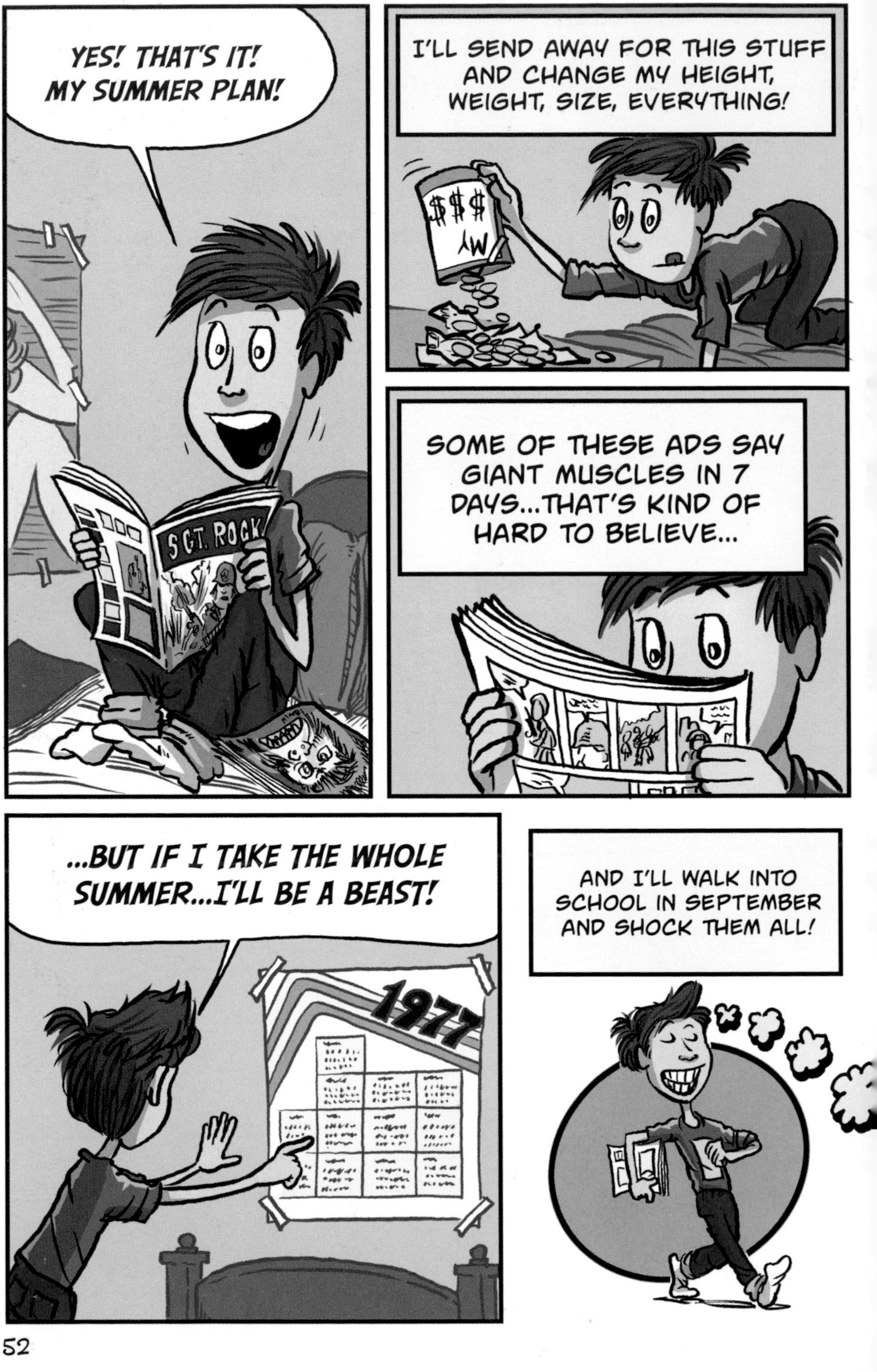
YES! THAT'S IT! MY SUMMER PLAN!
S.G.T. ROCK
I'LL SEND AWAY FOR THIS STUFF AND CHANGE MY HEIGHT, WEIGHT, SIZE, EVERYTHING!
$$$
MY
SOME OF THESE ADS SAY GIANT MUSCLES IN 7 DAYS...THAT'S KIND OF HARD TO BELIEVE...
...BUT IF I TAKE THE WHOLE SUMMER...I'LL BE A BEAST!
1977
AND I'LL WALK INTO SCHOOL IN SEPTEMBER AND SHOCK THEM ALL!

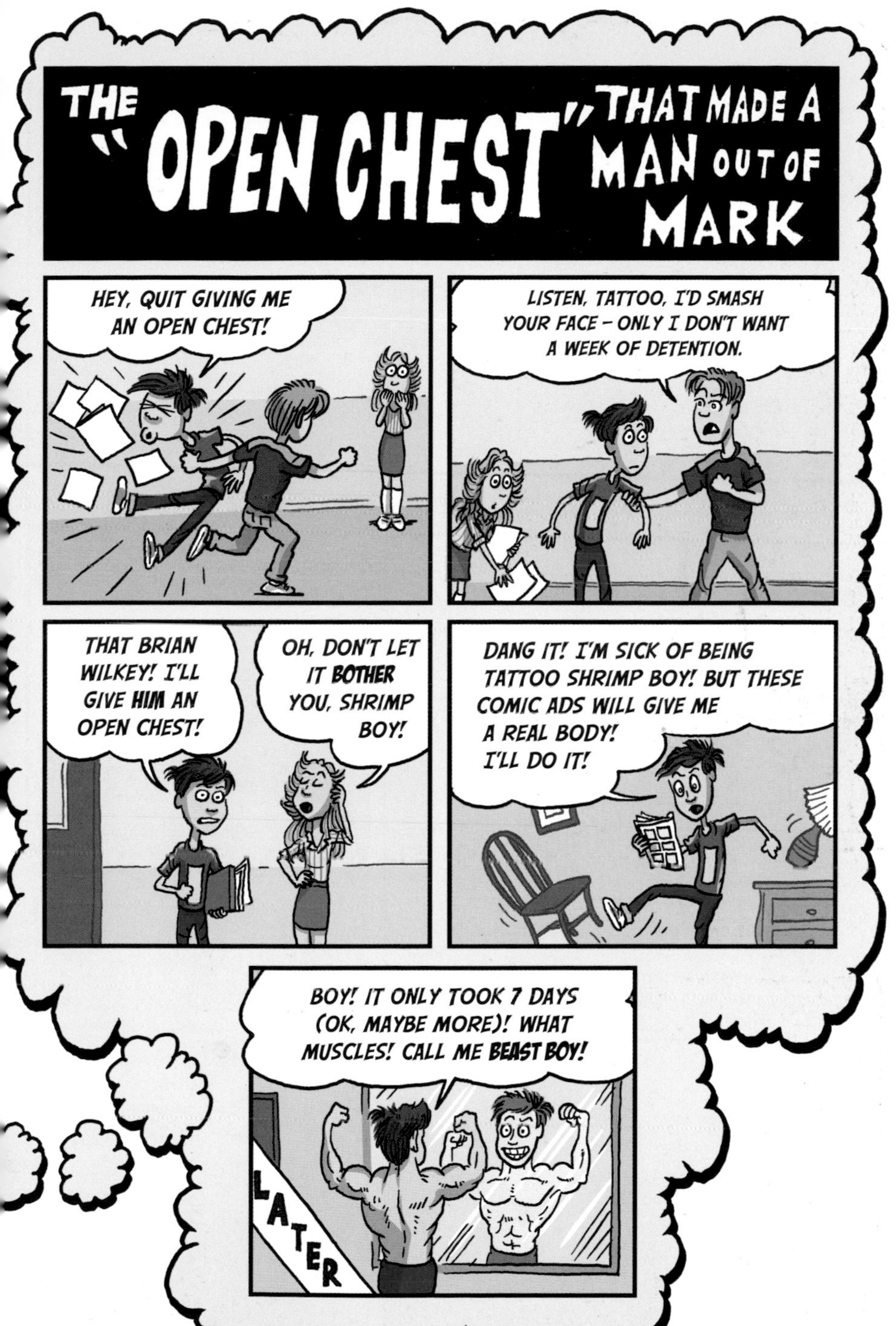
THE "OPEN CHEST" THAT MADE A MAN OUT OF MARK
HEY, QUIT GIVING ME AN OPEN CHEST!
LISTEN, TATTOO, I'D SMASH YOUR FACE – ONLY I DON'T WANT A WEEK OF DETENTION.
THAT BRIAN WILKEY! I'LL GIVE HIM AN OPEN CHEST!
OH, DON'T LET IT BOTHER YOU, SHRIMP BOY!
DANG IT! I'M SICK OF BEING TATTOO SHRIMP BOY! BUT THESE COMIC ADS WILL GIVE ME A REAL BODY! I'LL DO IT!
BOY! IT ONLY TOOK 7 DAYS (OK, MAYBE MORE)! WHAT MUSCLES! CALL ME BEAST BOY!
LATER

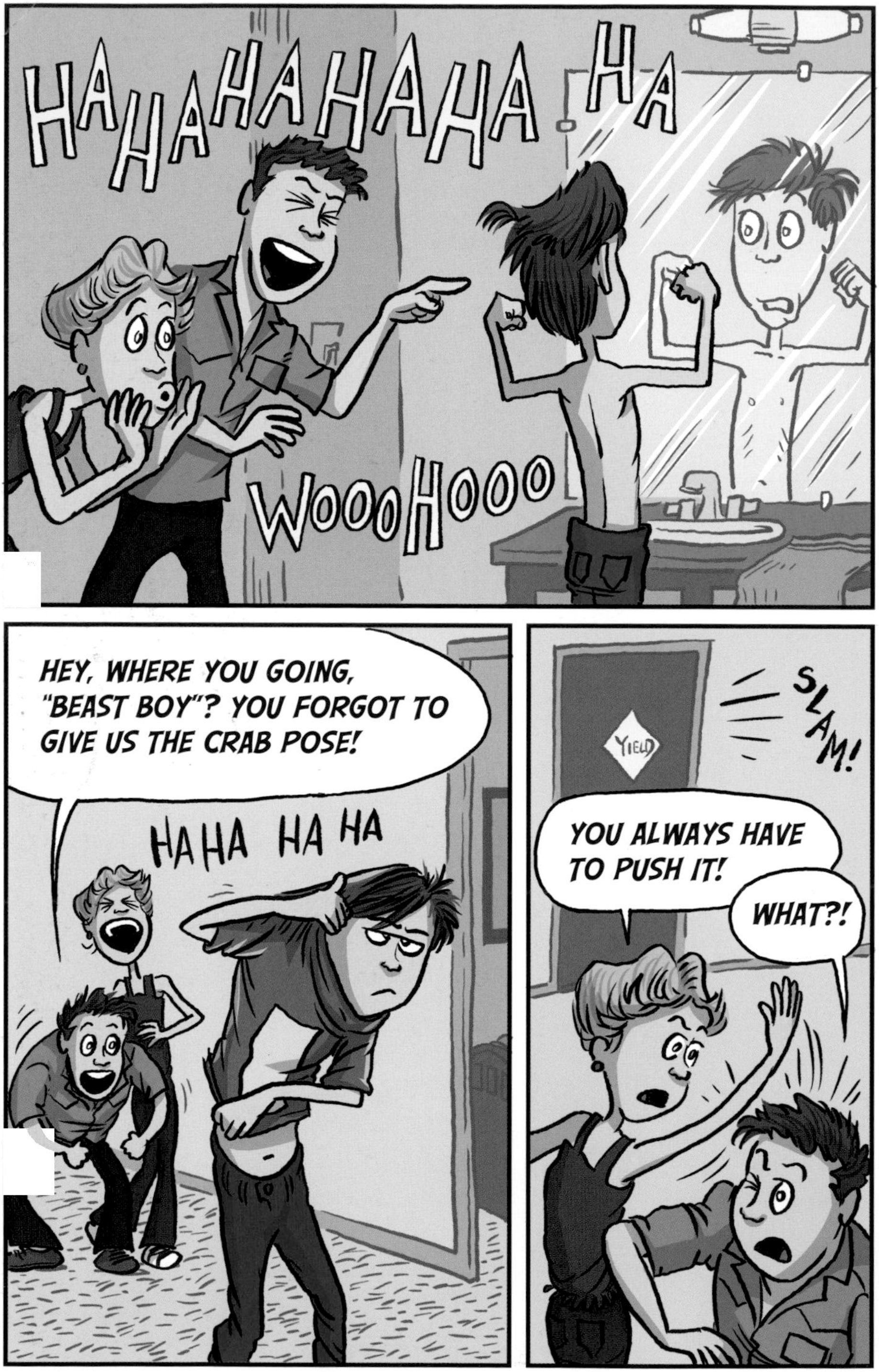

HAHAHAHAHAHA HA
WOOOHOOO
HEY, WHERE YOU GOING, "BEAST BOY"? YOU FORGOT TO GIVE US THE CRAB POSE!
HAHA HA HA
YIELD
SLAM!
YOU ALWAYS HAVE TO PUSH IT!
WHAT?!

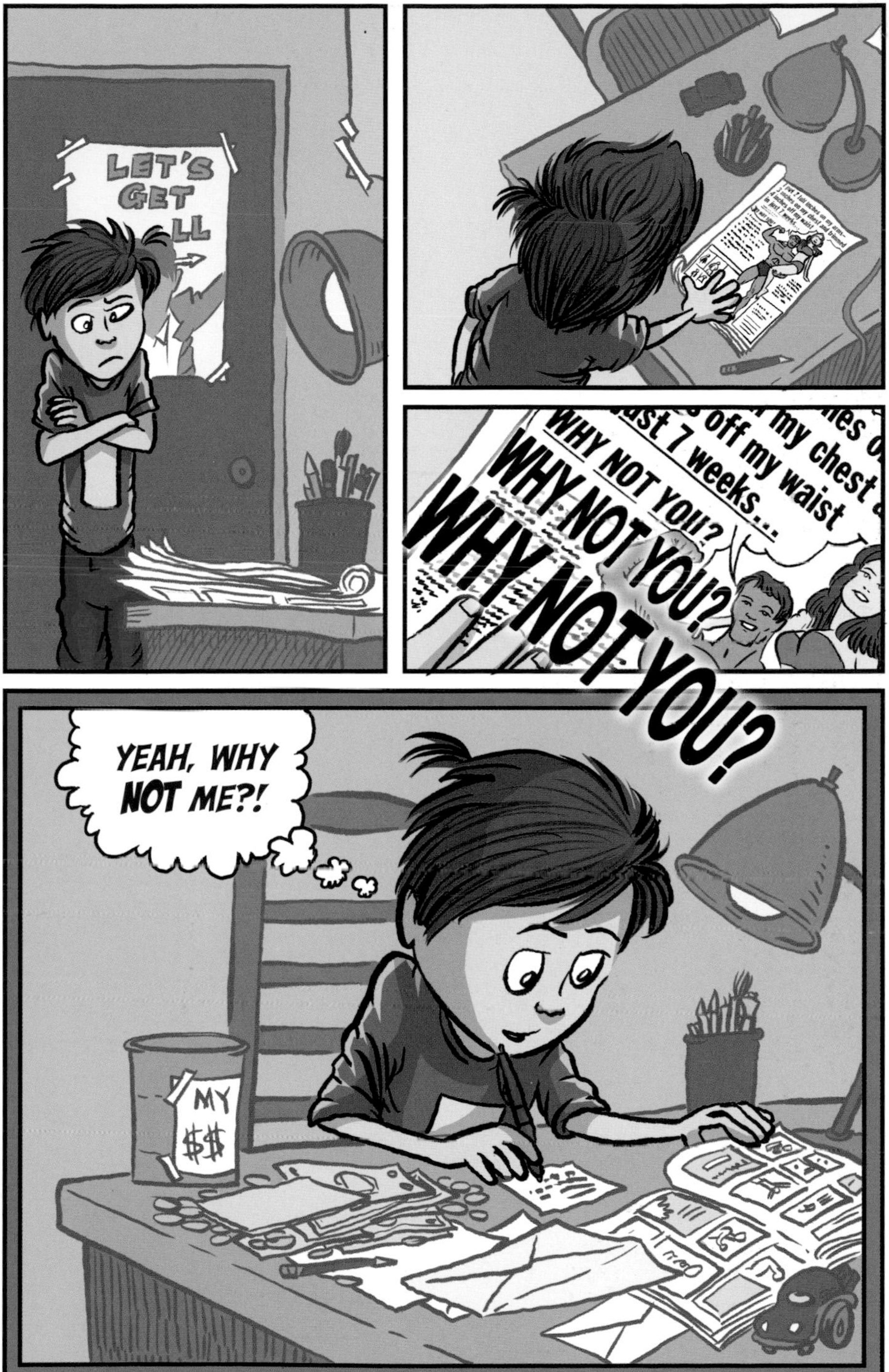
LET'S GET
WHY NOT YOU?
WHY NOT YOU?
WHY NOT YOU?
YEAH, WHY NOT ME?!
MY $$

CHAPTER 5

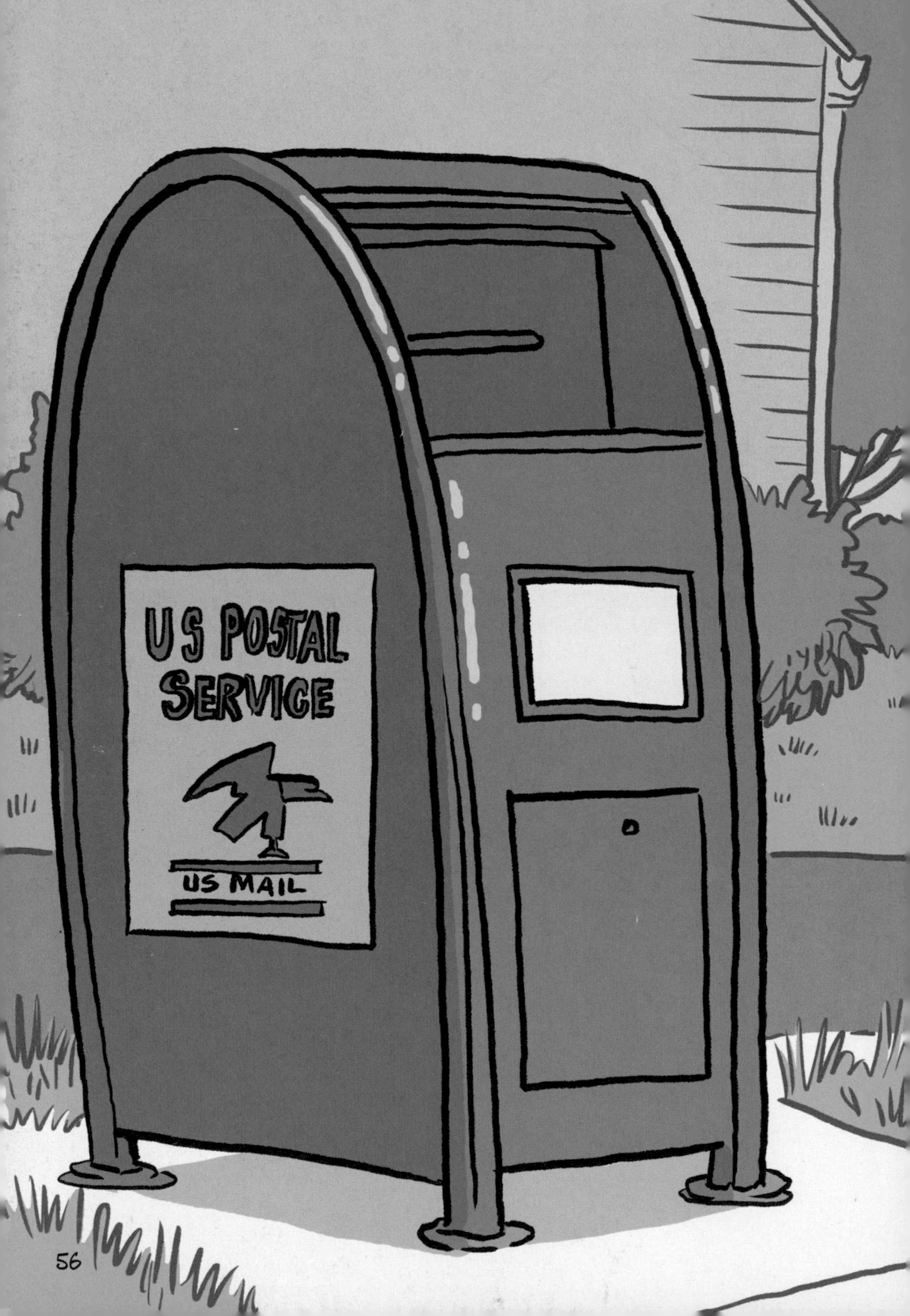
U S POSTAL SERVICE
US MAIL

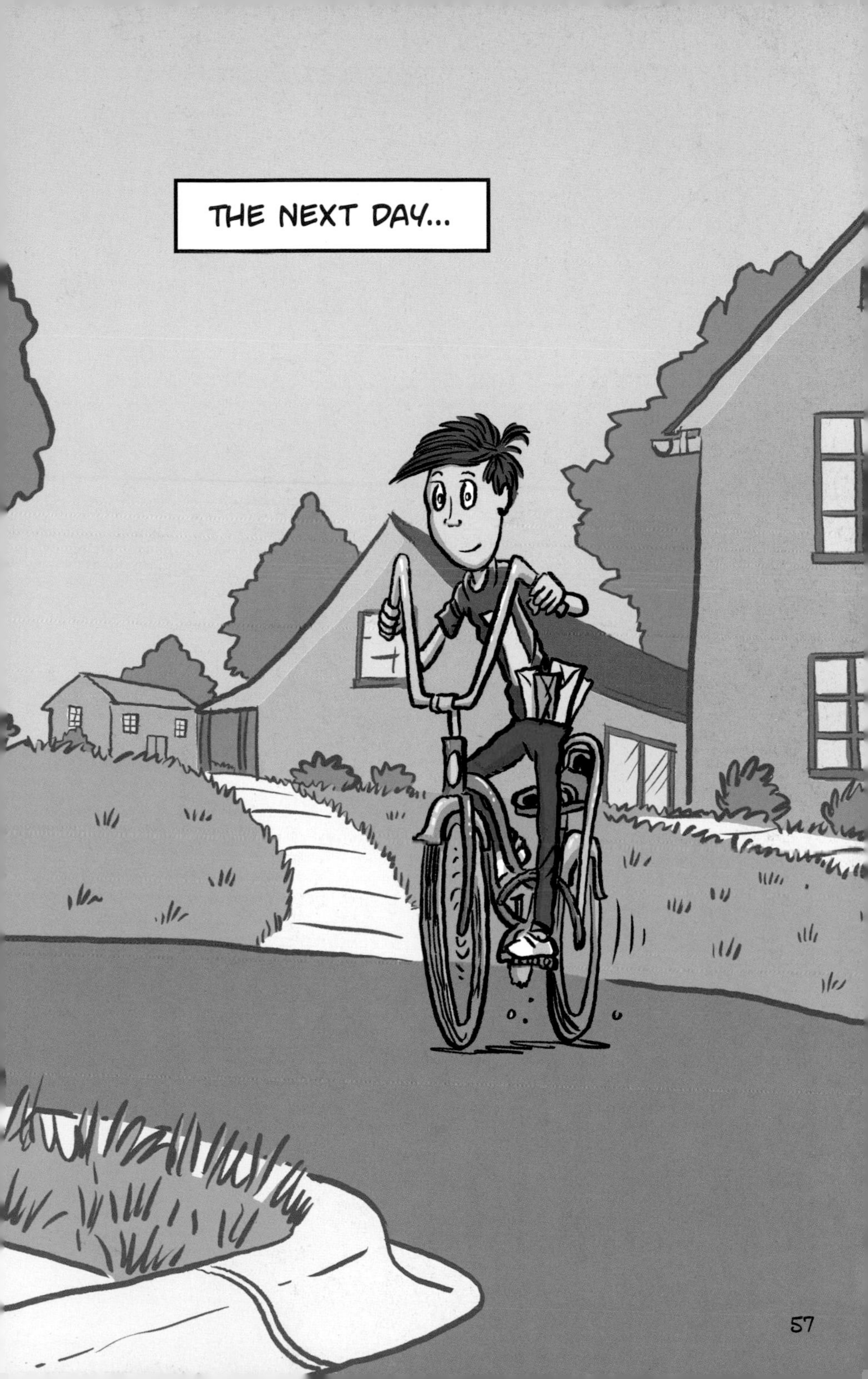
THE NEXT DAY...

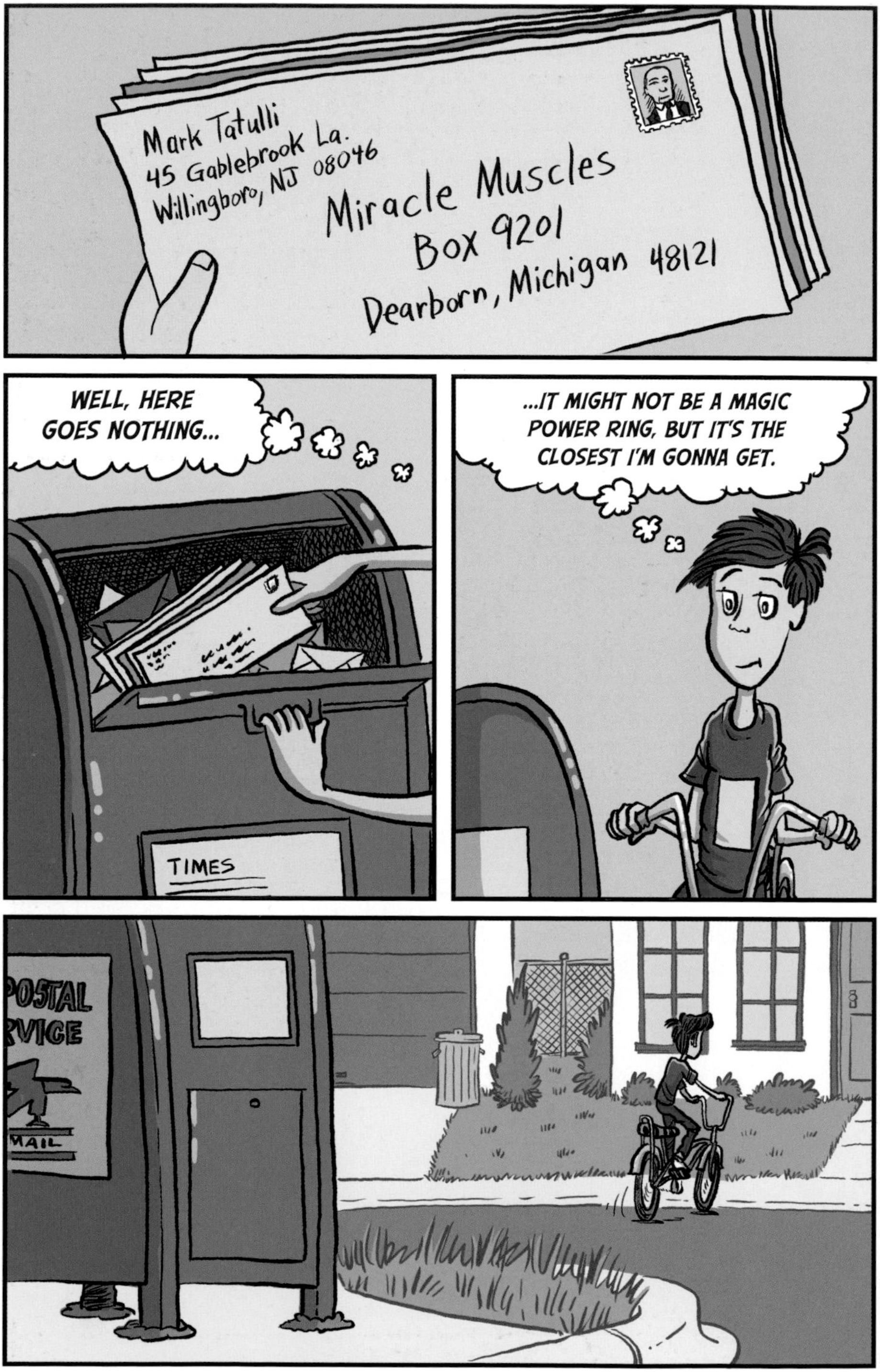
Mark Tatulli
45 Gablebrook La.
Willingboro, NJ 08046
Miracle Muscles
Box 9201
Dearborn, Michigan 48121
WELL, HERE GOES NOTHING...
TIMES
...IT MIGHT NOT BE A MAGIC POWER RING, BUT IT'S THE CLOSEST I'M GONNA GET.
POSTAL
RVICE
MAIL

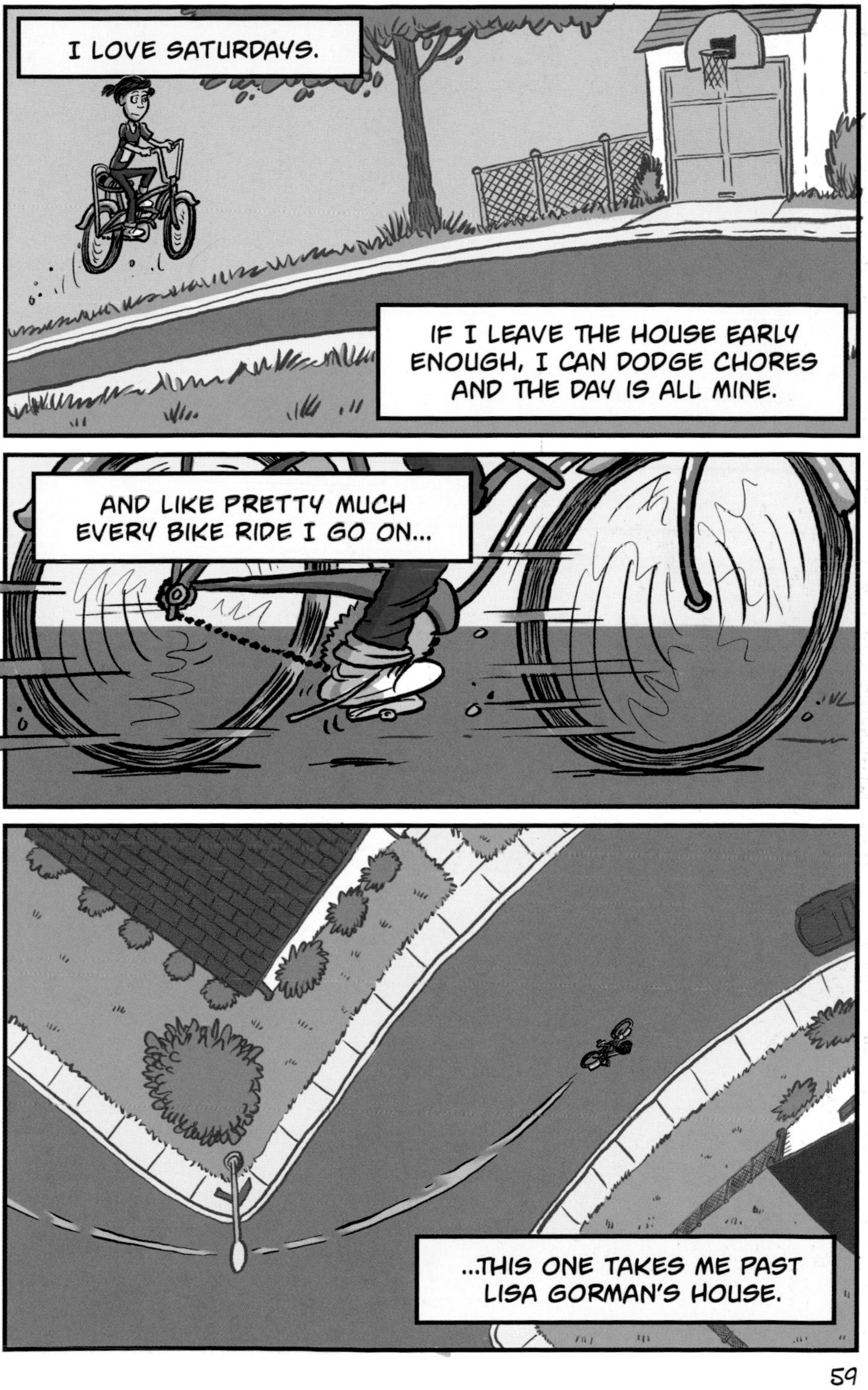
I LOVE SATURDAYS.
IF I LEAVE THE HOUSE EARLY ENOUGH, I CAN DODGE CHORES AND THE DAY IS ALL MINE.
AND LIKE PRETTY MUCH EVERY BIKE RIDE I GO ON...
...THIS ONE TAKES ME PAST LISA GORMAN'S HOUSE.

I SLOW DOWN...

...BUT NOT TOO SLOW...

...DON'T WANT TO BE OBVIOUS...

...I'M JUST HOPING FOR A GLIMPSE...

HEY!

OOOF!

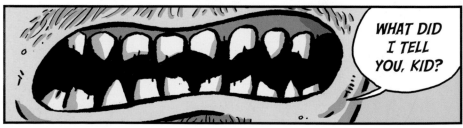

WHAT DID I TELL YOU, KID?

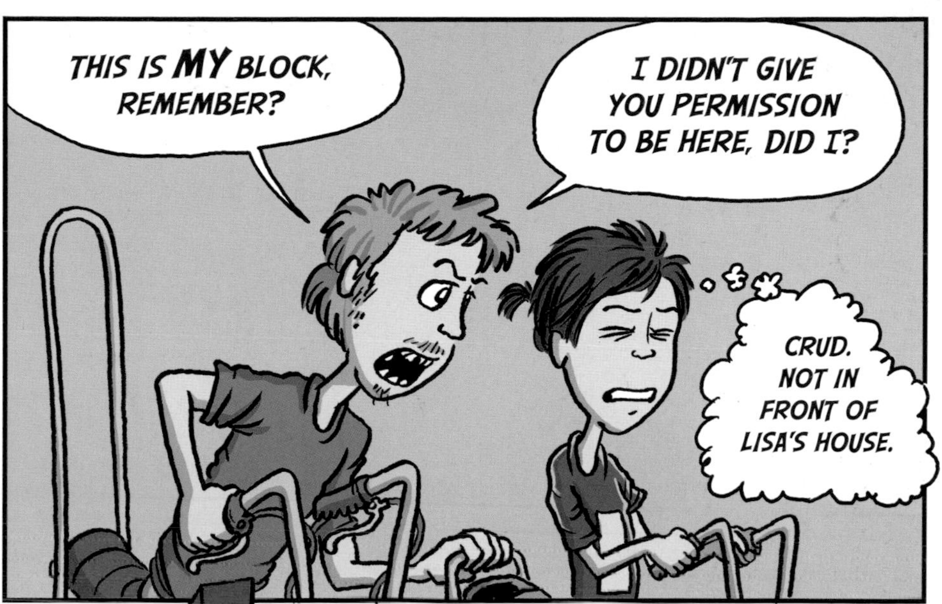
THIS IS MY BLOCK, REMEMBER?
I DIDN'T GIVE YOU PERMISSION TO BE HERE, DID I?
CRUD. NOT IN FRONT OF LISA'S HOUSE.

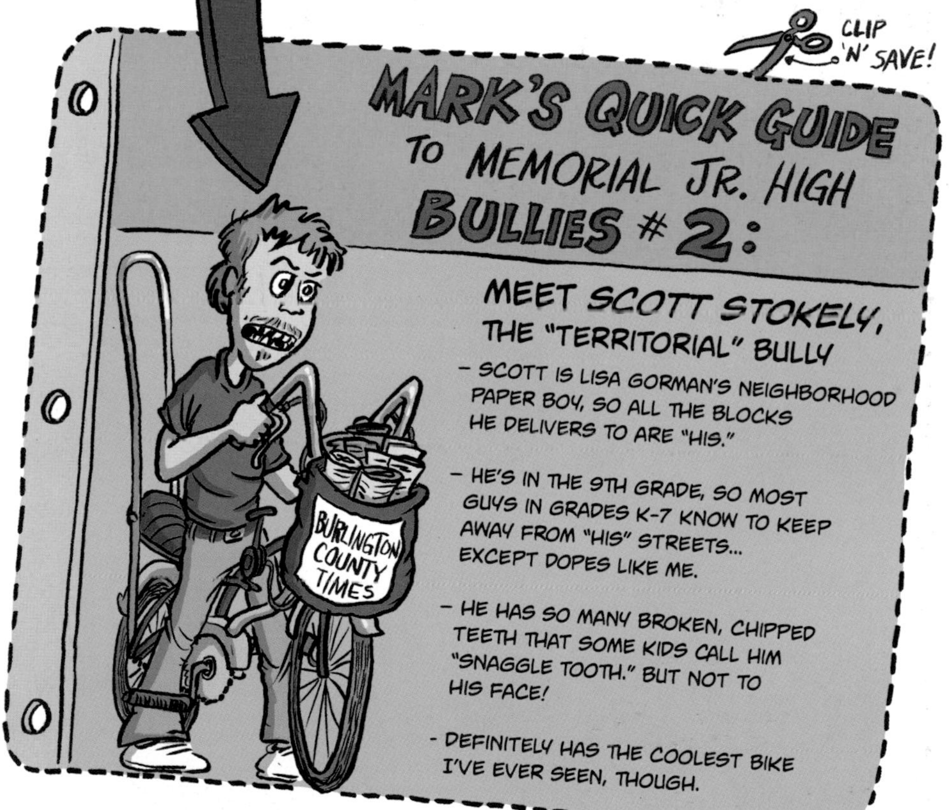
CLIP 'N' SAVE!
MARK'S QUICK GUIDE TO MEMORIAL JR. HIGH BULLIES # 2:
MEET SCOTT STOKELY, THE "TERRITORIAL" BULLY
- SCOTT IS LISA GORMAN'S NEIGHBORHOOD PAPER BOY, SO ALL THE BLOCKS HE DELIVERS TO ARE "HIS."
- HE'S IN THE 9TH GRADE, SO MOST GUYS IN GRADES K-7 KNOW TO KEEP AWAY FROM "HIS" STREETS... EXCEPT DOPES LIKE ME.
- HE HAS SO MANY BROKEN, CHIPPED TEETH THAT SOME KIDS CALL HIM "SNAGGLE TOOTH." BUT NOT TO HIS FACE!
- DEFINITELY HAS THE COOLEST BIKE I'VE EVER SEEN, THOUGH.
BURLINGTON COUNTY TIMES

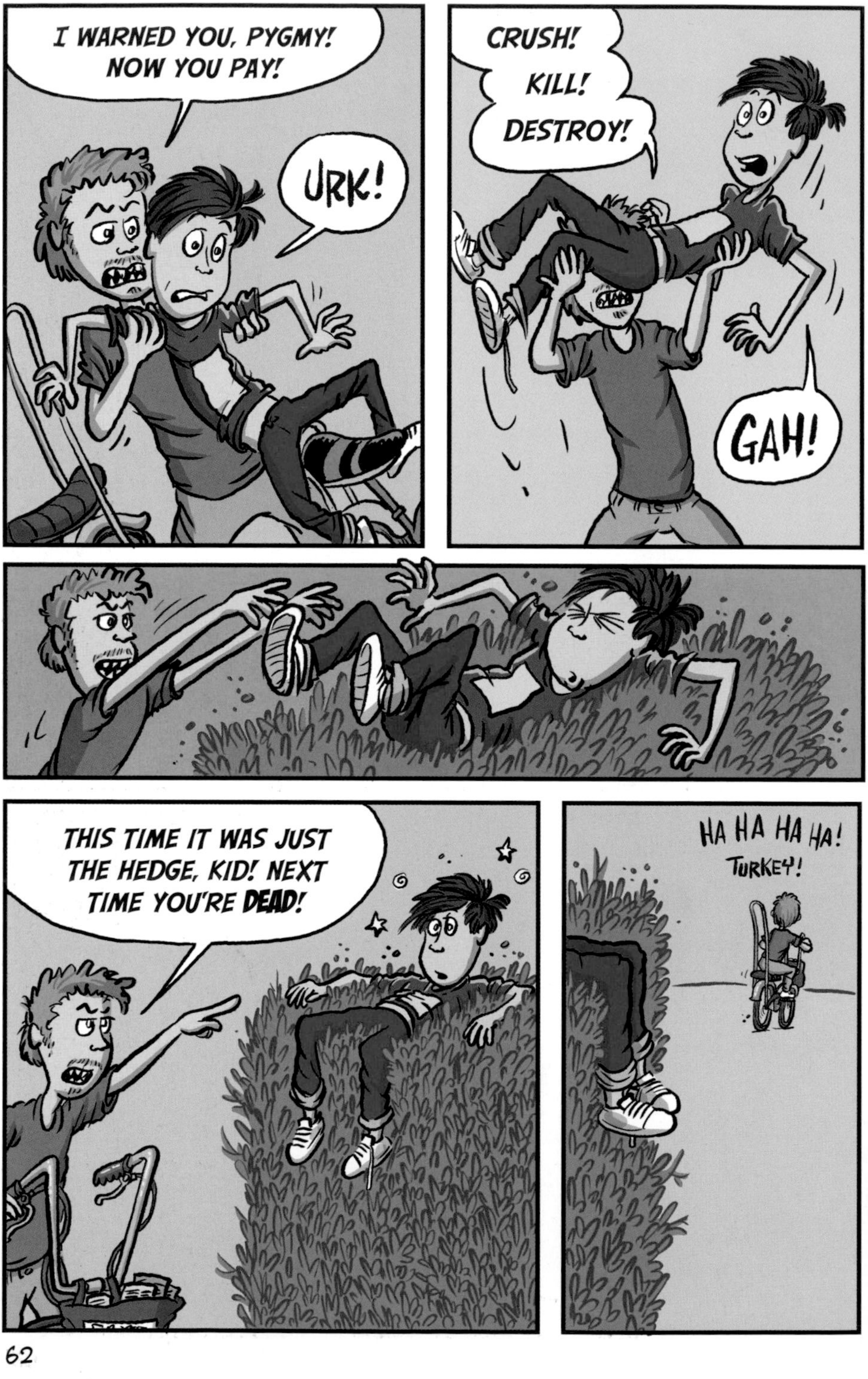
I WARNED YOU, PYGMY! NOW YOU PAY!
URK!
CRUSH!
KILL!
DESTROY!
GAH!
THIS TIME IT WAS JUST THE HEDGE, KID! NEXT TIME YOU'RE **DEAD**!
HA HA HA HA!
TURKEY!

CRUD.

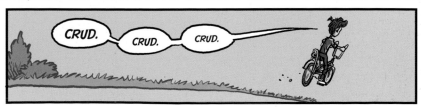

CRUD. CRUD. CRUD.

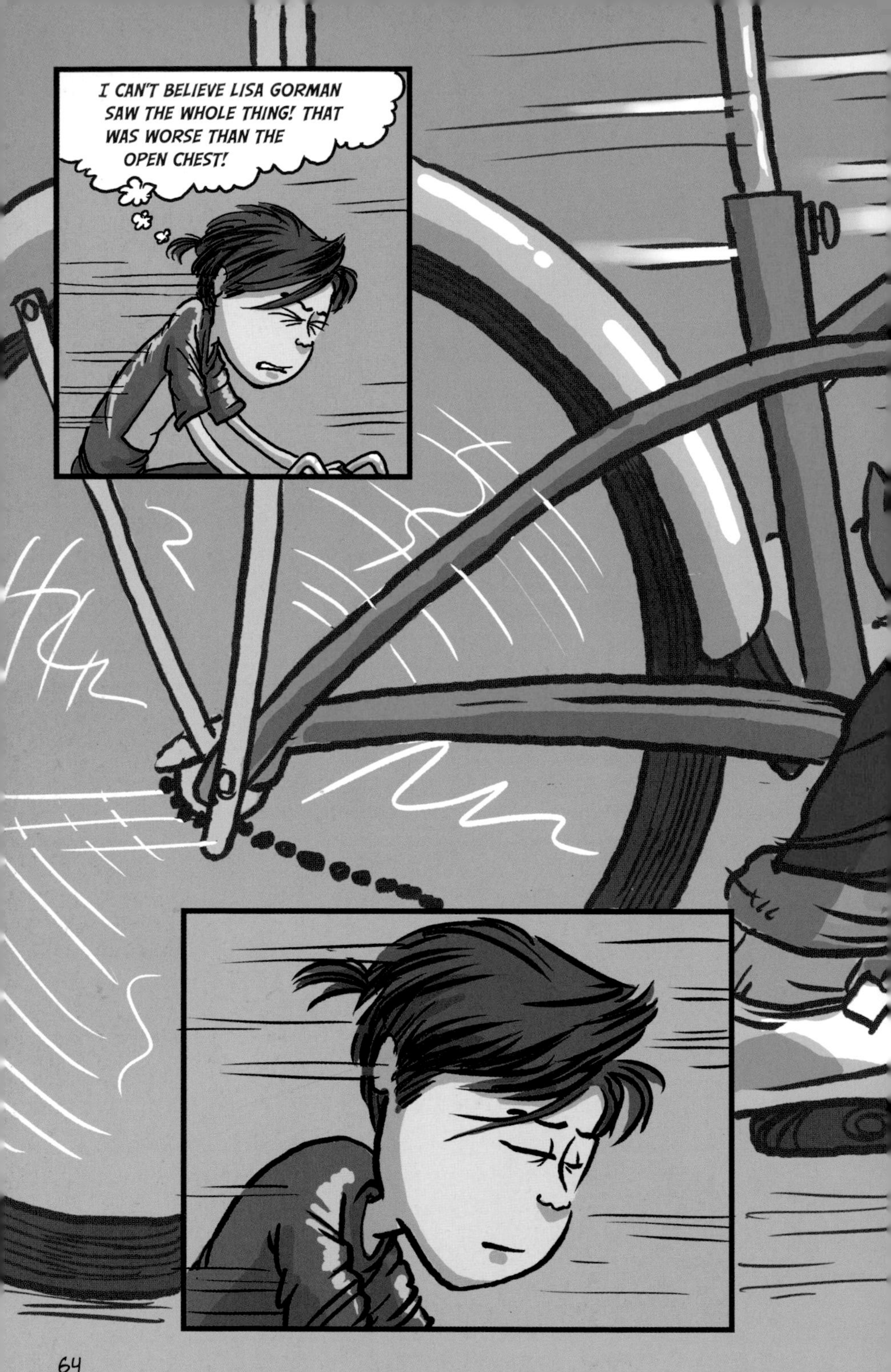
I CAN'T BELIEVE LISA GORMAN SAW THE WHOLE THING! THAT WAS WORSE THAN THE OPEN CHEST!

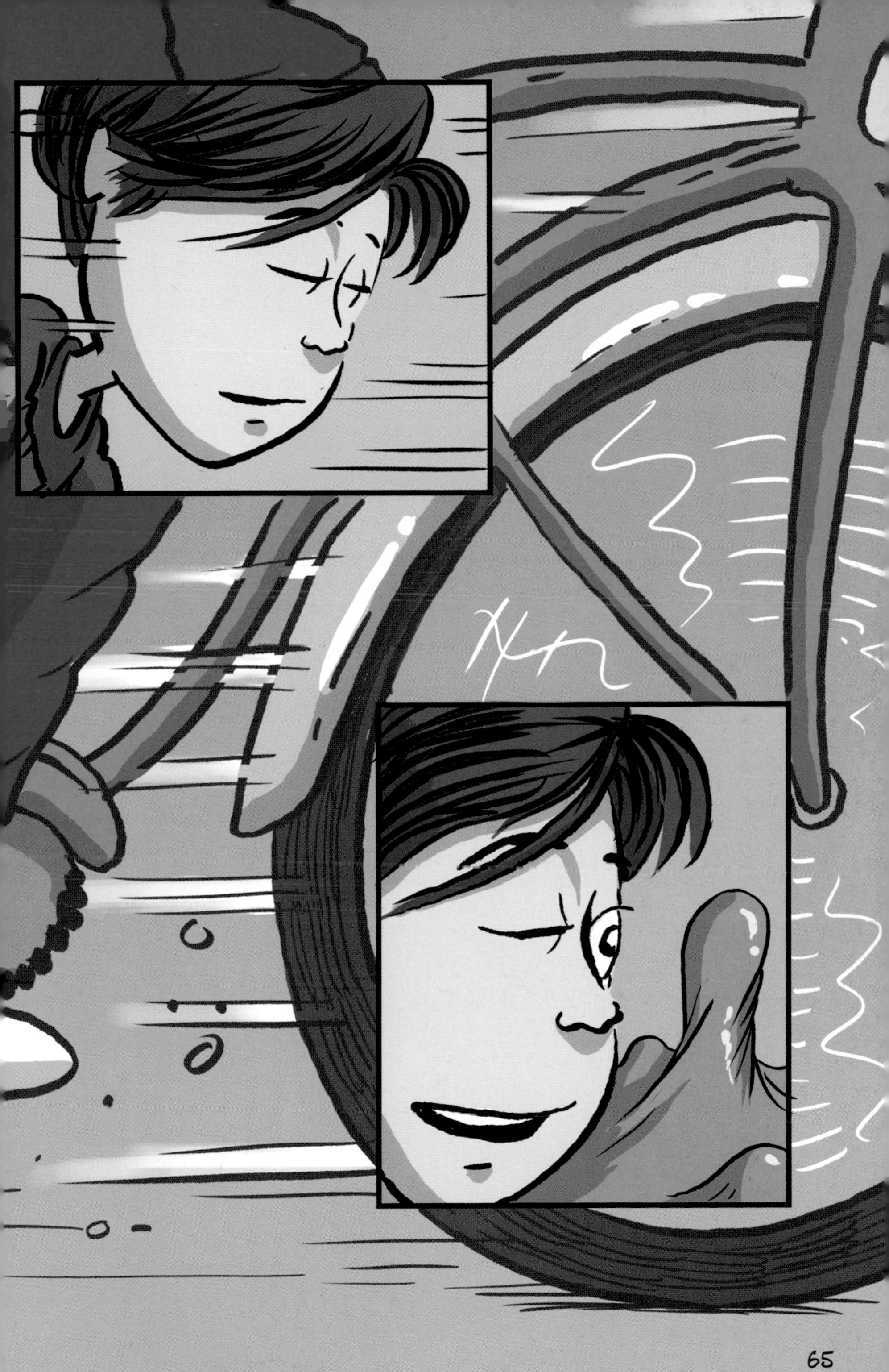
Hn

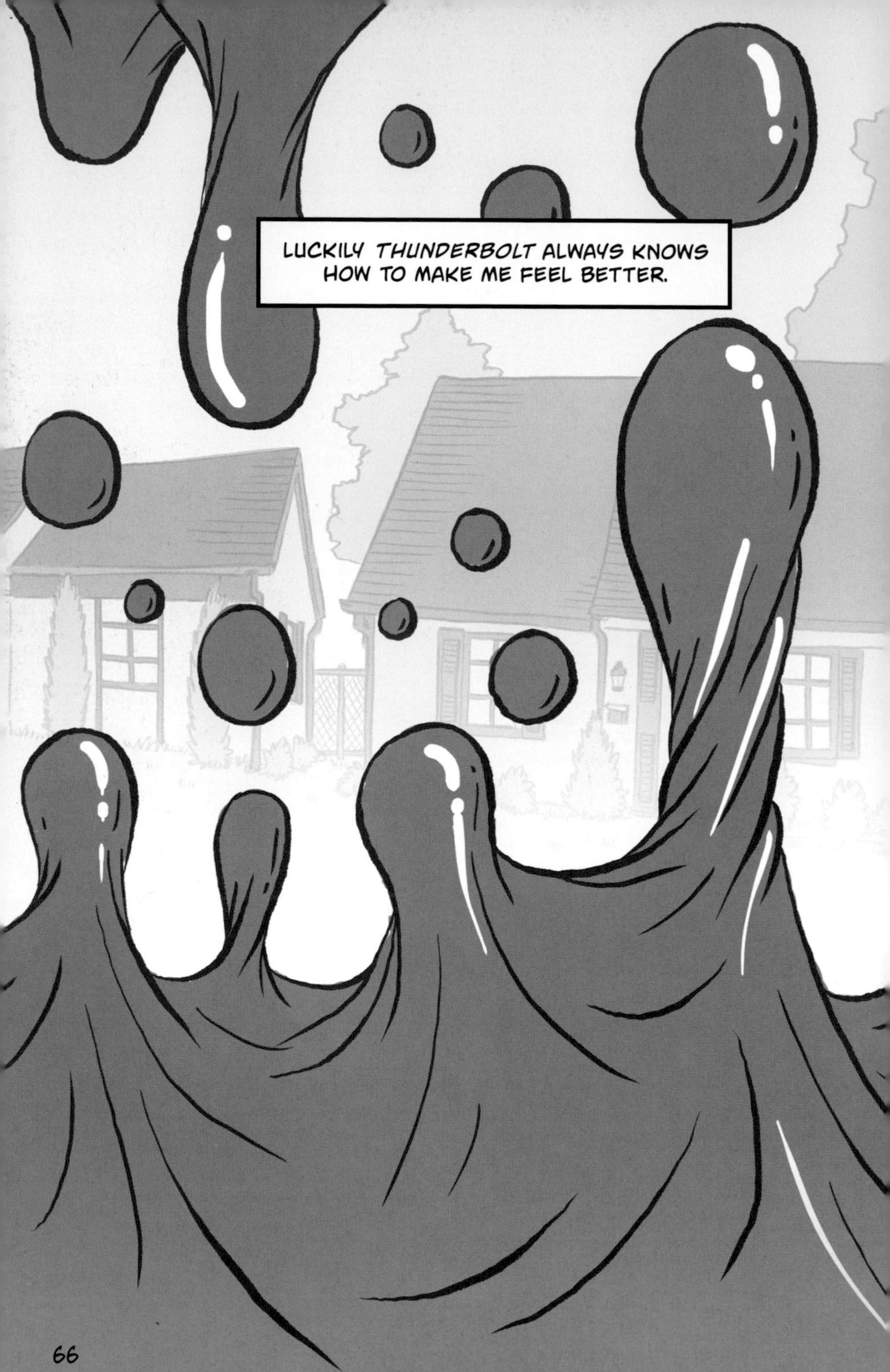
LUCKILY *THUNDERBOLT* ALWAYS KNOWS HOW TO MAKE ME FEEL BETTER.

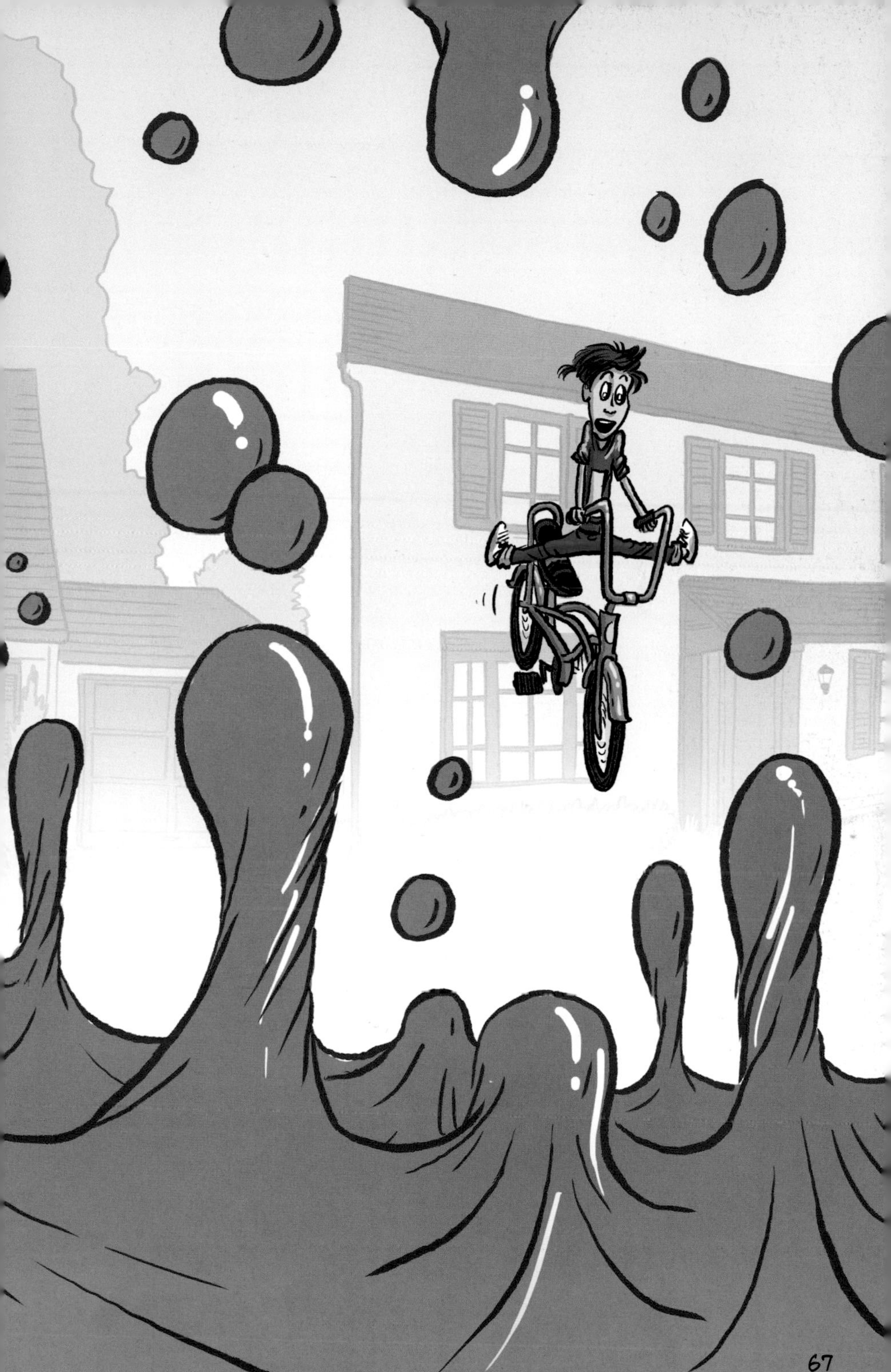

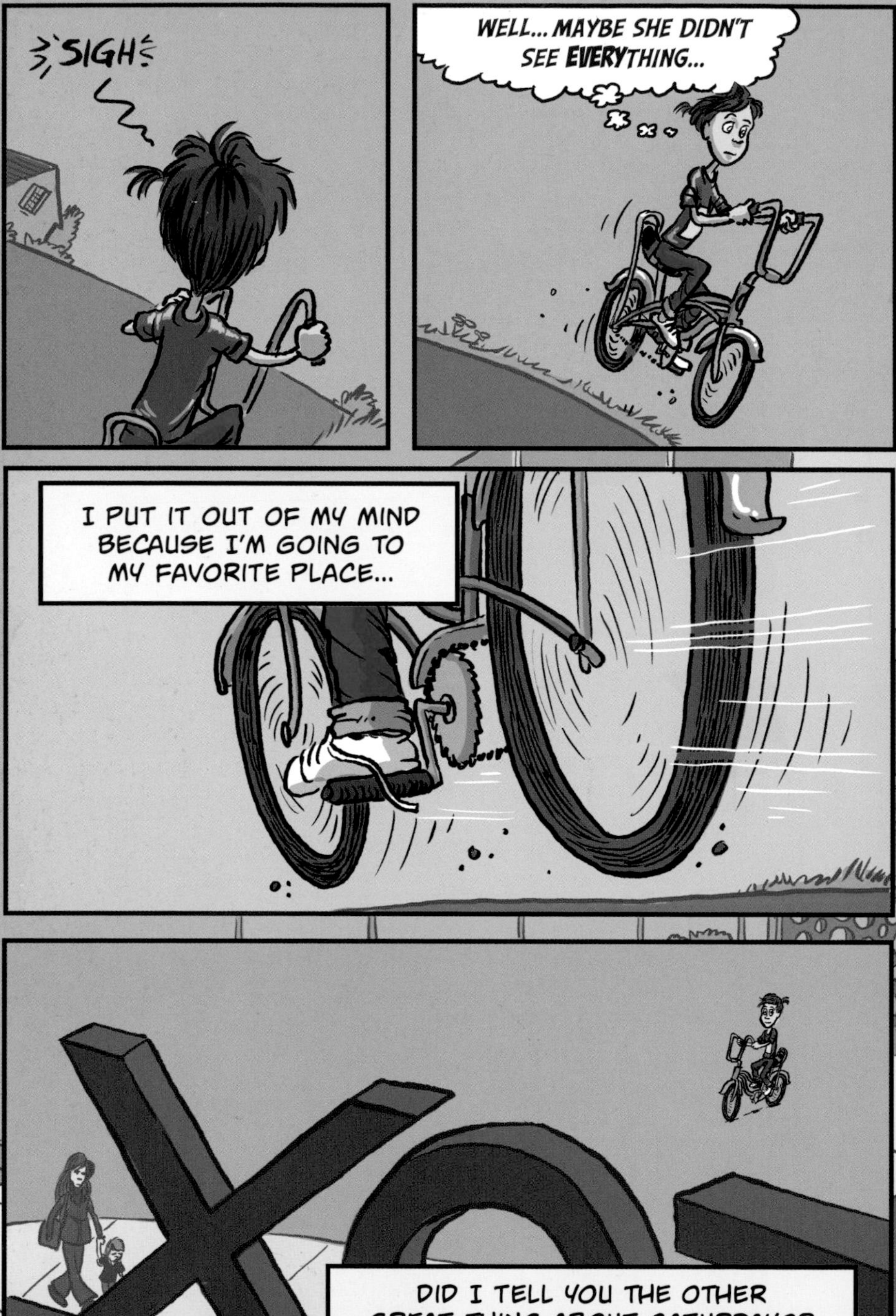
SIGH
WELL... MAYBE SHE DIDN'T SEE EVERYTHING...
I PUT IT OUT OF MY MIND BECAUSE I'M GOING TO MY FAVORITE PLACE...
DID I TELL YOU THE OTHER GREAT THING ABOUT SATURDAYS?

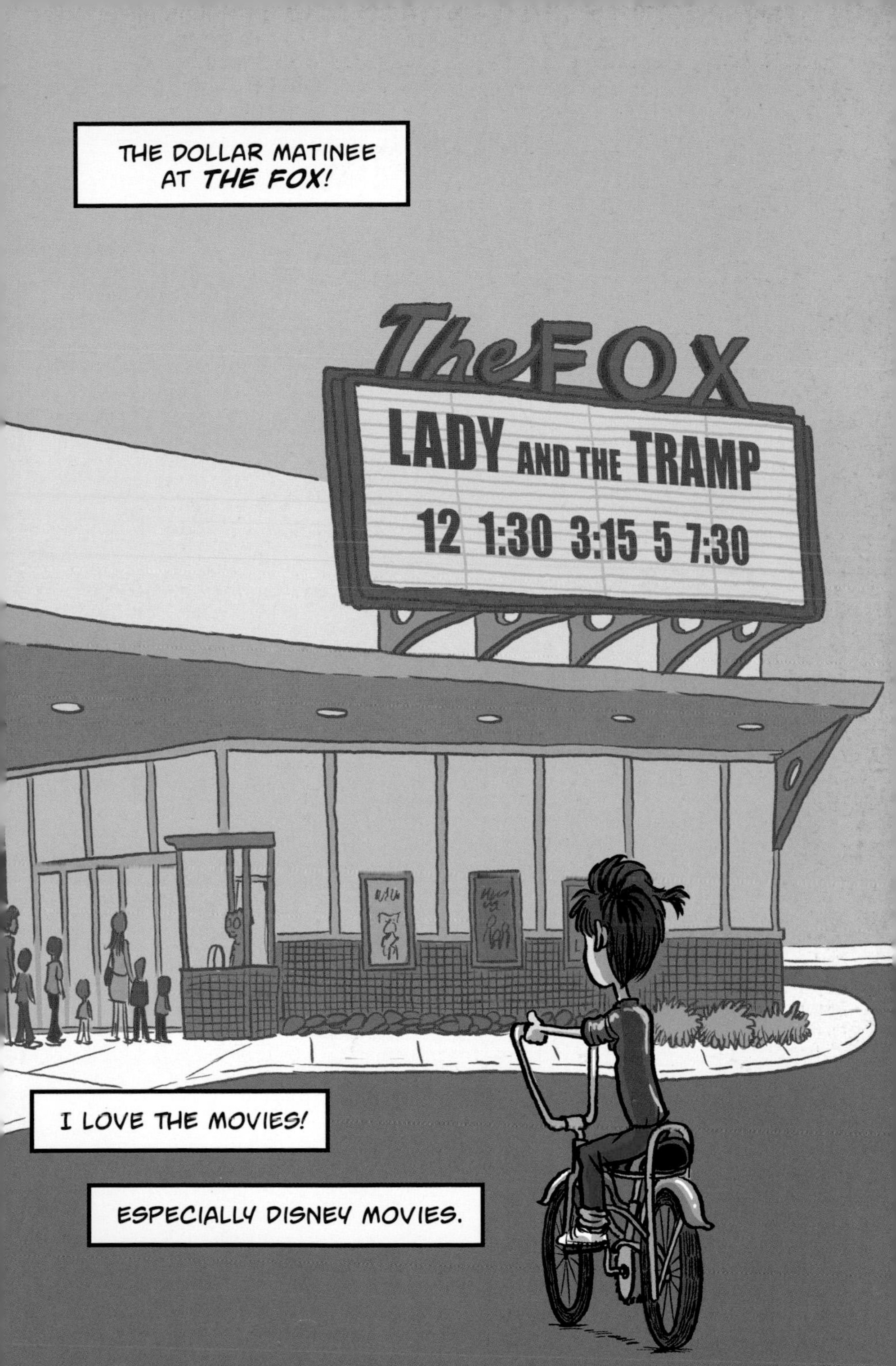
THE DOLLAR MATINEE AT *THE FOX*!
The FOX
LADY AND THE TRAMP
12 1:30 3:15 5 7:30
I LOVE THE MOVIES!
ESPECIALLY DISNEY MOVIES.

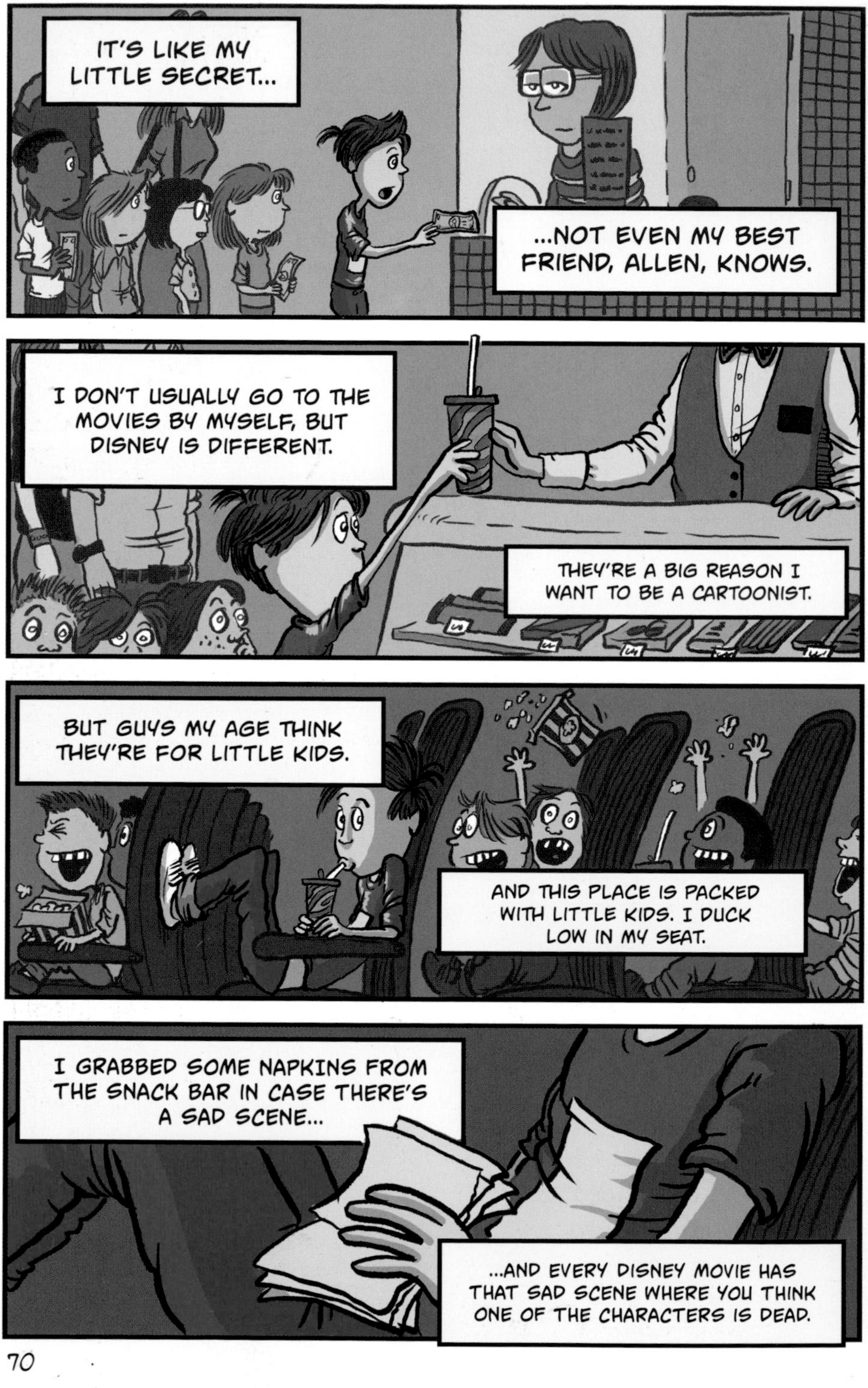
IT'S LIKE MY LITTLE SECRET...
...NOT EVEN MY BEST FRIEND, ALLEN, KNOWS.
I DON'T USUALLY GO TO THE MOVIES BY MYSELF, BUT DISNEY IS DIFFERENT.
THEY'RE A BIG REASON I WANT TO BE A CARTOONIST.
BUT GUYS MY AGE THINK THEY'RE FOR LITTLE KIDS.
AND THIS PLACE IS PACKED WITH LITTLE KIDS. I DUCK LOW IN MY SEAT.
I GRABBED SOME NAPKINS FROM THE SNACK BAR IN CASE THERE'S A SAD SCENE...
...AND EVERY DISNEY MOVIE HAS THAT SAD SCENE WHERE YOU THINK ONE OF THE CHARACTERS IS DEAD.

IT'S BAD ENOUGH SOMEBODY MIGHT SPOT ME AT A KIDDIE MOVIE—I DON'T NEED THEM TO SEE ME CRYING OVER SOME CARTOON DOG.

OOOOO! SHOWTIME!

PREVUES OF COMING ATTRACTIONS

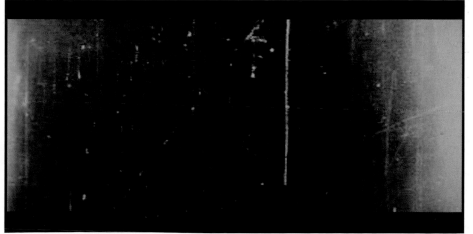

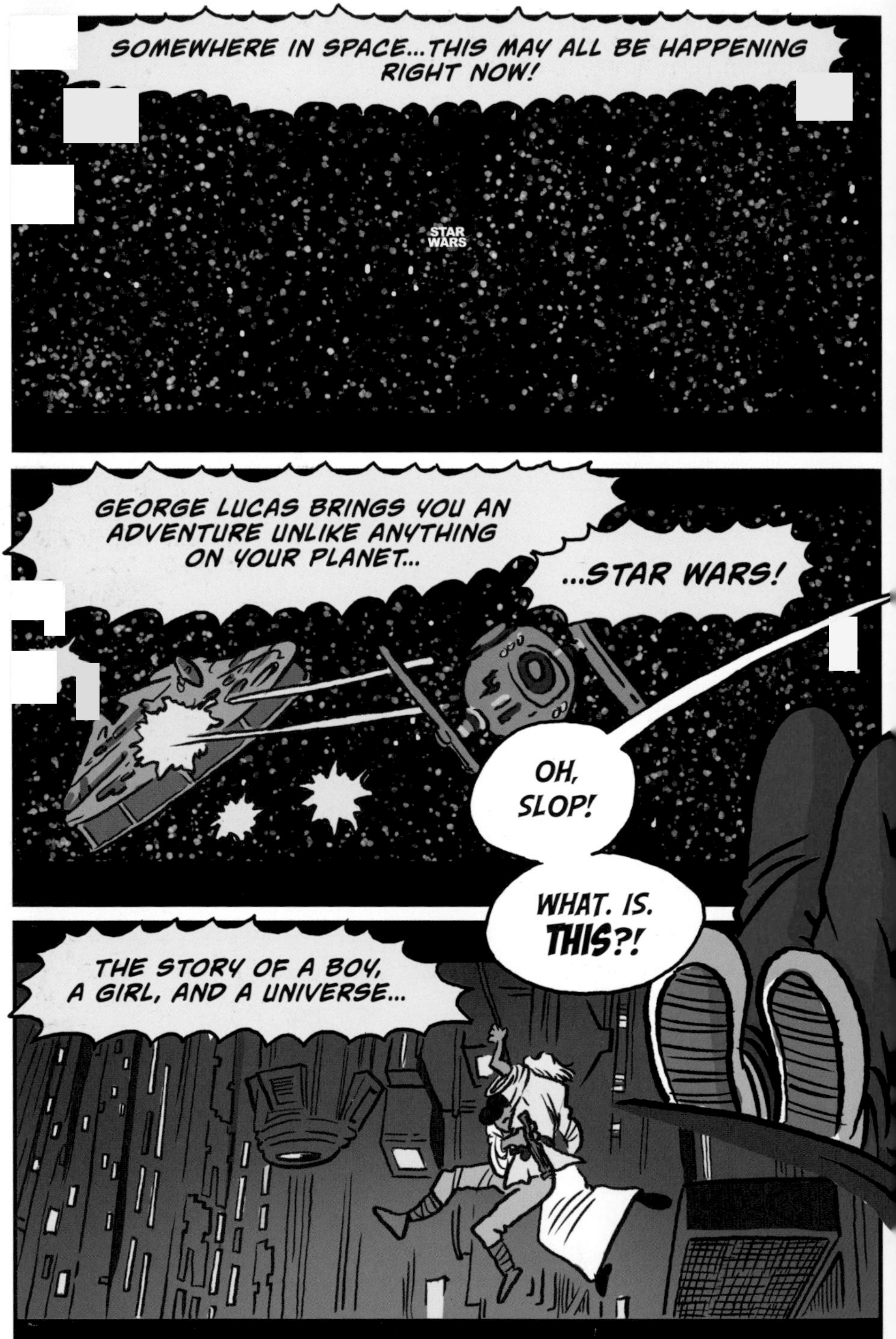
SOMEWHERE IN SPACE...THIS MAY ALL BE HAPPENING RIGHT NOW!
STAR WARS
GEORGE LUCAS BRINGS YOU AN ADVENTURE UNLIKE ANYTHING ON YOUR PLANET...
...STAR WARS!
OH, SLOP!
WHAT. IS. THIS?!
THE STORY OF A BOY, A GIRL, AND A UNIVERSE...

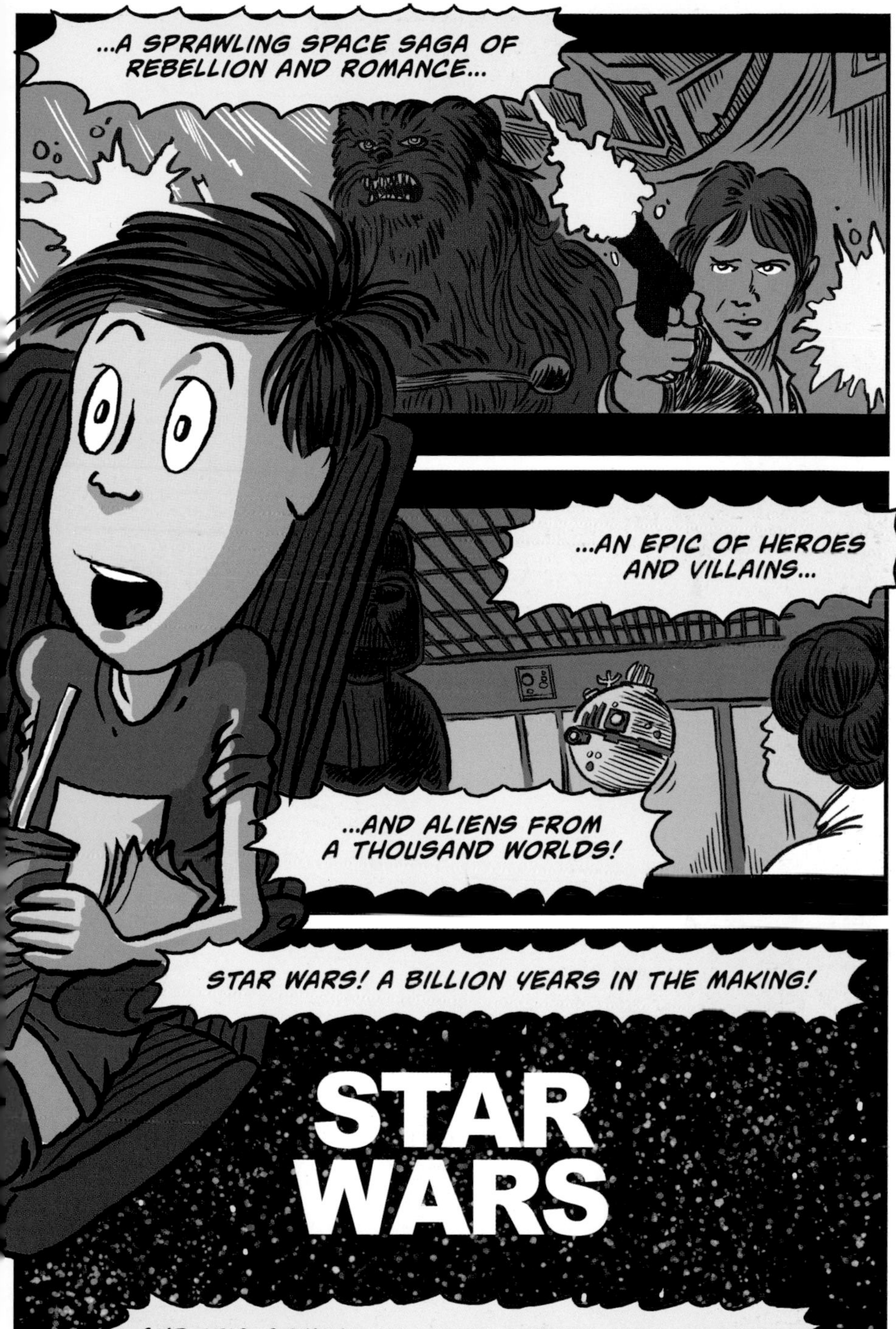
...A SPRAWLING SPACE SAGA OF REBELLION AND ROMANCE...
...AN EPIC OF HEROES AND VILLAINS...
...AND ALIENS FROM A THOUSAND WORLDS!
STAR WARS! A BILLION YEARS IN THE MAKING!
STAR WARS
AND IT'S COMING TO YOUR GALAXY THIS SUMMER!

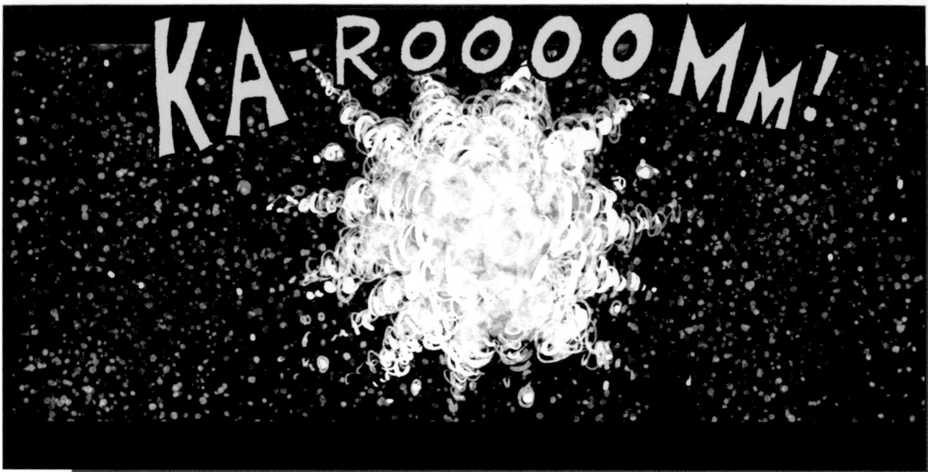
KA-ROOOOMM!

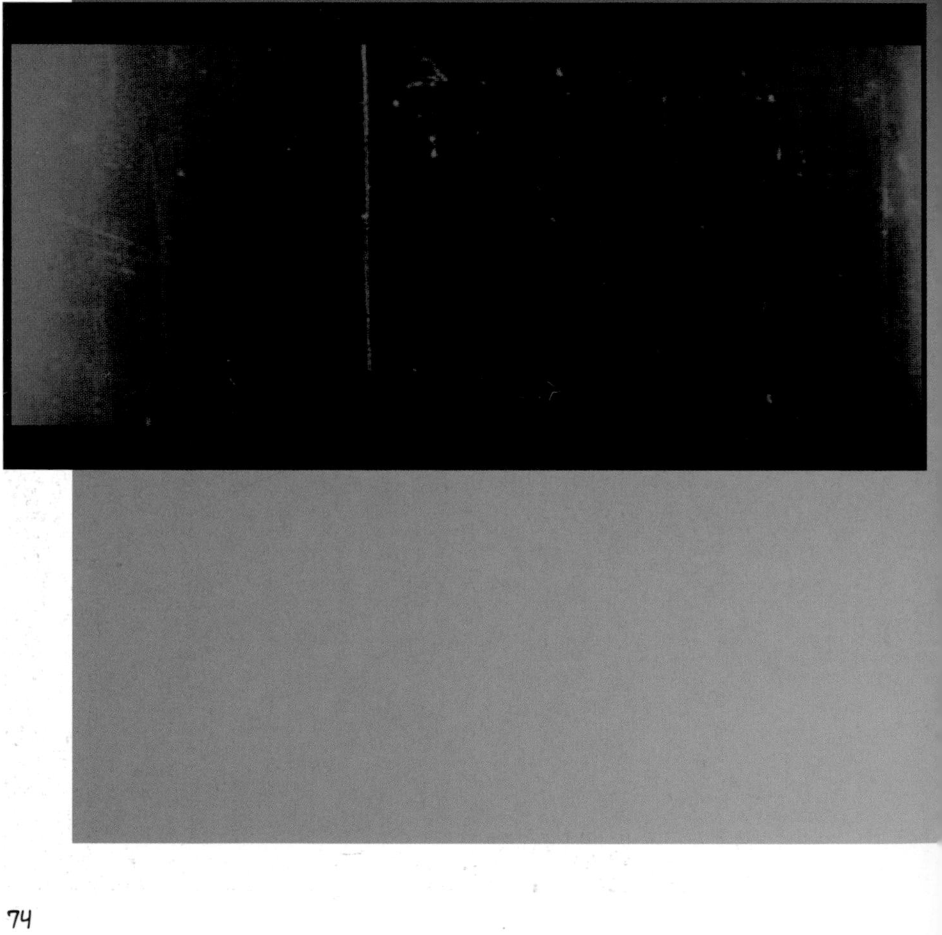

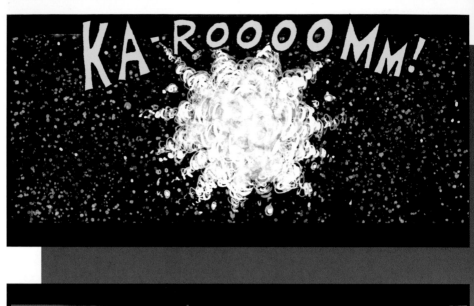

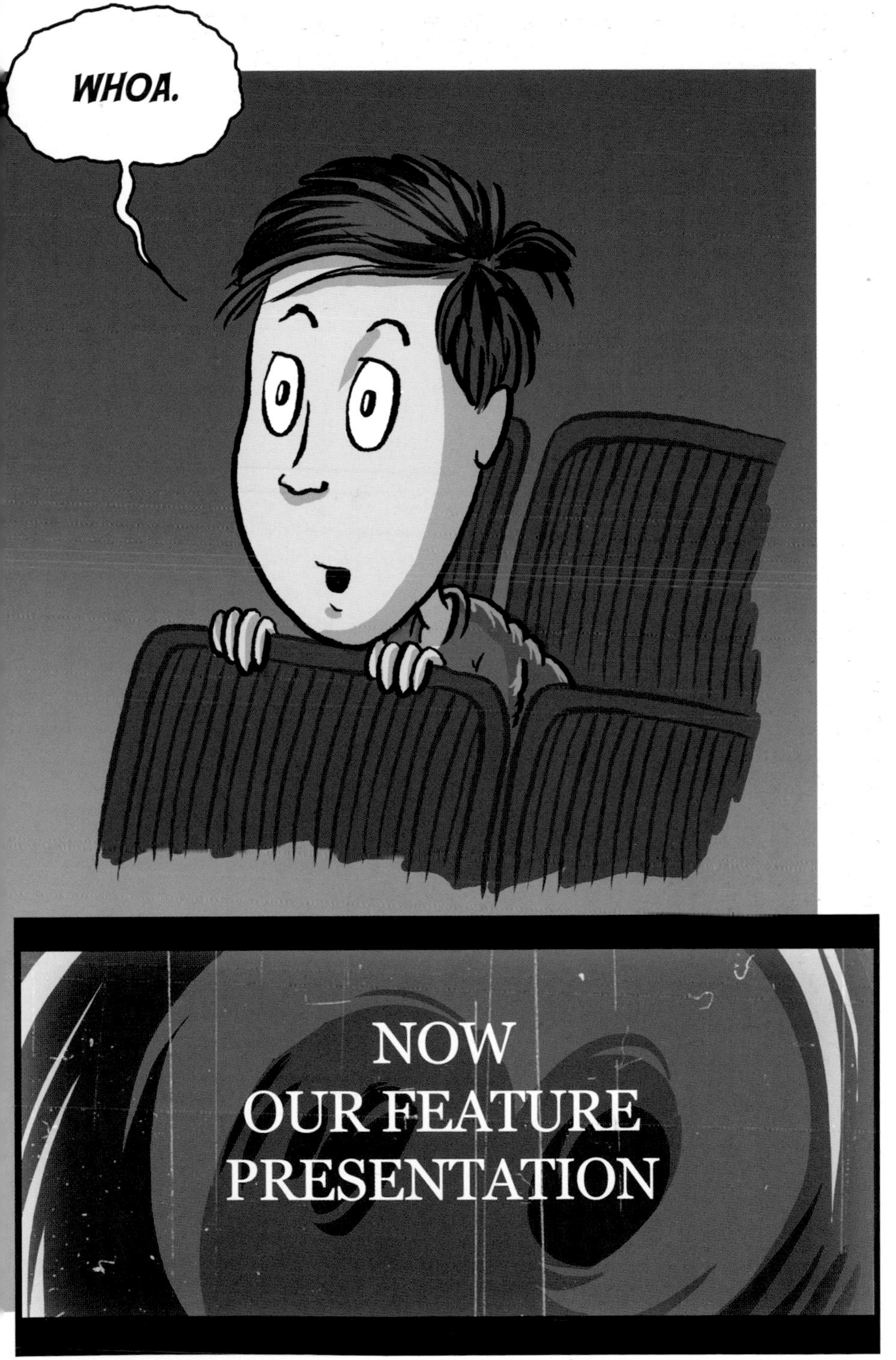
WHOA.
NOW
OUR FEATURE
PRESENTATION

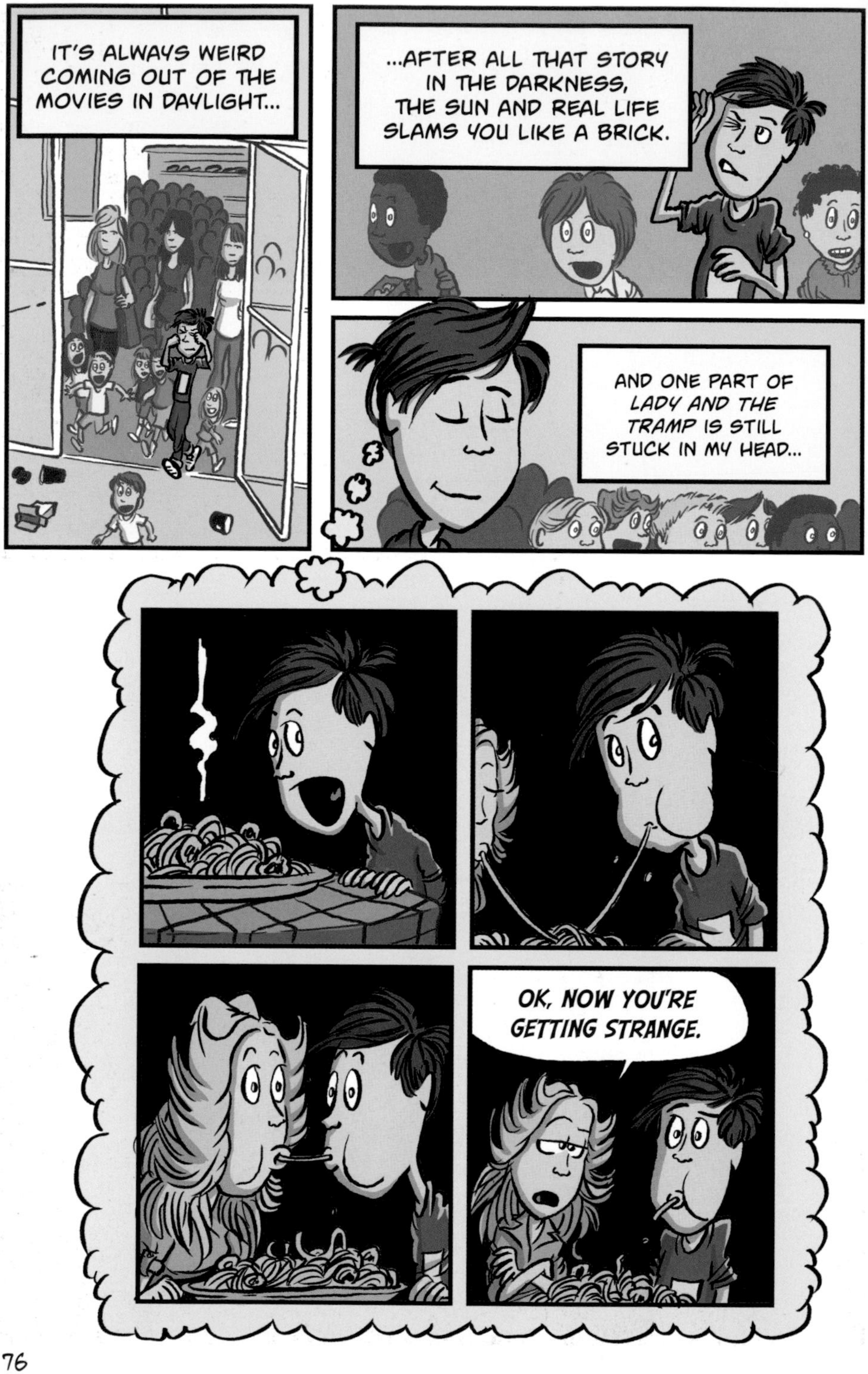
IT'S ALWAYS WEIRD COMING OUT OF THE MOVIES IN DAYLIGHT...
...AFTER ALL THAT STORY IN THE DARKNESS, THE SUN AND REAL LIFE SLAMS YOU LIKE A BRICK.
AND ONE PART OF *LADY AND THE TRAMP* IS STILL STUCK IN MY HEAD...
OK, NOW YOU'RE GETTING STRANGE.

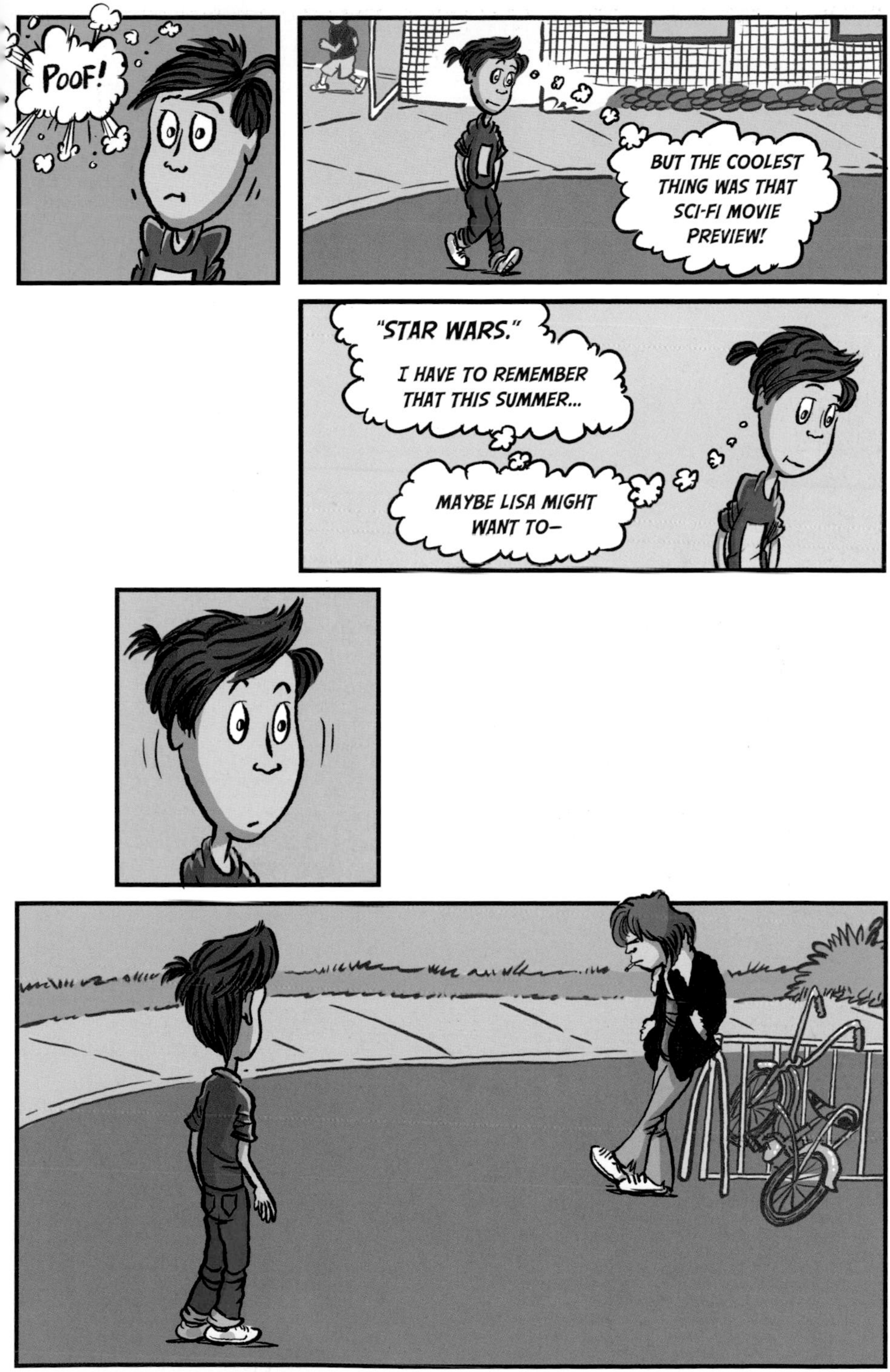
POOF!
BUT THE COOLEST THING WAS THAT SCI-FI MOVIE PREVIEW!
"STAR WARS."
I HAVE TO REMEMBER THAT THIS SUMMER...
MAYBE LISA MIGHT WANT TO–

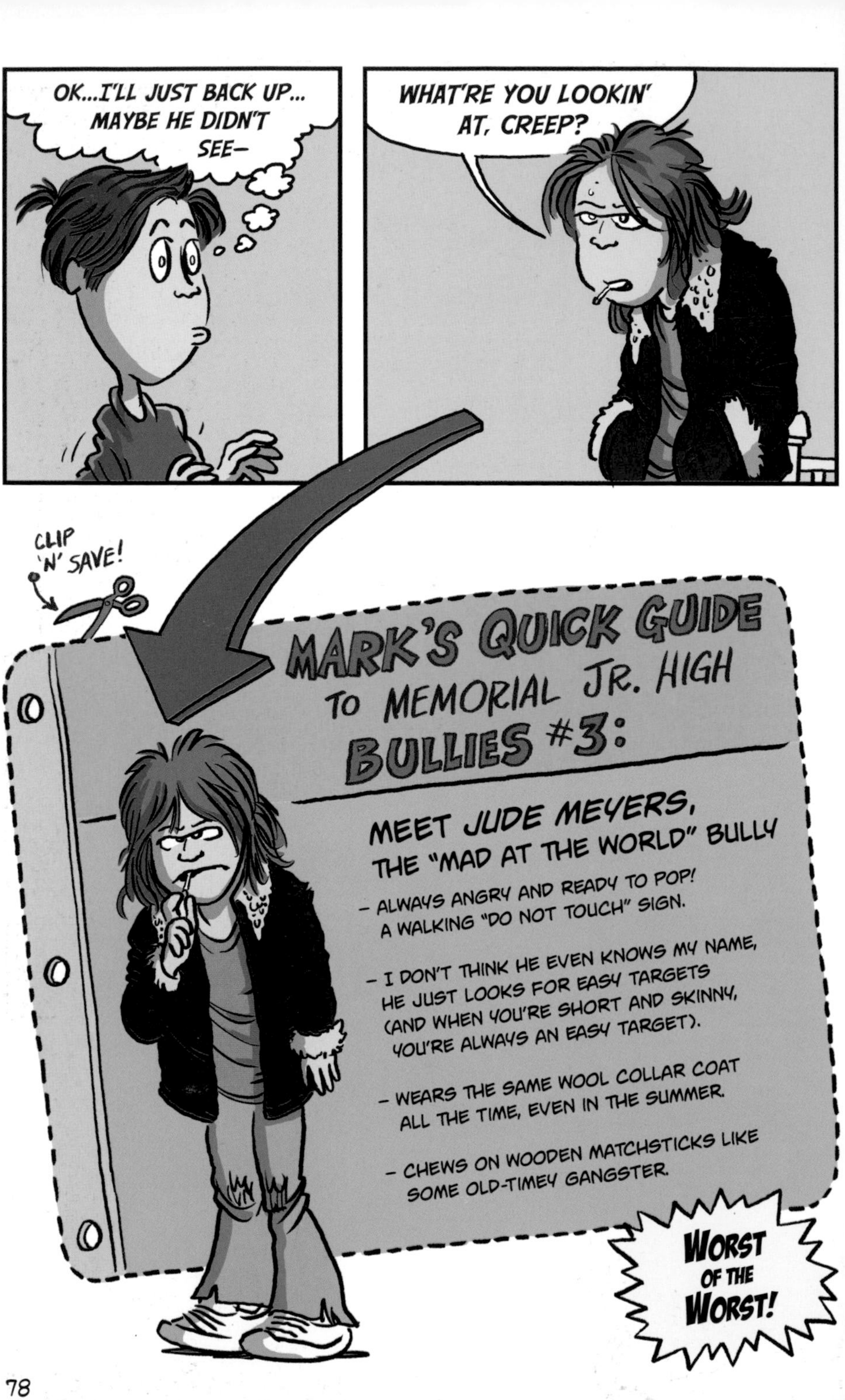
OK...I'LL JUST BACK UP... MAYBE HE DIDN'T SEE–
WHAT'RE YOU LOOKIN' AT, CREEP?
CLIP 'N' SAVE!
MARK'S QUICK GUIDE TO MEMORIAL JR. HIGH BULLIES #3:
MEET JUDE MEYERS, THE "MAD AT THE WORLD" BULLY
– ALWAYS ANGRY AND READY TO POP! A WALKING "DO NOT TOUCH" SIGN.
– I DON'T THINK HE EVEN KNOWS MY NAME, HE JUST LOOKS FOR EASY TARGETS (AND WHEN YOU'RE SHORT AND SKINNY, YOU'RE ALWAYS AN EASY TARGET).
– WEARS THE SAME WOOL COLLAR COAT ALL THE TIME, EVEN IN THE SUMMER.
– CHEWS ON WOODEN MATCHSTICKS LIKE SOME OLD-TIMEY GANGSTER.
WORST OF THE WORST!

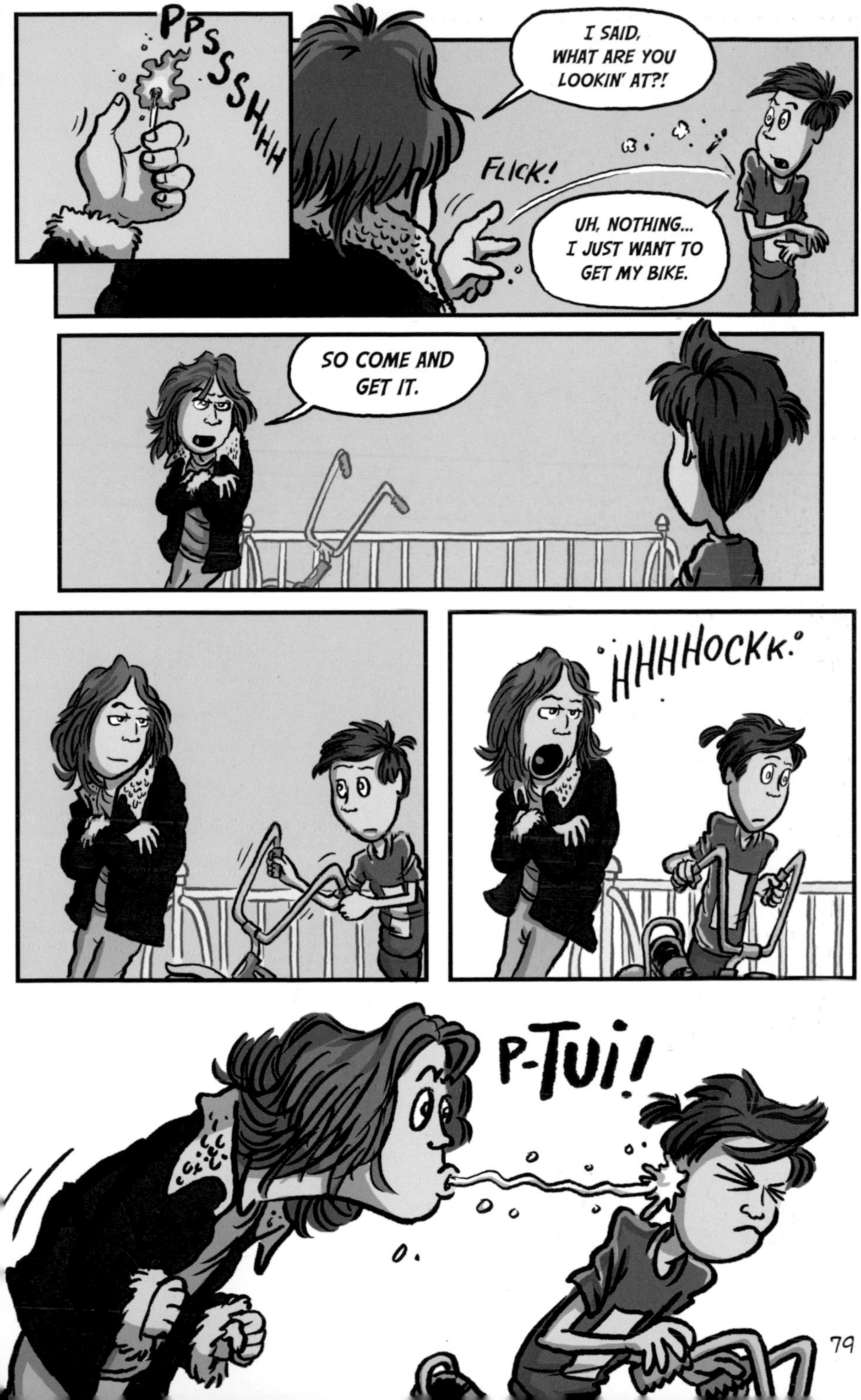
PPSSSHHH
I SAID, WHAT ARE YOU LOOKIN' AT?!
FLICK!
UH, NOTHING... I JUST WANT TO GET MY BIKE.
SO COME AND GET IT.
HHHHOCKK.
P-TUI!

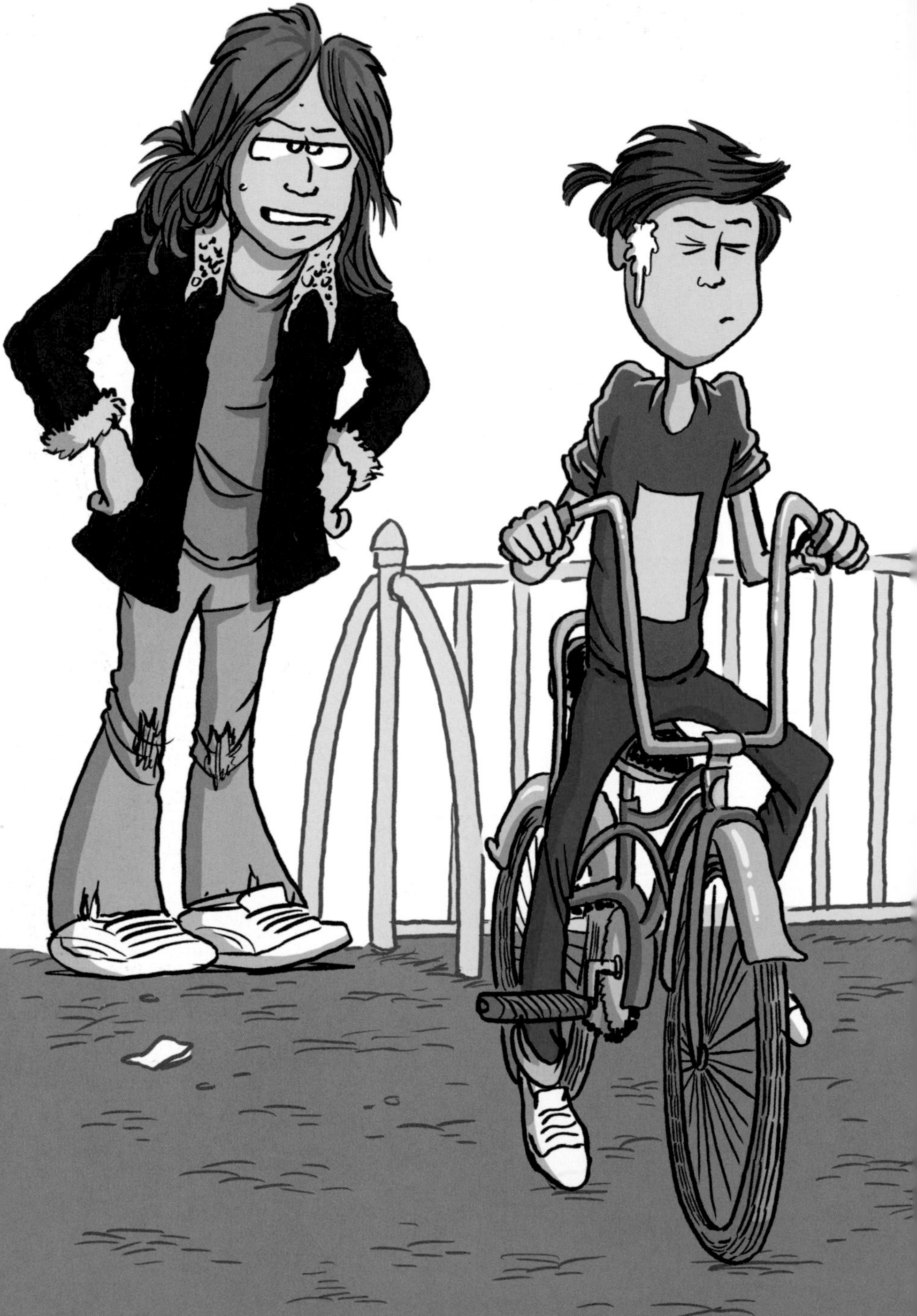

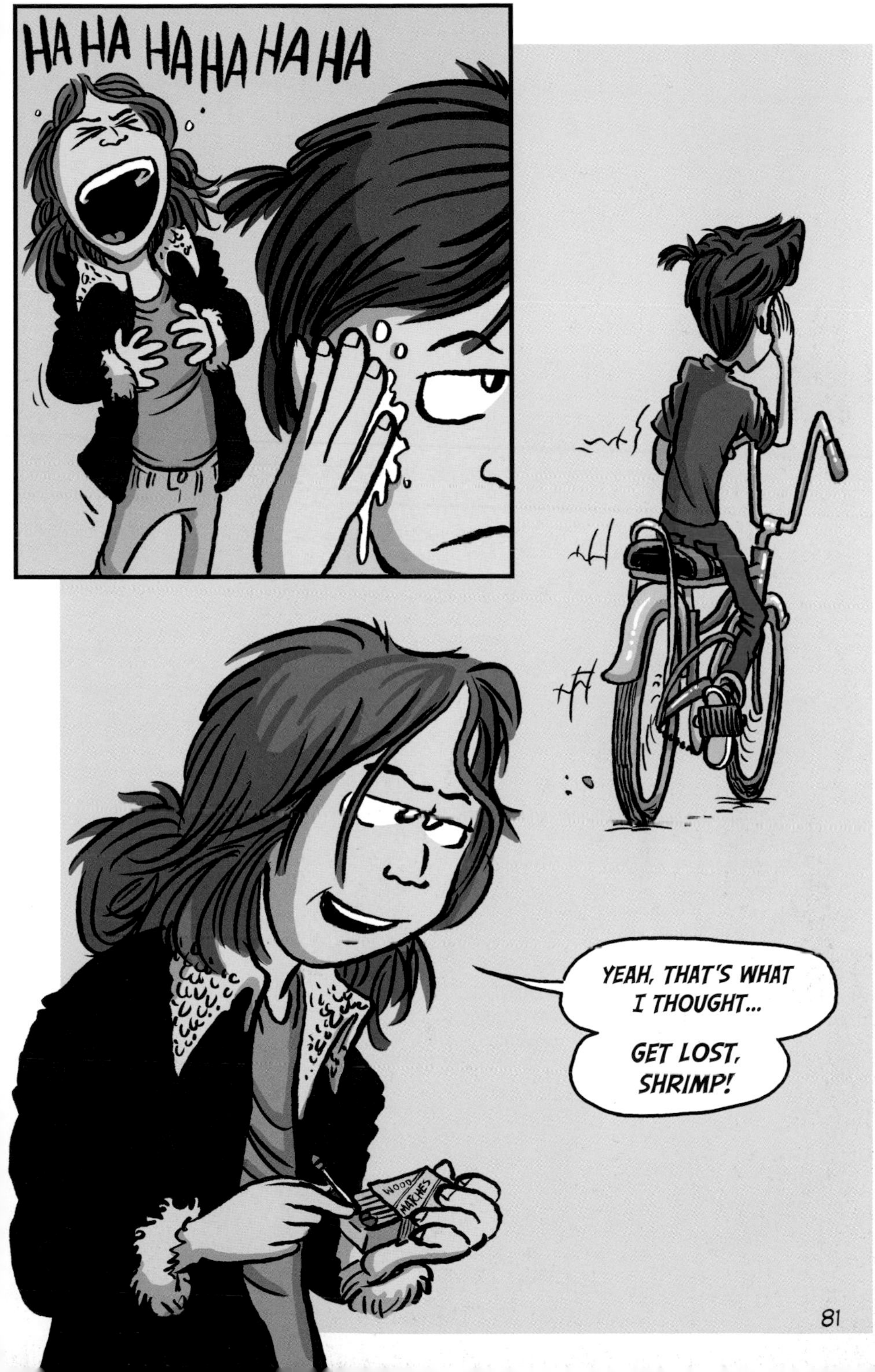
HA HA HA HA HA HA
YEAH, THAT'S WHAT I THOUGHT...
GET LOST, SHRIMP!
WOOD MATCHES

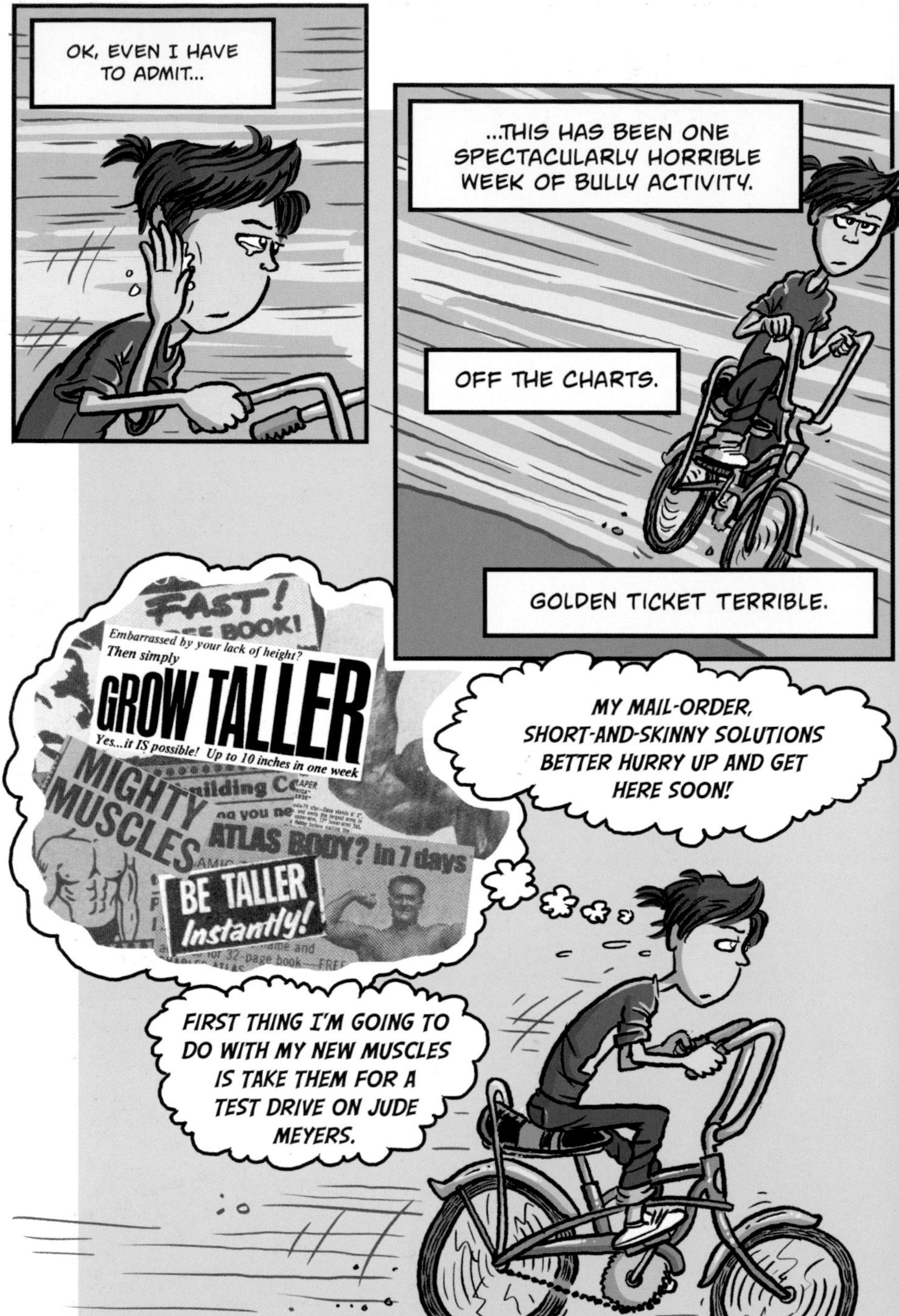
OK, EVEN I HAVE TO ADMIT...
...THIS HAS BEEN ONE SPECTACULARLY HORRIBLE WEEK OF BULLY ACTIVITY.
OFF THE CHARTS.
GOLDEN TICKET TERRIBLE.
FAST!
Embarrassed by your lack of height? Then simply
GROW TALLER
Yes...it IS possible! Up to 10 inches in one week
MIGHTY MUSCLES
ATLAS BODY? in 7 days
BE TALLER Instantly!
MY MAIL-ORDER, SHORT-AND-SKINNY SOLUTIONS BETTER HURRY UP AND GET HERE SOON!
FIRST THING I'M GOING TO DO WITH MY NEW MUSCLES IS TAKE THEM FOR A TEST DRIVE ON JUDE MEYERS.

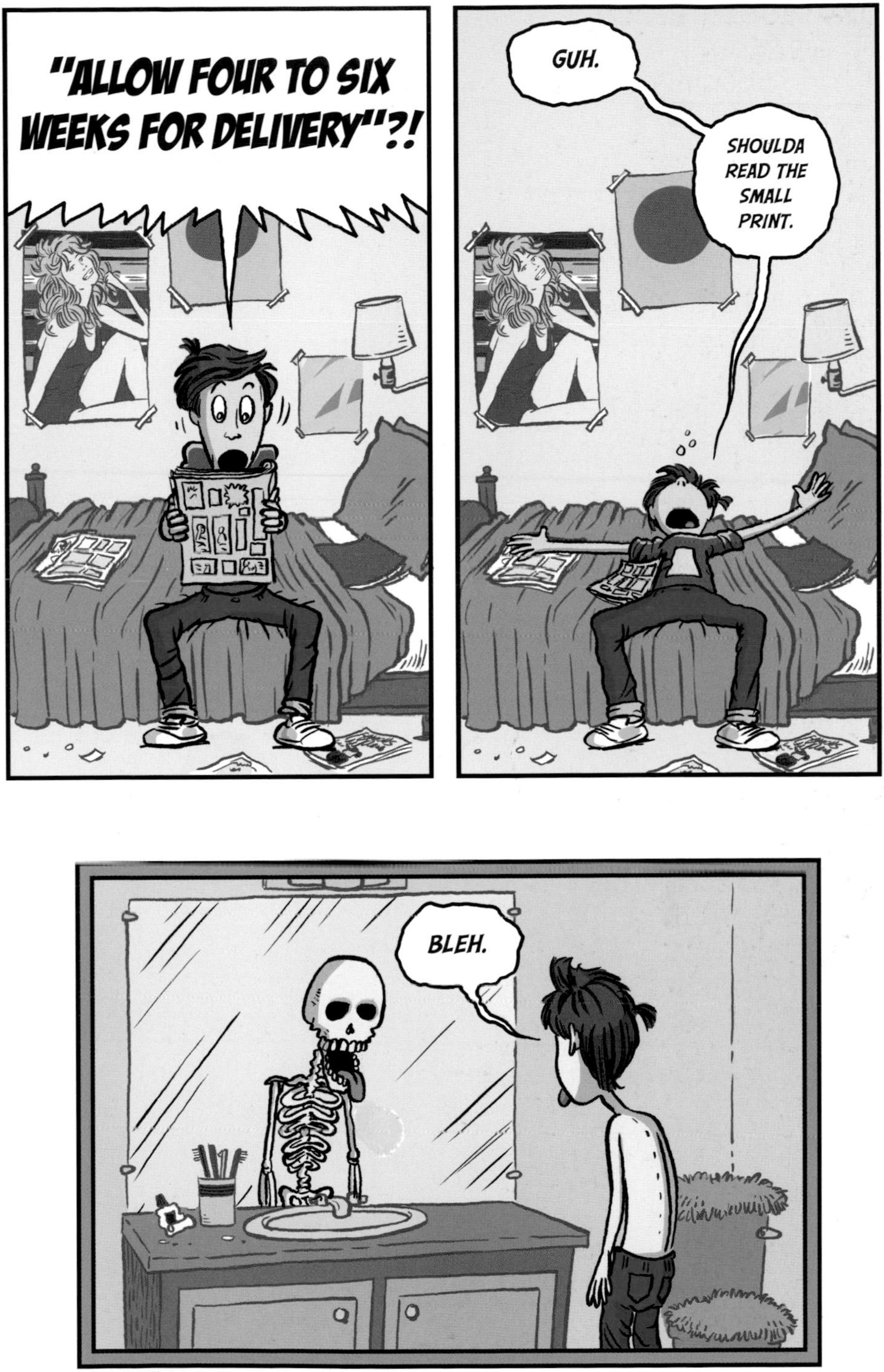
"ALLOW FOUR TO SIX WEEKS FOR DELIVERY"?!
GUH.
SHOULDA READ THE SMALL PRINT.
BLEH.

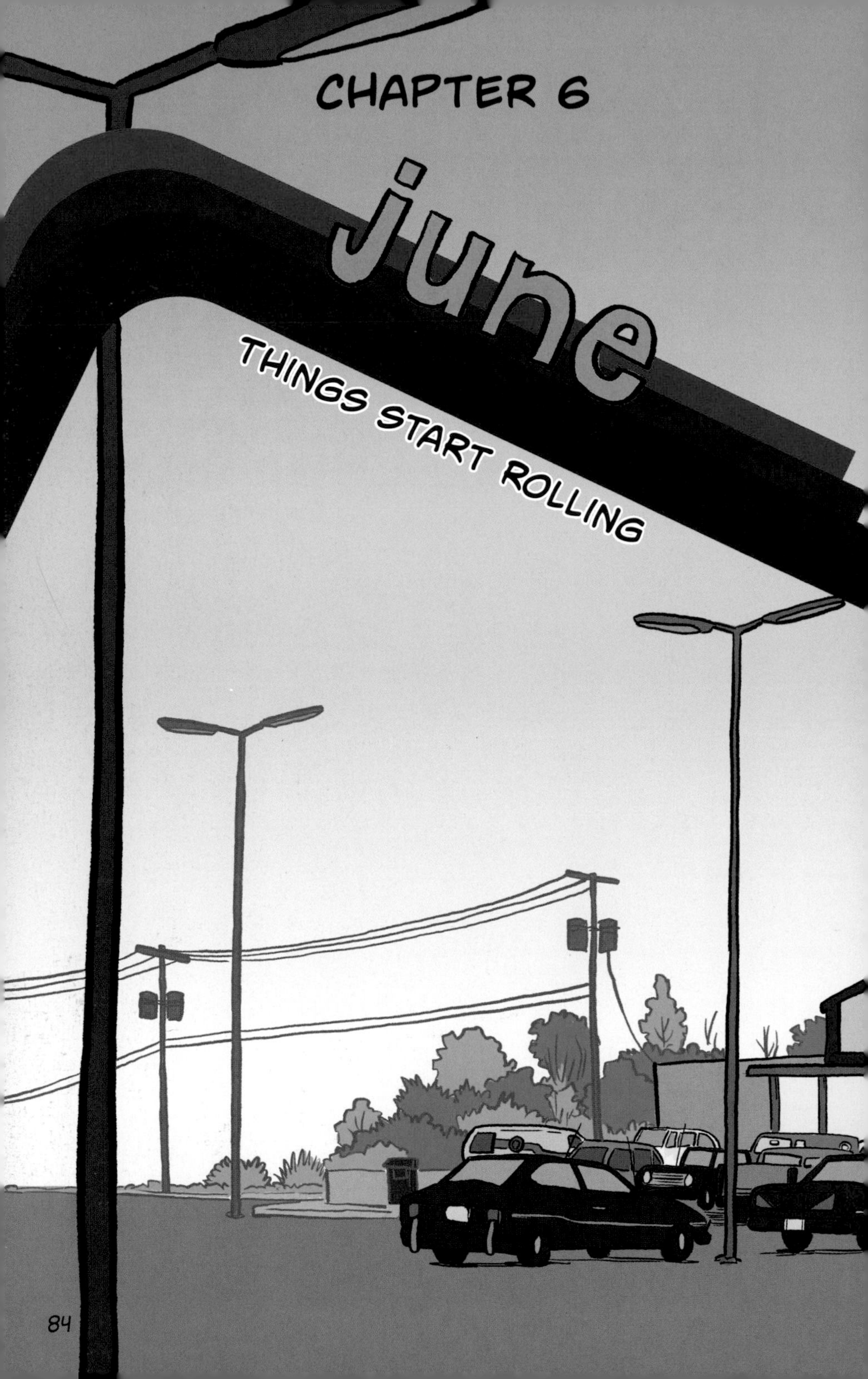
CHAPTER 6
june
THINGS START ROLLING

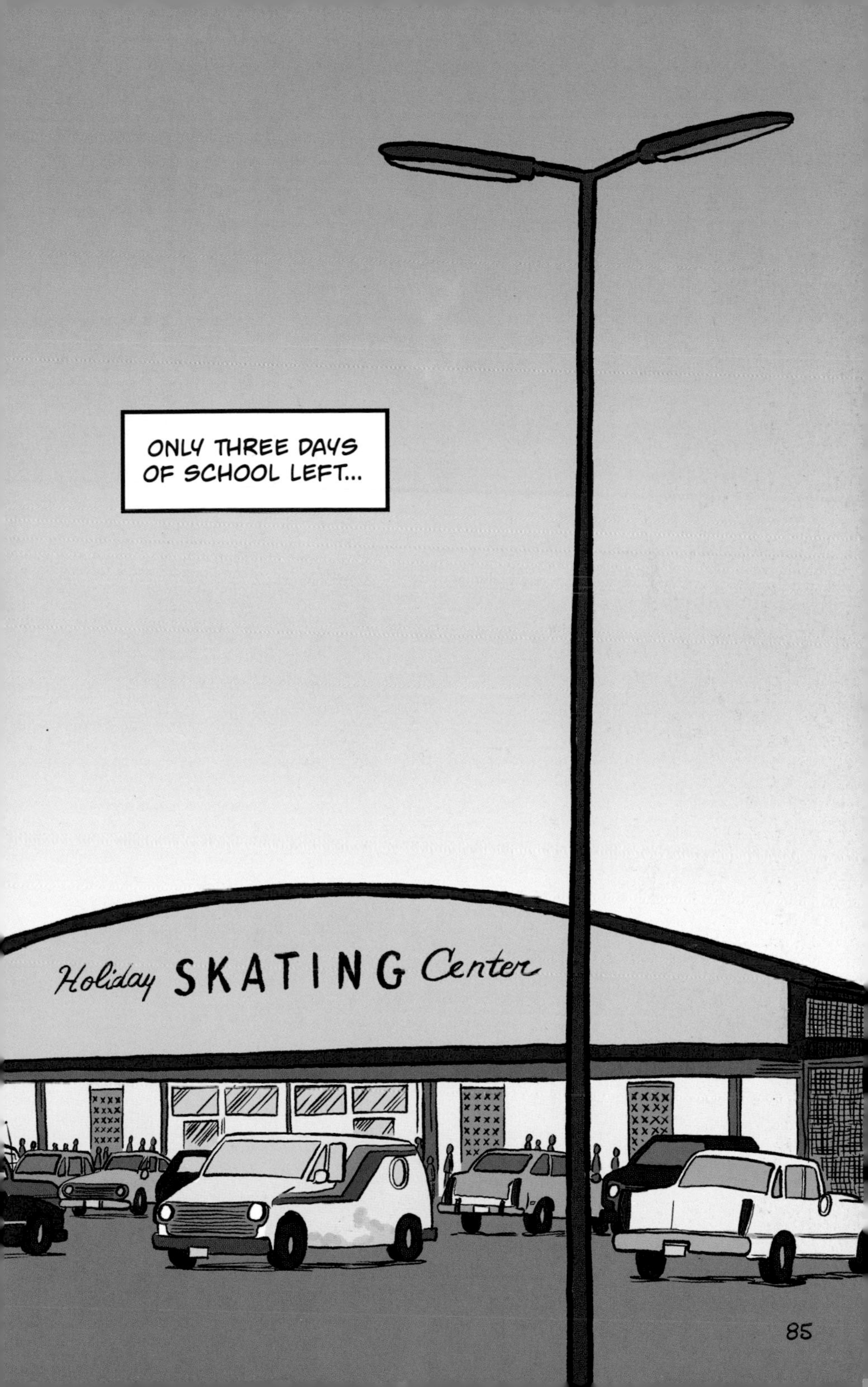
ONLY THREE DAYS OF SCHOOL LEFT...
Holiday SKATING Center

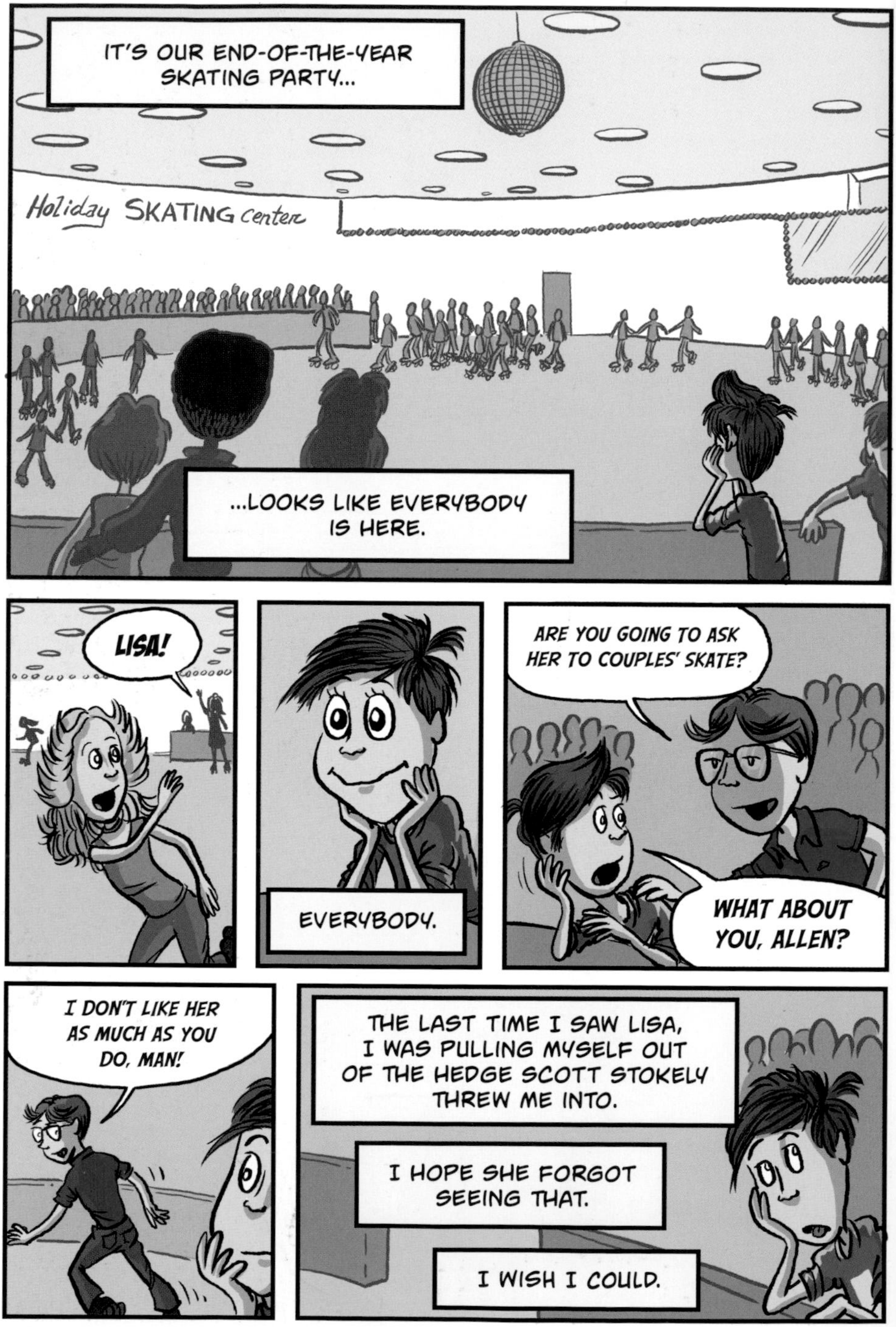
IT'S OUR END-OF-THE-YEAR SKATING PARTY...
Holiday SKATING center
...LOOKS LIKE EVERYBODY IS HERE.
LISA!
EVERYBODY.
ARE YOU GOING TO ASK HER TO COUPLES' SKATE?
WHAT ABOUT YOU, ALLEN?
I DON'T LIKE HER AS MUCH AS YOU DO, MAN!
THE LAST TIME I SAW LISA, I WAS PULLING MYSELF OUT OF THE HEDGE SCOTT STOKELY THREW ME INTO.
I HOPE SHE FORGOT SEEING THAT.
I WISH I COULD.

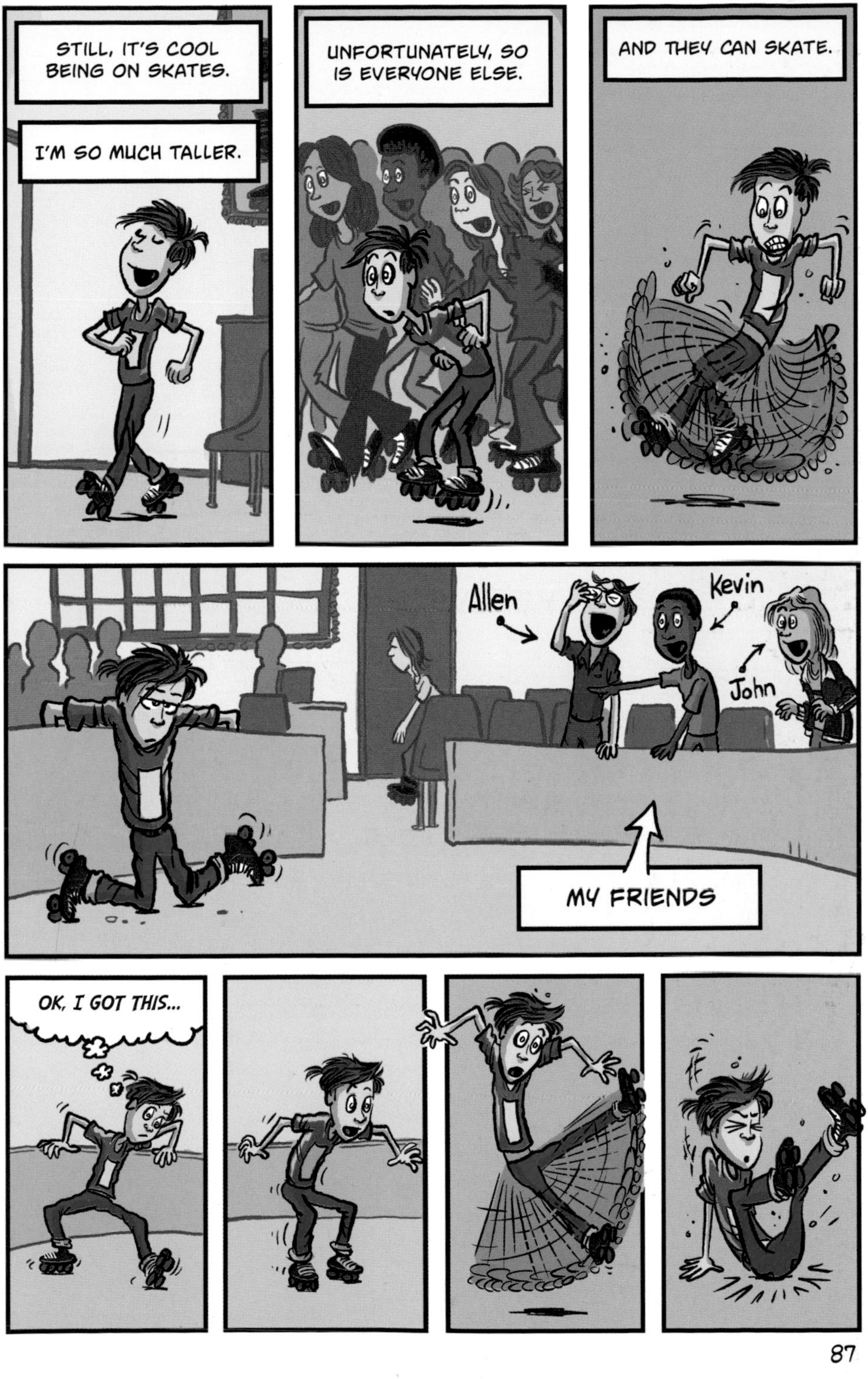
STILL, IT'S COOL BEING ON SKATES.
I'M SO MUCH TALLER.
UNFORTUNATELY, SO IS EVERYONE ELSE.
AND THEY CAN SKATE.
Allen
Kevin
John
MY FRIENDS
OK, I GOT THIS...

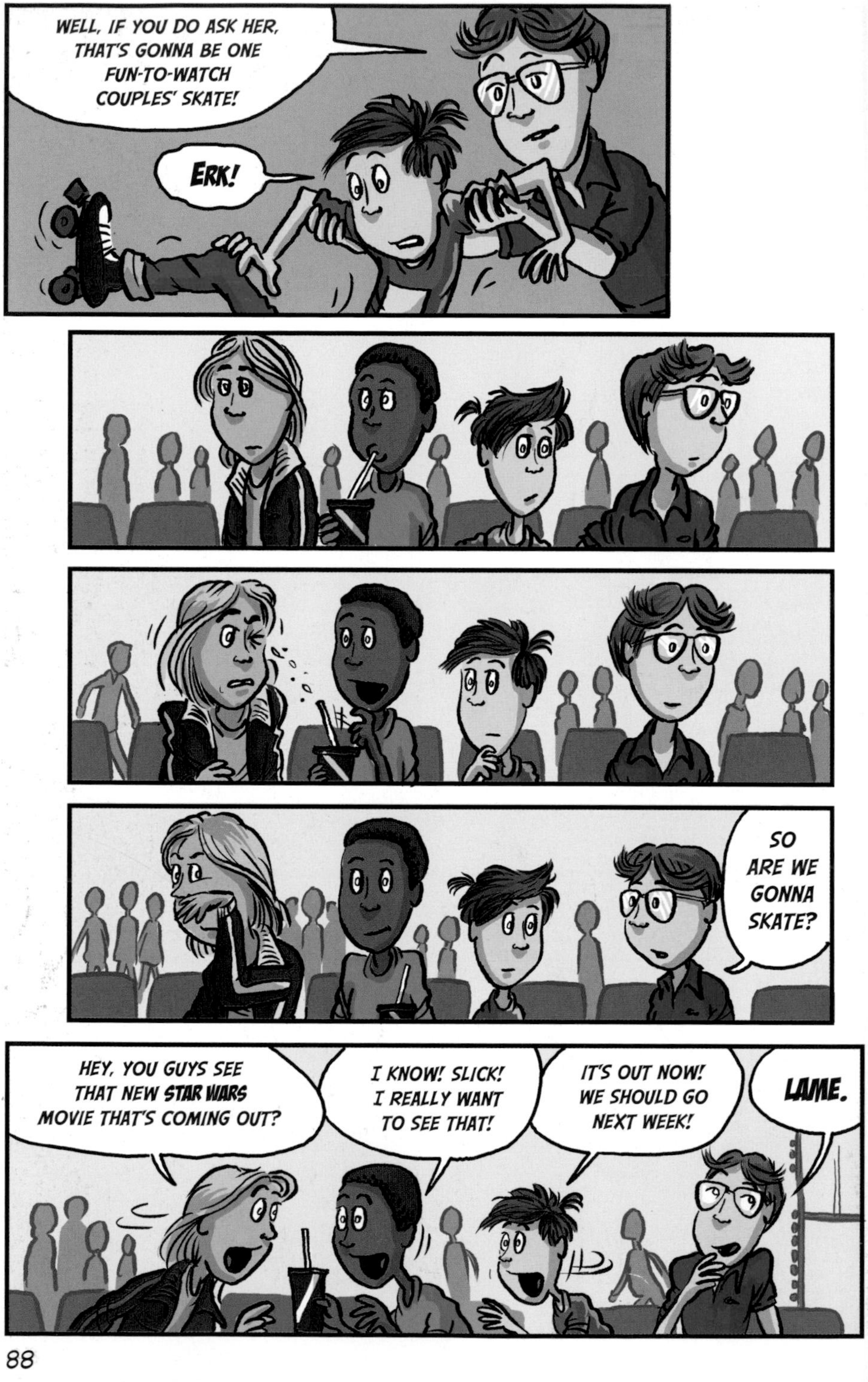
WELL, IF YOU DO ASK HER, THAT'S GONNA BE ONE FUN-TO-WATCH COUPLES' SKATE!
ERK!
SO ARE WE GONNA SKATE?
HEY, YOU GUYS SEE THAT NEW STAR WARS MOVIE THAT'S COMING OUT?
I KNOW! SLICK! I REALLY WANT TO SEE THAT!
IT'S OUT NOW! WE SHOULD GO NEXT WEEK!
LAME.

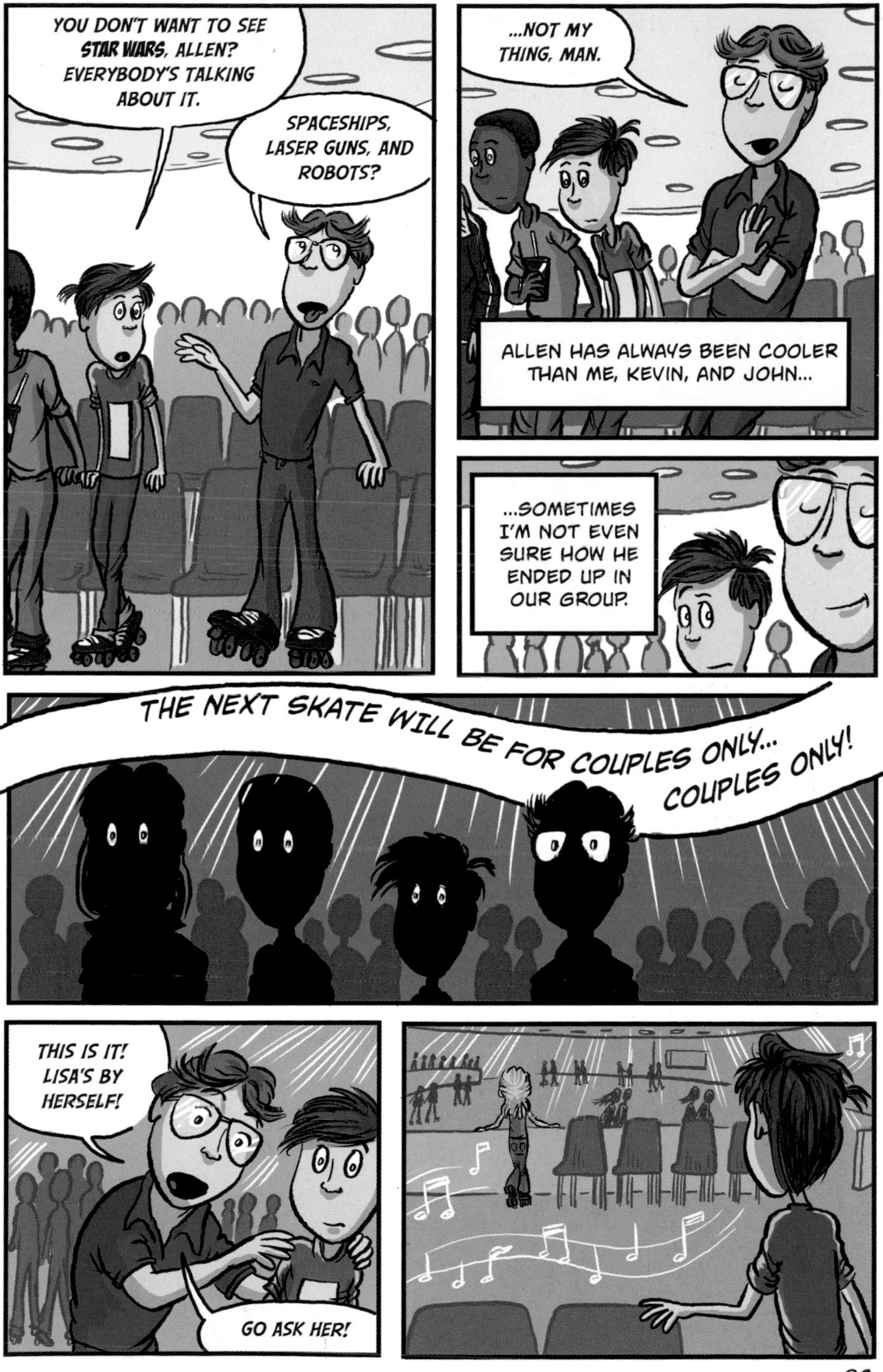

YOU DON'T WANT TO SEE STAR WARS, ALLEN? EVERYBODY'S TALKING ABOUT IT.
SPACESHIPS, LASER GUNS, AND ROBOTS?
...NOT MY THING, MAN.
ALLEN HAS ALWAYS BEEN COOLER THAN ME, KEVIN, AND JOHN...
...SOMETIMES I'M NOT EVEN SURE HOW HE ENDED UP IN OUR GROUP.
THE NEXT SKATE WILL BE FOR COUPLES ONLY... COUPLES ONLY!
THIS IS IT! LISA'S BY HERSELF!
GO ASK HER!

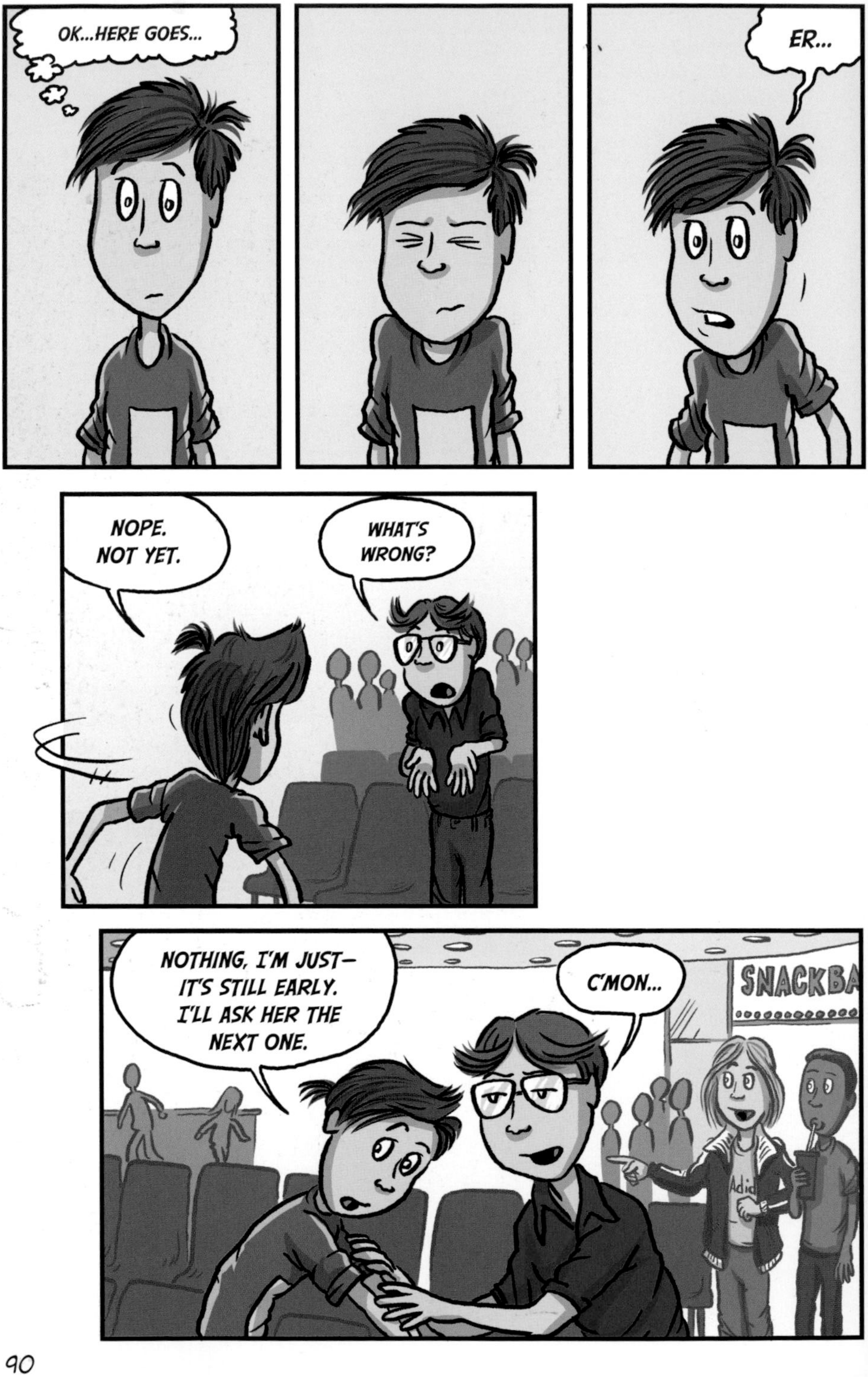
OK...HERE GOES...
ER...
NOPE. NOT YET.
WHAT'S WRONG?
NOTHING, I'M JUST— IT'S STILL EARLY. I'LL ASK HER THE NEXT ONE.
C'MON...
SNACKBA

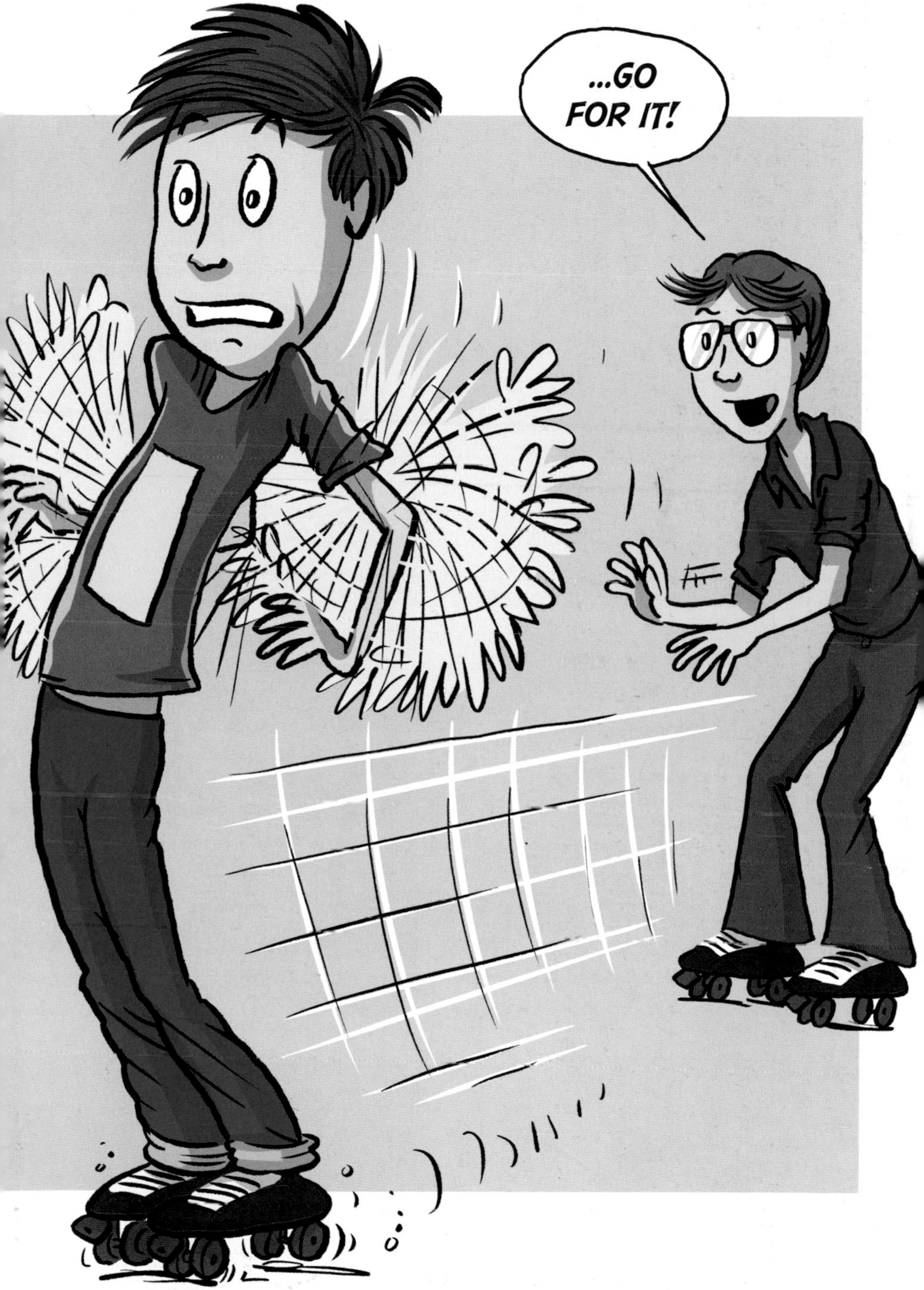
...GO FOR IT!

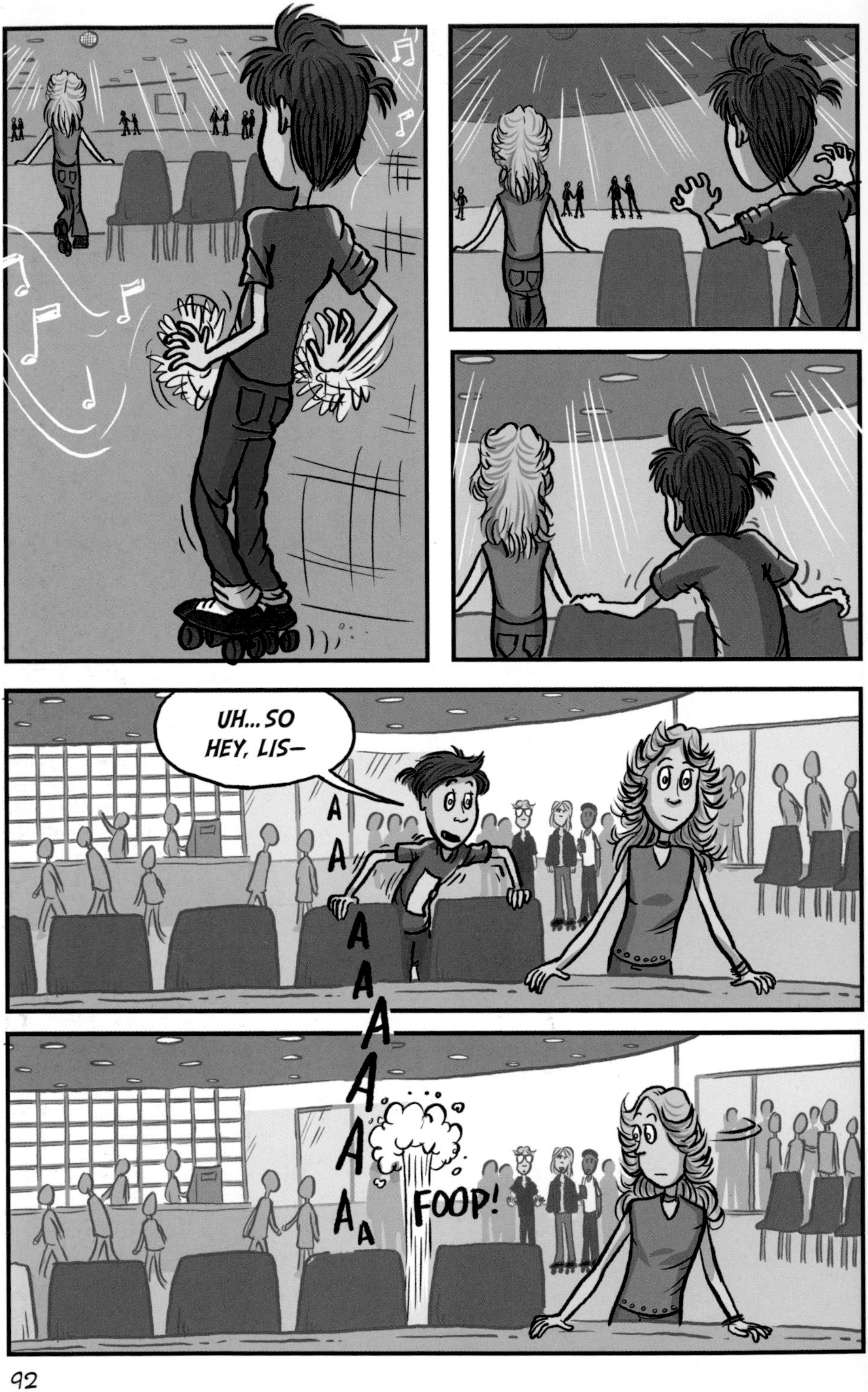
UH... SO
HEY, LIS—
AAAAAAAAAA
FOOP!

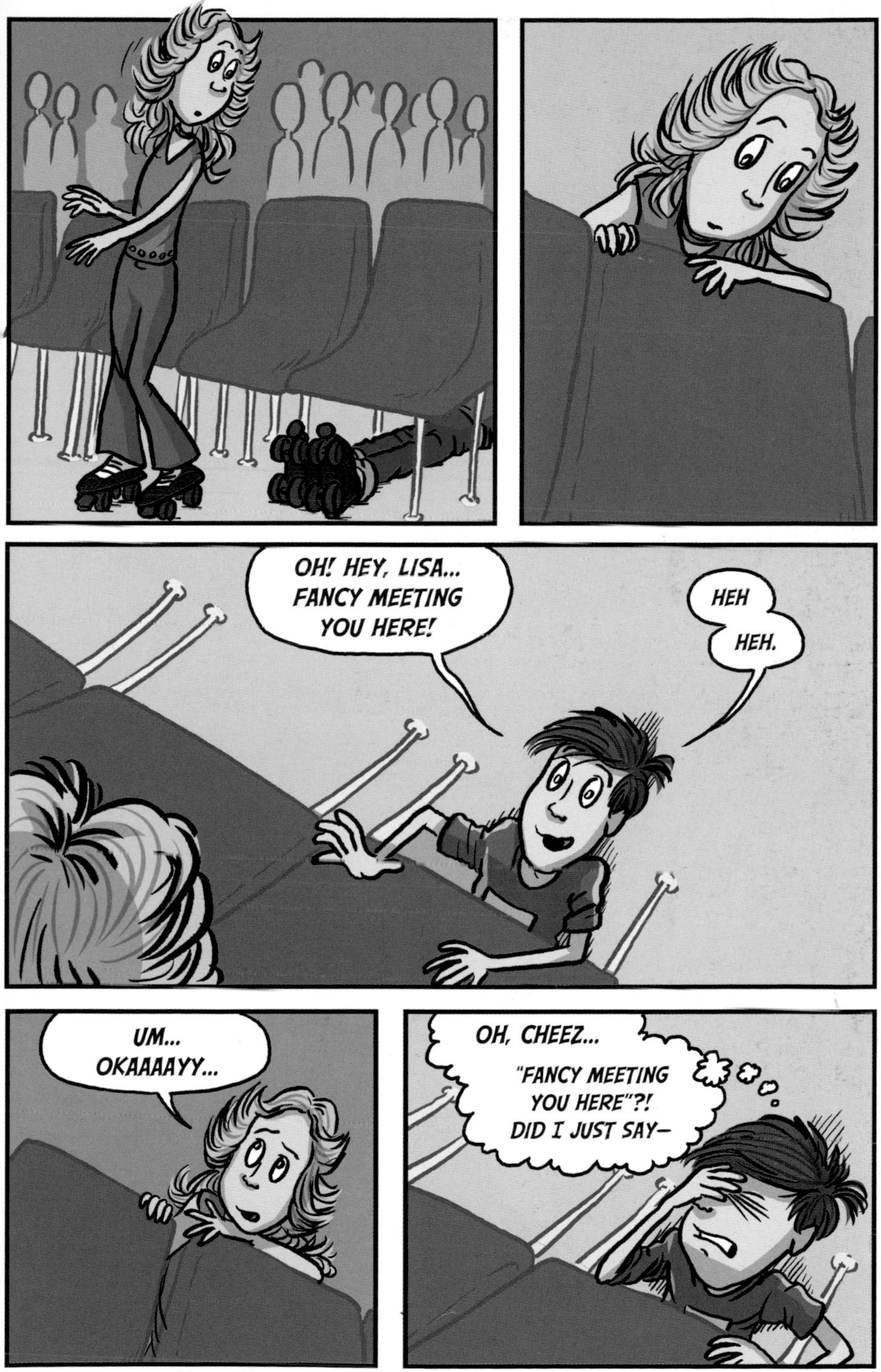
OH! HEY, LISA... FANCY MEETING YOU HERE!
HEH
HEH.
UM... OKAAAAYY...
OH, CHEEZ...
"FANCY MEETING YOU HERE"?! DID I JUST SAY–

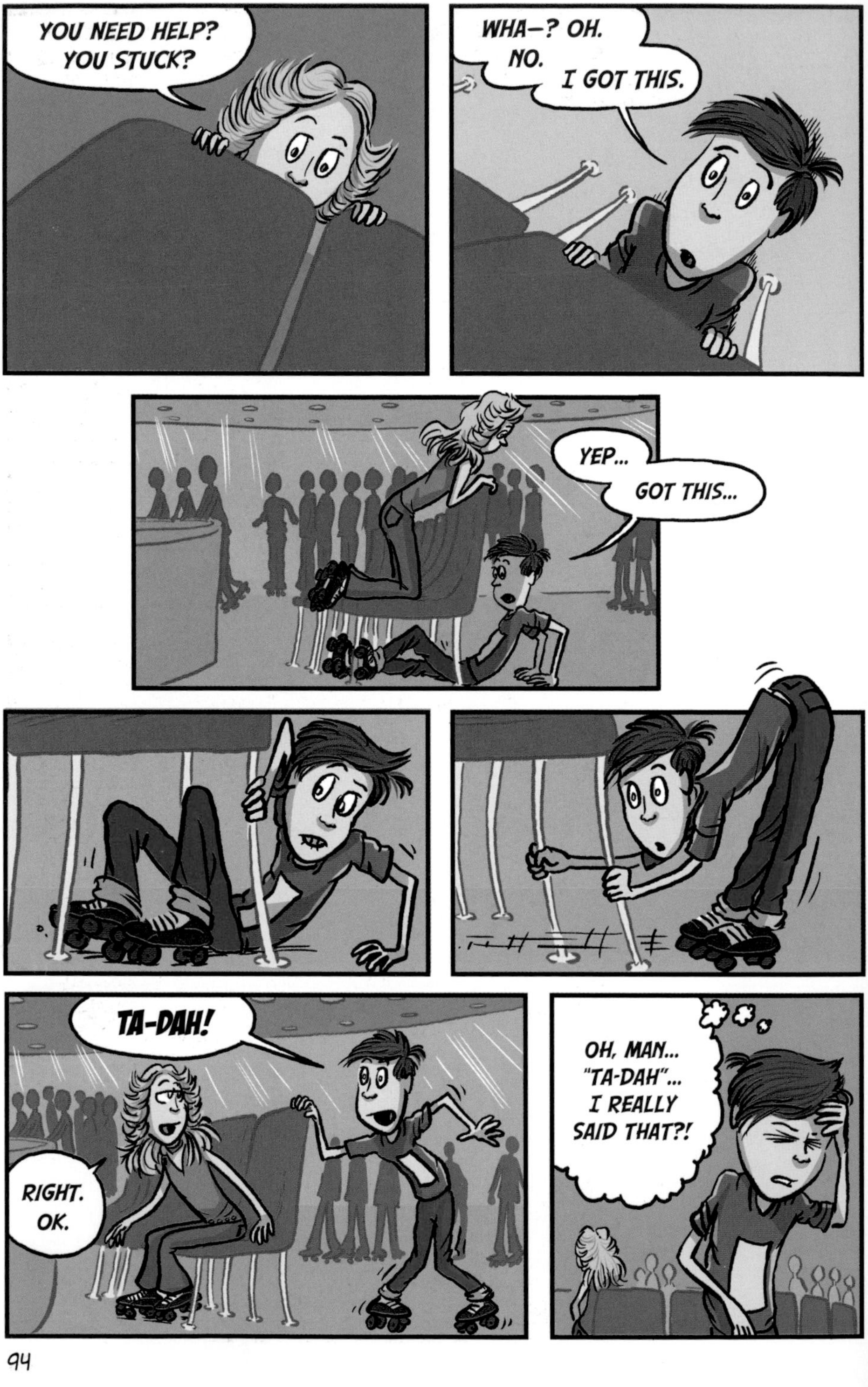
YOU NEED HELP? YOU STUCK?
WHA—? OH. NO.
I GOT THIS.
YEP...
GOT THIS...
TA-DAH!
RIGHT. OK.
OH, MAN... "TA-DAH"... I REALLY SAID THAT?!

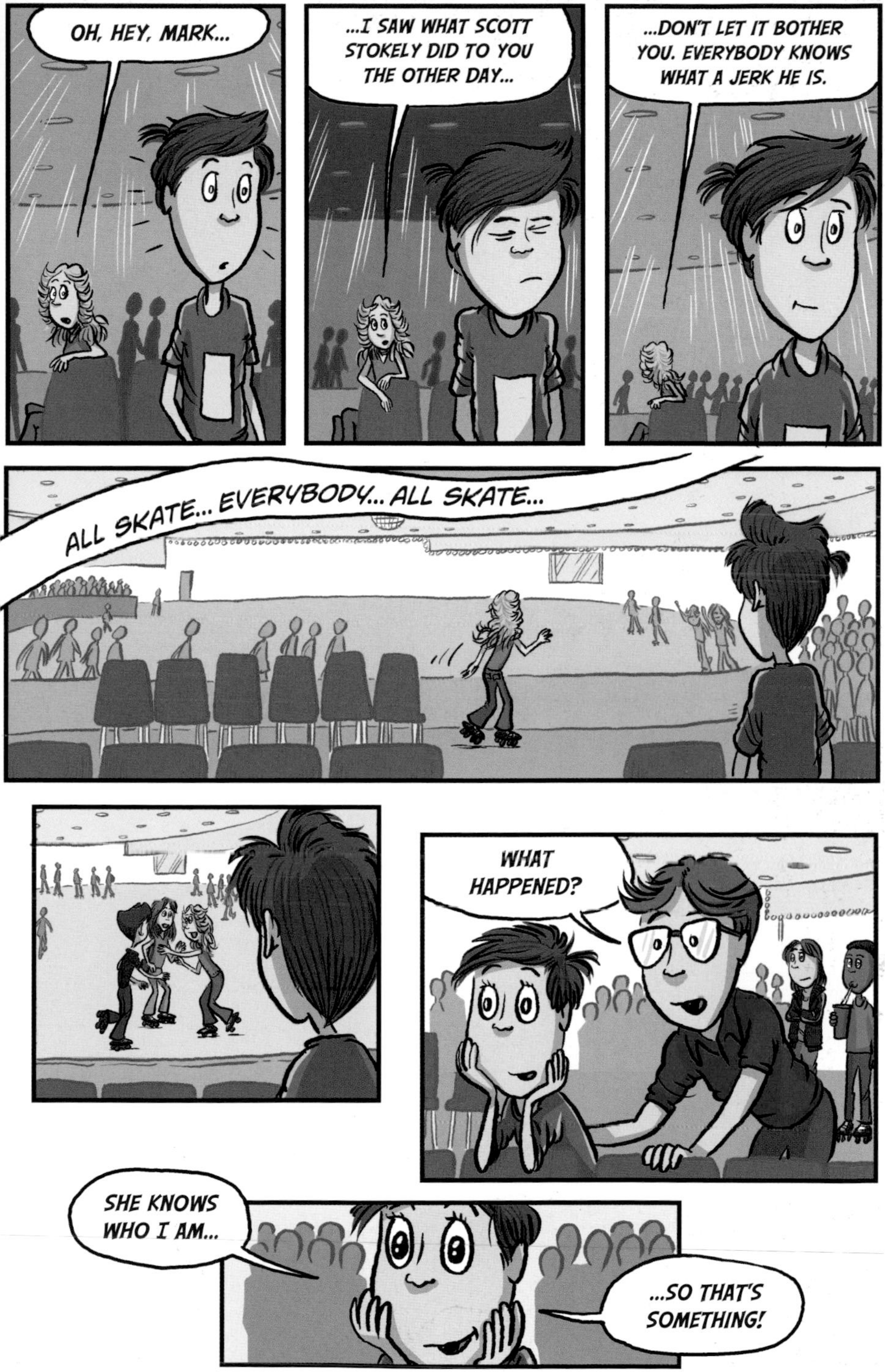
OH, HEY, MARK...
...I SAW WHAT SCOTT STOKELY DID TO YOU THE OTHER DAY...
...DON'T LET IT BOTHER YOU. EVERYBODY KNOWS WHAT A JERK HE IS.
ALL SKATE... EVERYBODY... ALL SKATE...
WHAT HAPPENED?
SHE KNOWS WHO I AM...
...SO THAT'S SOMETHING!

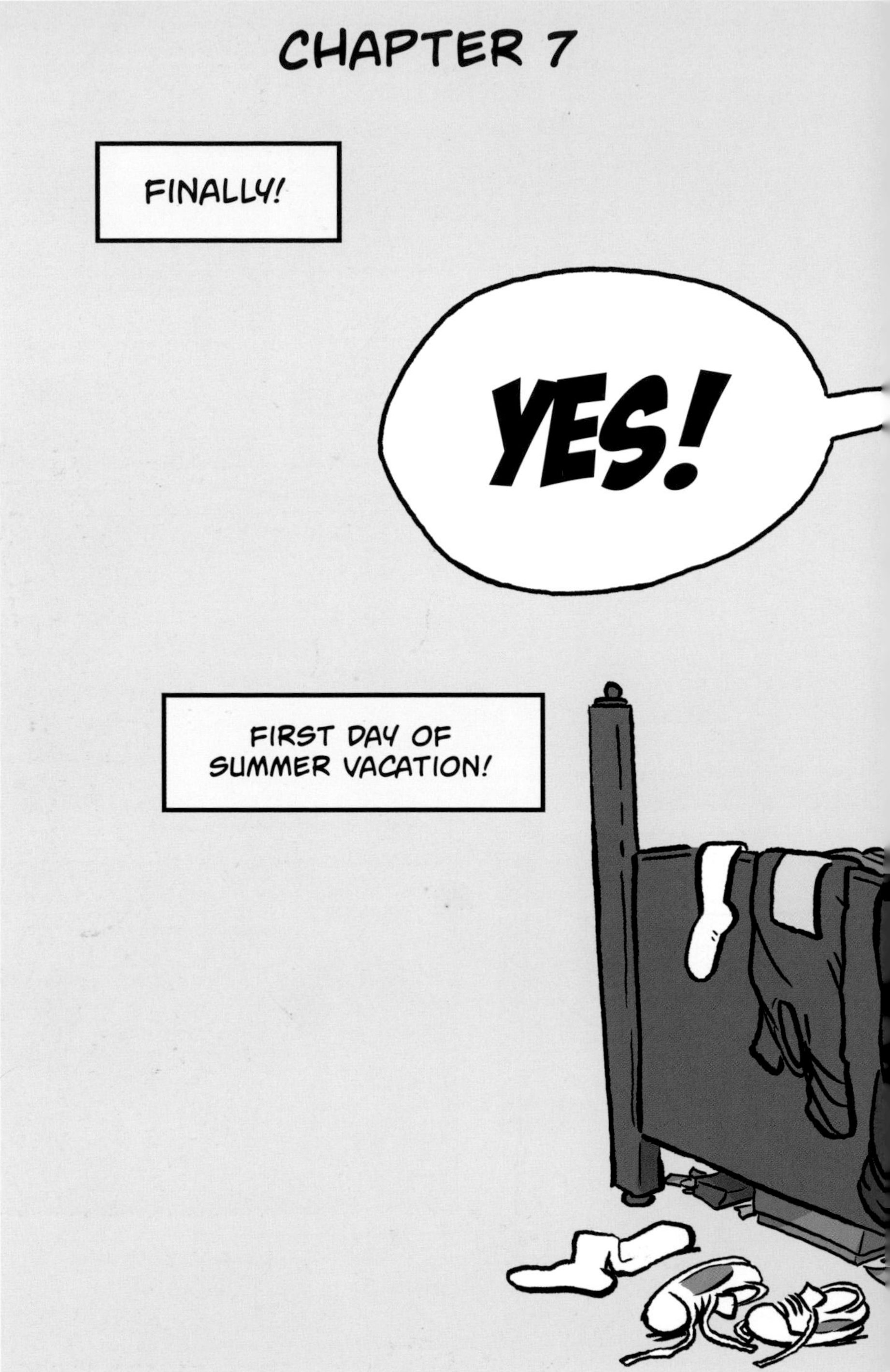
CHAPTER 7
FINALLY!
YES!
FIRST DAY OF SUMMER VACATION!

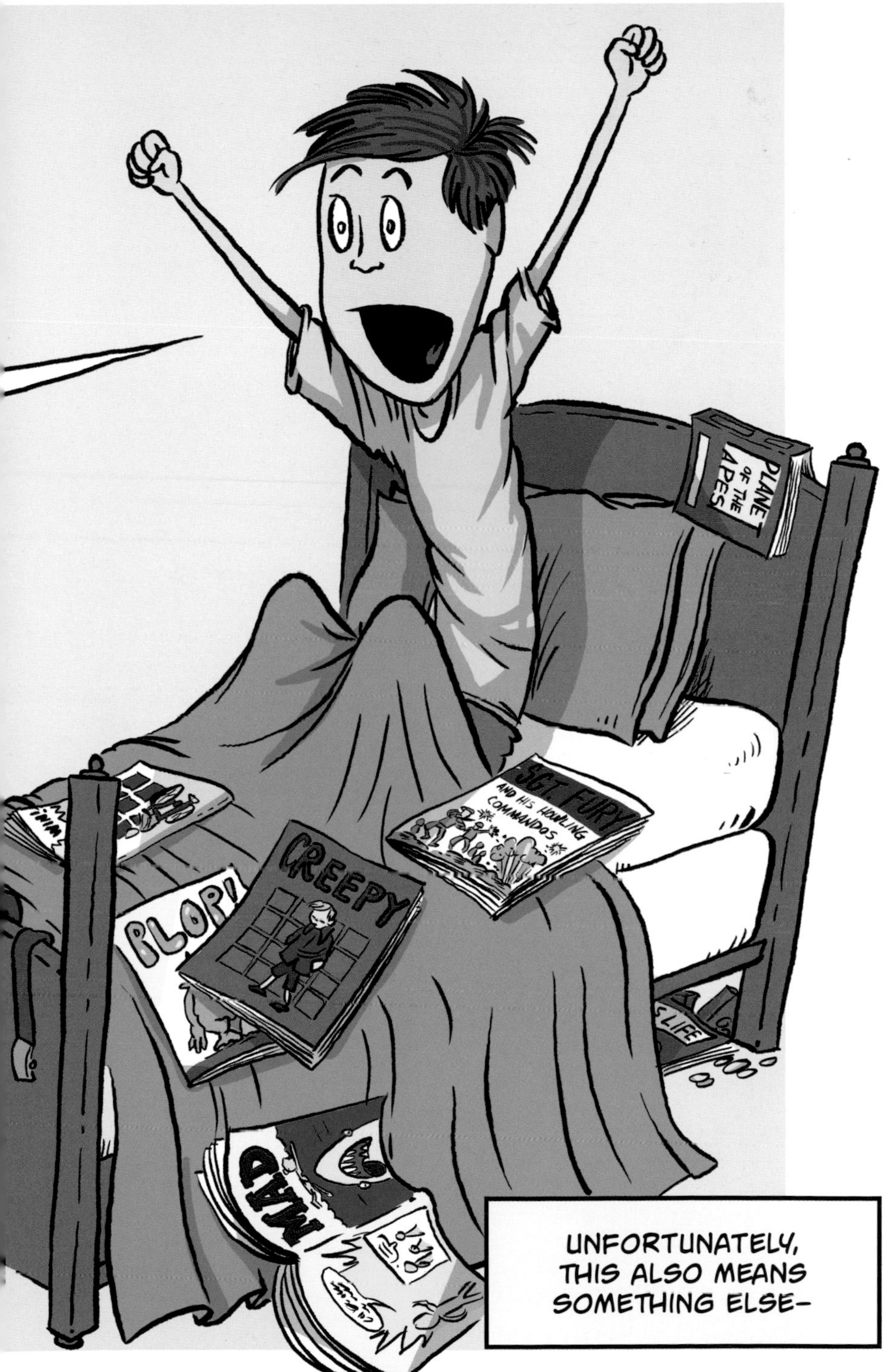
PLANE OF THE APES
SGT. FURY
AND HIS HOWLING COMMANDOS
CREEPY
PLOP!
MAD
UNFORTUNATELY, THIS ALSO MEANS SOMETHING ELSE–

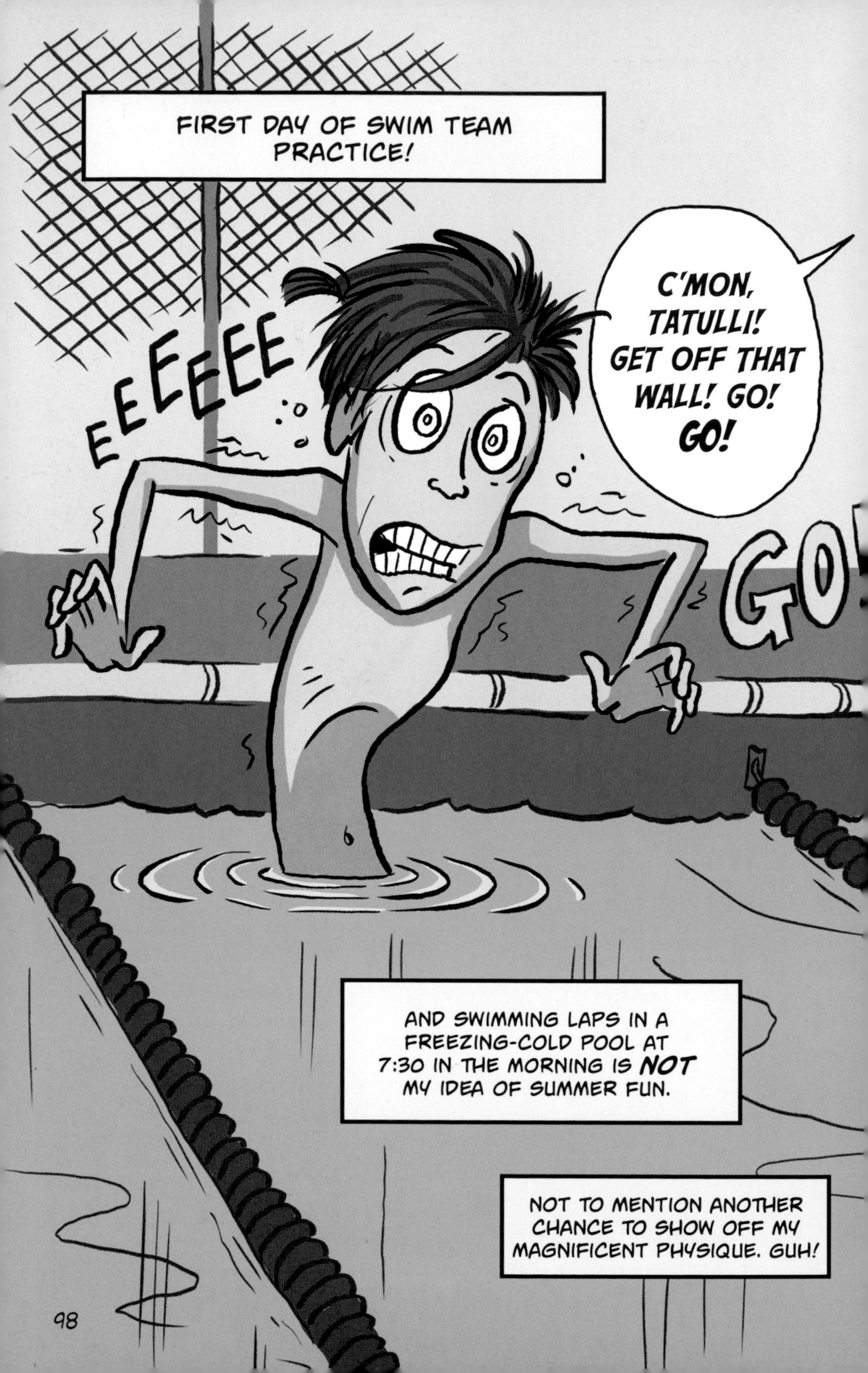
FIRST DAY OF SWIM TEAM PRACTICE!
EEEEEEE
C'MON, TATULLI! GET OFF THAT WALL! GO! GO!
GO!
AND SWIMMING LAPS IN A FREEZING-COLD POOL AT 7:30 IN THE MORNING IS NOT MY IDEA OF SUMMER FUN.
NOT TO MENTION ANOTHER CHANCE TO SHOW OFF MY MAGNIFICENT PHYSIQUE. GUH!

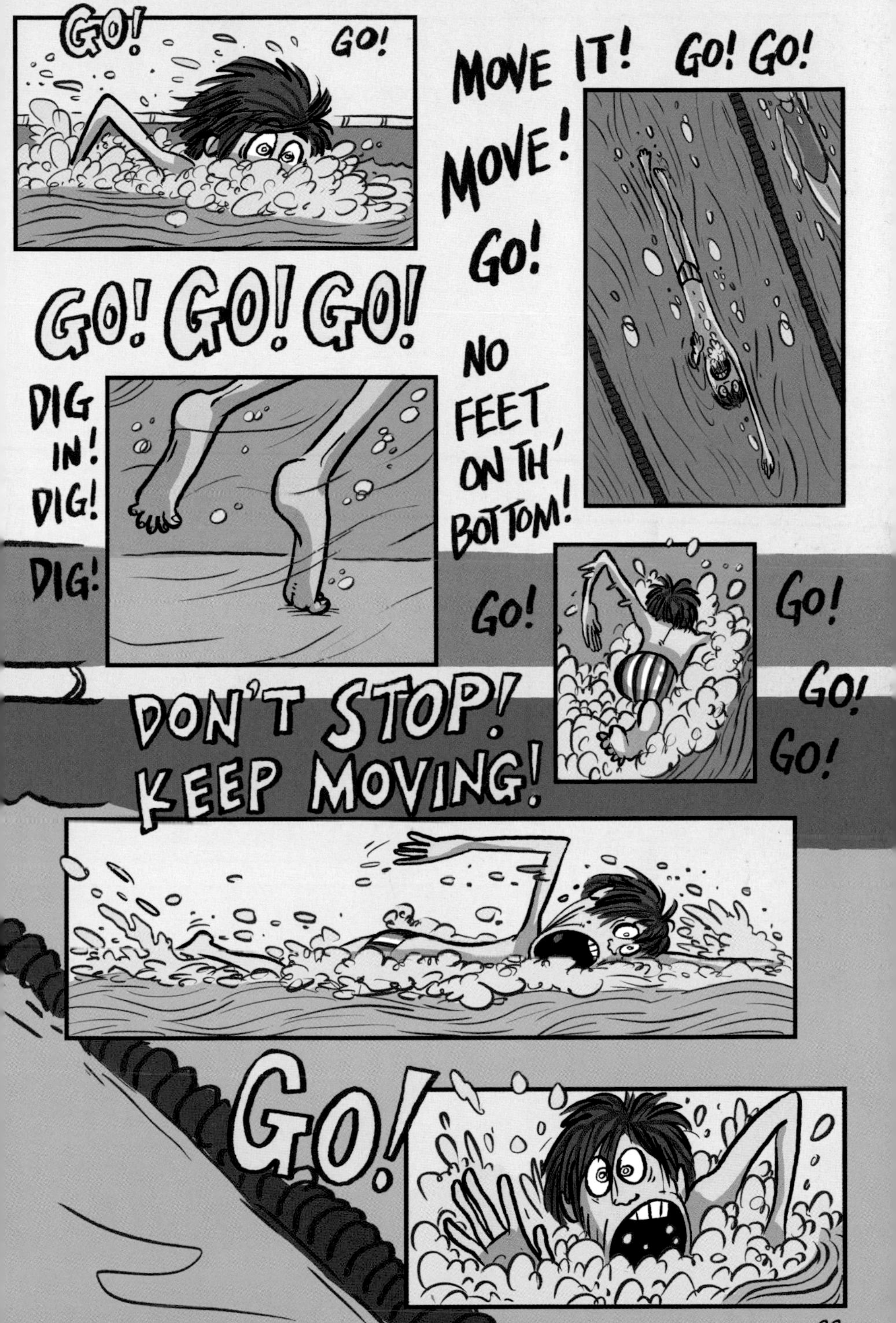
GO!
GO!
MOVE IT! GO! GO!
MOVE!
GO!
GO! GO! GO!
NO FEET ON TH' BOTTOM!
DIG IN! DIG!
DIG!
GO!
GO!
GO!
GO!
DON'T STOP! KEEP MOVING!
GO!

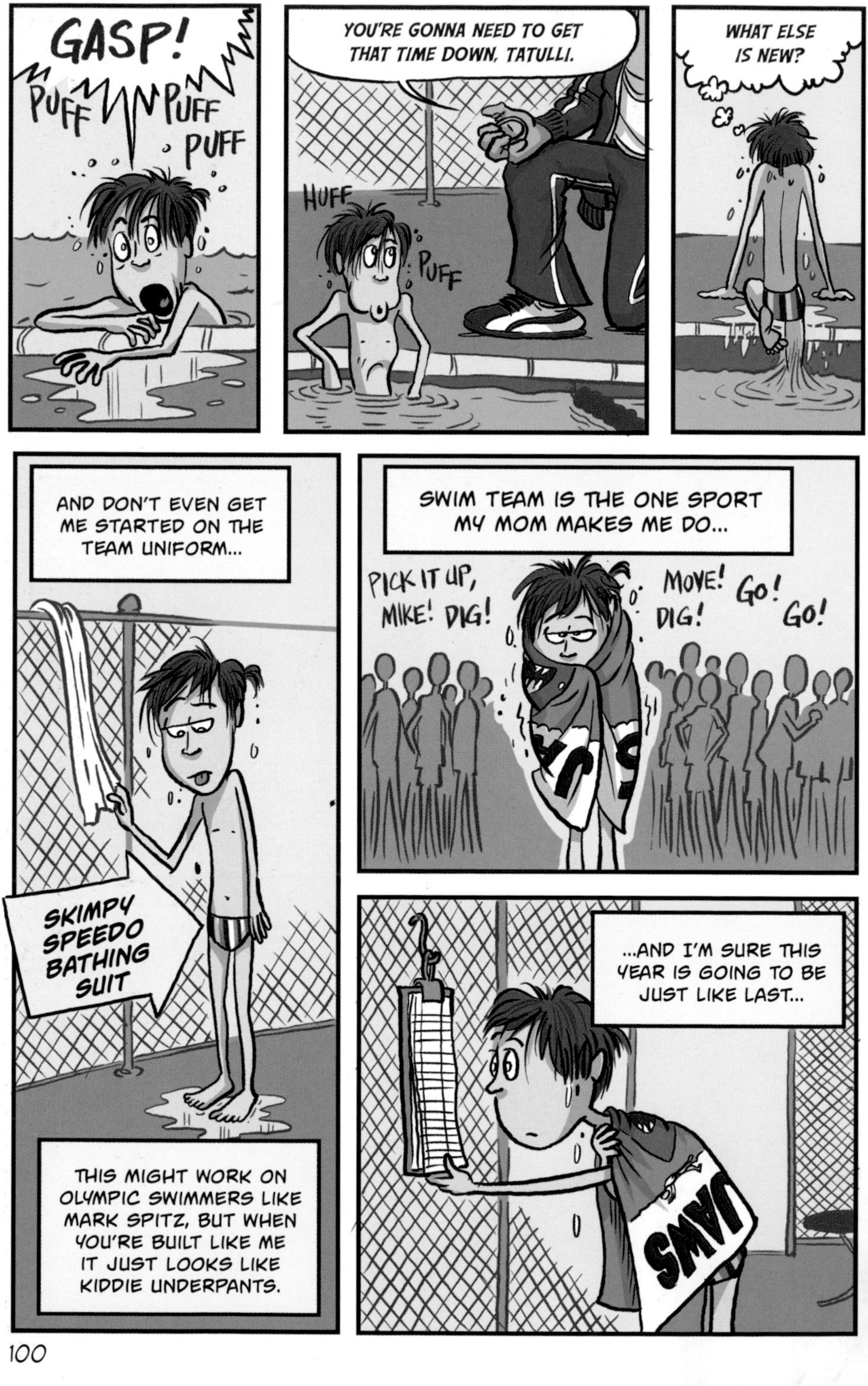
GASP!
PUFF PUFF
PUFF
YOU'RE GONNA NEED TO GET THAT TIME DOWN, TATULLI.
HUFF
PUFF
WHAT ELSE IS NEW?
AND DON'T EVEN GET ME STARTED ON THE TEAM UNIFORM...
SKIMPY SPEEDO BATHING SUIT
THIS MIGHT WORK ON OLYMPIC SWIMMERS LIKE MARK SPITZ, BUT WHEN YOU'RE BUILT LIKE ME IT JUST LOOKS LIKE KIDDIE UNDERPANTS.
SWIM TEAM IS THE ONE SPORT MY MOM MAKES ME DO...
PICK IT UP, MIKE! DIG!
MOVE! DIG!
GO! GO!
...AND I'M SURE THIS YEAR IS GOING TO BE JUST LIKE LAST...
JAWS

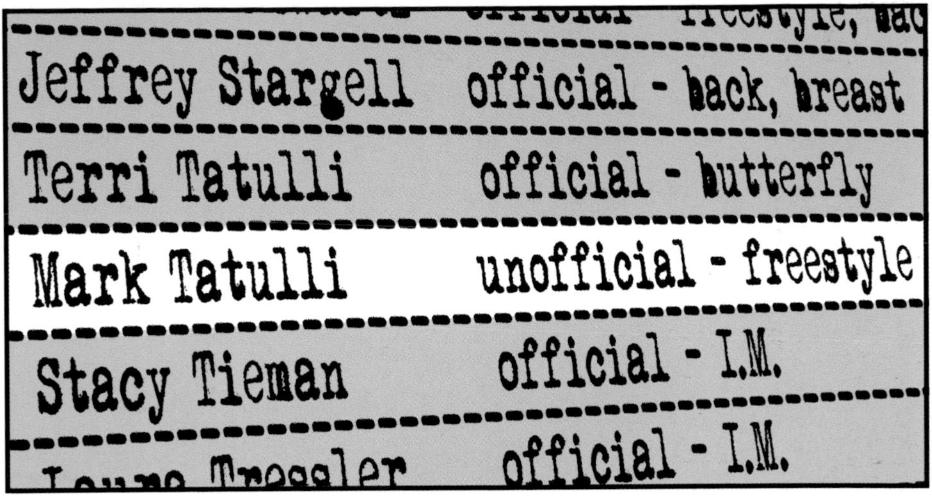
Jeffrey Stargell official - back, breast
Terri Tatulli official - butterfly
Mark Tatulli unofficial - freestyle
Stacy Tieman official - I.M.
official - I.M.

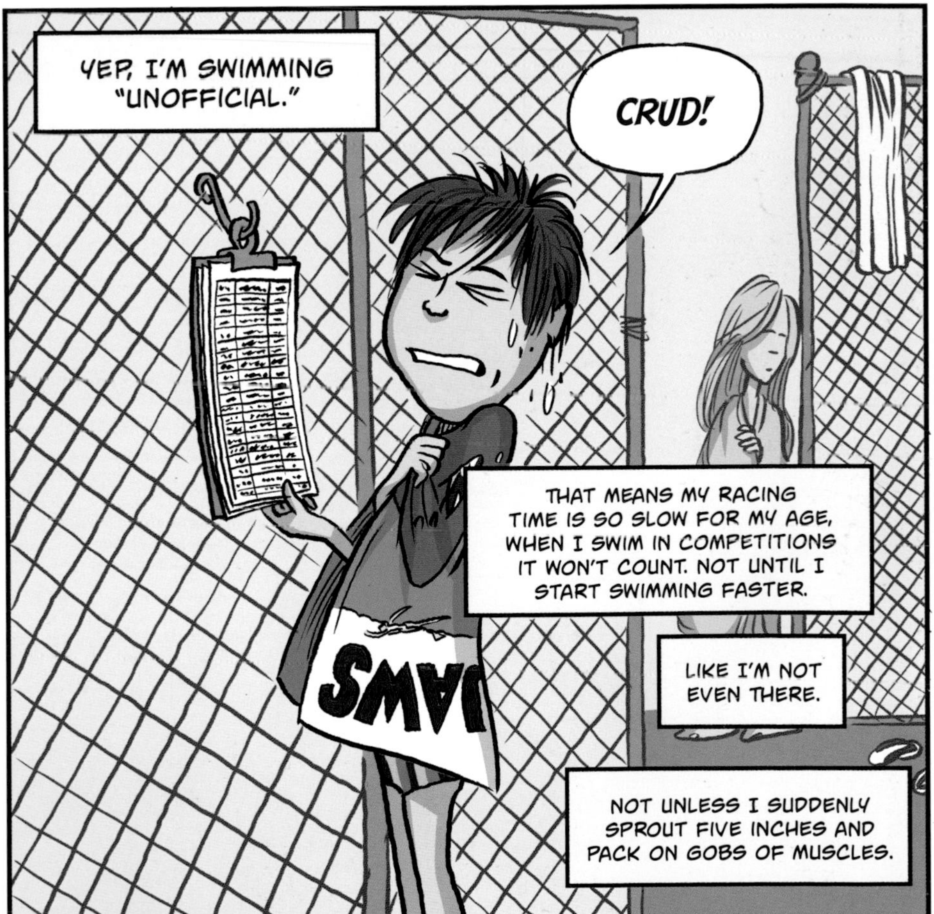
YEP, I'M SWIMMING "UNOFFICIAL."
CRUD!
THAT MEANS MY RACING TIME IS SO SLOW FOR MY AGE, WHEN I SWIM IN COMPETITIONS IT WON'T COUNT. NOT UNTIL I START SWIMMING FASTER.
LIKE I'M NOT EVEN THERE.
NOT UNLESS I SUDDENLY SPROUT FIVE INCHES AND PACK ON GOBS OF MUSCLES.

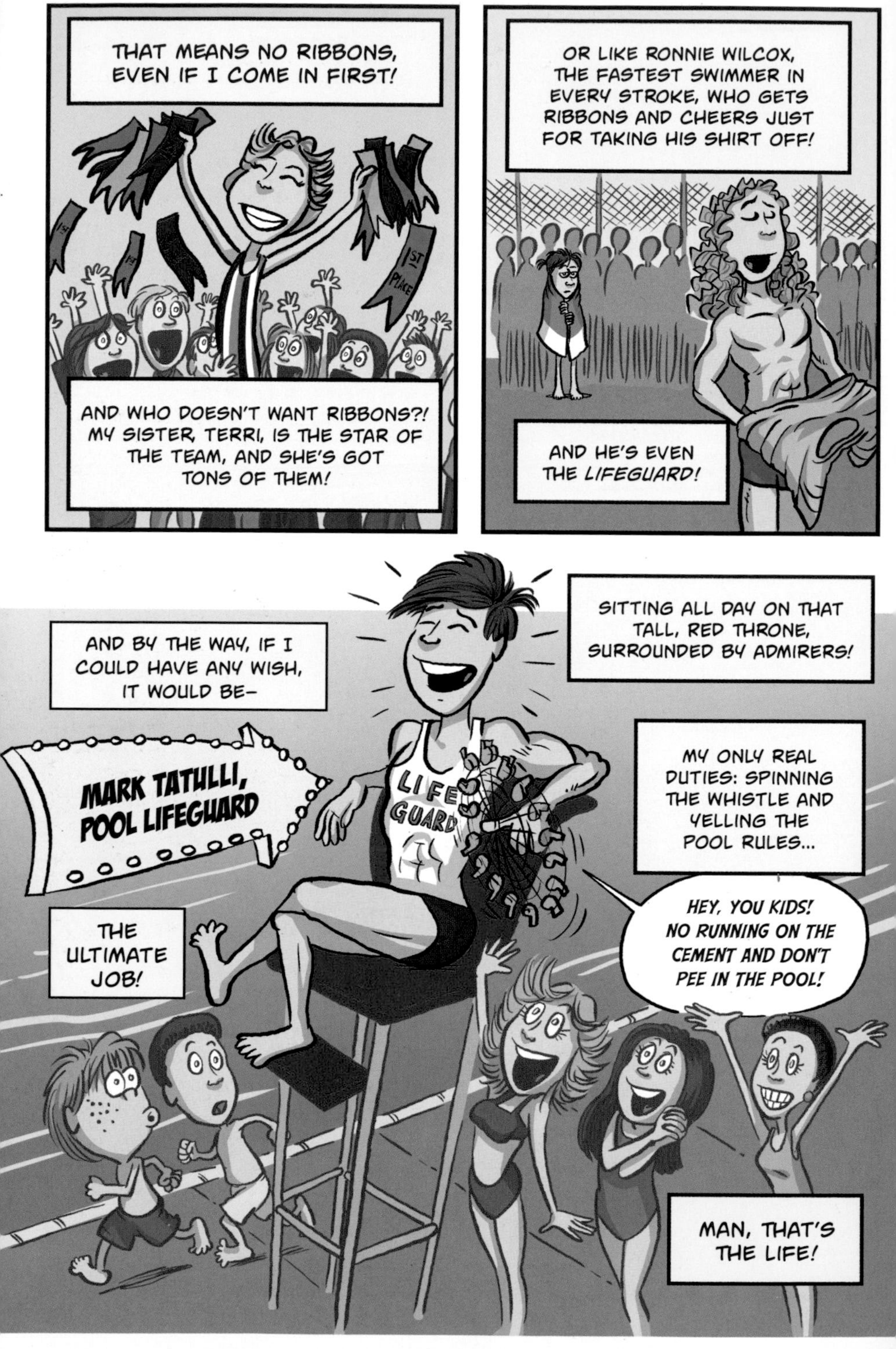

THAT MEANS NO RIBBONS, EVEN IF I COME IN FIRST!
1ST PLACE
AND WHO DOESN'T WANT RIBBONS?! MY SISTER, TERRI, IS THE STAR OF THE TEAM, AND SHE'S GOT TONS OF THEM!
OR LIKE RONNIE WILCOX, THE FASTEST SWIMMER IN EVERY STROKE, WHO GETS RIBBONS AND CHEERS JUST FOR TAKING HIS SHIRT OFF!
AND HE'S EVEN THE *LIFEGUARD*!
AND BY THE WAY, IF I COULD HAVE ANY WISH, IT WOULD BE–
MARK TATULLI, POOL LIFEGUARD
SITTING ALL DAY ON THAT TALL, RED THRONE, SURROUNDED BY ADMIRERS!
LIFE GUARD
MY ONLY REAL DUTIES: SPINNING THE WHISTLE AND YELLING THE POOL RULES...
THE ULTIMATE JOB!
HEY, YOU KIDS! NO RUNNING ON THE CEMENT AND DON'T PEE IN THE POOL!
MAN, THAT'S THE LIFE!

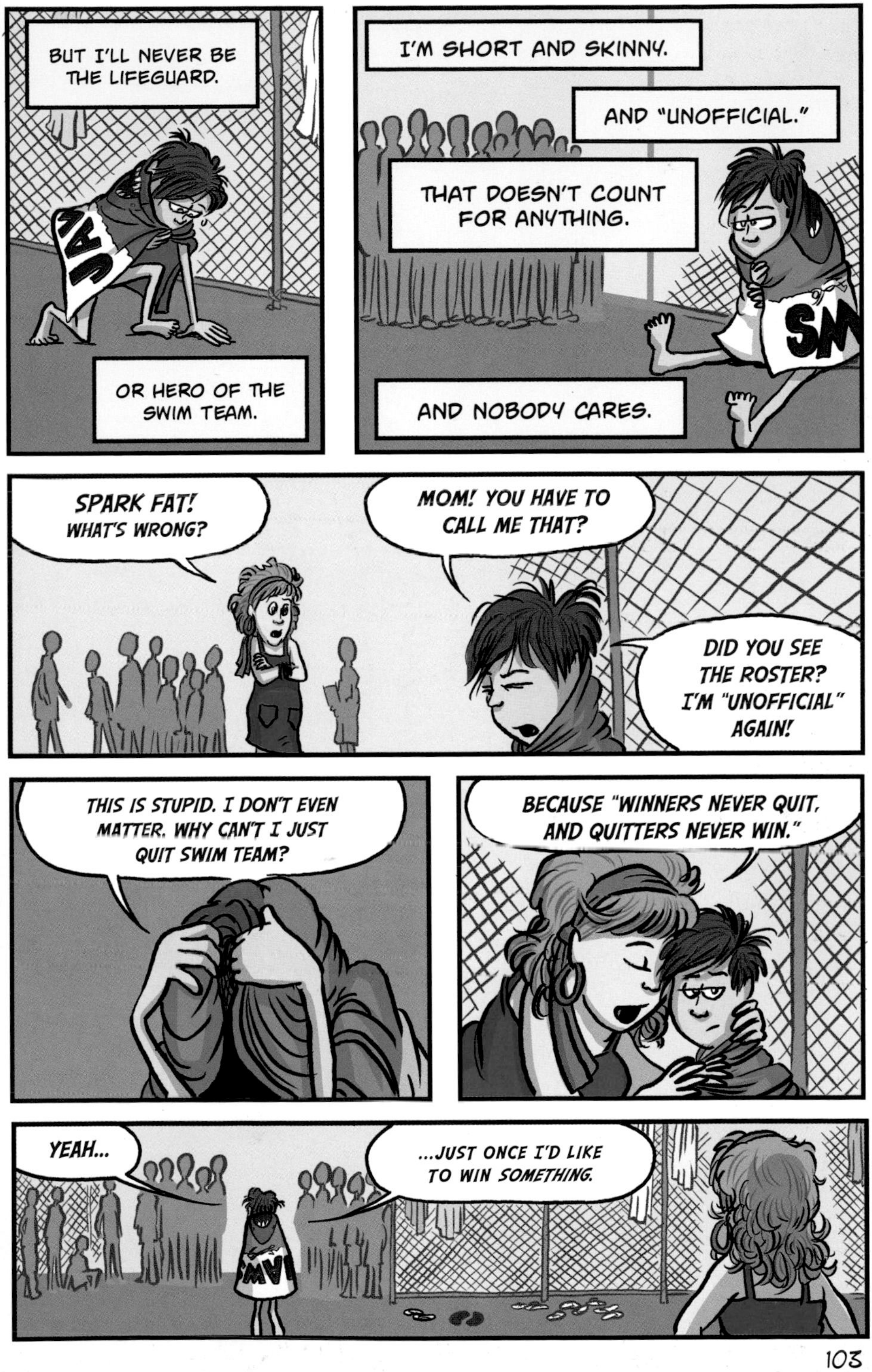
BUT I'LL NEVER BE THE LIFEGUARD.
JAY
OR HERO OF THE SWIM TEAM.
I'M SHORT AND SKINNY.
AND "UNOFFICIAL."
THAT DOESN'T COUNT FOR ANYTHING.
SM
AND NOBODY CARES.
SPARK FAT! WHAT'S WRONG?
MOM! YOU HAVE TO CALL ME THAT?
DID YOU SEE THE ROSTER? I'M "UNOFFICIAL" AGAIN!
THIS IS STUPID. I DON'T EVEN MATTER. WHY CAN'T I JUST QUIT SWIM TEAM?
BECAUSE "WINNERS NEVER QUIT, AND QUITTERS NEVER WIN."
YEAH...
...JUST ONCE I'D LIKE TO WIN SOMETHING.

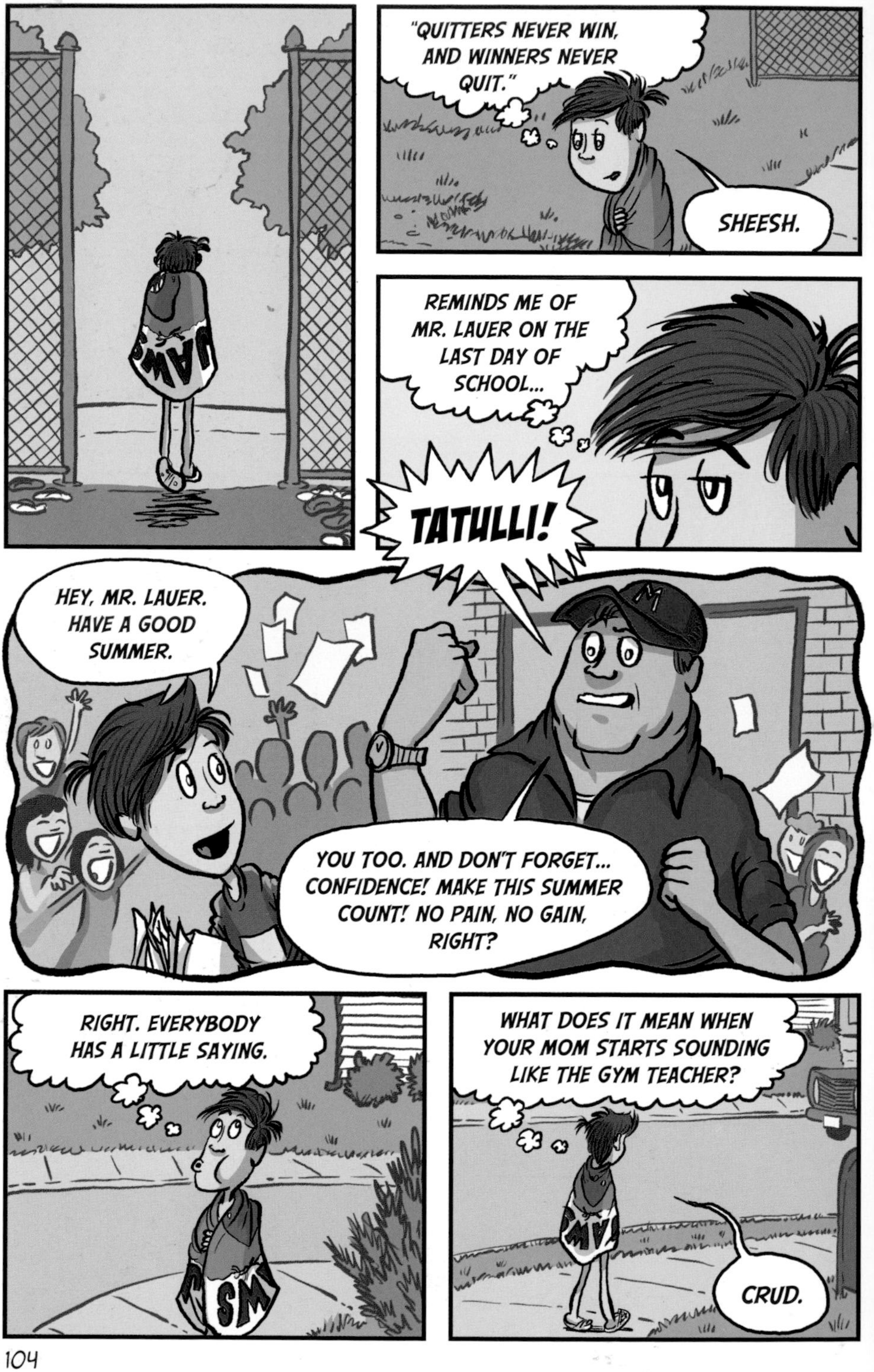
"QUITTERS NEVER WIN, AND WINNERS NEVER QUIT."
SHEESH.
REMINDS ME OF MR. LAUER ON THE LAST DAY OF SCHOOL...
TATULLI!
HEY, MR. LAUER. HAVE A GOOD SUMMER.
YOU TOO. AND DON'T FORGET... CONFIDENCE! MAKE THIS SUMMER COUNT! NO PAIN, NO GAIN, RIGHT?
RIGHT. EVERYBODY HAS A LITTLE SAYING.
WHAT DOES IT MEAN WHEN YOUR MOM STARTS SOUNDING LIKE THE GYM TEACHER?
CRUD.

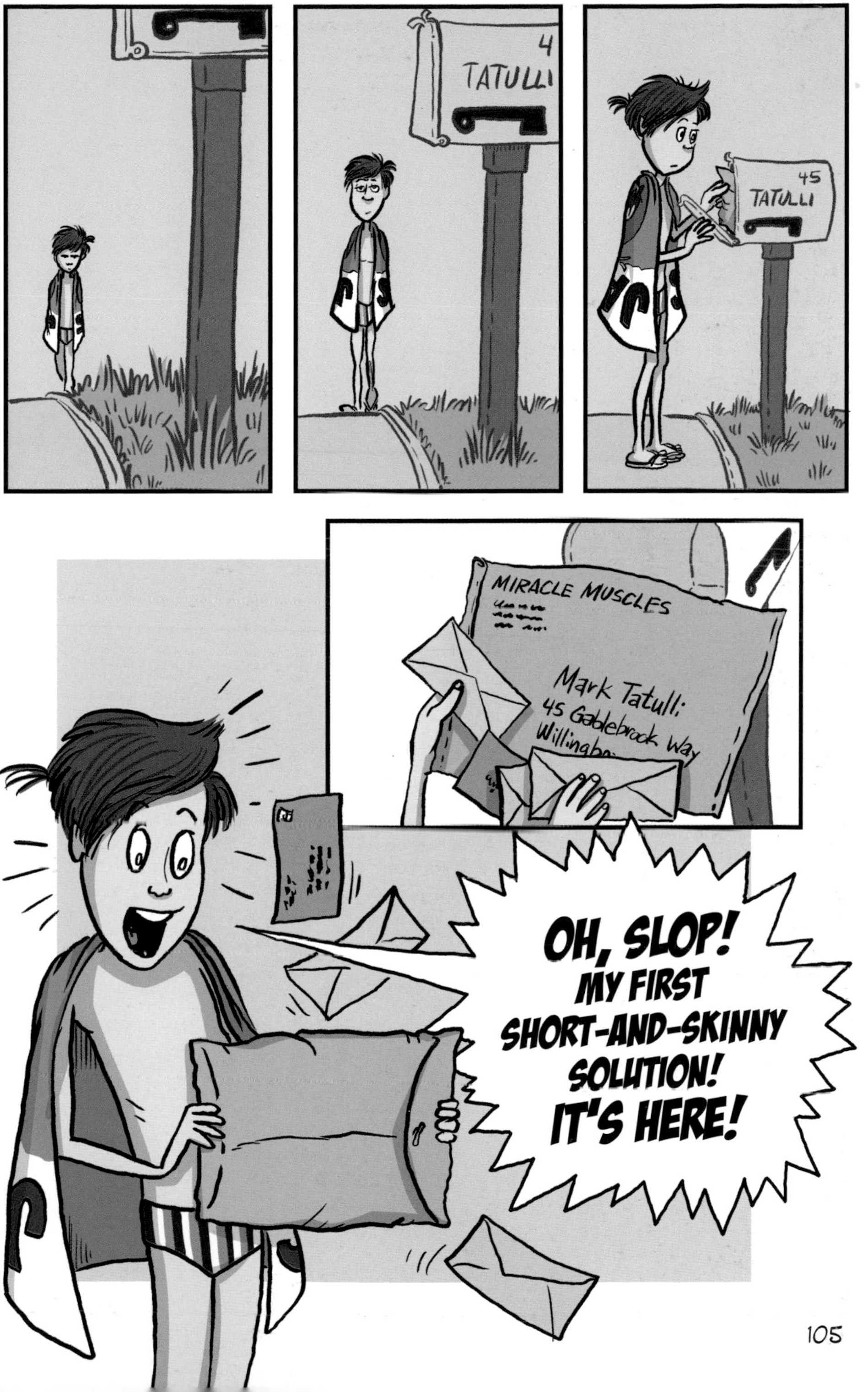
4
TATULLI
45
TATULLI
MIRACLE MUSCLES
Mark Tatulli
45 Gablebrook Way
OH, SLOP! MY FIRST SHORT-AND-SKINNY SOLUTION! IT'S HERE!

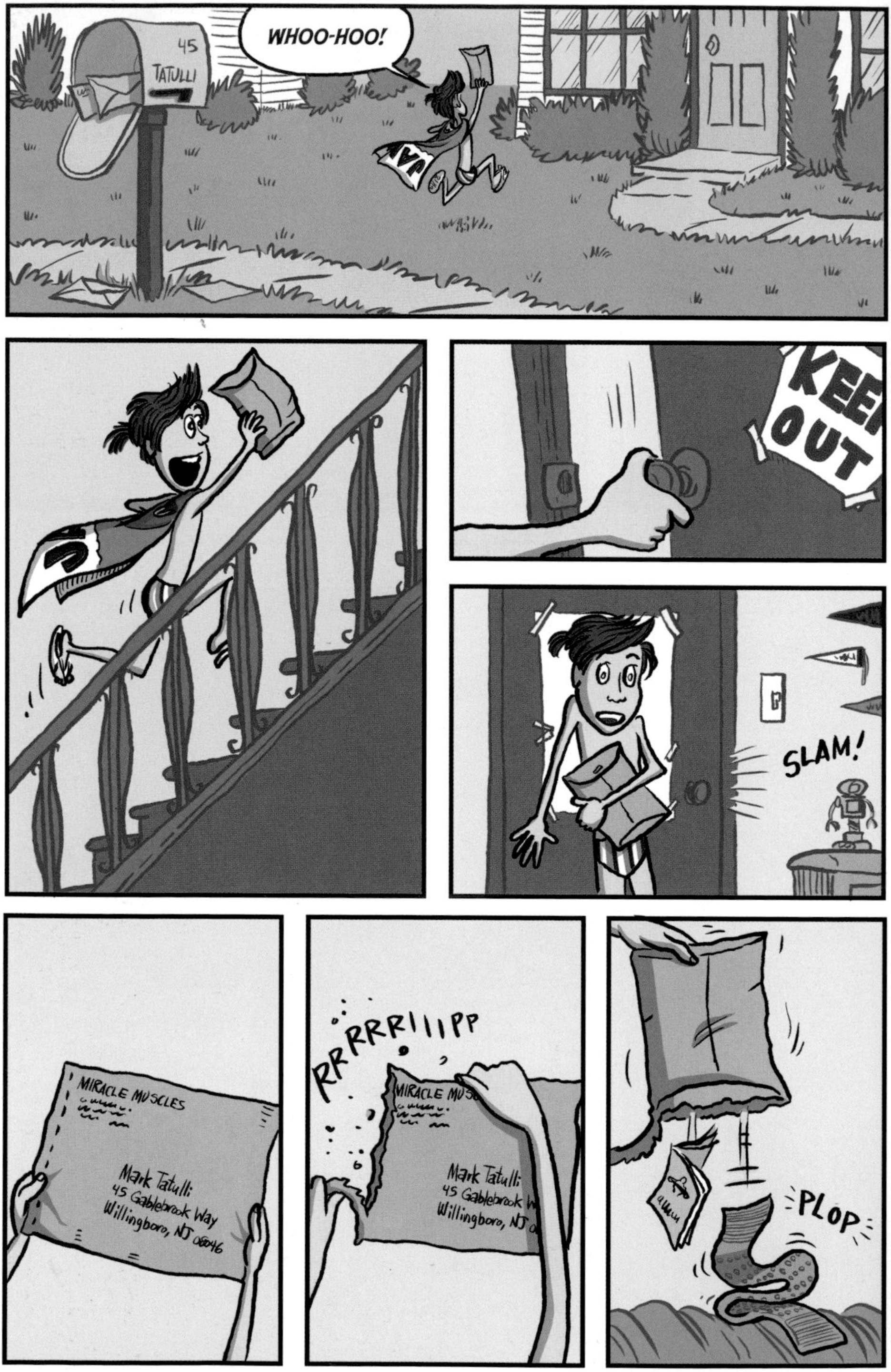

45
TATULLI
[redacted]
WHOO-HOO!
KEE
OUT
SLAM!
MIRACLE MUSCLES
Mark Tatulli
45 Gablebrook Way
Willingboro, NJ 08046
RRRRRIIIPP
MIRACLE MUS
Mark Tatulli
45 Gablebrook W
Willingboro, NJ 0
PLOP

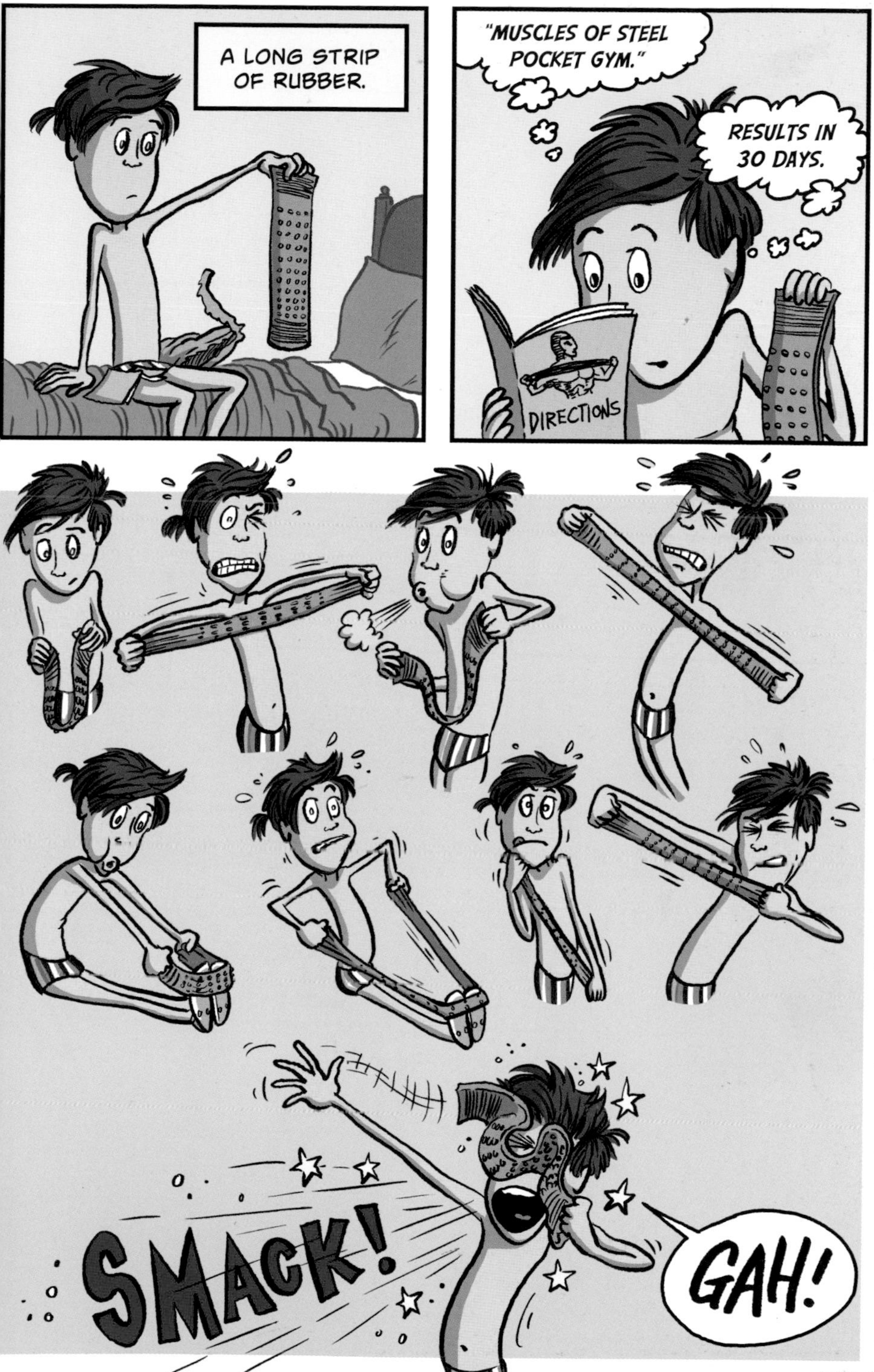
A LONG STRIP OF RUBBER.
"MUSCLES OF STEEL POCKET GYM."
RESULTS IN 30 DAYS.
DIRECTIONS
SMACK!
GAH!

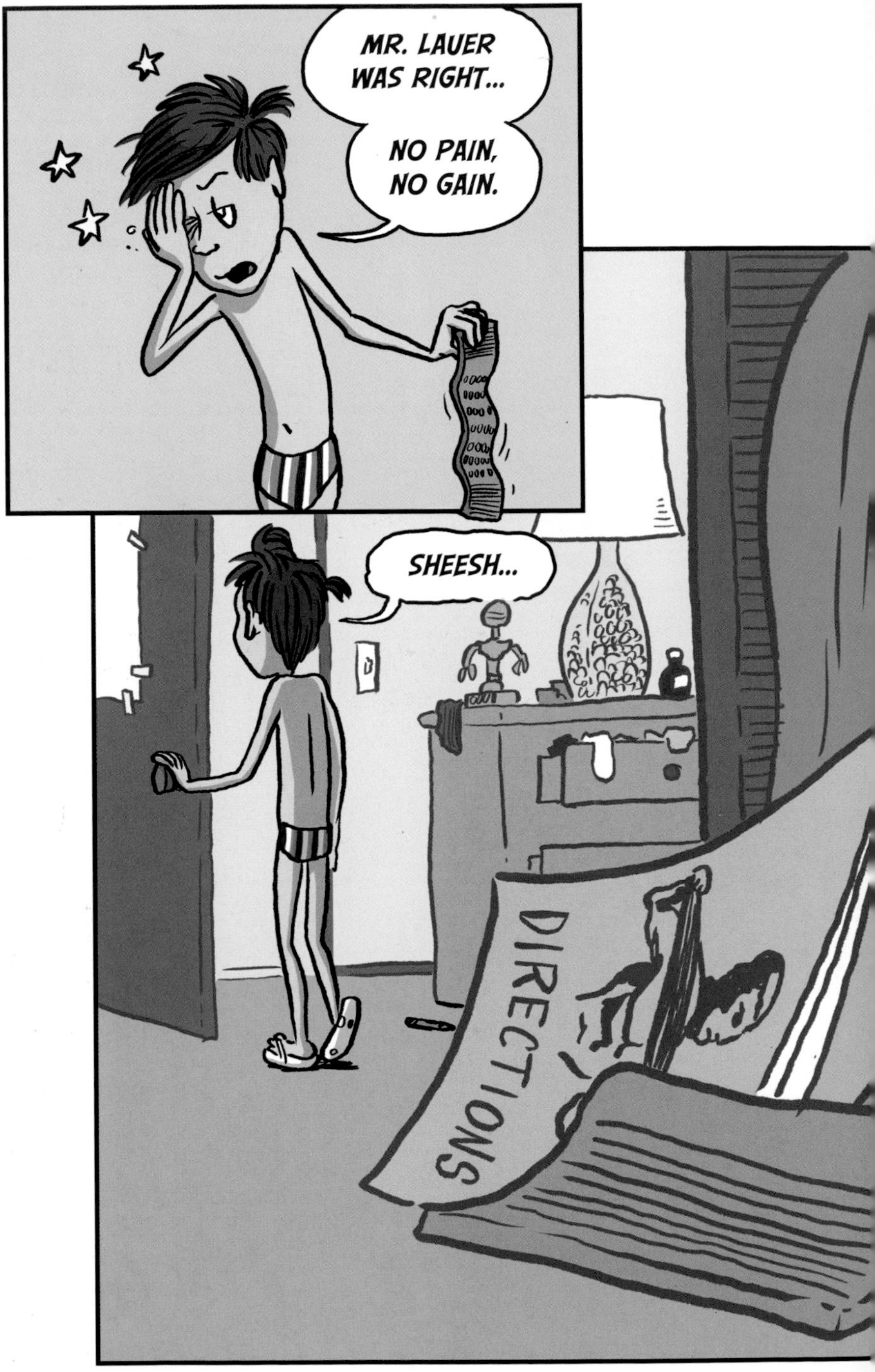
MR. LAUER WAS RIGHT...
NO PAIN, NO GAIN.
SHEESH...
DIRECTIONS

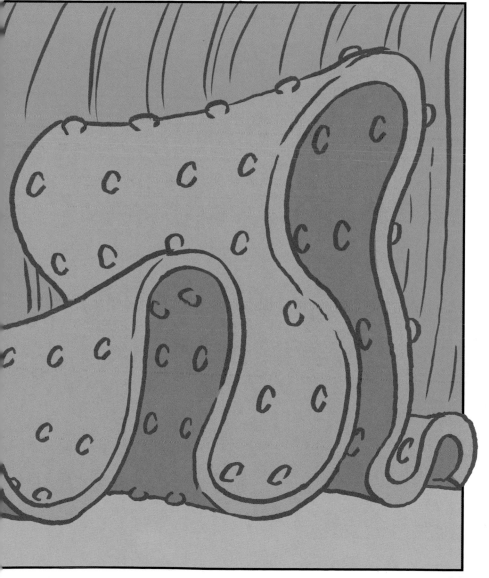

CHAPTER 8

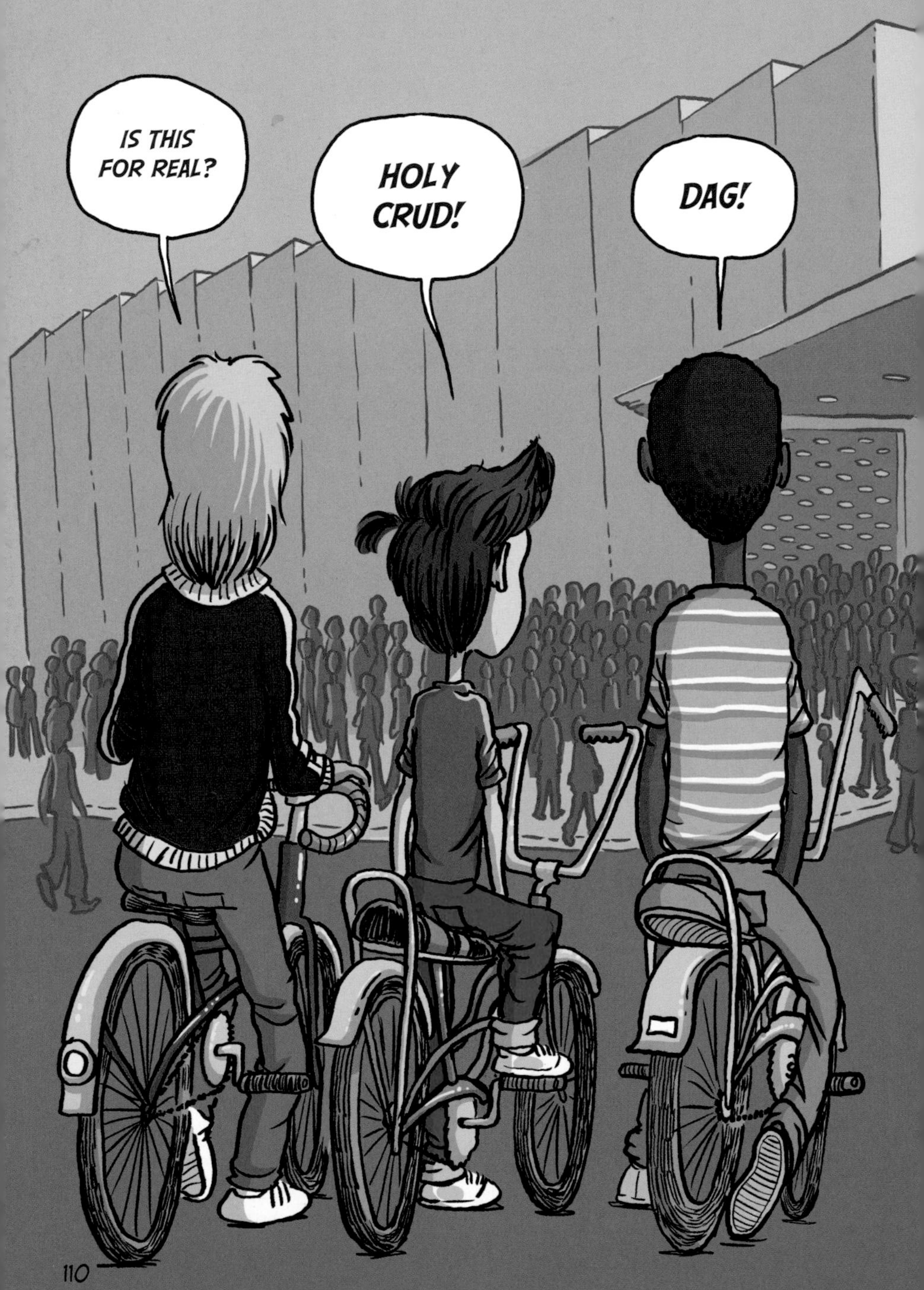
IS THIS FOR REAL?
HOLY CRUD!
DAG!

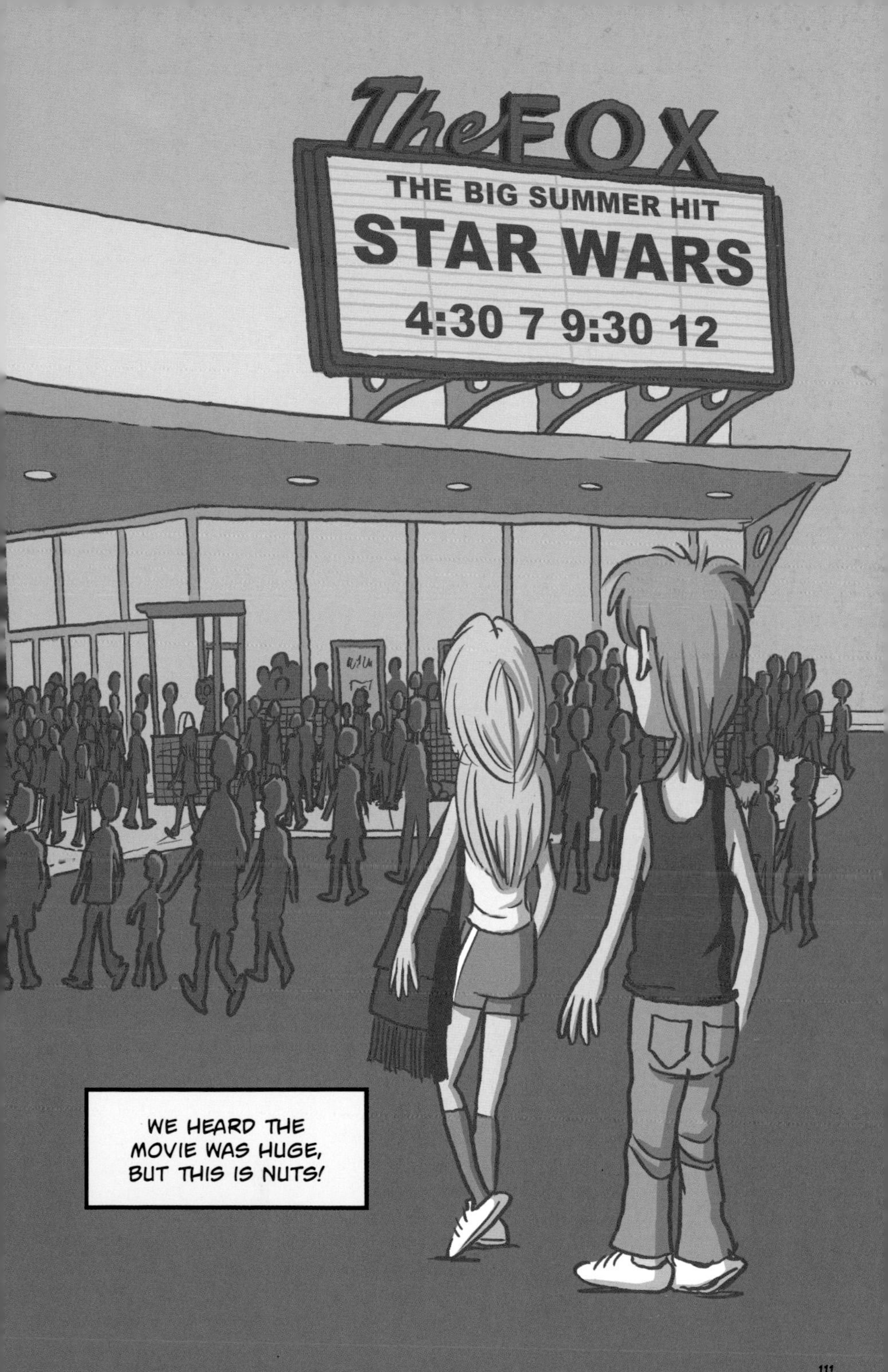

The FOX
THE BIG SUMMER HIT
STAR WARS
4:30 7 9:30 12
WE HEARD THE MOVIE WAS HUGE, BUT THIS IS NUTS!

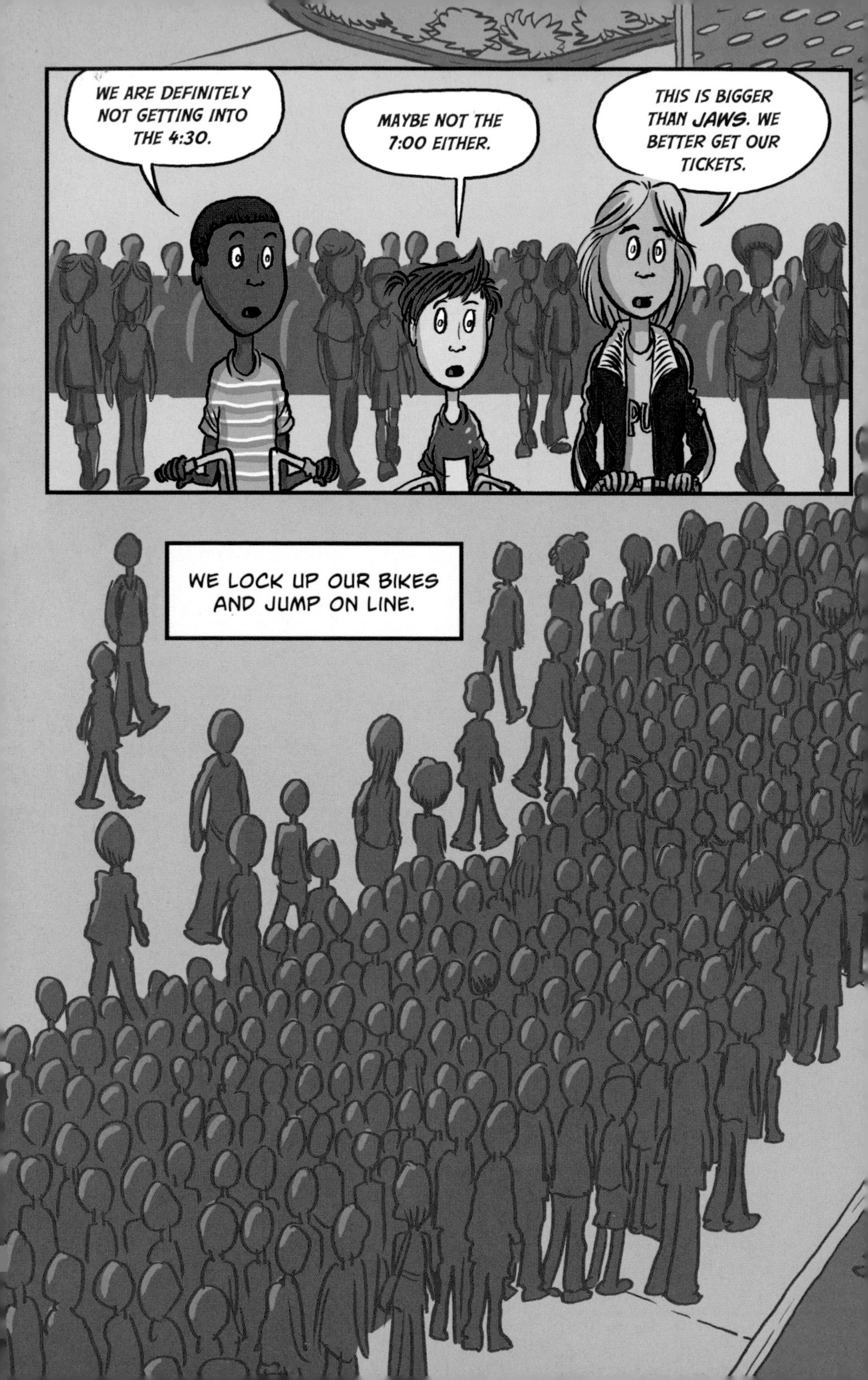
WE ARE DEFINITELY NOT GETTING INTO THE 4:30.
MAYBE NOT THE 7:00 EITHER.
THIS IS BIGGER THAN JAWS. WE BETTER GET OUR TICKETS.
WE LOCK UP OUR BIKES AND JUMP ON LINE.

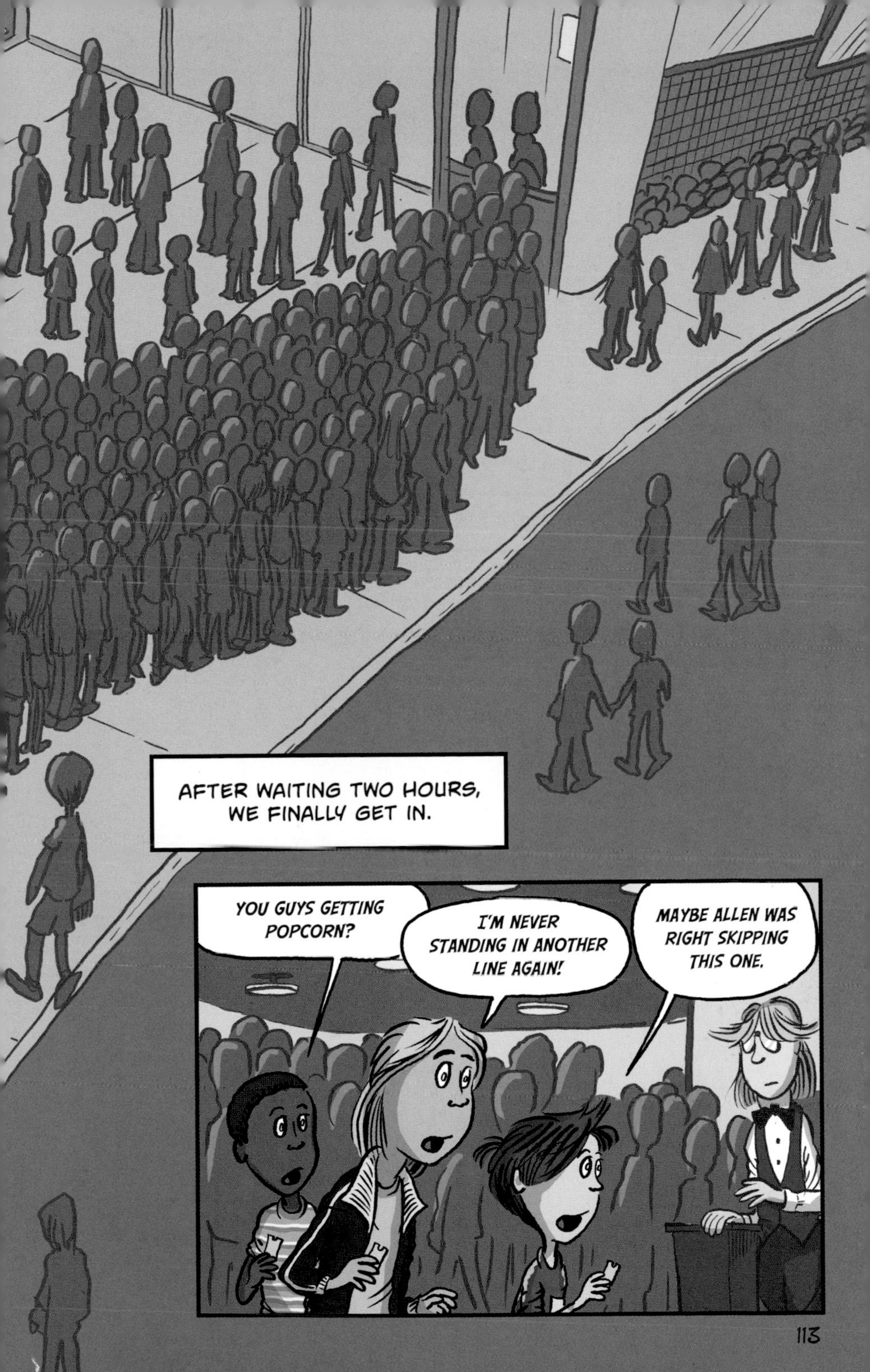
AFTER WAITING TWO HOURS, WE FINALLY GET IN.
YOU GUYS GETTING POPCORN?
I'M NEVER STANDING IN ANOTHER LINE AGAIN!
MAYBE ALLEN WAS RIGHT SKIPPING THIS ONE.

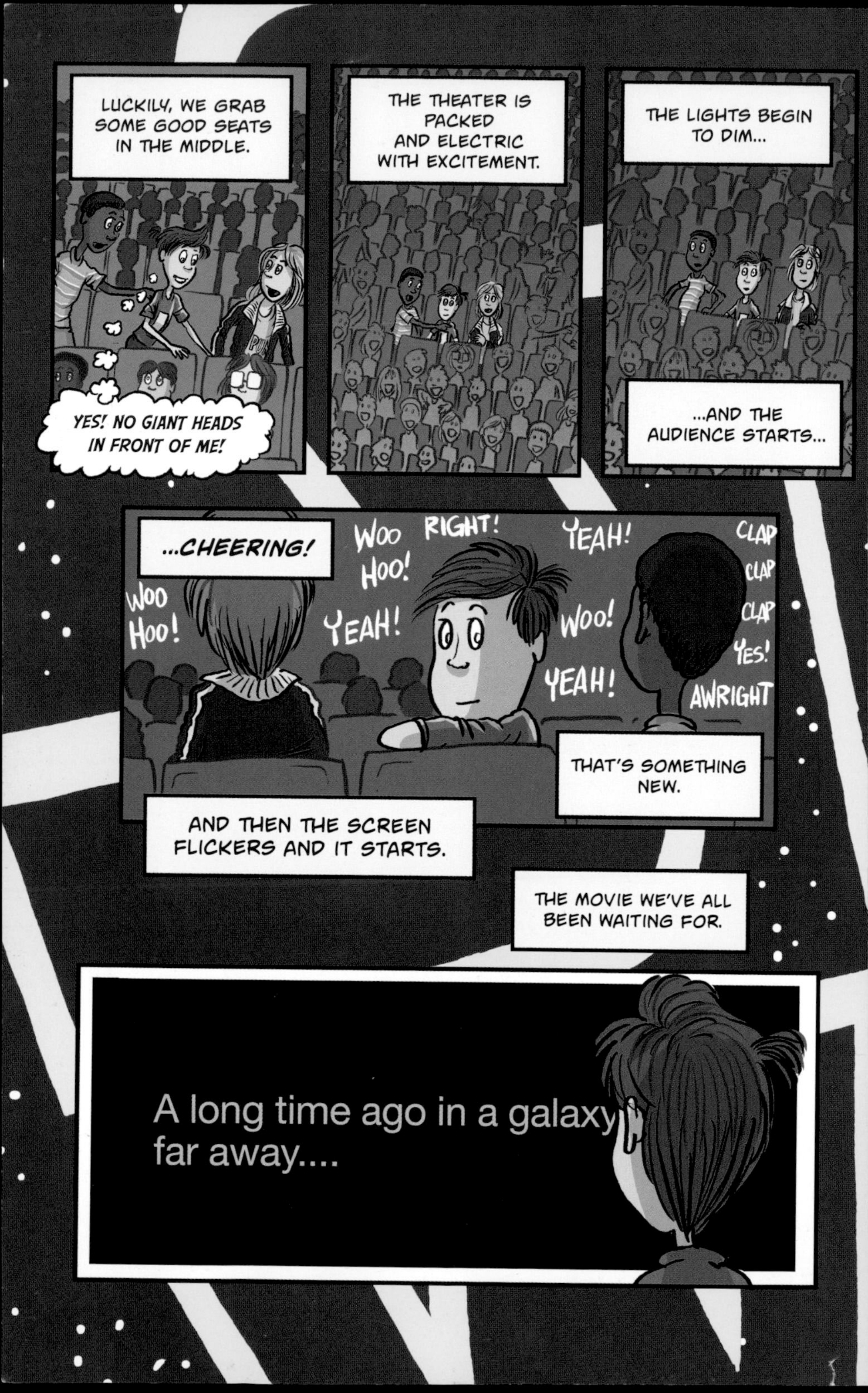
LUCKILY, WE GRAB SOME GOOD SEATS IN THE MIDDLE.
YES! NO GIANT HEADS IN FRONT OF ME!
THE THEATER IS PACKED AND ELECTRIC WITH EXCITEMENT.
THE LIGHTS BEGIN TO DIM...
...AND THE AUDIENCE STARTS...
...CHEERING!
WOO HOO!
WOO HOO!
RIGHT!
YEAH!
YEAH!
WOO!
YEAH!
CLAP
CLAP
CLAP
YES!
AWRIGHT
THAT'S SOMETHING NEW.
AND THEN THE SCREEN FLICKERS AND IT STARTS.
THE MOVIE WE'VE ALL BEEN WAITING FOR.
A long time ago in a galaxy far away....

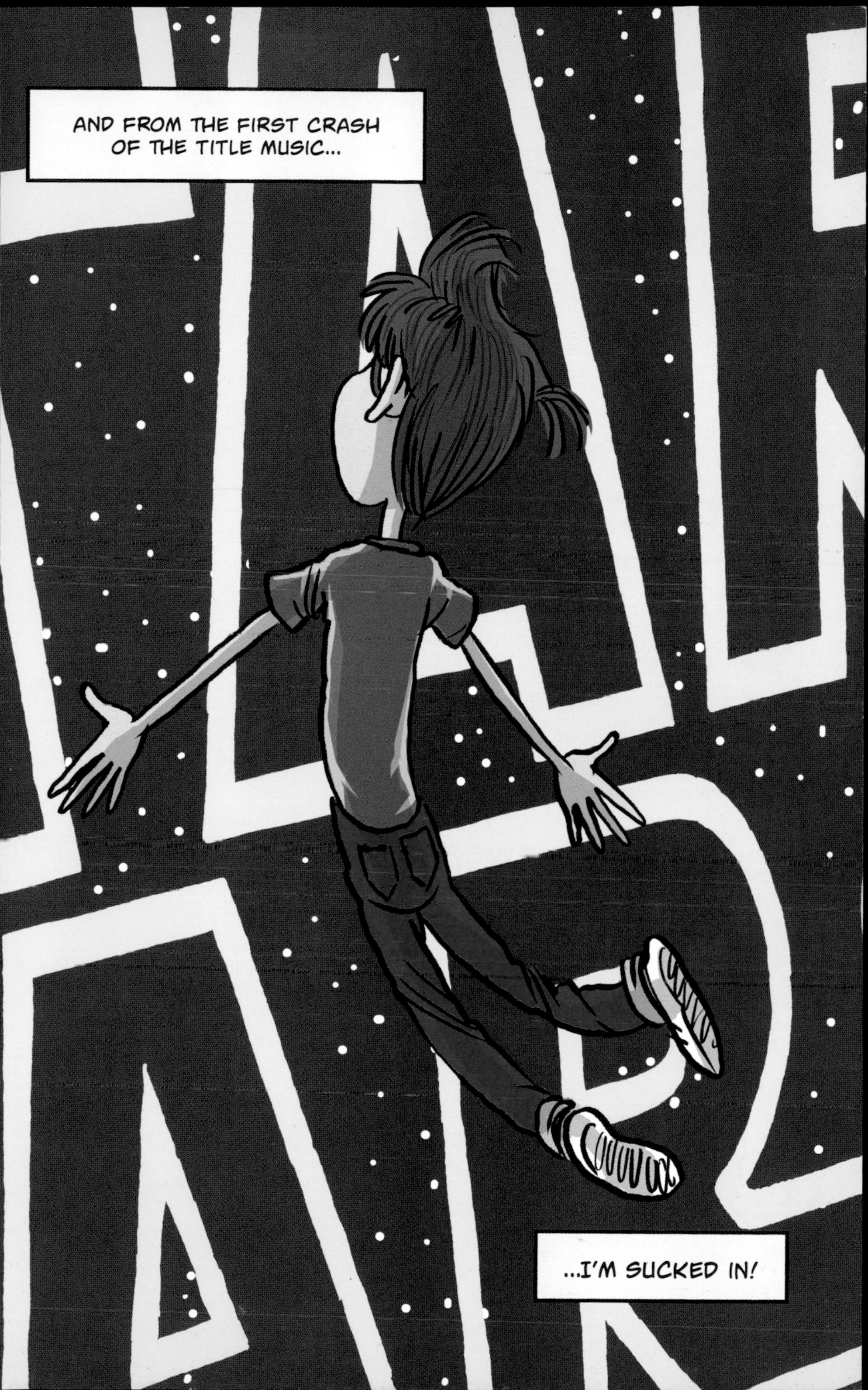
AND FROM THE FIRST CRASH OF THE TITLE MUSIC...
...I'M SUCKED IN!

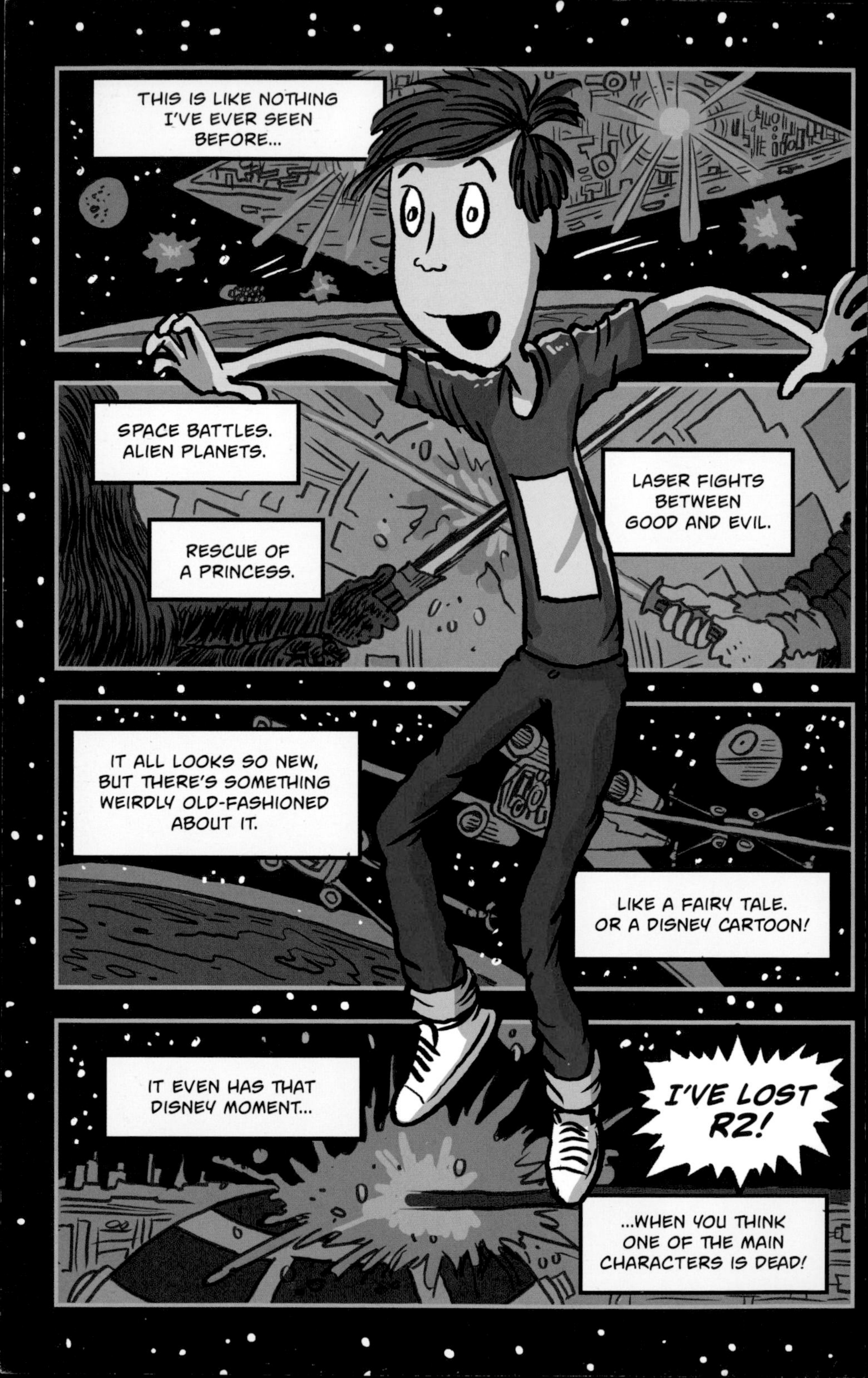
THIS IS LIKE NOTHING I'VE EVER SEEN BEFORE...
SPACE BATTLES. ALIEN PLANETS.
RESCUE OF A PRINCESS.
LASER FIGHTS BETWEEN GOOD AND EVIL.
IT ALL LOOKS SO NEW, BUT THERE'S SOMETHING WEIRDLY OLD-FASHIONED ABOUT IT.
LIKE A FAIRY TALE. OR A DISNEY CARTOON!
IT EVEN HAS THAT DISNEY MOMENT...
I'VE LOST R2!
...WHEN YOU THINK ONE OF THE MAIN CHARACTERS IS DEAD!

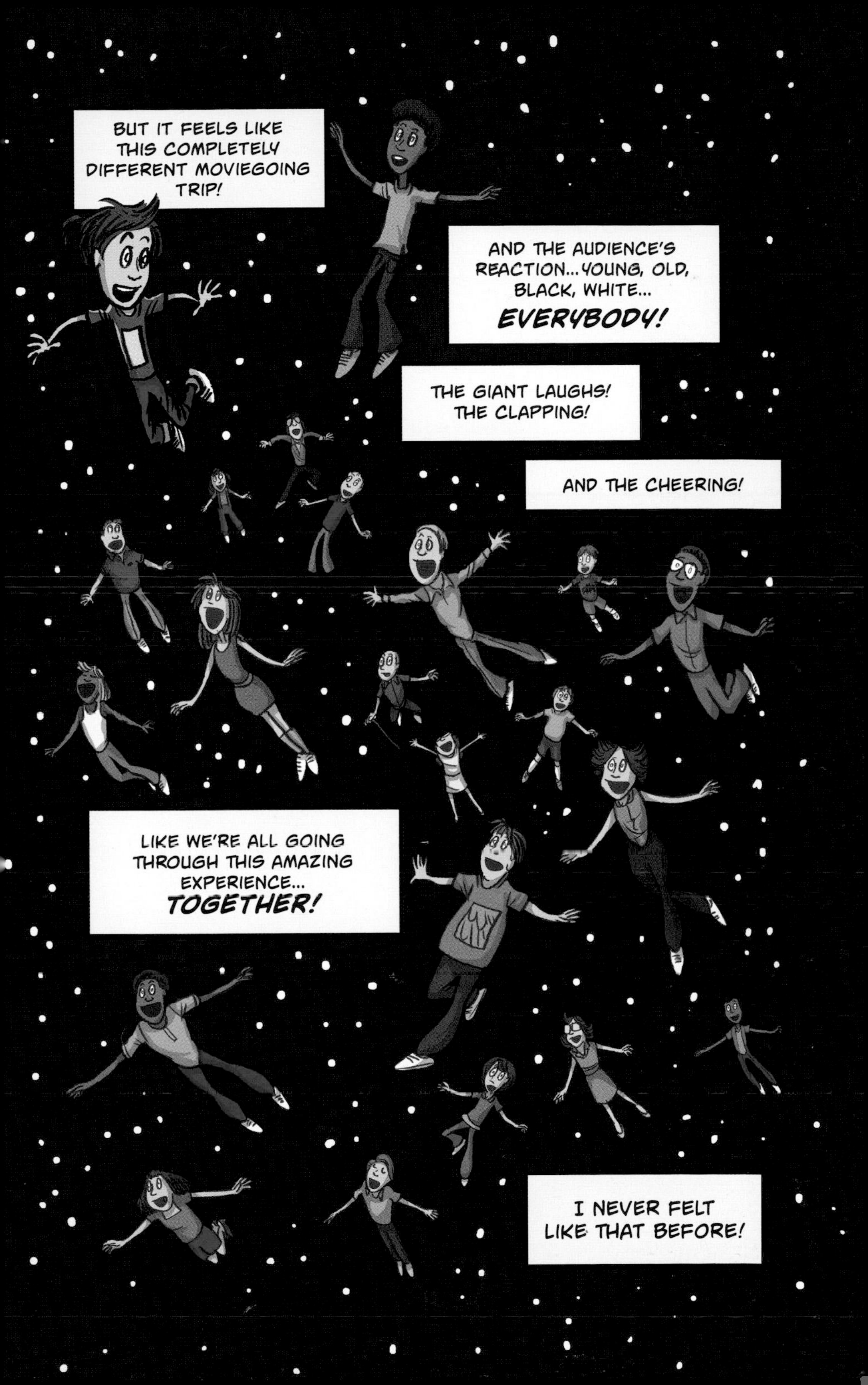
BUT IT FEELS LIKE THIS COMPLETELY DIFFERENT MOVIEGOING TRIP!
AND THE AUDIENCE'S REACTION... YOUNG, OLD, BLACK, WHITE... EVERYBODY!
THE GIANT LAUGHS! THE CLAPPING!
AND THE CHEERING!
LIKE WE'RE ALL GOING THROUGH THIS AMAZING EXPERIENCE... TOGETHER!
I NEVER FELT LIKE THAT BEFORE!

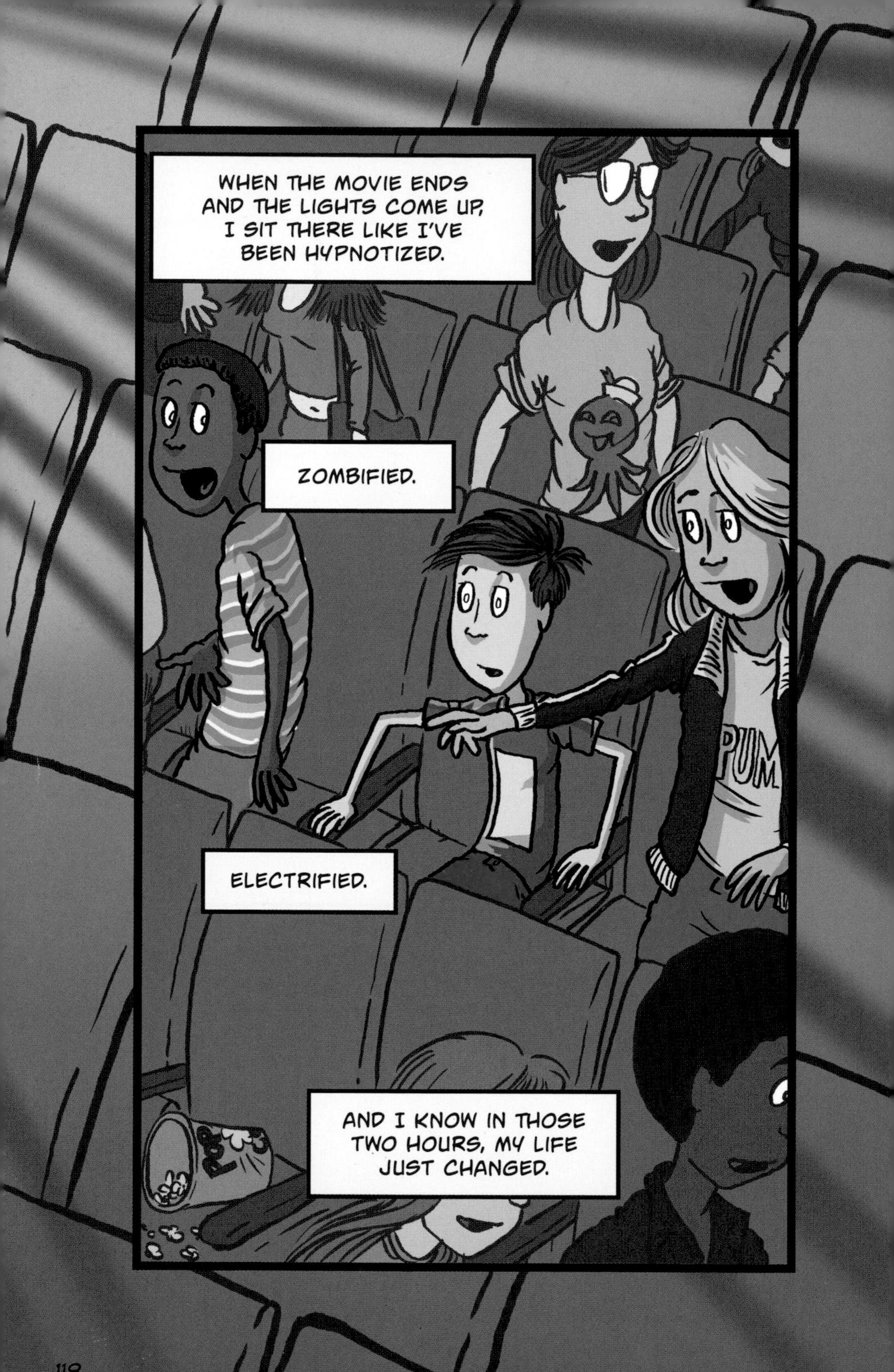
WHEN THE MOVIE ENDS AND THE LIGHTS COME UP, I SIT THERE LIKE I'VE BEEN HYPNOTIZED.
ZOMBIFIED.
ELECTRIFIED.
AND I KNOW IN THOSE TWO HOURS, MY LIFE JUST CHANGED.

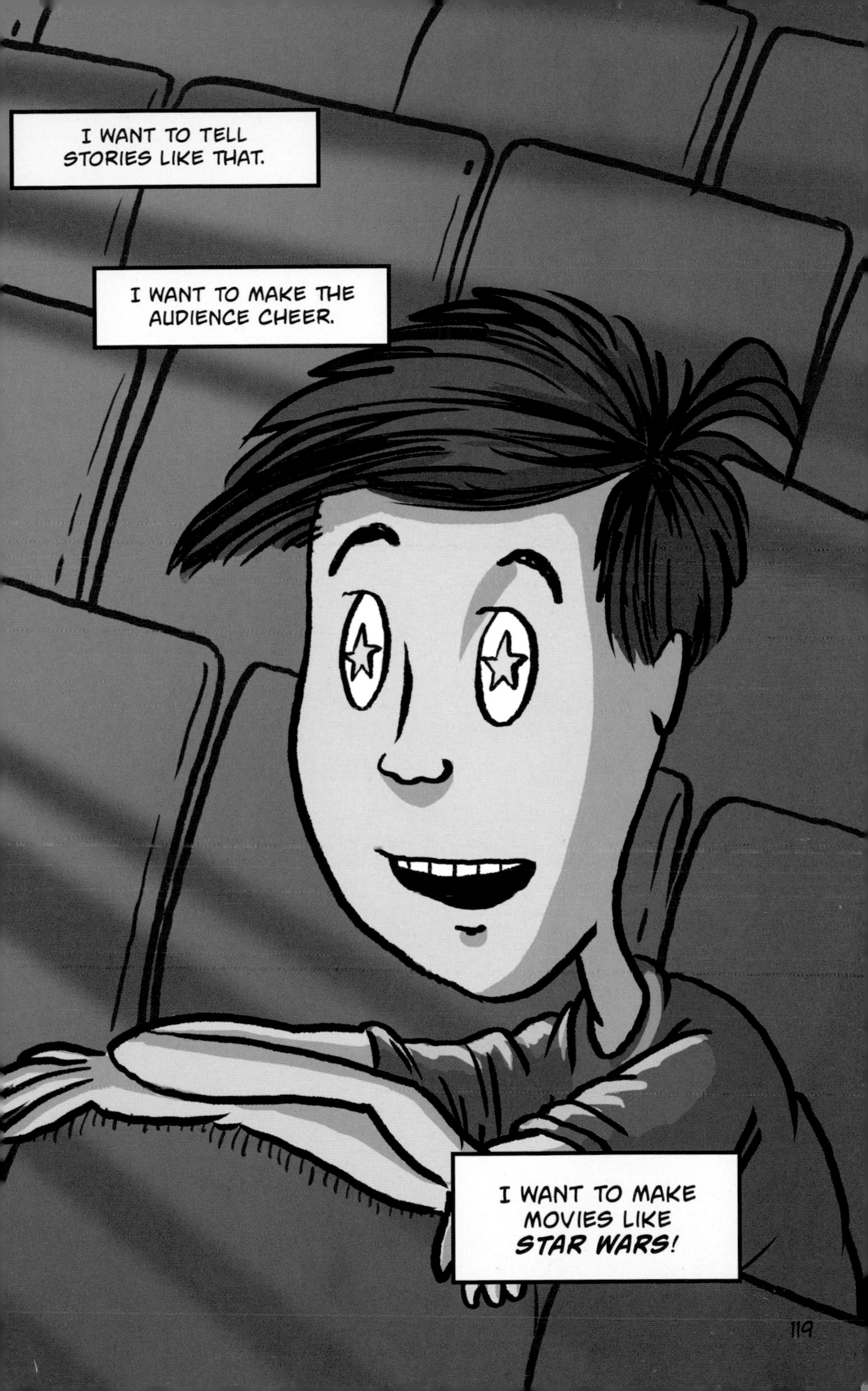
I WANT TO TELL STORIES LIKE THAT.
I WANT TO MAKE THE AUDIENCE CHEER.
I WANT TO MAKE MOVIES LIKE STAR WARS!

CHAPTER 9

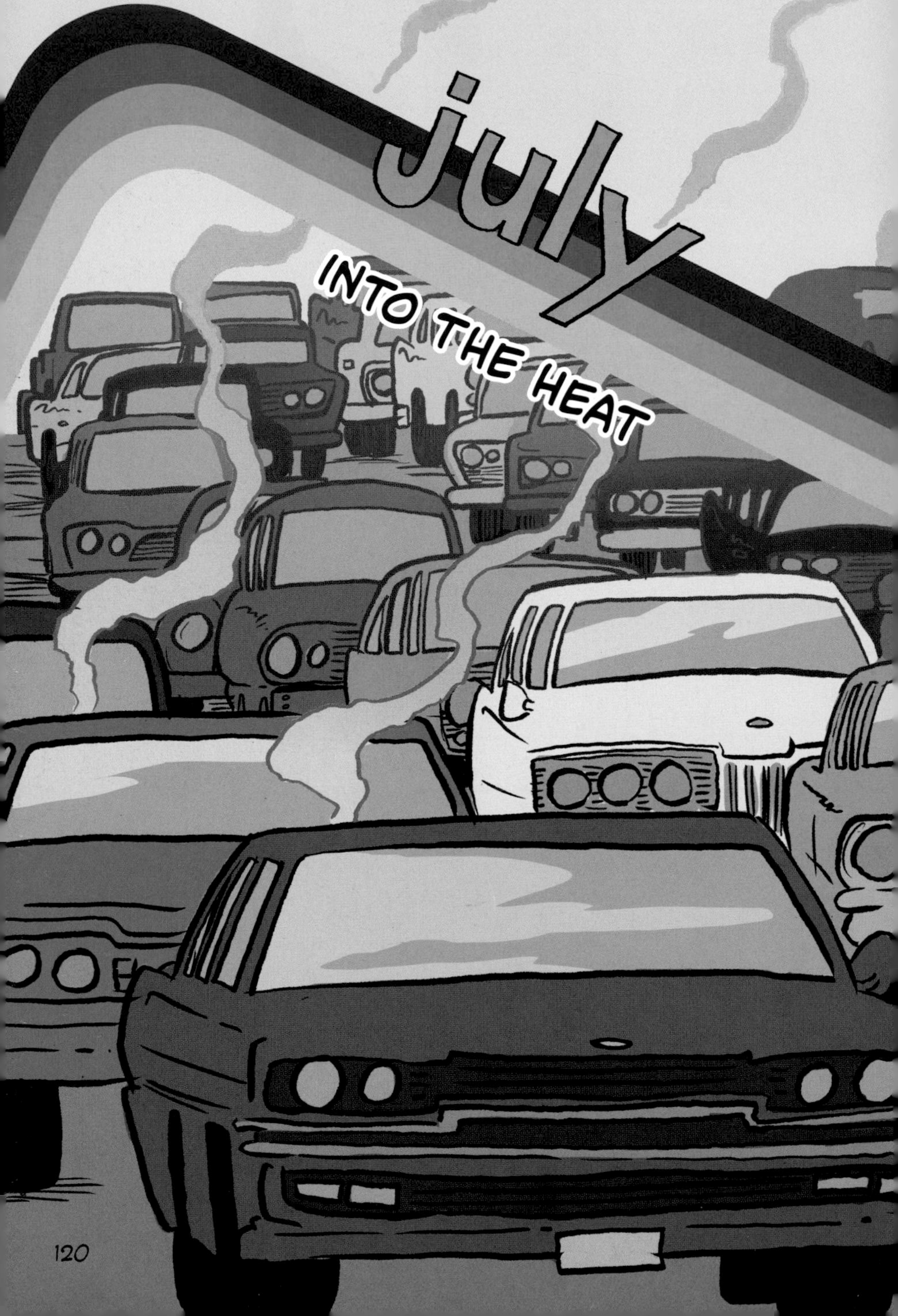
july
INTO THE HEAT

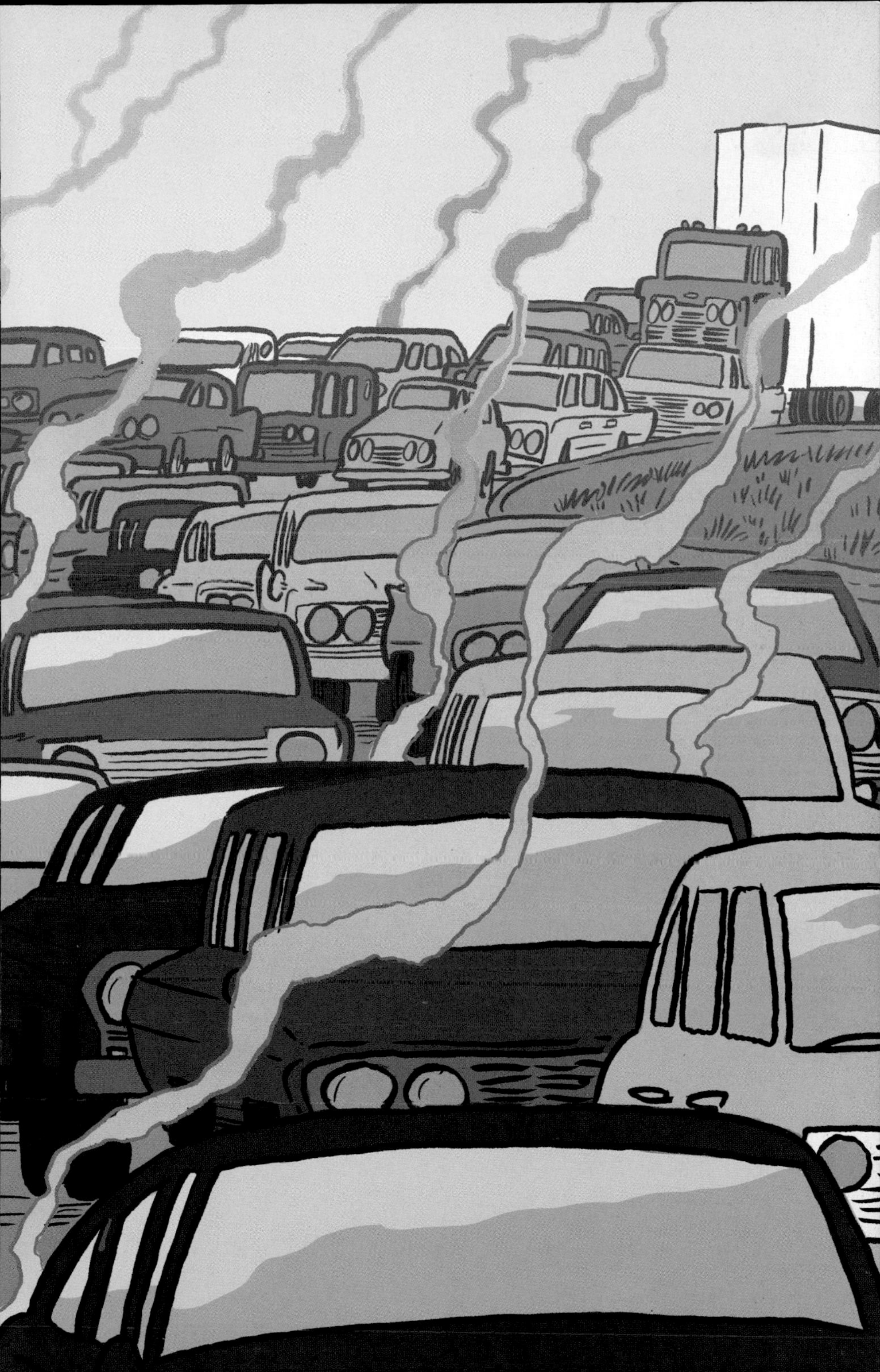

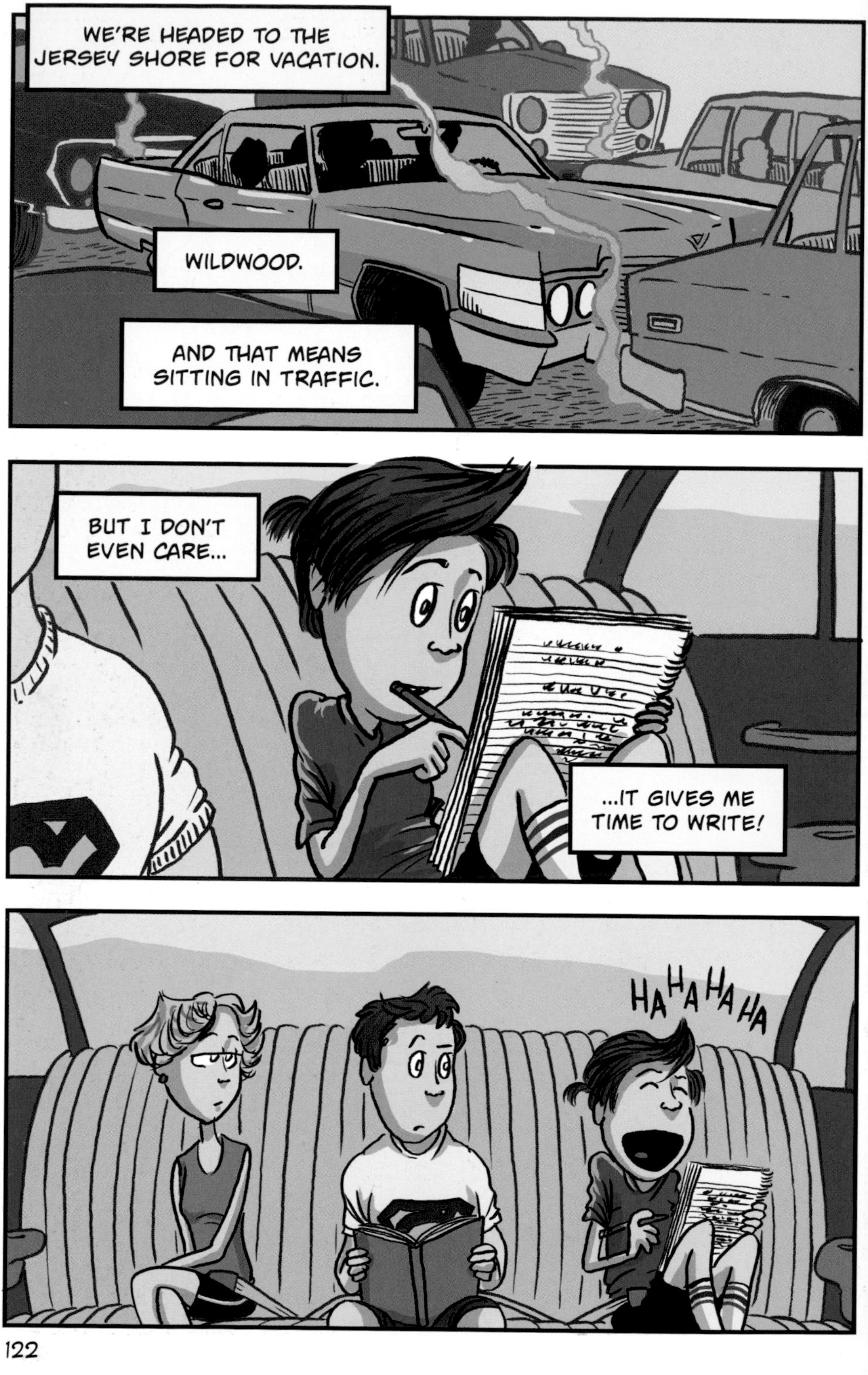
WE'RE HEADED TO THE JERSEY SHORE FOR VACATION.
WILDWOOD.
AND THAT MEANS SITTING IN TRAFFIC.
BUT I DON'T EVEN CARE...
...IT GIVES ME TIME TO WRITE!
HAHAHAHAHA

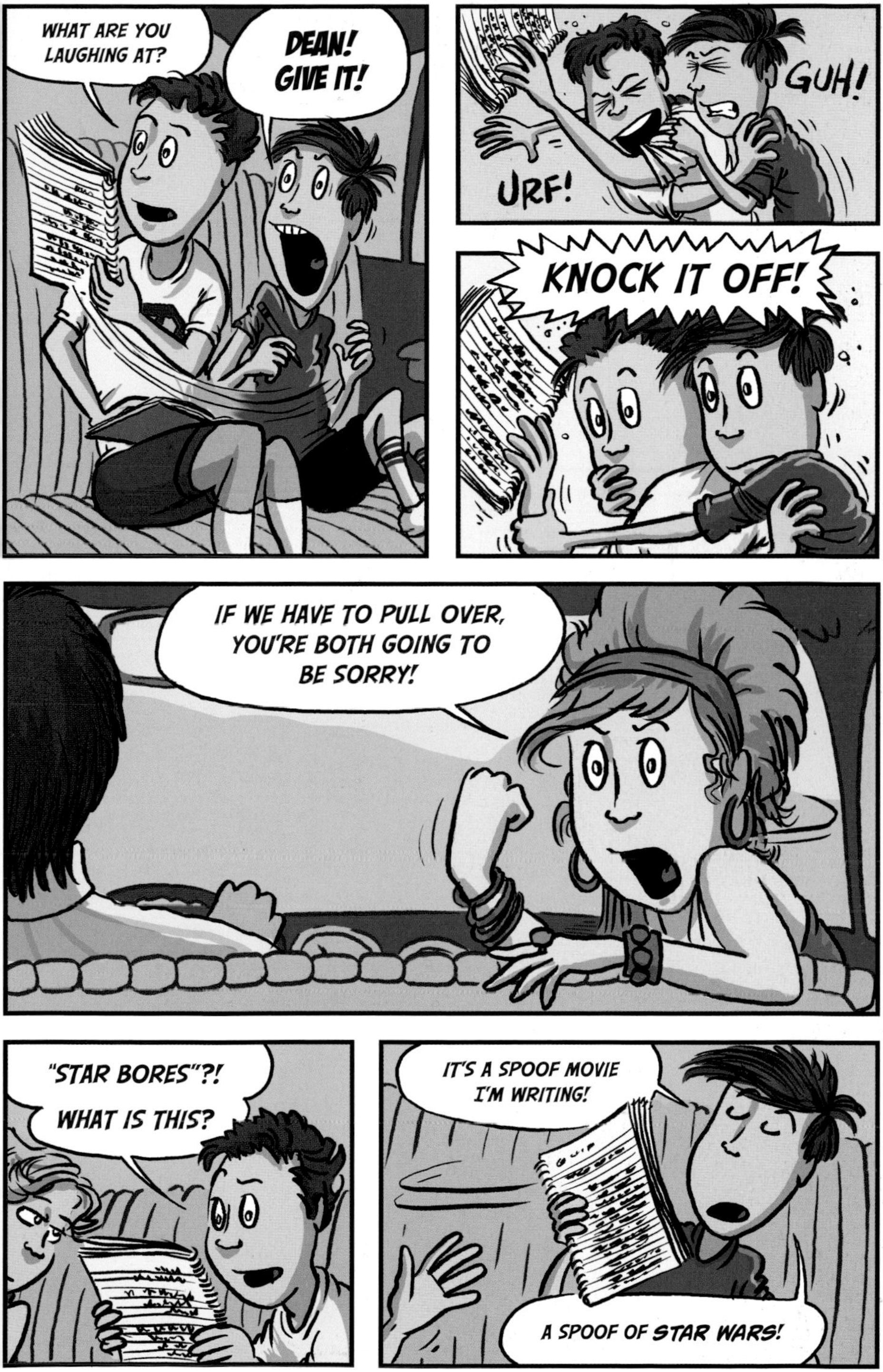

WHAT ARE YOU LAUGHING AT?
DEAN! GIVE IT!
GUH!
URF!
KNOCK IT OFF!
IF WE HAVE TO PULL OVER, YOU'RE BOTH GOING TO BE SORRY!
"STAR BORES"?!
WHAT IS THIS?
IT'S A SPOOF MOVIE I'M WRITING!
A SPOOF OF STAR WARS!

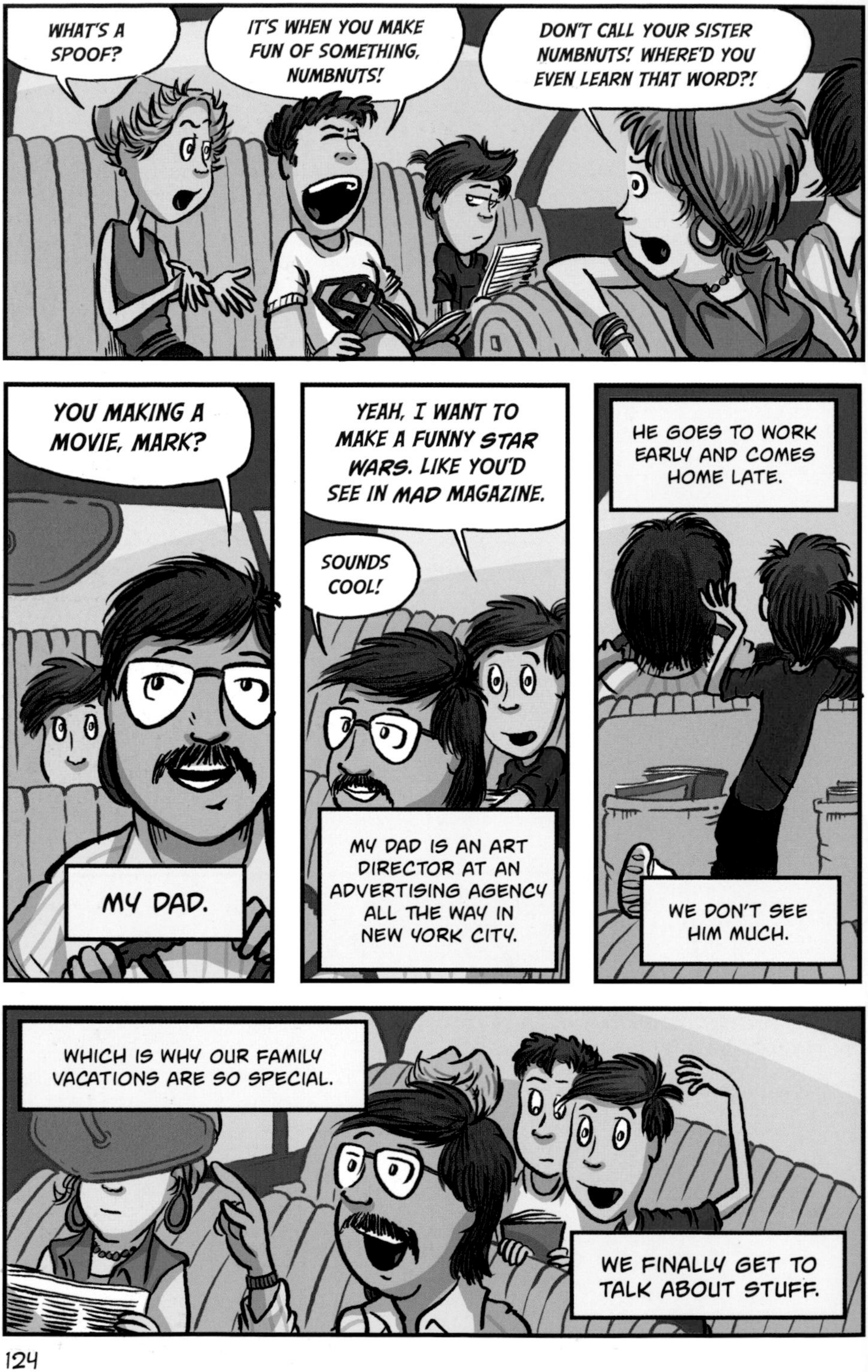
WHAT'S A SPOOF?
IT'S WHEN YOU MAKE FUN OF SOMETHING, NUMBNUTS!
DON'T CALL YOUR SISTER NUMBNUTS! WHERE'D YOU EVEN LEARN THAT WORD?!
YOU MAKING A MOVIE, MARK?
MY DAD.
YEAH, I WANT TO MAKE A FUNNY STAR WARS. LIKE YOU'D SEE IN MAD MAGAZINE.
SOUNDS COOL!
MY DAD IS AN ART DIRECTOR AT AN ADVERTISING AGENCY ALL THE WAY IN NEW YORK CITY.
HE GOES TO WORK EARLY AND COMES HOME LATE.
WE DON'T SEE HIM MUCH.
WHICH IS WHY OUR FAMILY VACATIONS ARE SO SPECIAL.
WE FINALLY GET TO TALK ABOUT STUFF.

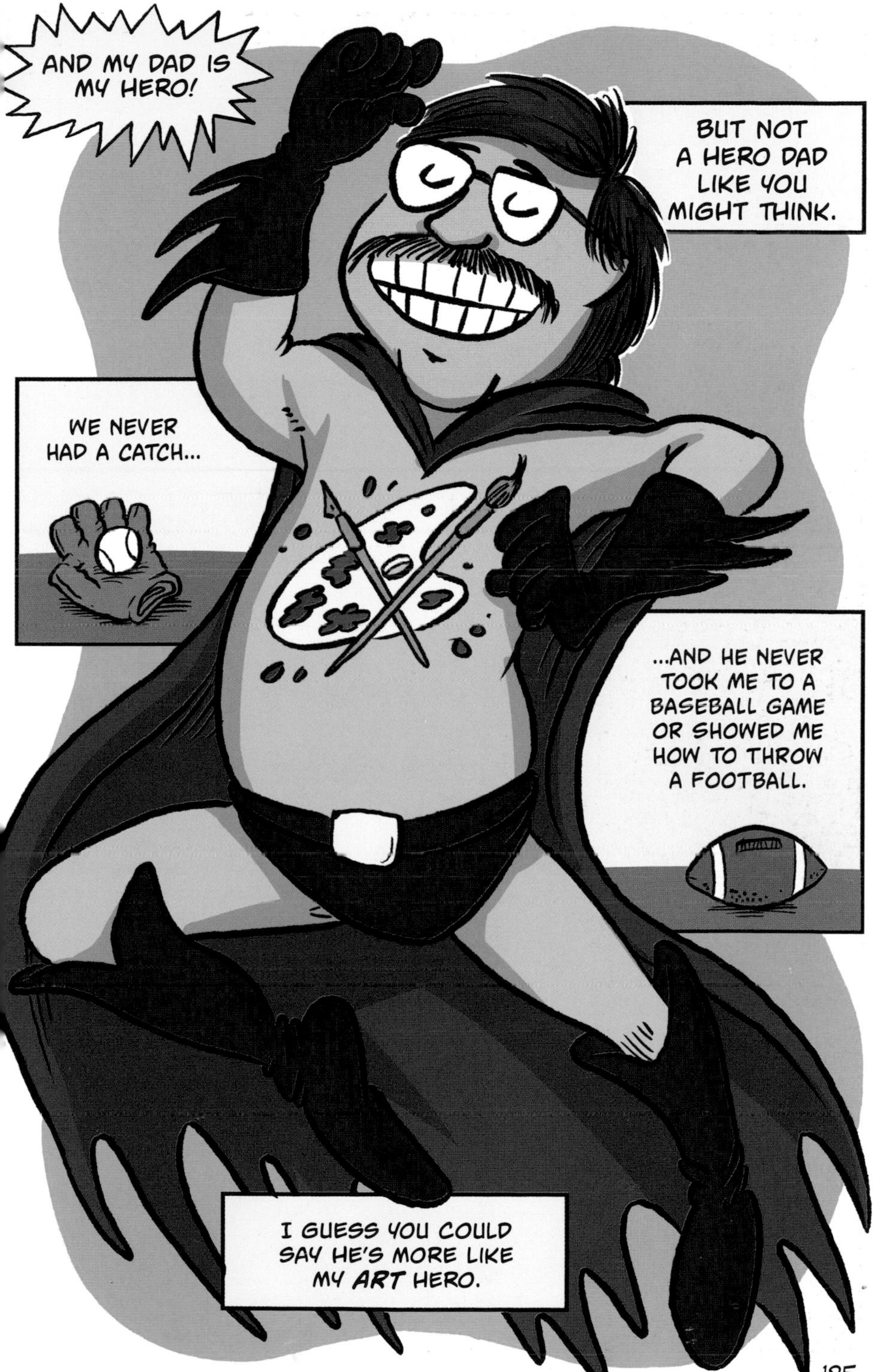
AND MY DAD IS MY HERO!
BUT NOT A HERO DAD LIKE YOU MIGHT THINK.
WE NEVER HAD A CATCH...
...AND HE NEVER TOOK ME TO A BASEBALL GAME OR SHOWED ME HOW TO THROW A FOOTBALL.
I GUESS YOU COULD SAY HE'S MORE LIKE MY *ART* HERO.

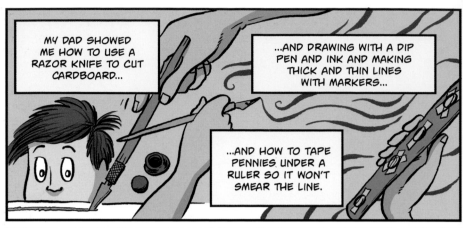

MY DAD SHOWED ME HOW TO USE A RAZOR KNIFE TO CUT CARDBOARD...

...AND DRAWING WITH A DIP PEN AND INK AND MAKING THICK AND THIN LINES WITH MARKERS...

...AND HOW TO TAPE PENNIES UNDER A RULER SO IT WON'T SMEAR THE LINE.

AND MADE ME MY FIRST CARTOON CAMERA STAND OUT OF AN OLD BAR STOOL!

OF COURSE, HE ALMOST BURNED THE HOUSE DOWN WHEN THE FLOOD-LIGHT CAUGHT FIRE. MOM'S STILL MAD ABOUT THE BURN MARK ON THE DINING ROOM CEILING.

OK, SO MY DAD'S NOT PERFECT, BUT HE'S MY ART HERO AND I KNOW HE'LL HAVE A TON OF COOL IDEAS FOR MY MOVIE.

I CAN'T WAIT TO READ THE SCRIPT WHEN YOU'RE DONE!

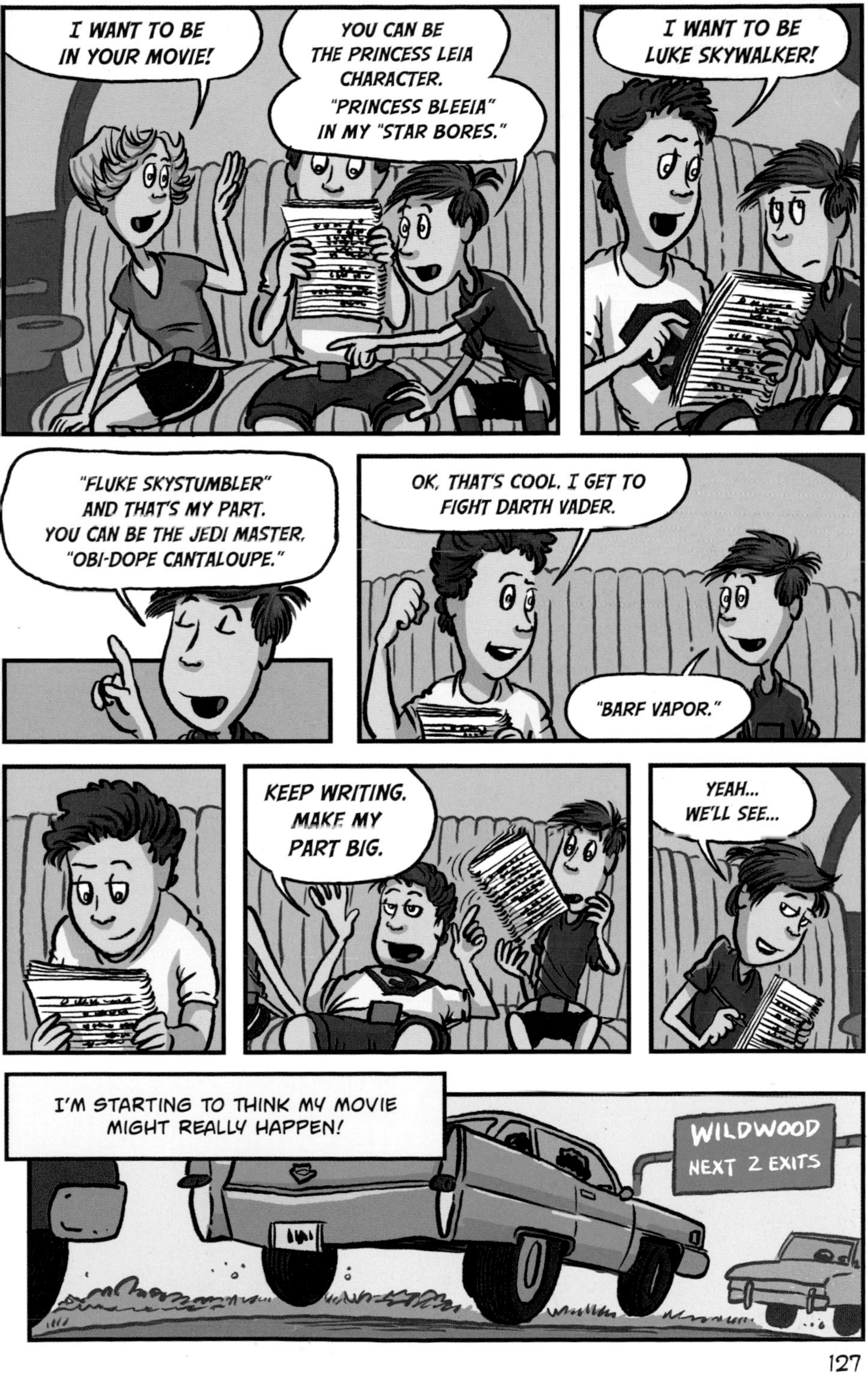
I WANT TO BE IN YOUR MOVIE!
YOU CAN BE THE PRINCESS LEIA CHARACTER.
"PRINCESS BLEEIA" IN MY "STAR BORES."
I WANT TO BE LUKE SKYWALKER!
"FLUKE SKYSTUMBLER" AND THAT'S MY PART. YOU CAN BE THE JEDI MASTER. "OBI-DOPE CANTALOUPE."
OK, THAT'S COOL. I GET TO FIGHT DARTH VADER.
"BARF VAPOR."
KEEP WRITING. MAKE MY PART BIG.
YEAH... WE'LL SEE...
I'M STARTING TO THINK MY MOVIE MIGHT REALLY HAPPEN!
WILDWOOD
NEXT 2 EXITS

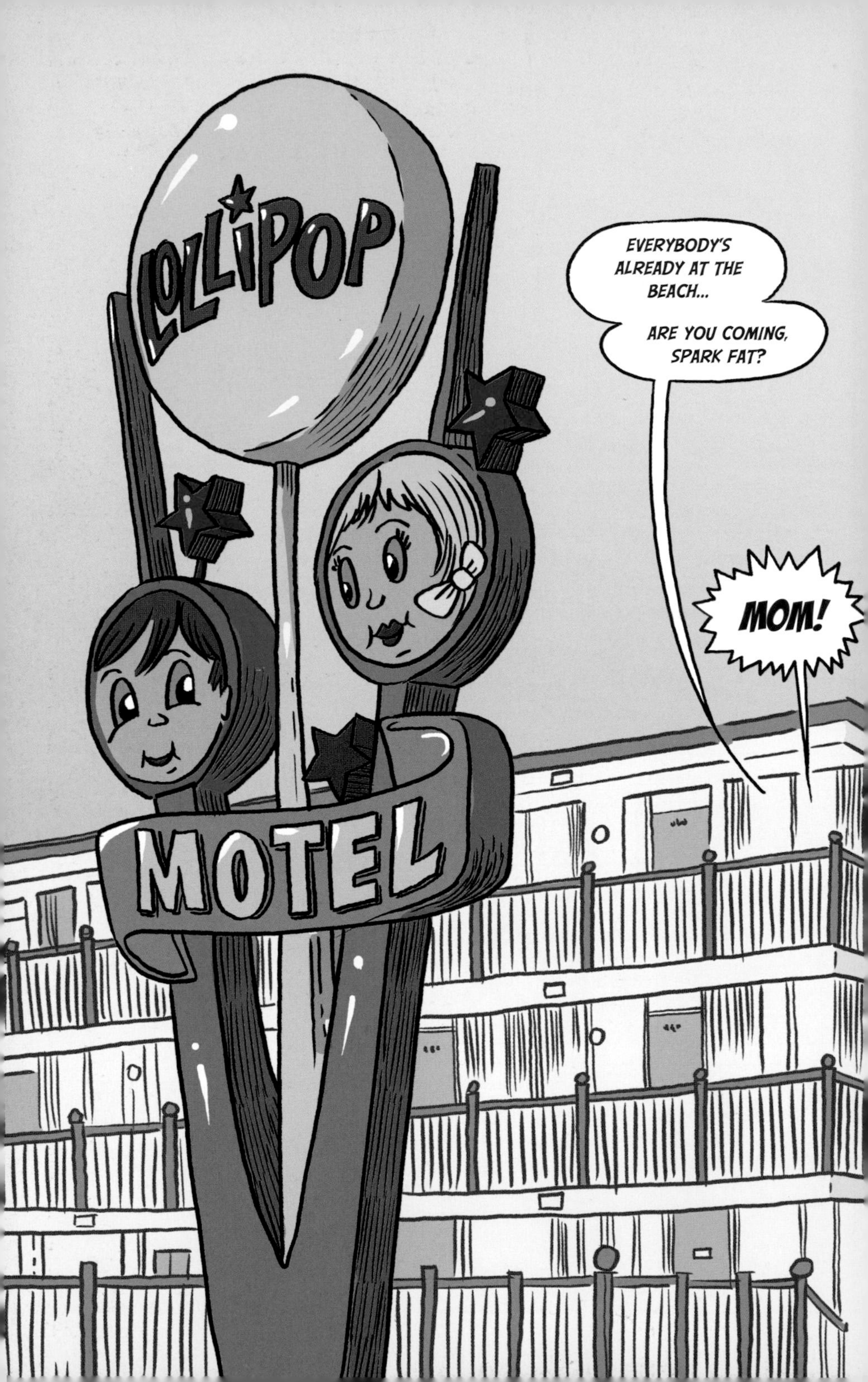
LOLLIPOP
MOTEL
EVERYBODY'S ALREADY AT THE BEACH...
ARE YOU COMING, SPARK FAT?
MOM!

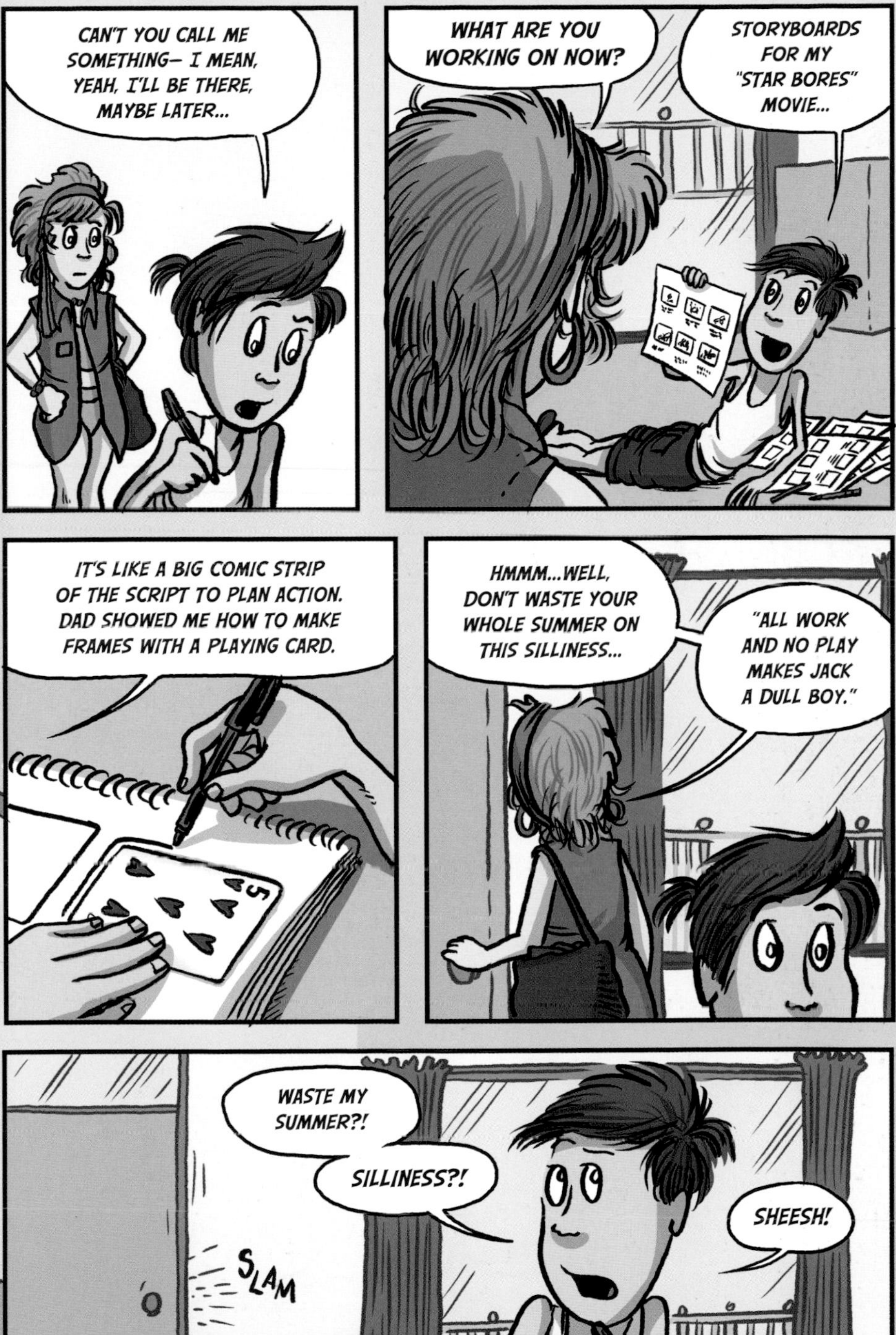
CAN'T YOU CALL ME SOMETHING– I MEAN, YEAH, I'LL BE THERE, MAYBE LATER...
WHAT ARE YOU WORKING ON NOW?
STORYBOARDS FOR MY "STAR BORES" MOVIE...
IT'S LIKE A BIG COMIC STRIP OF THE SCRIPT TO PLAN ACTION. DAD SHOWED ME HOW TO MAKE FRAMES WITH A PLAYING CARD.
HMMM...WELL, DON'T WASTE YOUR WHOLE SUMMER ON THIS SILLINESS...
"ALL WORK AND NO PLAY MAKES JACK A DULL BOY."
WASTE MY SUMMER?!
SILLINESS?!
SLAM
SHEESH!

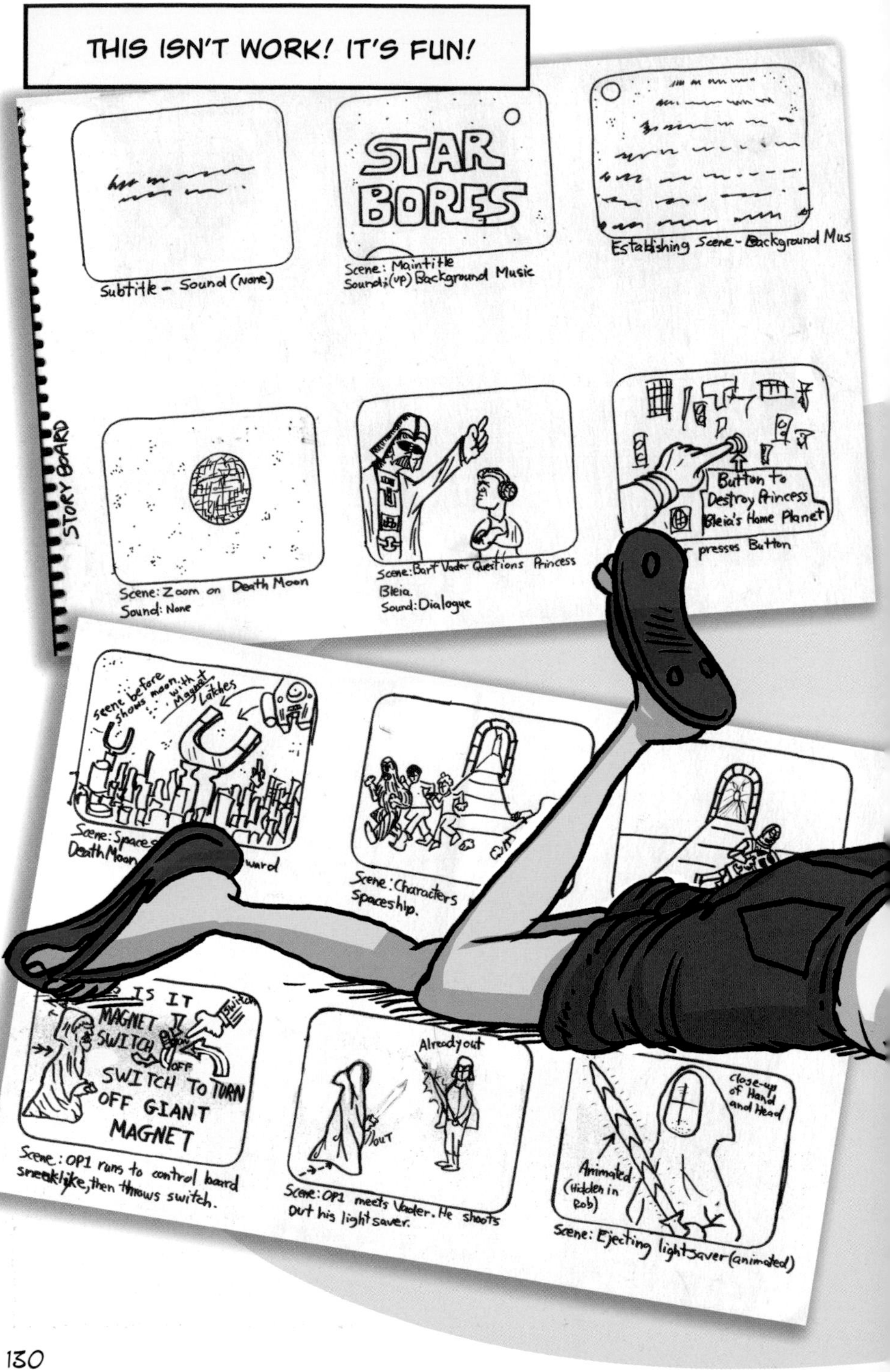
THIS ISN'T WORK! IT'S FUN!
STORY BOARD
Subtitle - Sound (None)
STAR BORES
Scene: Maintitle
Sound: (up) Background Music
Establishing Scene - Background Mus
Scene: Zoom on Death Moon
Sound: None
Scene: Bart Vader Questions Princess Bleia.
Sound: Dialogue
Button to Destroy Princess Bleia's Home Planet
presses Button
scene before shows moon with Magnet
Latches
Scene: Spaces
Death Moon
ward
Scene: Characters
Spaceship.
IS IT MAGNET SWITCH
Switch
OFF
SWITCH TO TURN OFF GIANT MAGNET
Scene: OP1 runs to control board sneaklike, then throws switch.
Already out
OUT
Scene: OP1 meets Vader. He shoots out his light saver.
Close-up of Hand and Head
Animated (Hidden in Rob)
Scene: Ejecting lightsaver (animated)

Scene: Head on view of cock pit. Ham Yoyo fidgits with dials and knobs. So does chompie.

Scene: Spaceship break away from Magnet.

Scene: Man explains pointing at mape at different areas. As he talks Fluke nods alot.

Scene: 3 ships fly off away from Camera. (Toward Death Moon)

Scene: 2 enemy ships fly camera in opposite direct

Scene: Barf Close-up in side space ship.

Scene: Close-up of Fluke Flying Space ship.

Scene: Top fire cracker blows is an animated crack.

Scene: close-up of Ham and Chompie flying their spaceship.

I THINK I MIGHT HAVE FOUND SOMETHING I'M GOOD AT!

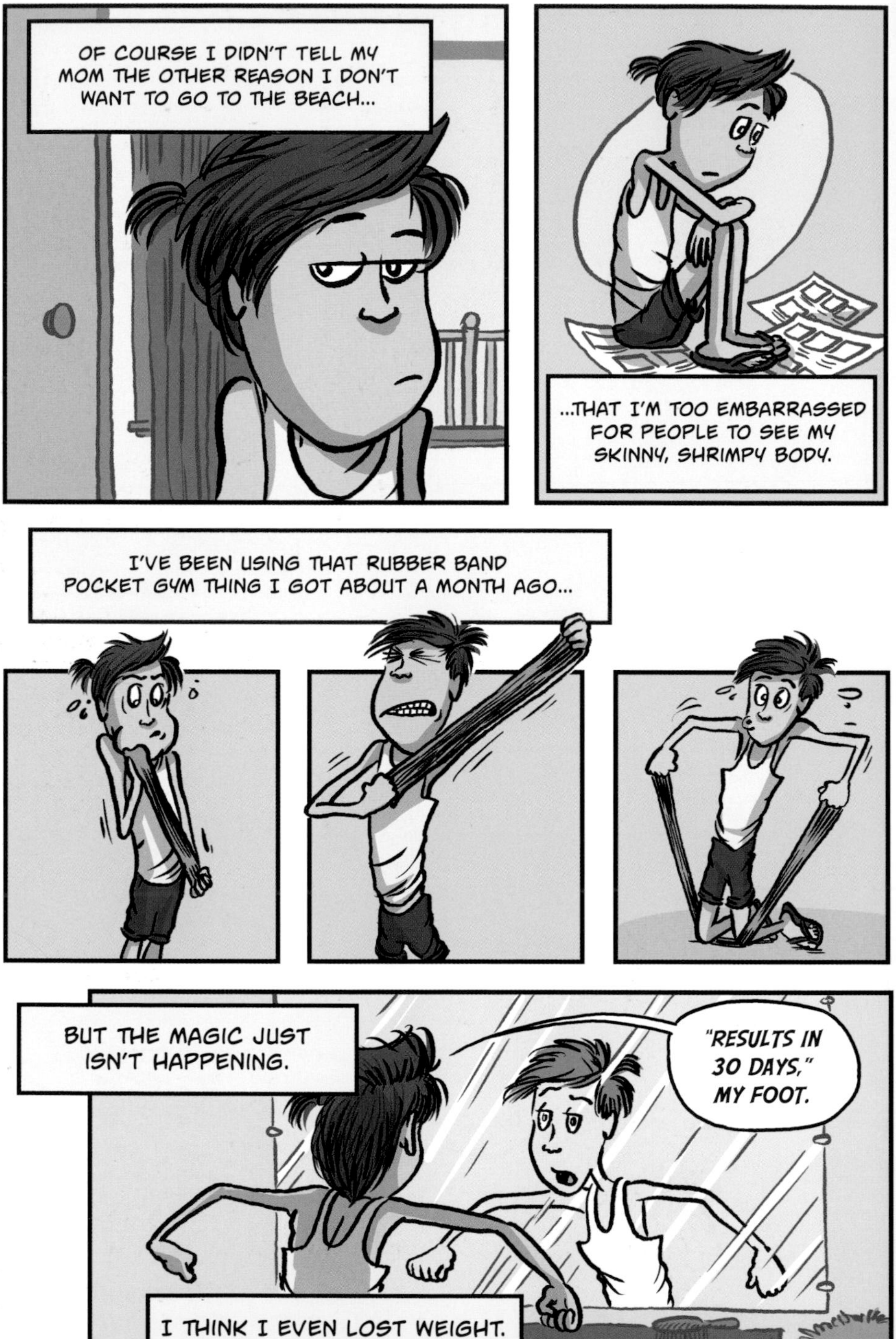
OF COURSE I DIDN'T TELL MY MOM THE OTHER REASON I DON'T WANT TO GO TO THE BEACH...
...THAT I'M TOO EMBARRASSED FOR PEOPLE TO SEE MY SKINNY, SHRIMPY BODY.
I'VE BEEN USING THAT RUBBER BAND POCKET GYM THING I GOT ABOUT A MONTH AGO...
BUT THE MAGIC JUST ISN'T HAPPENING.
"RESULTS IN 30 DAYS," MY FOOT.
I THINK I EVEN LOST WEIGHT.

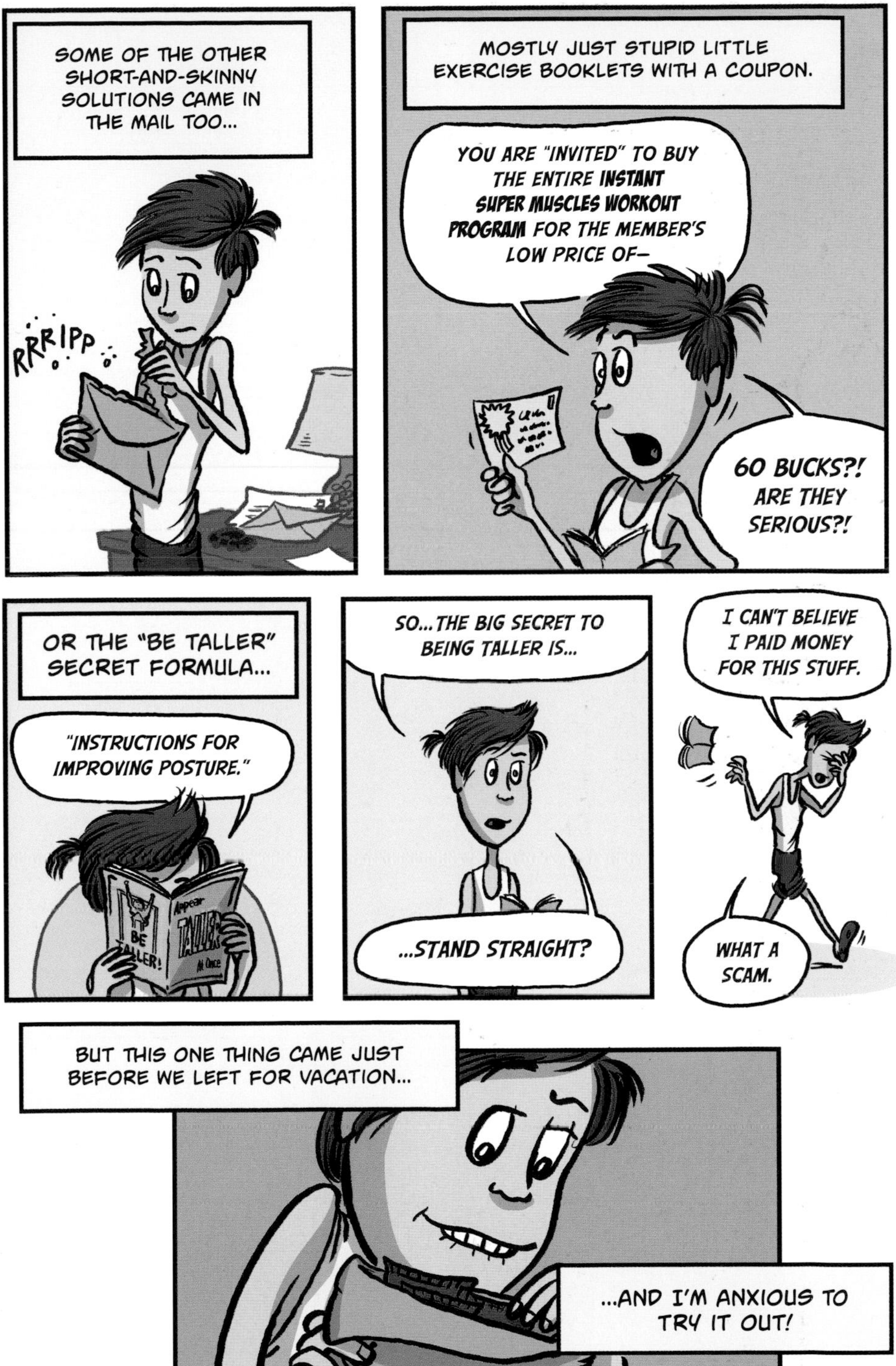
SOME OF THE OTHER SHORT-AND-SKINNY SOLUTIONS CAME IN THE MAIL TOO...
RRRIPP
MOSTLY JUST STUPID LITTLE EXERCISE BOOKLETS WITH A COUPON.
YOU ARE "INVITED" TO BUY THE ENTIRE INSTANT SUPER MUSCLES WORKOUT PROGRAM FOR THE MEMBER'S LOW PRICE OF—
60 BUCKS?! ARE THEY SERIOUS?!
OR THE "BE TALLER" SECRET FORMULA...
"INSTRUCTIONS FOR IMPROVING POSTURE."
BE TALLER!
Appear TALLER At Once
SO...THE BIG SECRET TO BEING TALLER IS...
...STAND STRAIGHT?
I CAN'T BELIEVE I PAID MONEY FOR THIS STUFF.
WHAT A SCAM.
BUT THIS ONE THING CAME JUST BEFORE WE LEFT FOR VACATION...
...AND I'M ANXIOUS TO TRY IT OUT!

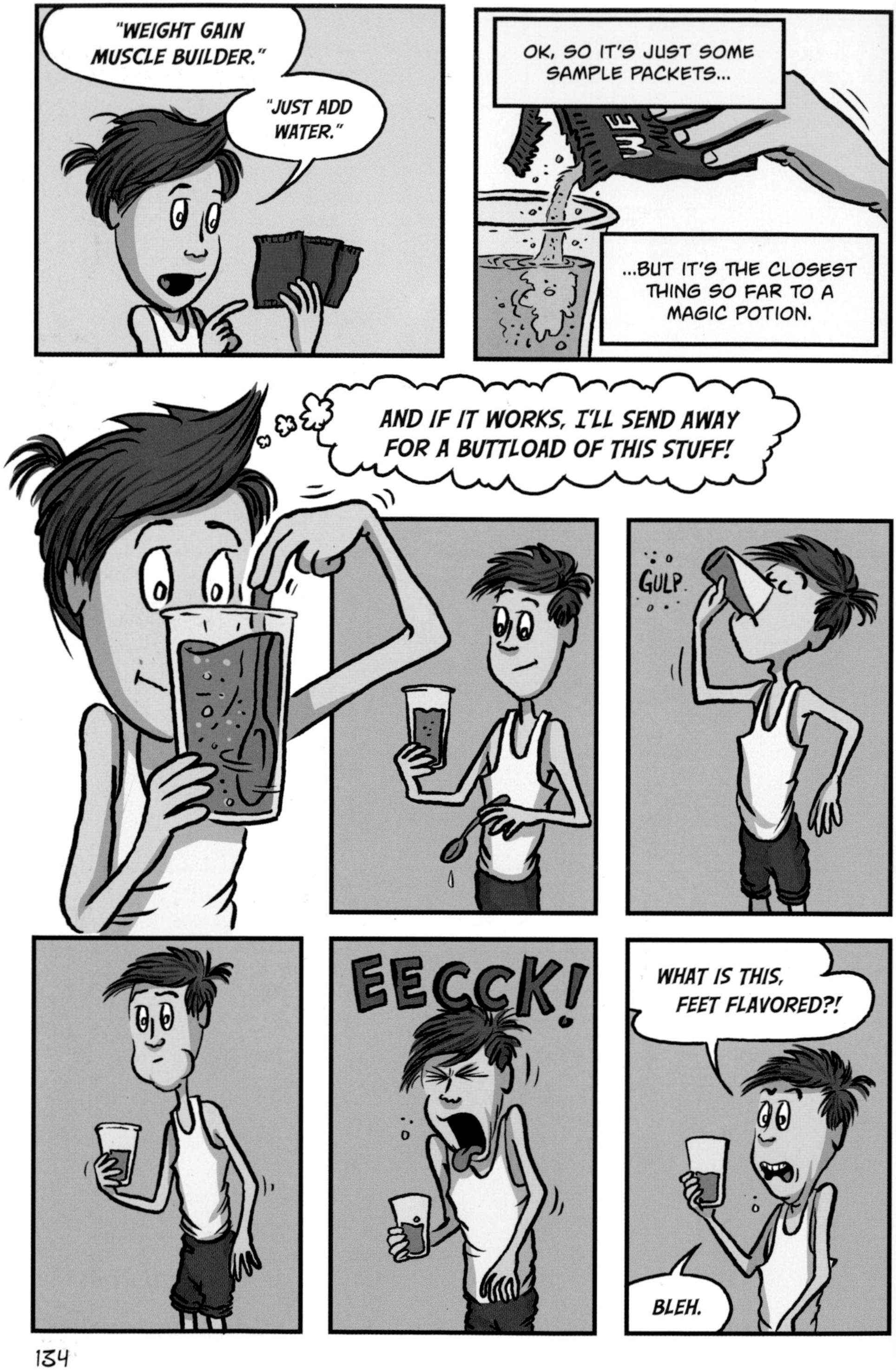
"WEIGHT GAIN MUSCLE BUILDER."
"JUST ADD WATER."
OK, SO IT'S JUST SOME SAMPLE PACKETS...
...BUT IT'S THE CLOSEST THING SO FAR TO A MAGIC POTION.
AND IF IT WORKS, I'LL SEND AWAY FOR A BUTTLOAD OF THIS STUFF!
GULP
EECCK!
WHAT IS THIS, FEET FLAVORED?!
BLEH.

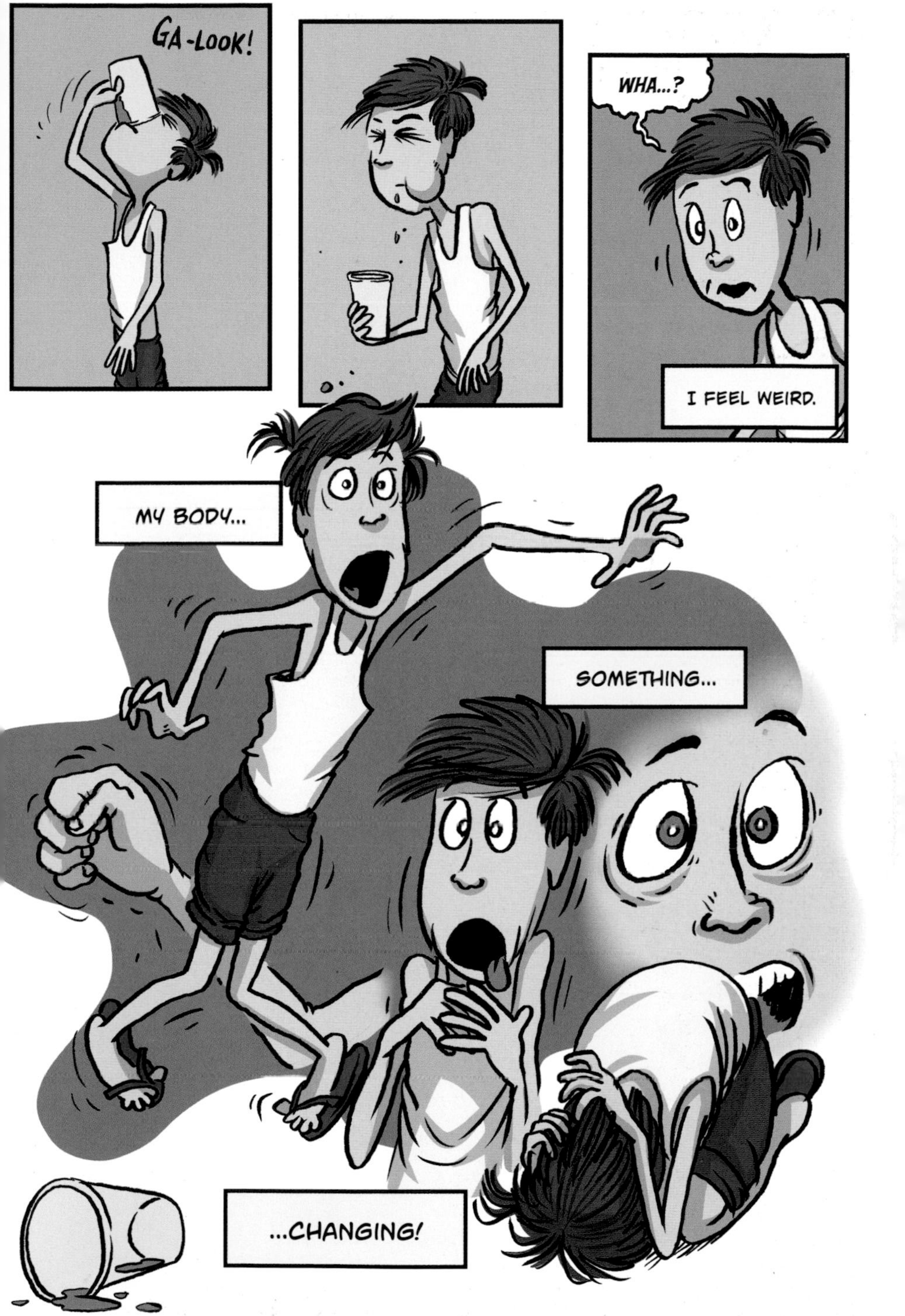
GA-LOOK!
WHA...?
I FEEL WEIRD.
MY BODY...
SOMETHING...
...CHANGING!

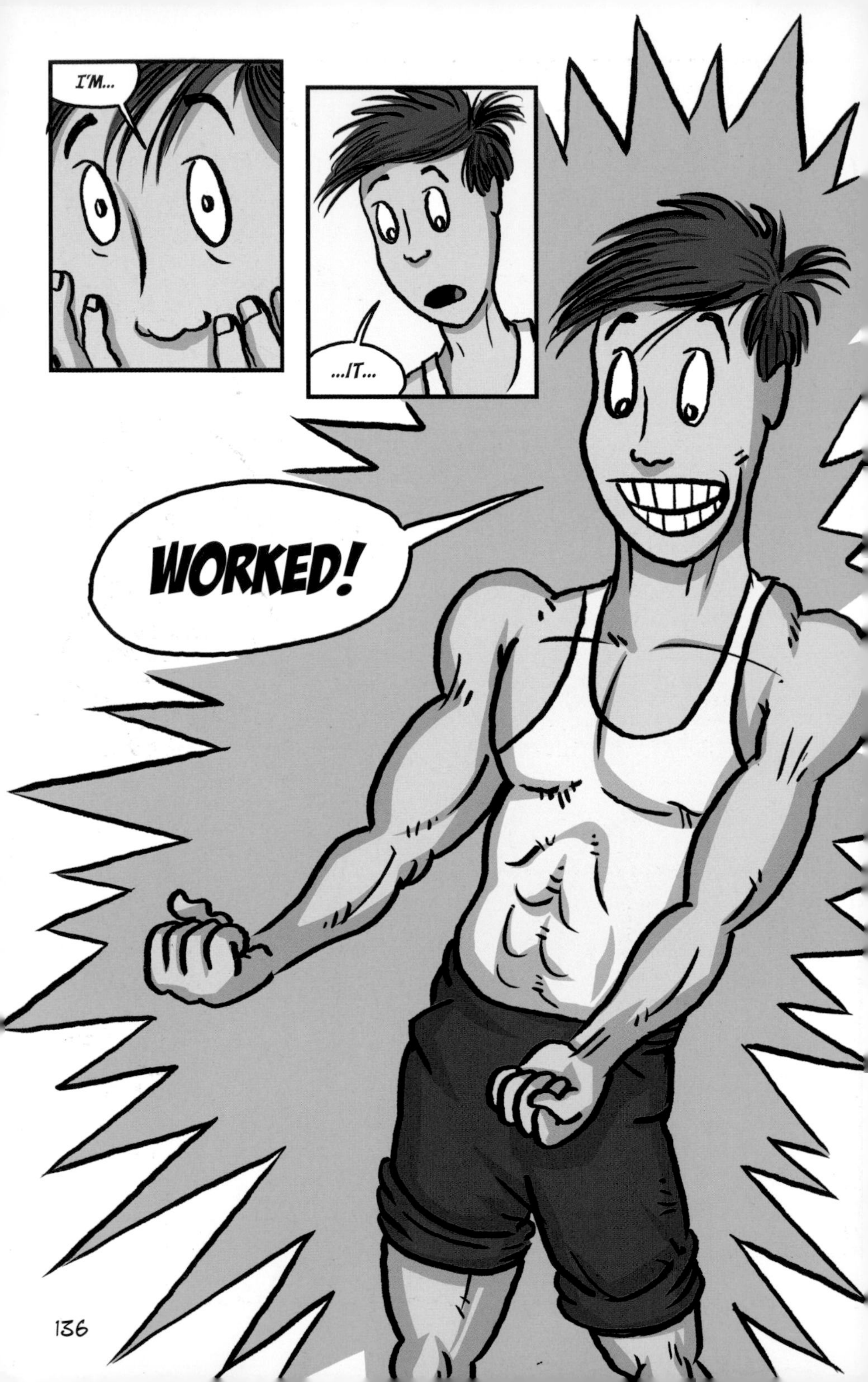
I'M...
...IT...
WORKED!

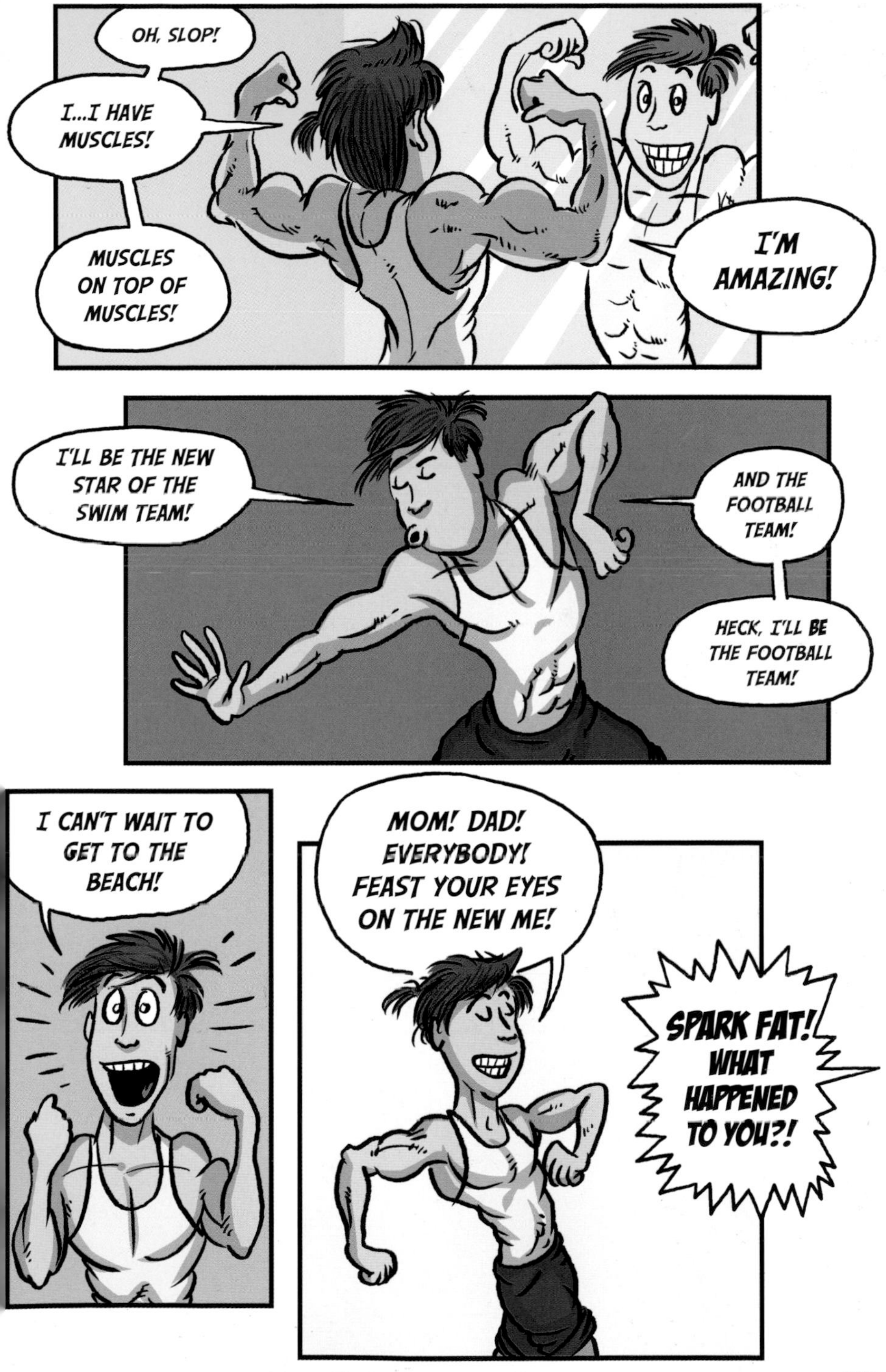
OH, SLOP!
I...I HAVE MUSCLES!
MUSCLES ON TOP OF MUSCLES!
I'M AMAZING!
I'LL BE THE NEW STAR OF THE SWIM TEAM!
AND THE FOOTBALL TEAM!
HECK, I'LL BE THE FOOTBALL TEAM!
I CAN'T WAIT TO GET TO THE BEACH!
MOM! DAD! EVERYBODY! FEAST YOUR EYES ON THE NEW ME!
SPARK FAT! WHAT HAPPENED TO YOU?!

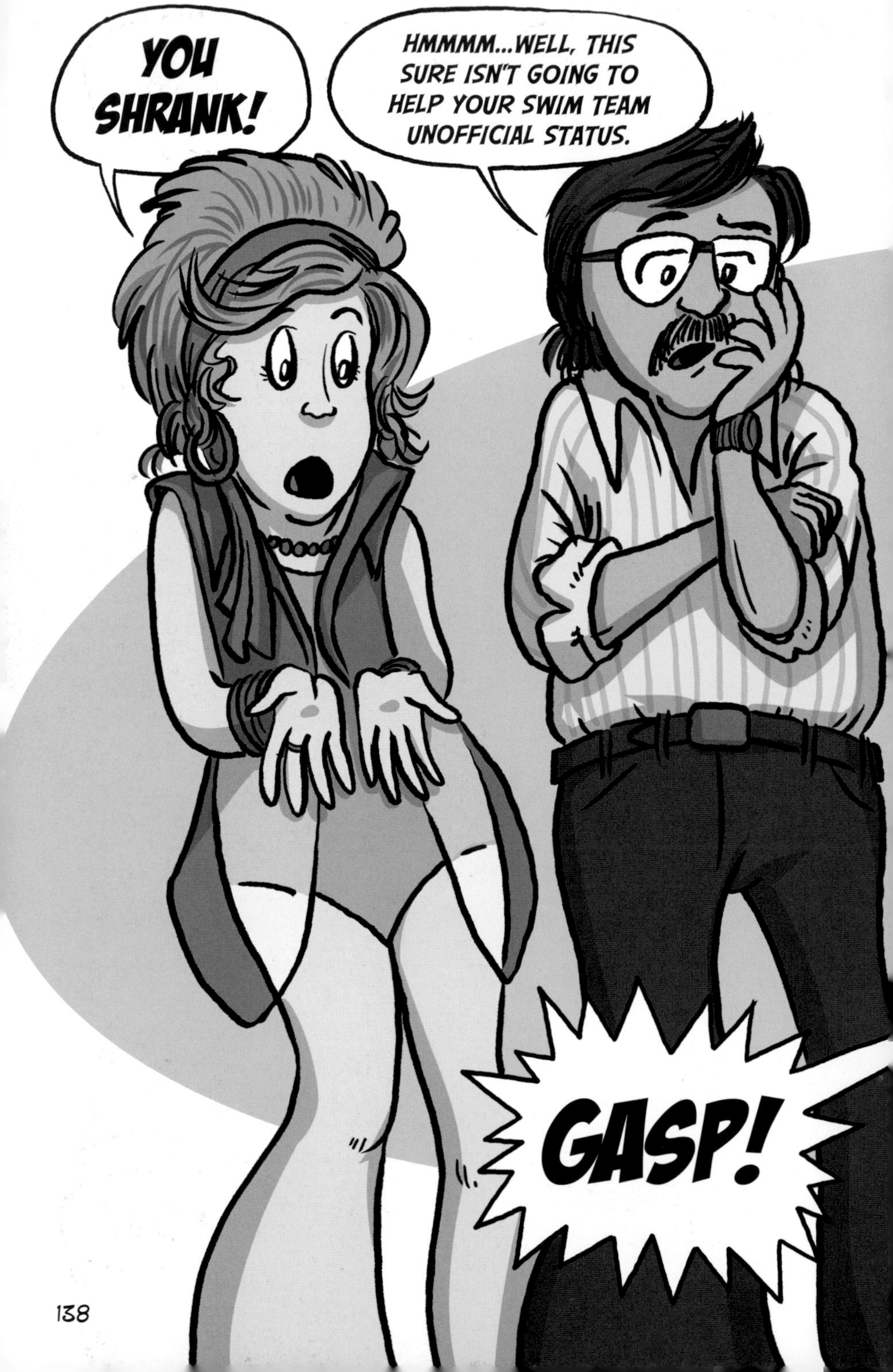
YOU SHRANK!
HMMMM...WELL, THIS SURE ISN'T GOING TO HELP YOUR SWIM TEAM UNOFFICIAL STATUS.
GASP!

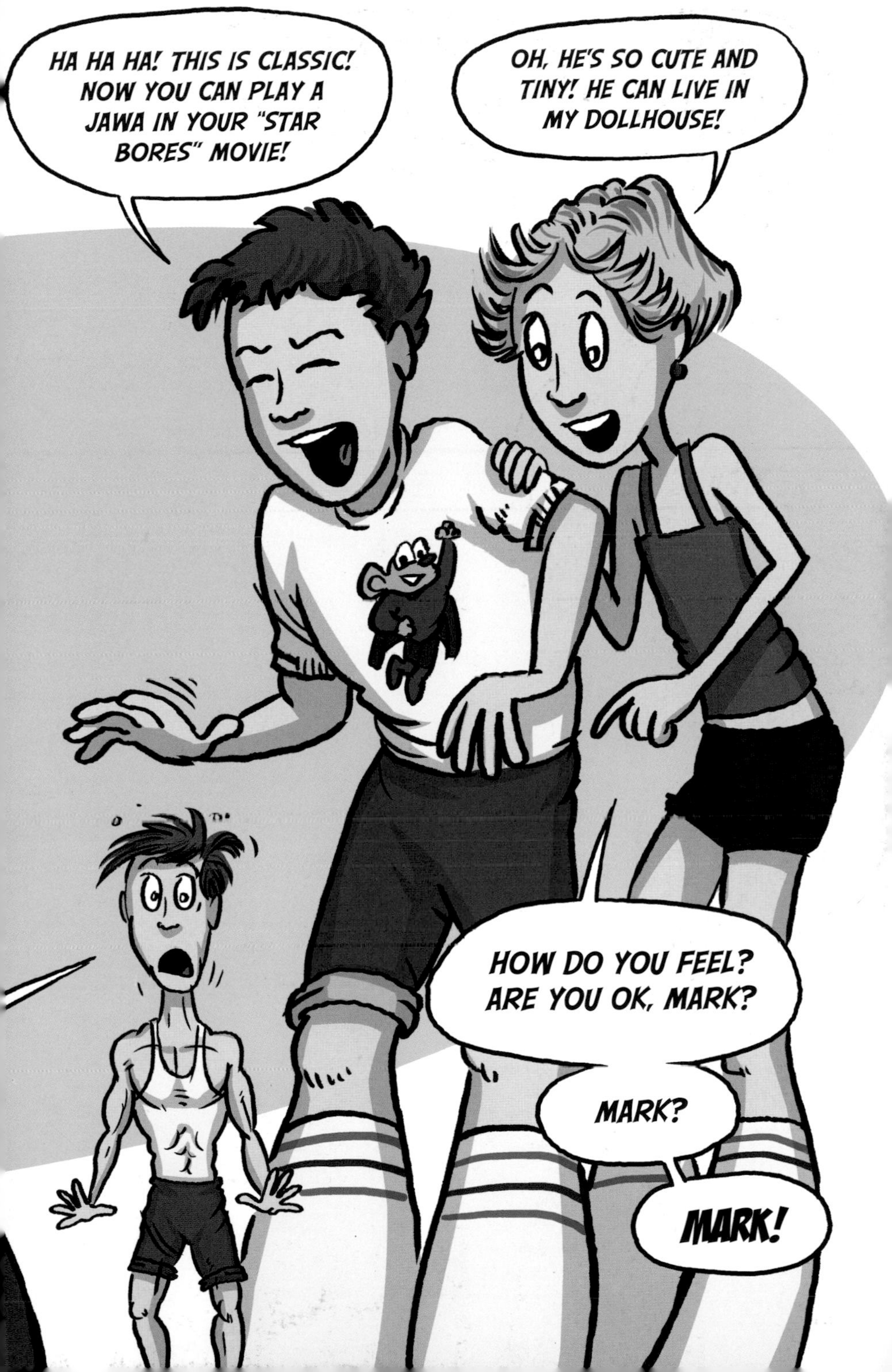
HA HA HA! THIS IS CLASSIC! NOW YOU CAN PLAY A JAWA IN YOUR "STAR BORES" MOVIE!
OH, HE'S SO CUTE AND TINY! HE CAN LIVE IN MY DOLLHOUSE!
HOW DO YOU FEEL? ARE YOU OK, MARK?
MARK?
MARK!

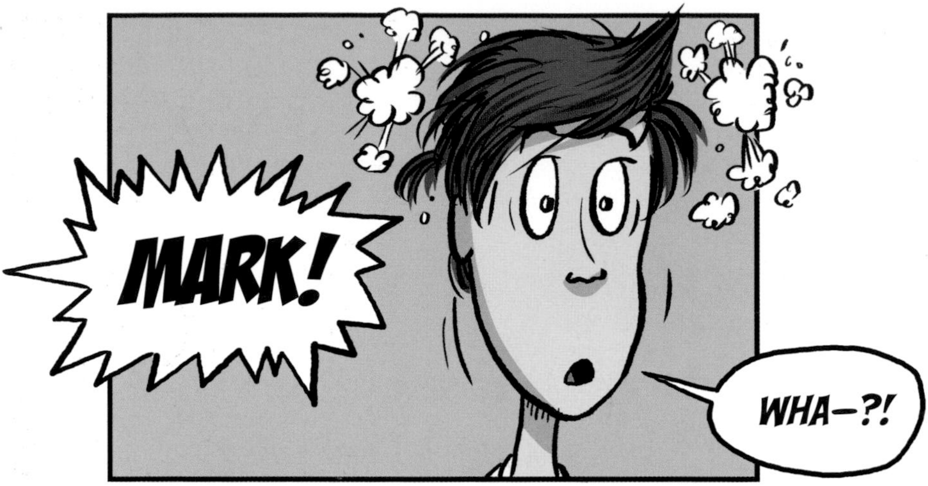
MARK!
WHA–?!

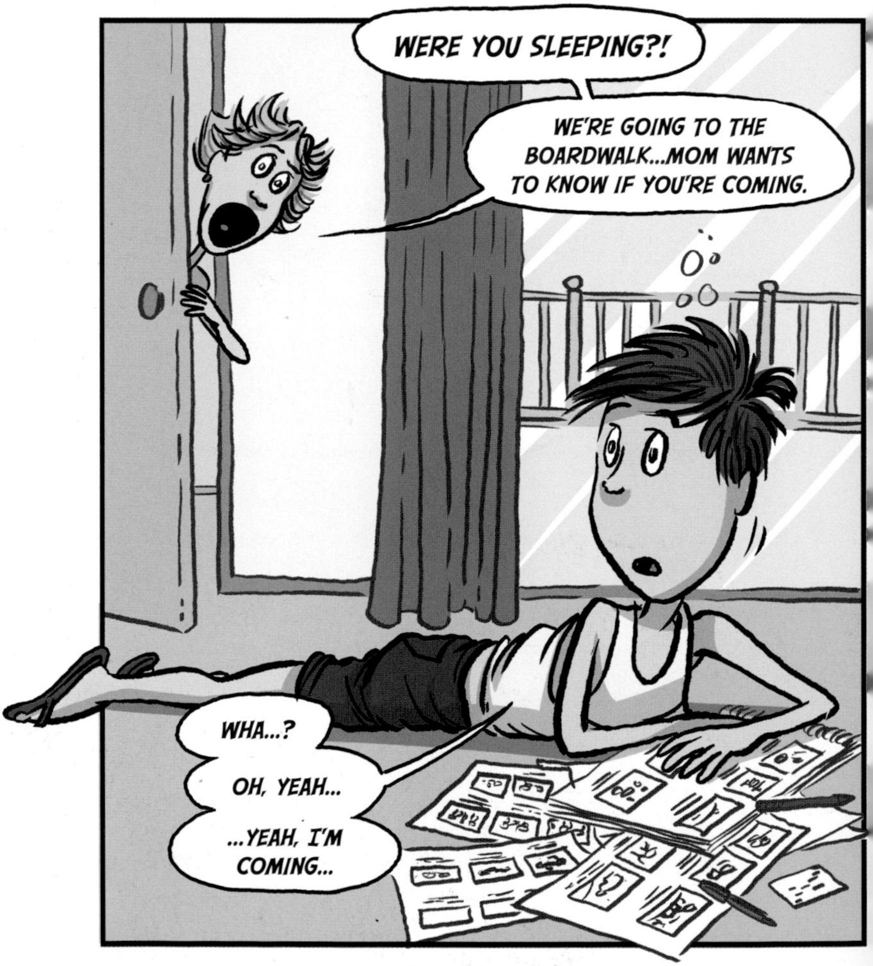
WERE YOU SLEEPING?!
WE'RE GOING TO THE BOARDWALK...MOM WANTS TO KNOW IF YOU'RE COMING.
WHA...?
OH, YEAH...
...YEAH, I'M COMING...

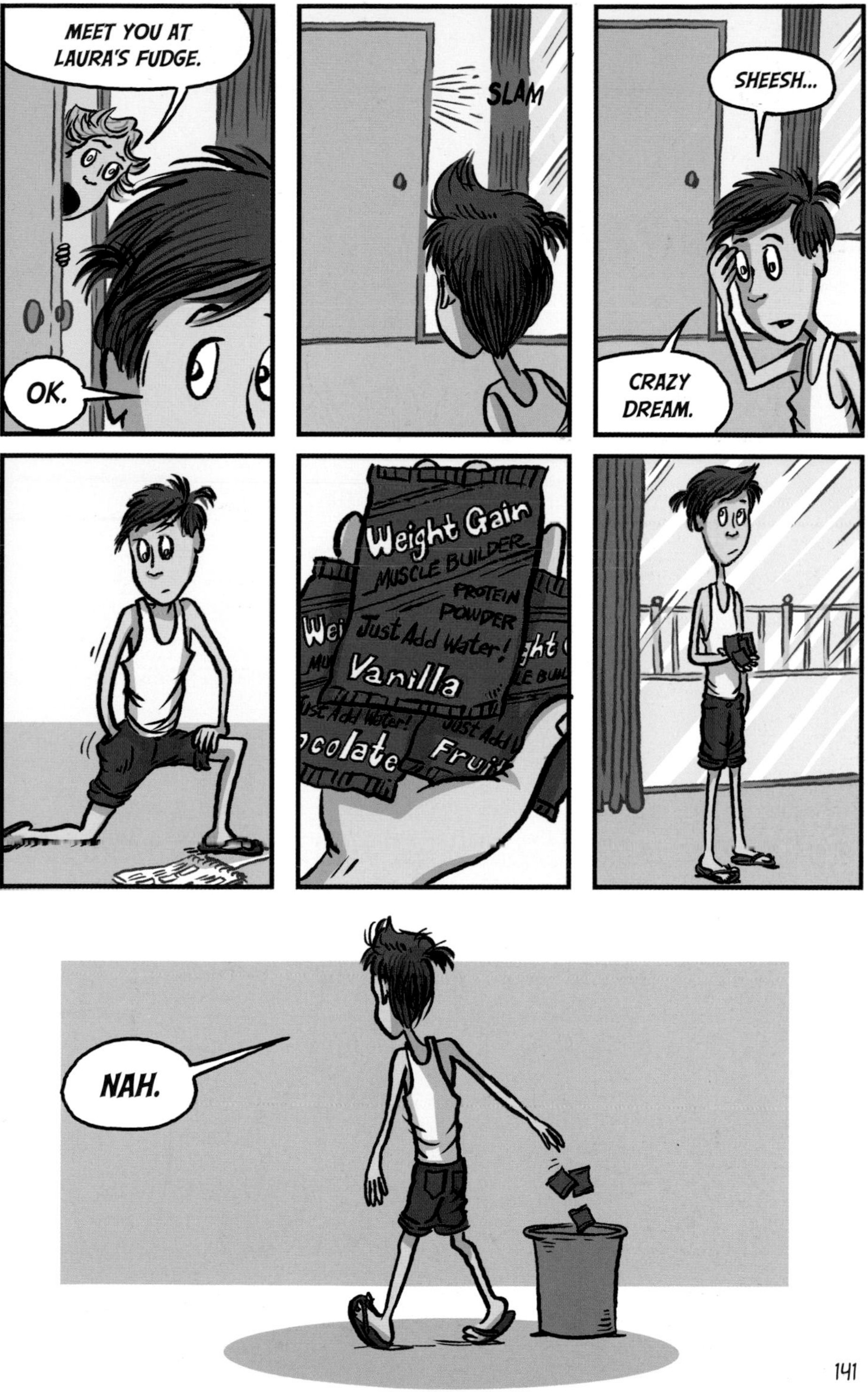
MEET YOU AT LAURA'S FUDGE.
OK.
SLAM
SHEESH...
CRAZY DREAM.
Weight Gain
MUSCLE BUILDER
PROTEIN POWDER
Just Add Water!
Vanilla
Just Add Water!
Just Add
NAH.

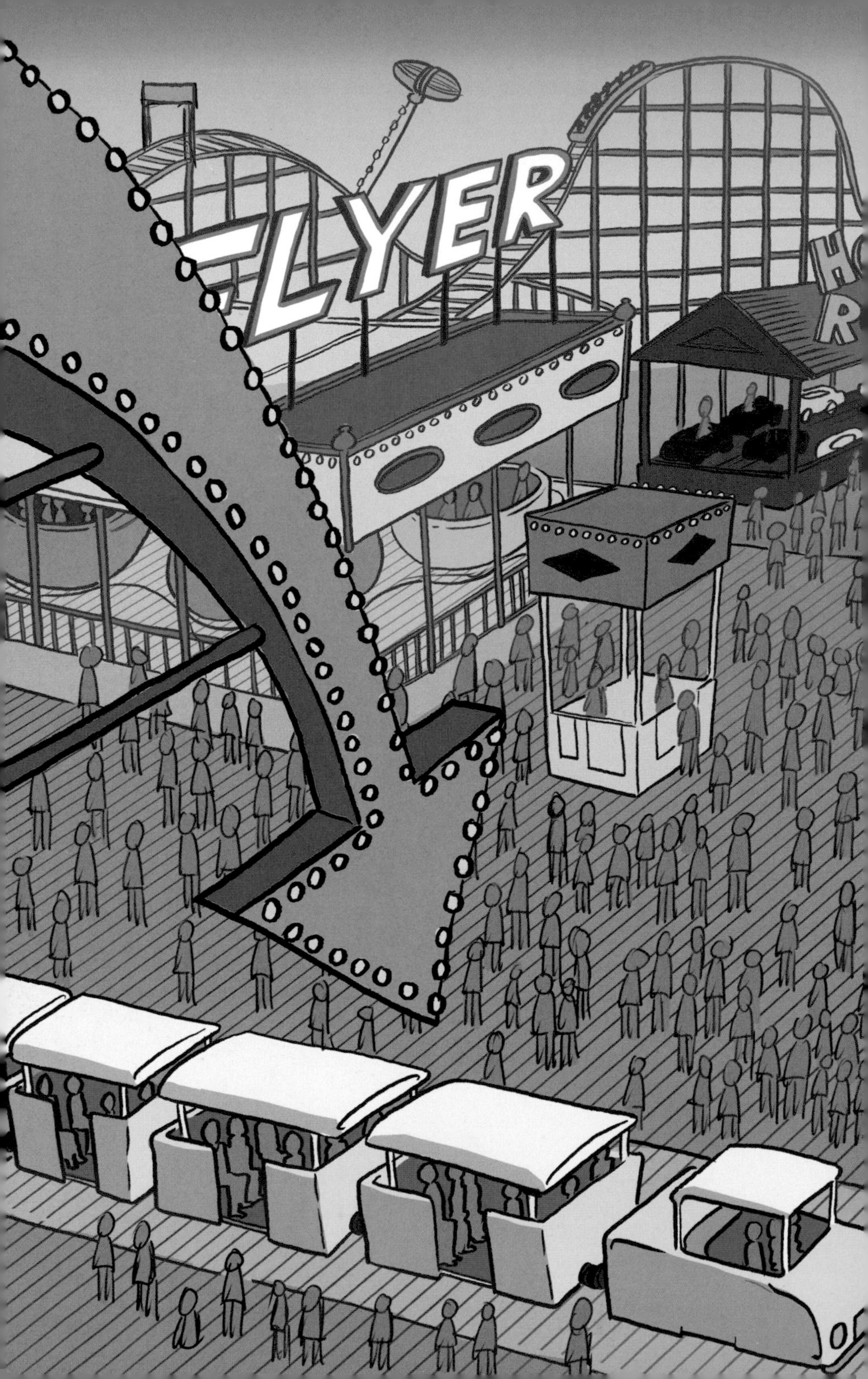
LYER

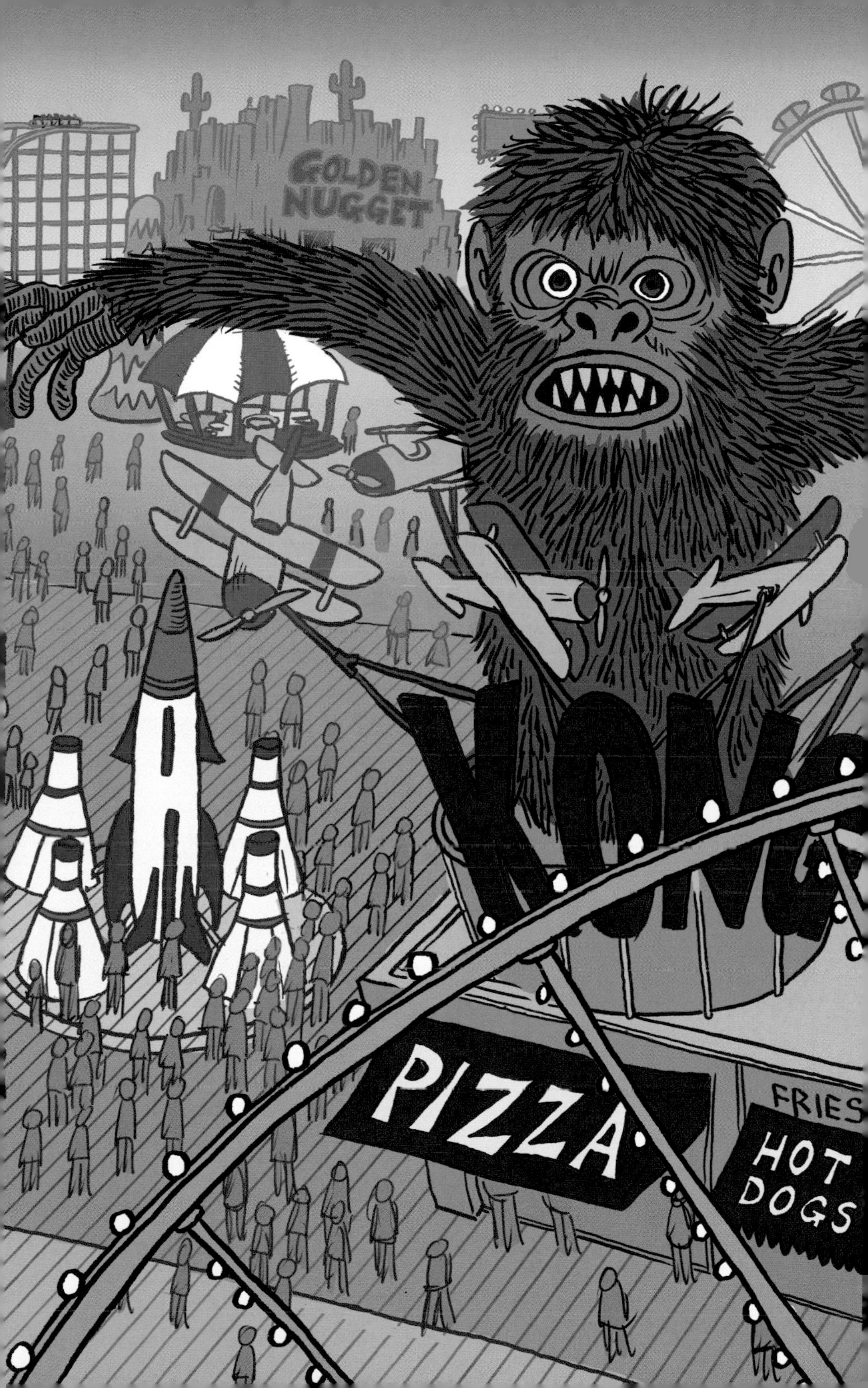
GOLDEN NUGGET
PIZZA
FRIES
HOT DOGS

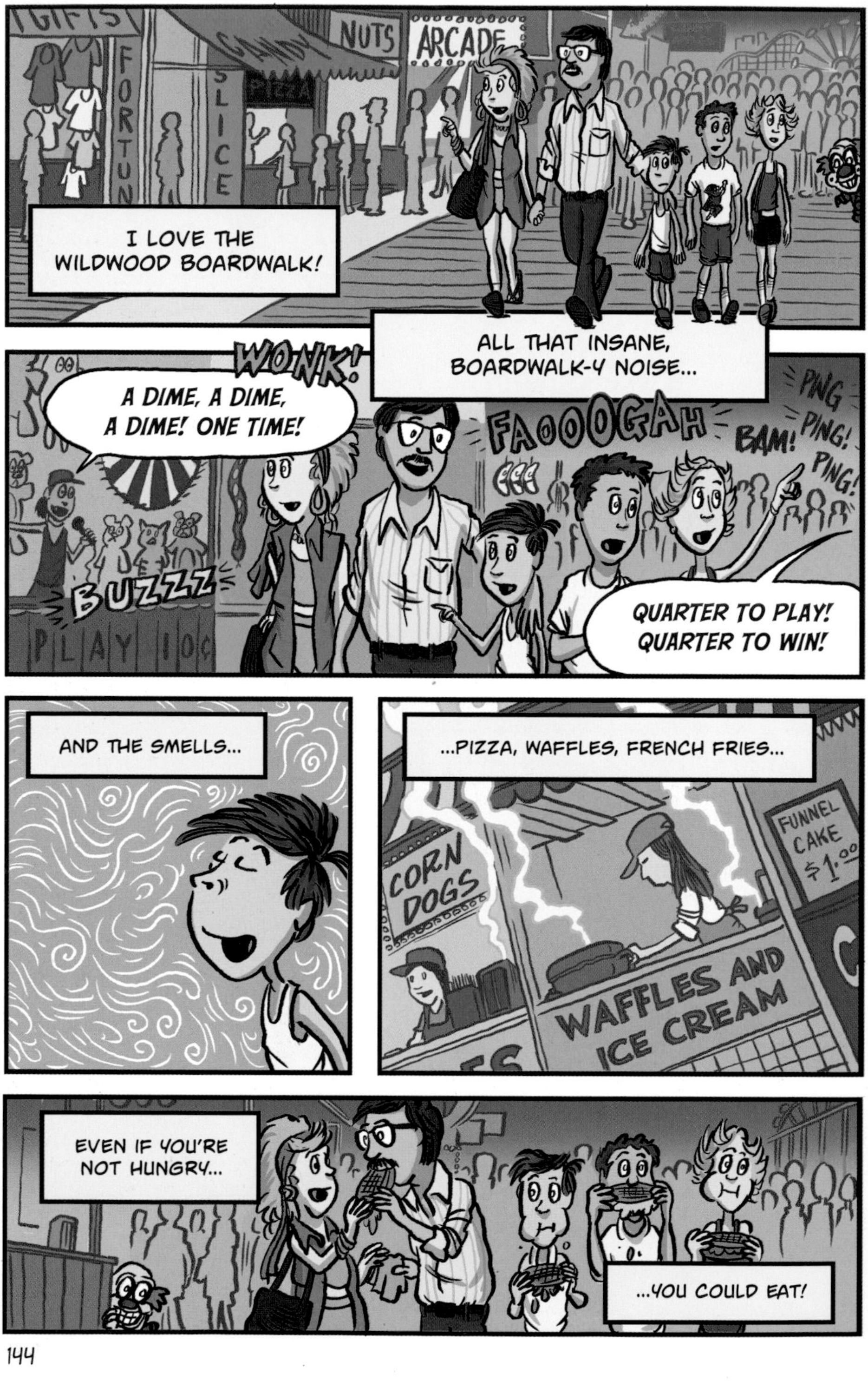

GIFTS
FORTUN
CANDY
SLICE
PIZZA
NUTS
ARCADE
I LOVE THE WILDWOOD BOARDWALK!
ALL THAT INSANE, BOARDWALK-Y NOISE...
WONK!
A DIME, A DIME, A DIME! ONE TIME!
FAOOOGAH
BAM!
PING PING! PING!
BUZZZ
PLAY 10¢
QUARTER TO PLAY! QUARTER TO WIN!
AND THE SMELLS...
...PIZZA, WAFFLES, FRENCH FRIES...
CORN DOGS
FUNNEL CAKE $1.00
WAFFLES AND ICE CREAM
EVEN IF YOU'RE NOT HUNGRY...
...YOU COULD EAT!

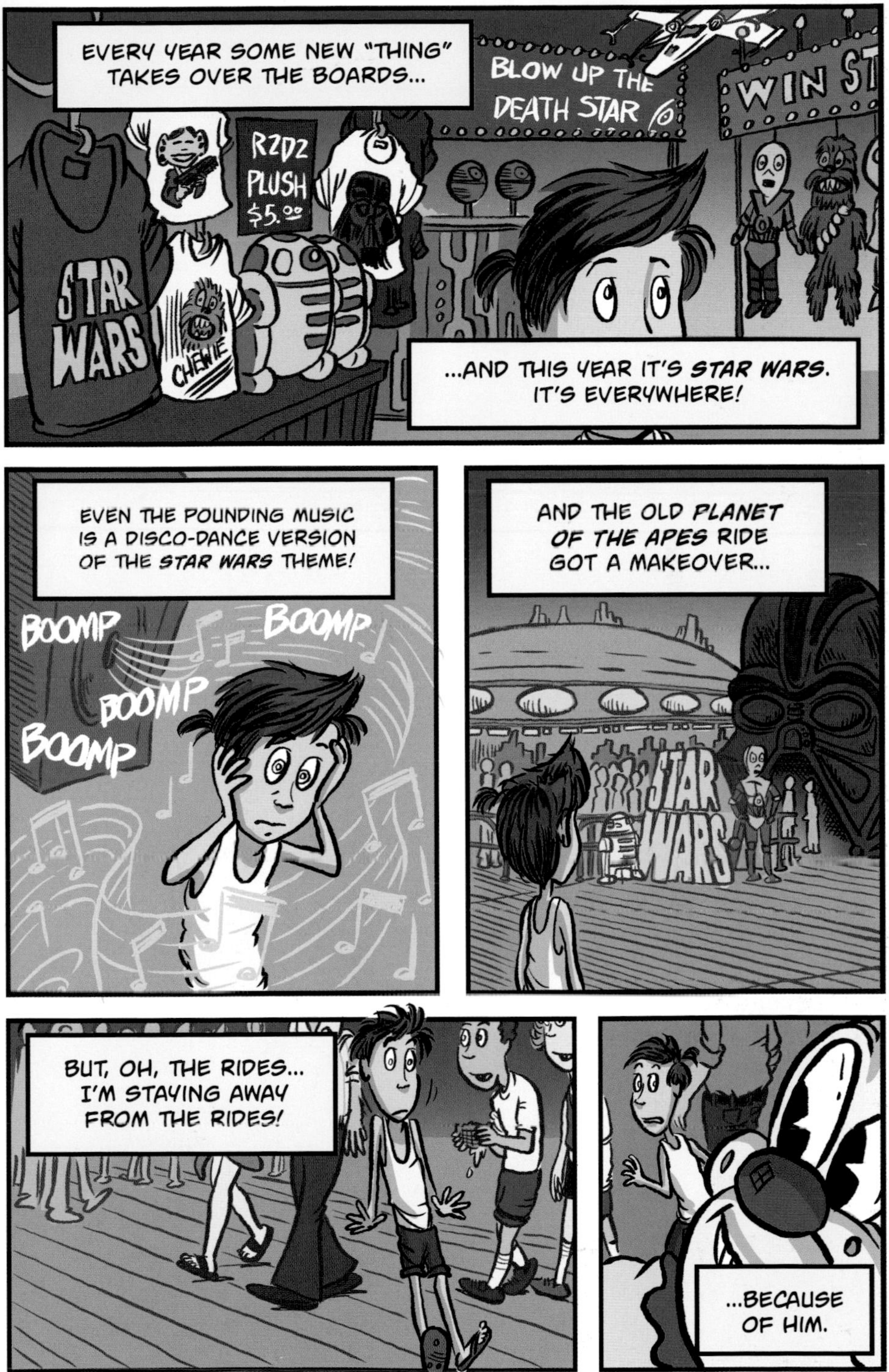
EVERY YEAR SOME NEW "THING" TAKES OVER THE BOARDS...
BLOW UP THE DEATH STAR
WIN ST
R2D2 PLUSH $5.00
STAR WARS
CHEWIE
...AND THIS YEAR IT'S *STAR WARS*. IT'S EVERYWHERE!
EVEN THE POUNDING MUSIC IS A DISCO-DANCE VERSION OF THE *STAR WARS* THEME!
BOOMP
BOOMP
BOOMP
BOOMP
AND THE OLD *PLANET OF THE APES* RIDE GOT A MAKEOVER...
STAR WARS
BUT, OH, THE RIDES... I'M STAYING AWAY FROM THE RIDES!
...BECAUSE OF HIM.

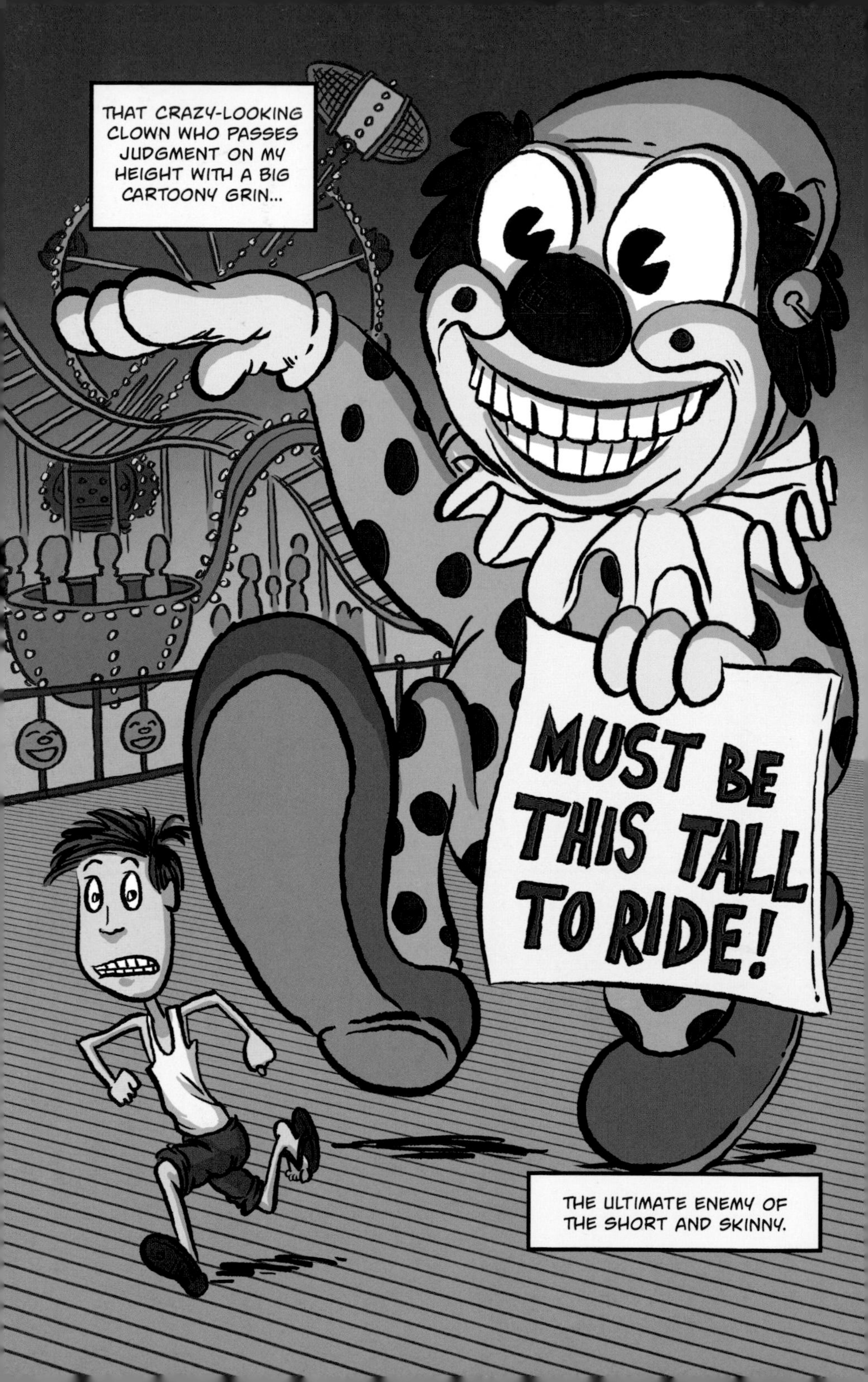
THAT CRAZY-LOOKING CLOWN WHO PASSES JUDGMENT ON MY HEIGHT WITH A BIG CARTOONY GRIN...
MUST BE THIS TALL TO RIDE!
THE ULTIMATE ENEMY OF THE SHORT AND SKINNY.

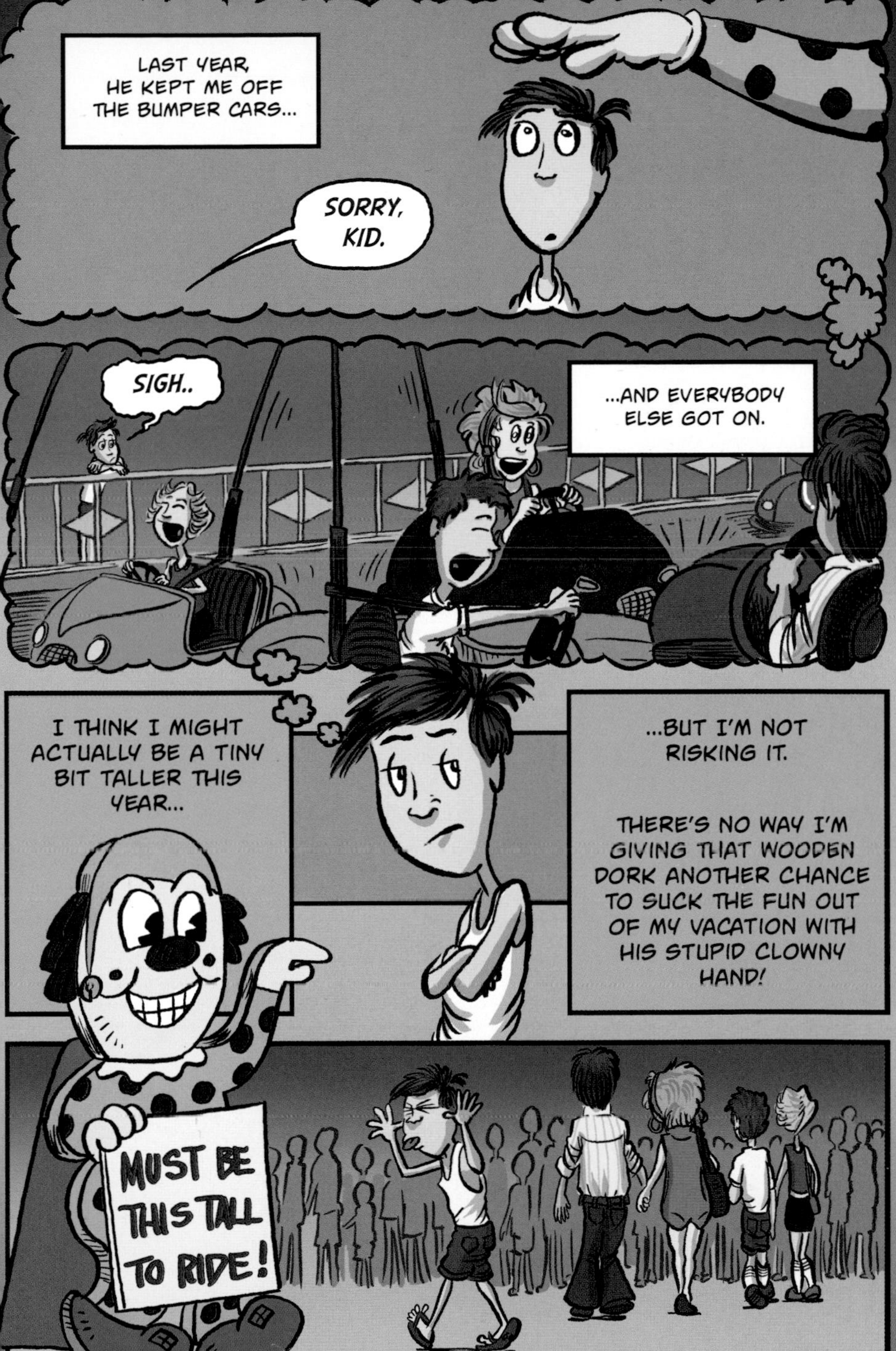

LAST YEAR, HE KEPT ME OFF THE BUMPER CARS...
SORRY, KID.
SIGH..
...AND EVERYBODY ELSE GOT ON.
I THINK I MIGHT ACTUALLY BE A TINY BIT TALLER THIS YEAR...
...BUT I'M NOT RISKING IT.
THERE'S NO WAY I'M GIVING THAT WOODEN DORK ANOTHER CHANCE TO SUCK THE FUN OUT OF MY VACATION WITH HIS STUPID CLOWNY HAND!
MUST BE THIS TALL TO RIDE!

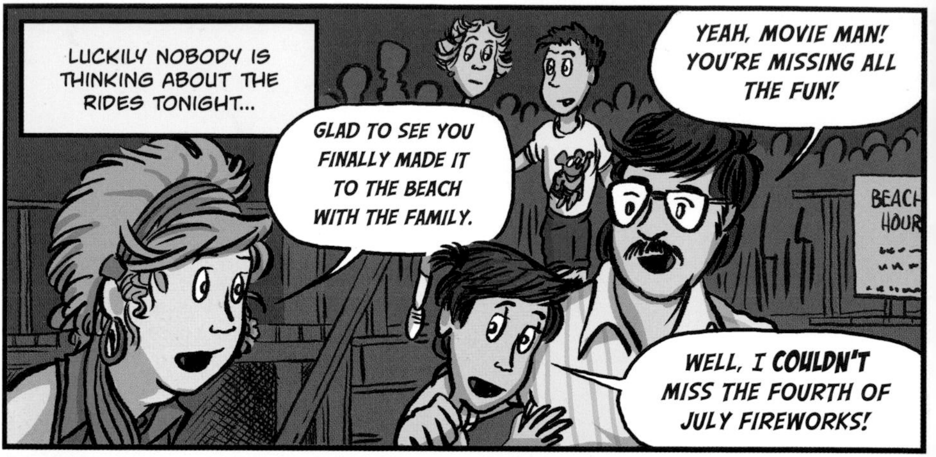
LUCKILY NOBODY IS THINKING ABOUT THE RIDES TONIGHT...
GLAD TO SEE YOU FINALLY MADE IT TO THE BEACH WITH THE FAMILY.
YEAH, MOVIE MAN! YOU'RE MISSING ALL THE FUN!
WELL, I COULDN'T MISS THE FOURTH OF JULY FIREWORKS!

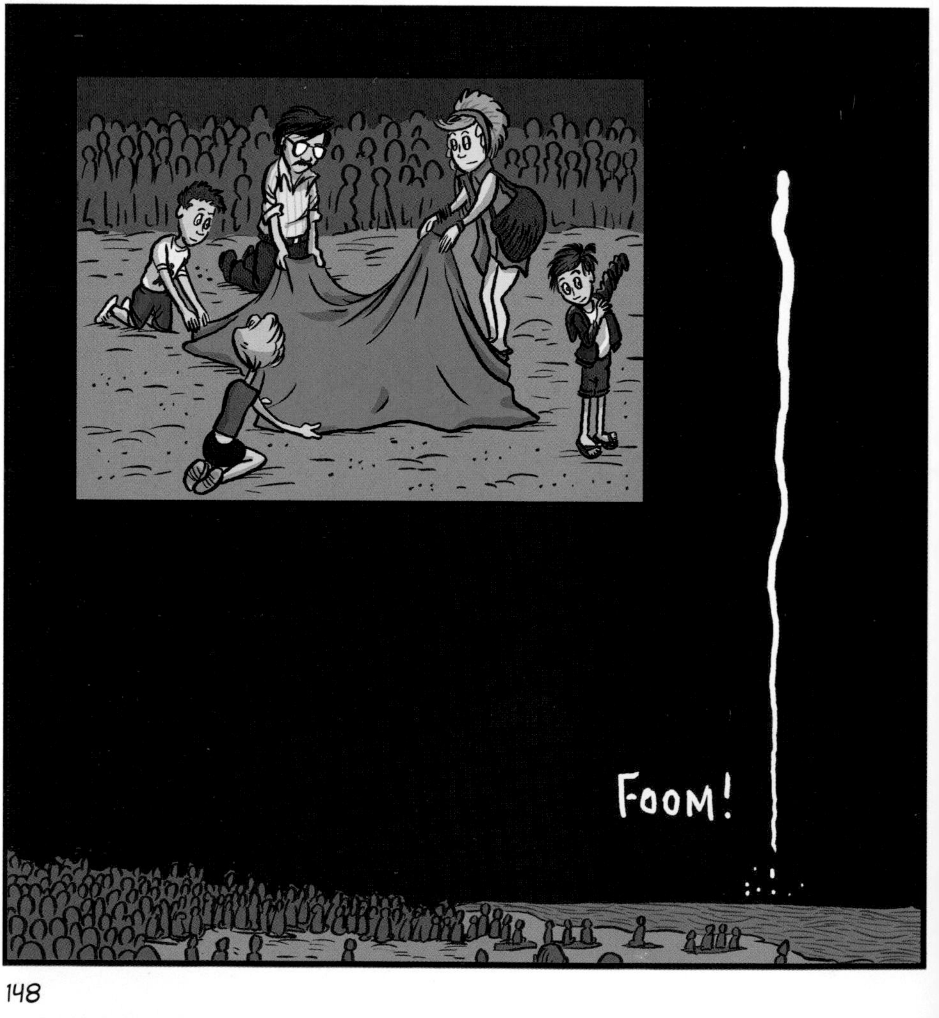
FOOM!

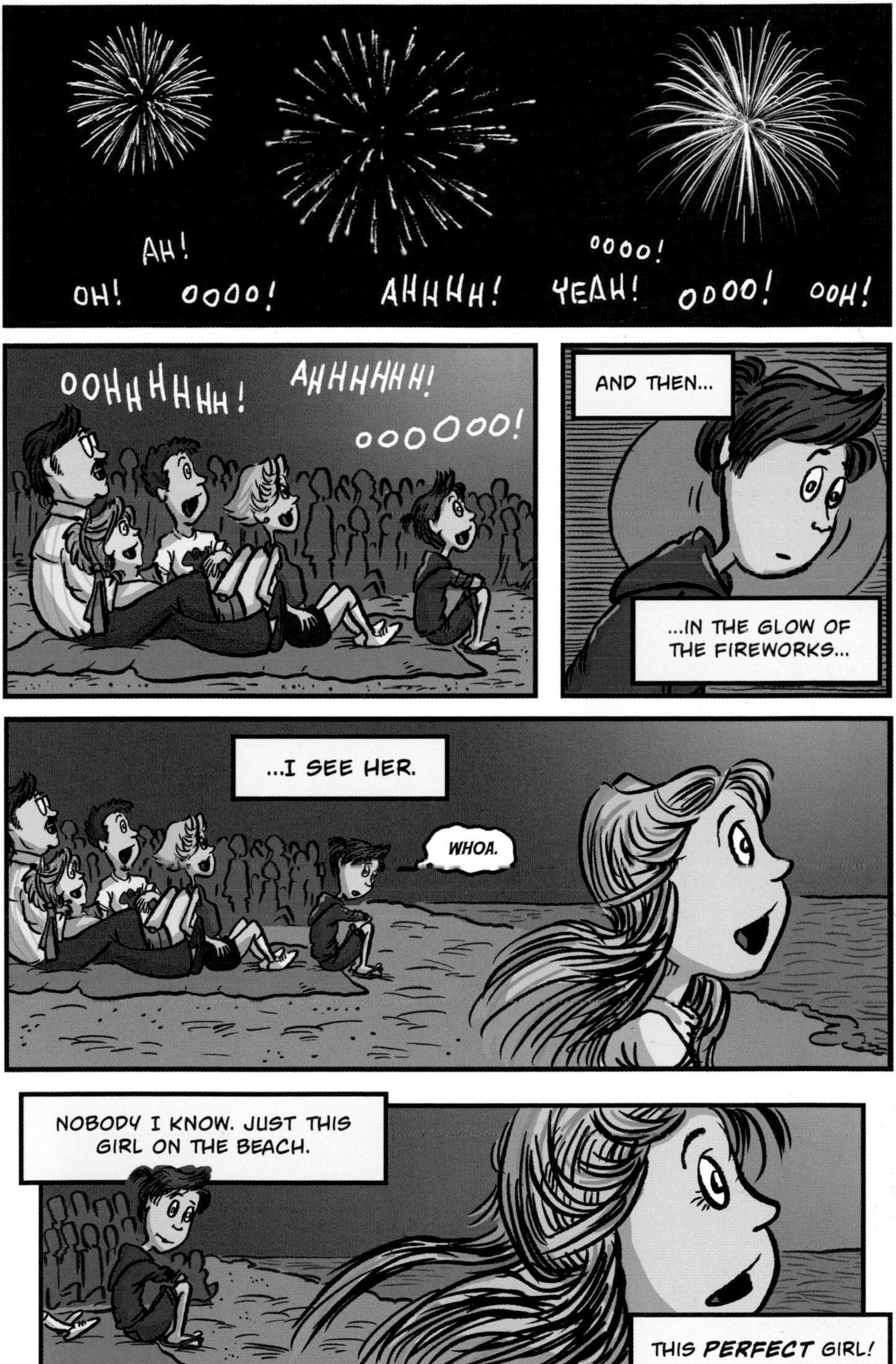

AH!
OH!
OOOO!
AHHHH!
OOOO!
YEAH!
OOOO!
OOH!
OOHHHHHH!
AHHHHHH!
OOOOOO!
AND THEN...
...IN THE GLOW OF THE FIREWORKS...
...I SEE HER.
WHOA.
NOBODY I KNOW. JUST THIS GIRL ON THE BEACH.
THIS PERFECT GIRL!

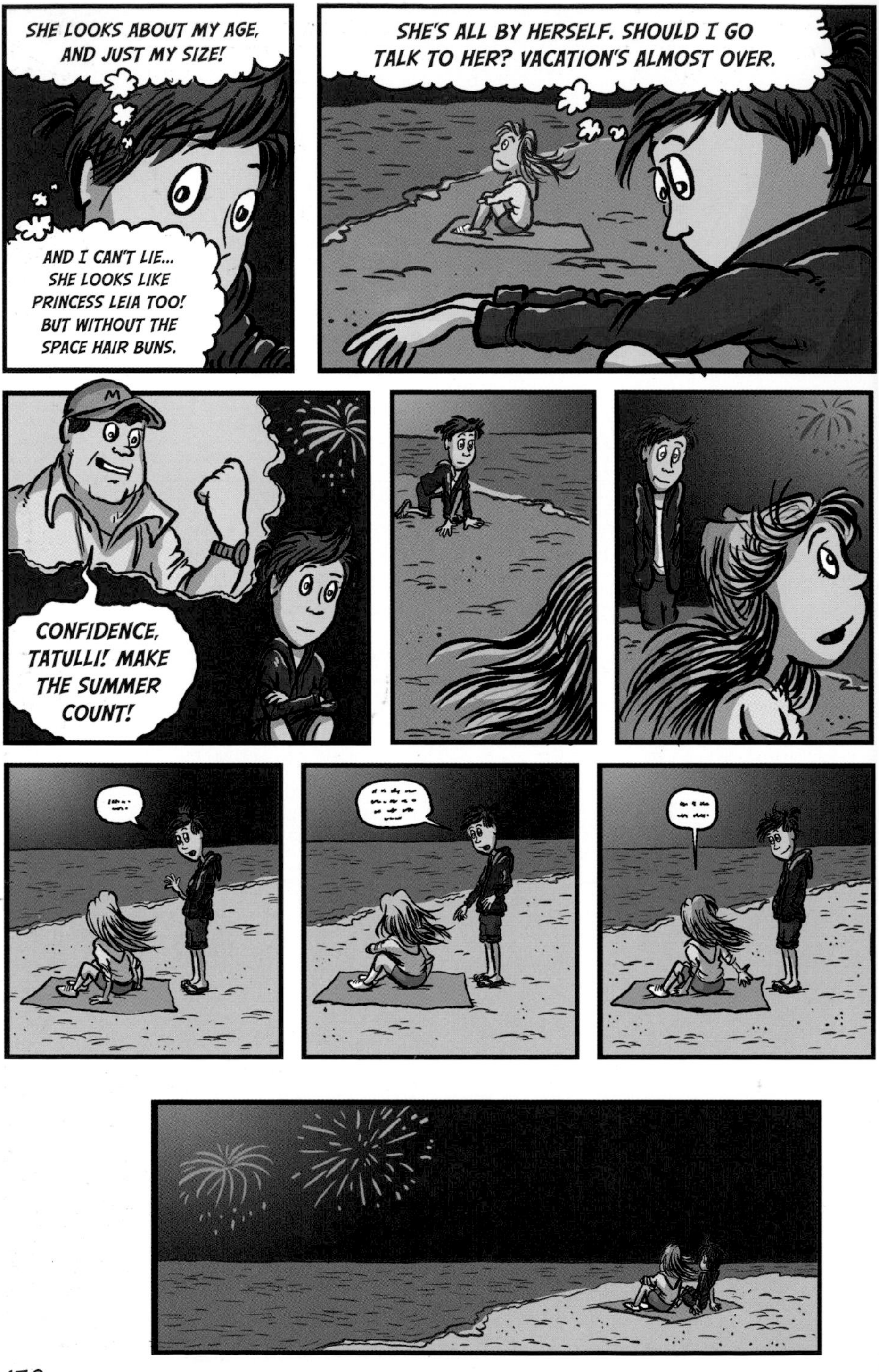
SHE LOOKS ABOUT MY AGE, AND JUST MY SIZE!
AND I CAN'T LIE... SHE LOOKS LIKE PRINCESS LEIA TOO! BUT WITHOUT THE SPACE HAIR BUNS.
SHE'S ALL BY HERSELF. SHOULD I GO TALK TO HER? VACATION'S ALMOST OVER.
M
CONFIDENCE, TATULLI! MAKE THE SUMMER COUNT!

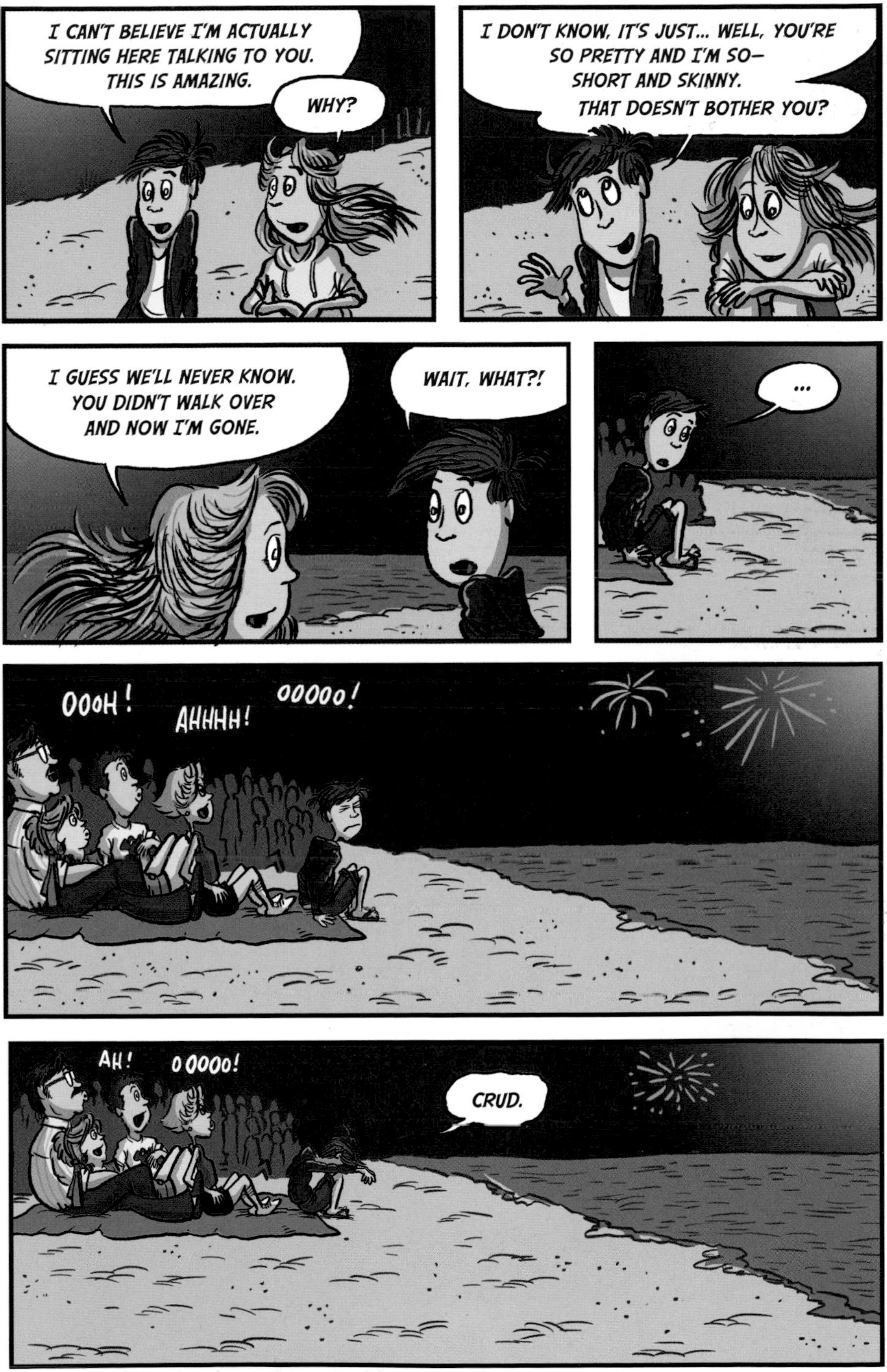
I CAN'T BELIEVE I'M ACTUALLY SITTING HERE TALKING TO YOU. THIS IS AMAZING.
WHY?
I DON'T KNOW, IT'S JUST... WELL, YOU'RE SO PRETTY AND I'M SO— SHORT AND SKINNY.
THAT DOESN'T BOTHER YOU?
I GUESS WE'LL NEVER KNOW. YOU DIDN'T WALK OVER AND NOW I'M GONE.
WAIT, WHAT?!
...
OOOH!
AHHHH!
OOOOO!
AH!
OOOOO!
CRUD.

CHAPTER 10

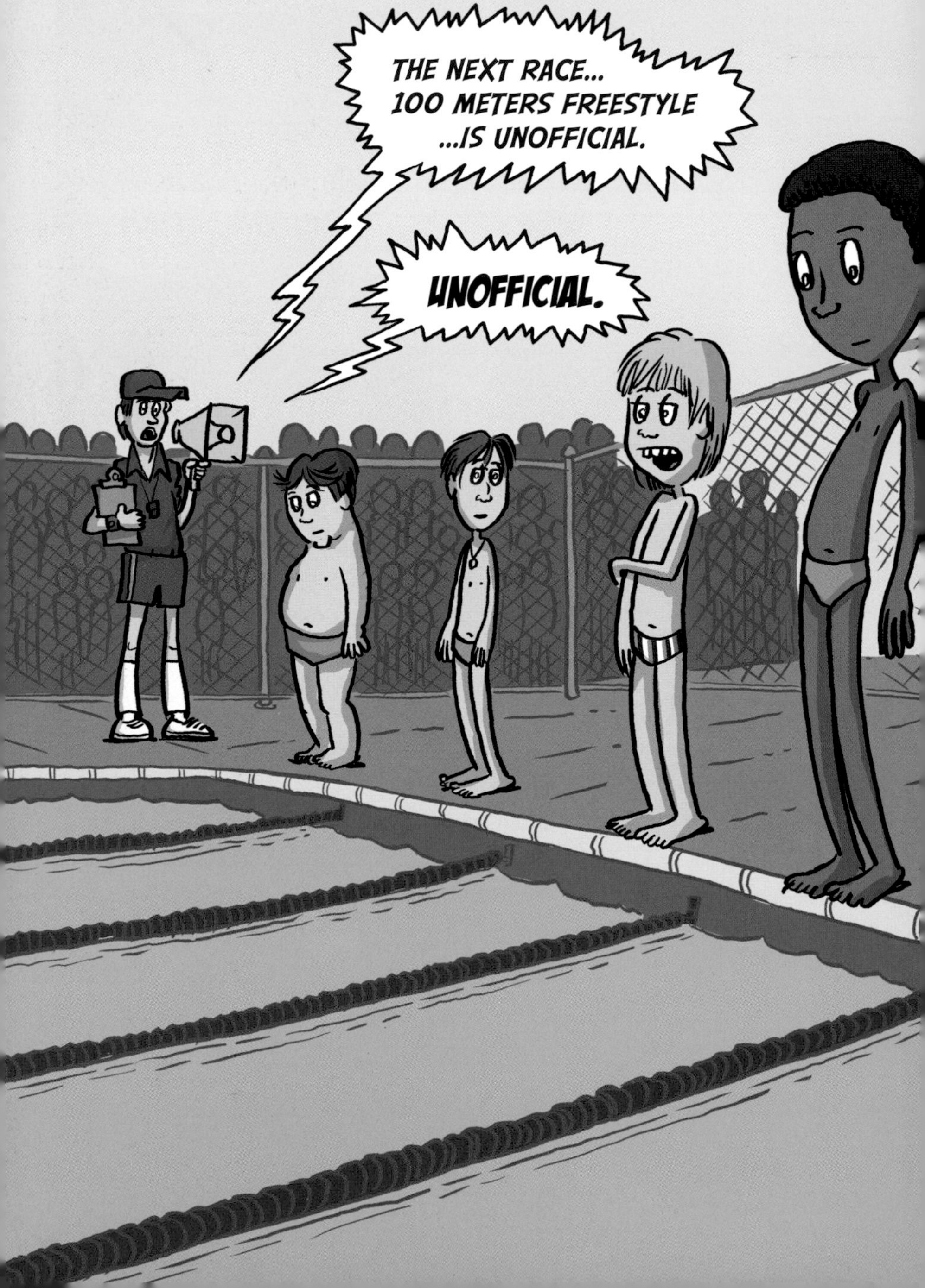
THE NEXT RACE... 100 METERS FREESTYLE ...IS UNOFFICIAL.
UNOFFICIAL.

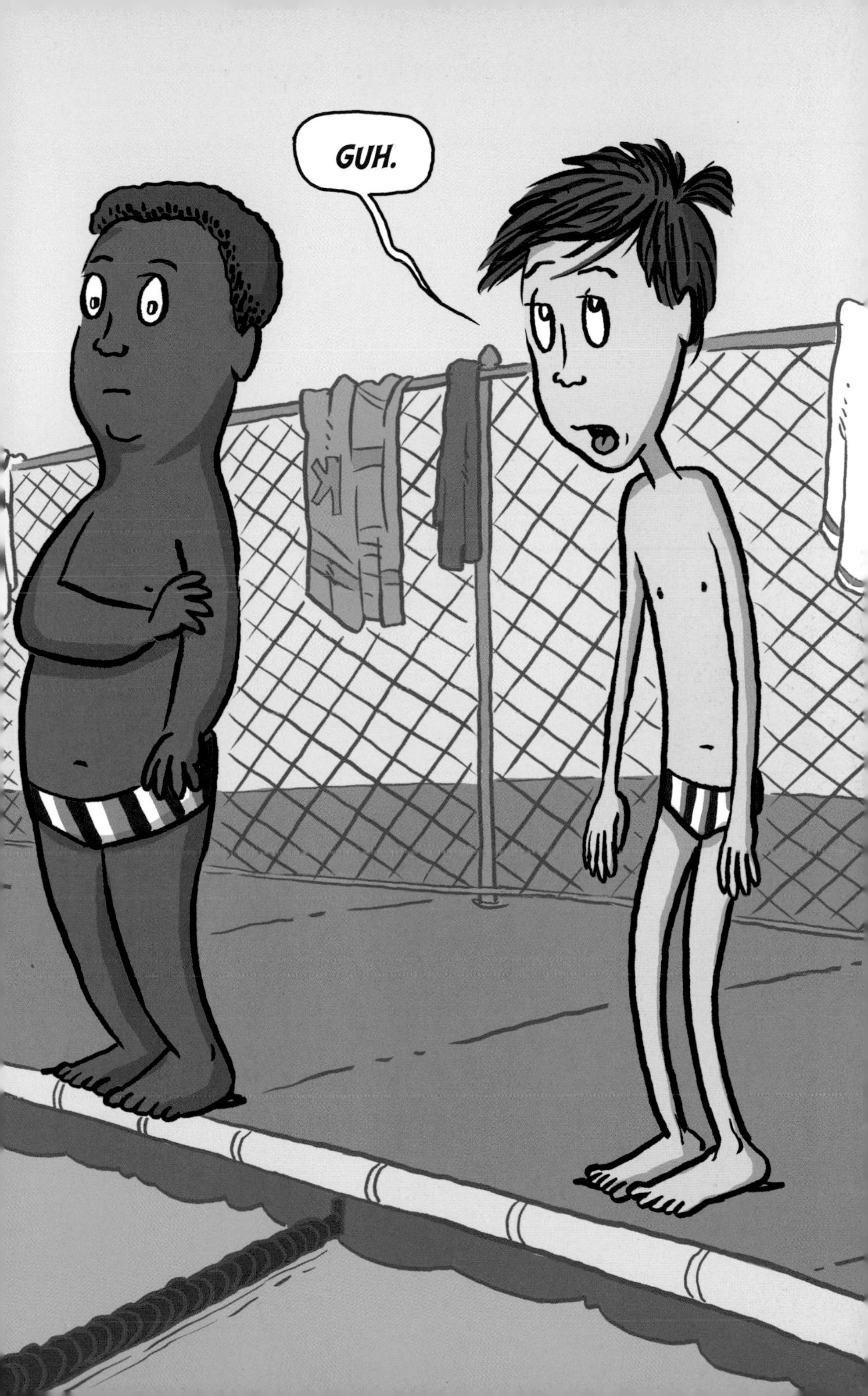
GUH.

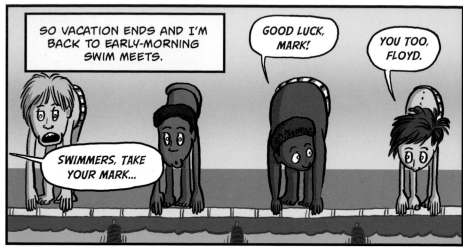

SO VACATION ENDS AND I'M BACK TO EARLY-MORNING SWIM MEETS.

GOOD LUCK, MARK!

YOU TOO, FLOYD.

SWIMMERS, TAKE YOUR MARK...

SWIMMING FOR TIME AT A MEET MEANS NO CHEERING OR CLAPPING CROWD...

IN FACT, UNOFFICIAL RACES ARE PRETTY MUCH WHEN EVERYBODY GOES TO THE BATHROOM.

WE'RE LIKE THE COMMERCIAL BREAK OF SWIM MEETS.

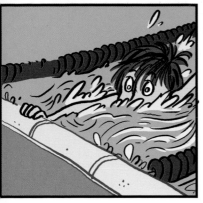

I COME IN FIRST PLACE...

...WHICH JUST MEANS I'M THE FASTEST OF THE SLOW KIDS.

FLOYD COMES IN FOURTH.

AFTERWARD, THEY GIVE RIBBONS TO THE WINNERS...

TERRI, FIRST PLACE...

MY SISTER GETS FIVE. MY BROTHER GETS TWO. I GET TO PRETEND LIKE I'M HAPPY.

I FEEL LIKE JAN BRADY.

MAYBE NEXT WEEK WE'LL SWIM OFFICIAL.

WE'LL GET RIBBONS NEXT WEEK, I BET.

YEAH, MAYBE, FLOYD.

MEANWHILE, MORE SHORT-AND-SKINNY SOLUTIONS COME IN THE MAIL...

45
TATULLI

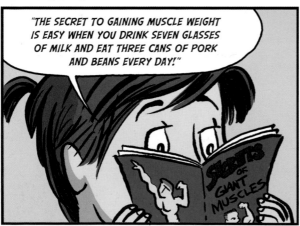

"THE SECRET TO GAINING MUSCLE WEIGHT IS EASY WHEN YOU DRINK SEVEN GLASSES OF MILK AND EAT THREE CANS OF PORK AND BEANS EVERY DAY!"

SECRETS OF GIANT MUSCLES

RIGHT.

THAT'S... NOT HAPPENING.

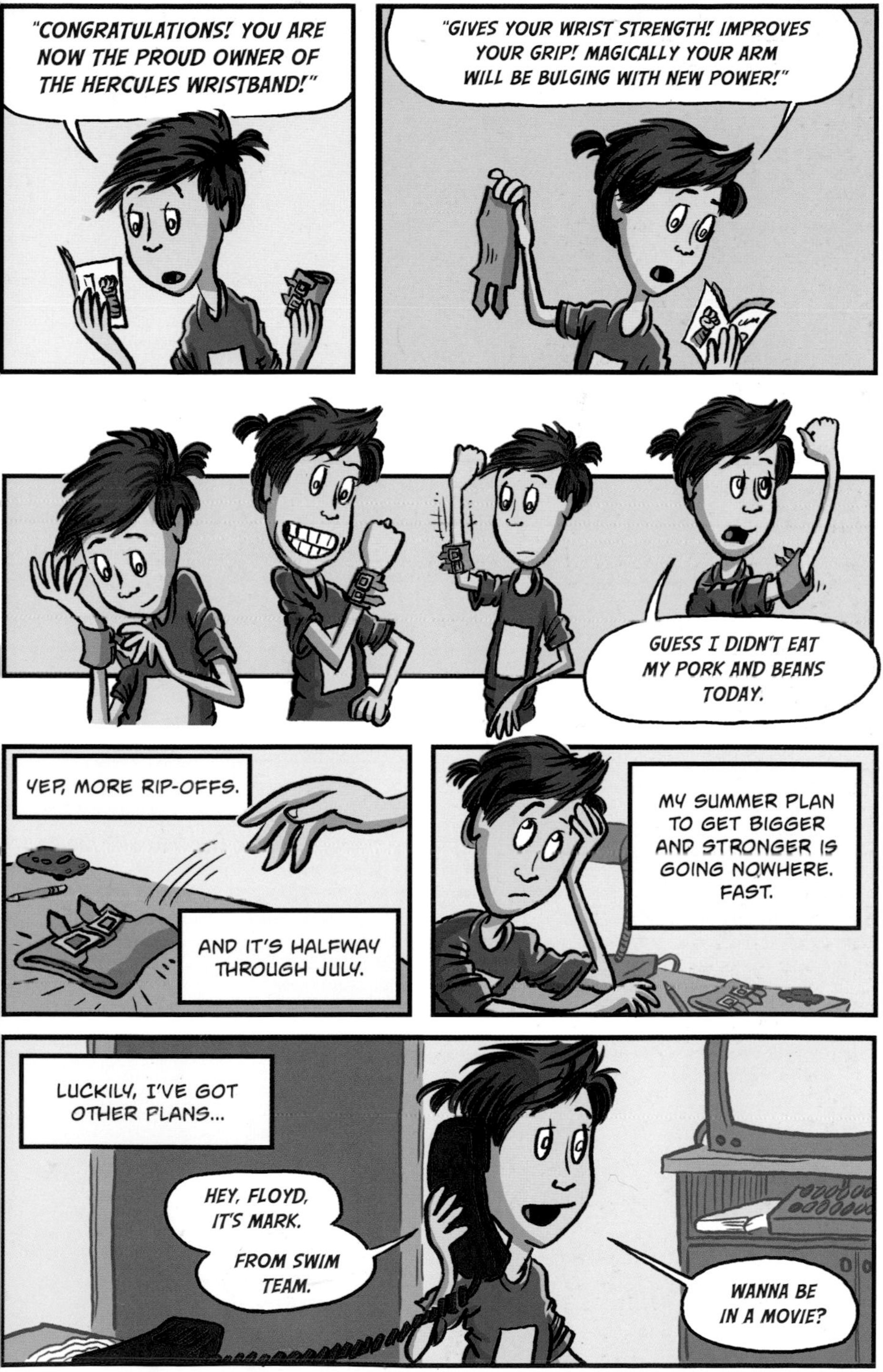
"CONGRATULATIONS! YOU ARE NOW THE PROUD OWNER OF THE HERCULES WRISTBAND!"
"GIVES YOUR WRIST STRENGTH! IMPROVES YOUR GRIP! MAGICALLY YOUR ARM WILL BE BULGING WITH NEW POWER!"
GUESS I DIDN'T EAT MY PORK AND BEANS TODAY.
YEP, MORE RIP-OFFS.
AND IT'S HALFWAY THROUGH JULY.
MY SUMMER PLAN TO GET BIGGER AND STRONGER IS GOING NOWHERE. FAST.
LUCKILY, I'VE GOT OTHER PLANS...
HEY, FLOYD, IT'S MARK.
FROM SWIM TEAM.
WANNA BE IN A MOVIE?

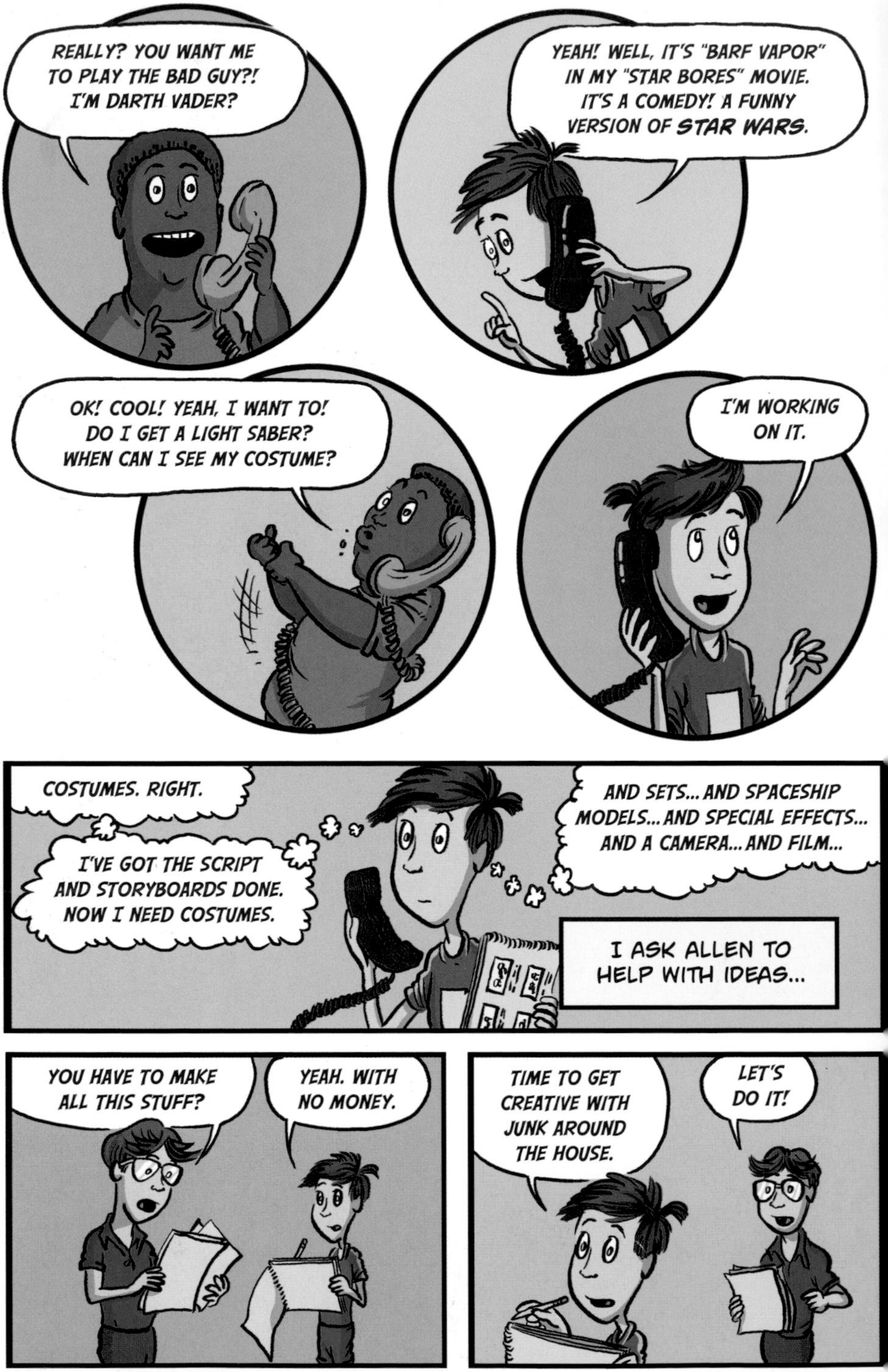
REALLY? YOU WANT ME TO PLAY THE BAD GUY?! I'M DARTH VADER?
YEAH! WELL, IT'S "BARF VAPOR" IN MY "STAR BORES" MOVIE. IT'S A COMEDY! A FUNNY VERSION OF STAR WARS.
OK! COOL! YEAH, I WANT TO! DO I GET A LIGHT SABER? WHEN CAN I SEE MY COSTUME?
I'M WORKING ON IT.
COSTUMES. RIGHT.
I'VE GOT THE SCRIPT AND STORYBOARDS DONE. NOW I NEED COSTUMES.
AND SETS... AND SPACESHIP MODELS... AND SPECIAL EFFECTS... AND A CAMERA... AND FILM...
I ASK ALLEN TO HELP WITH IDEAS...
YOU HAVE TO MAKE ALL THIS STUFF?
YEAH. WITH NO MONEY.
TIME TO GET CREATIVE WITH JUNK AROUND THE HOUSE.
LET'S DO IT!

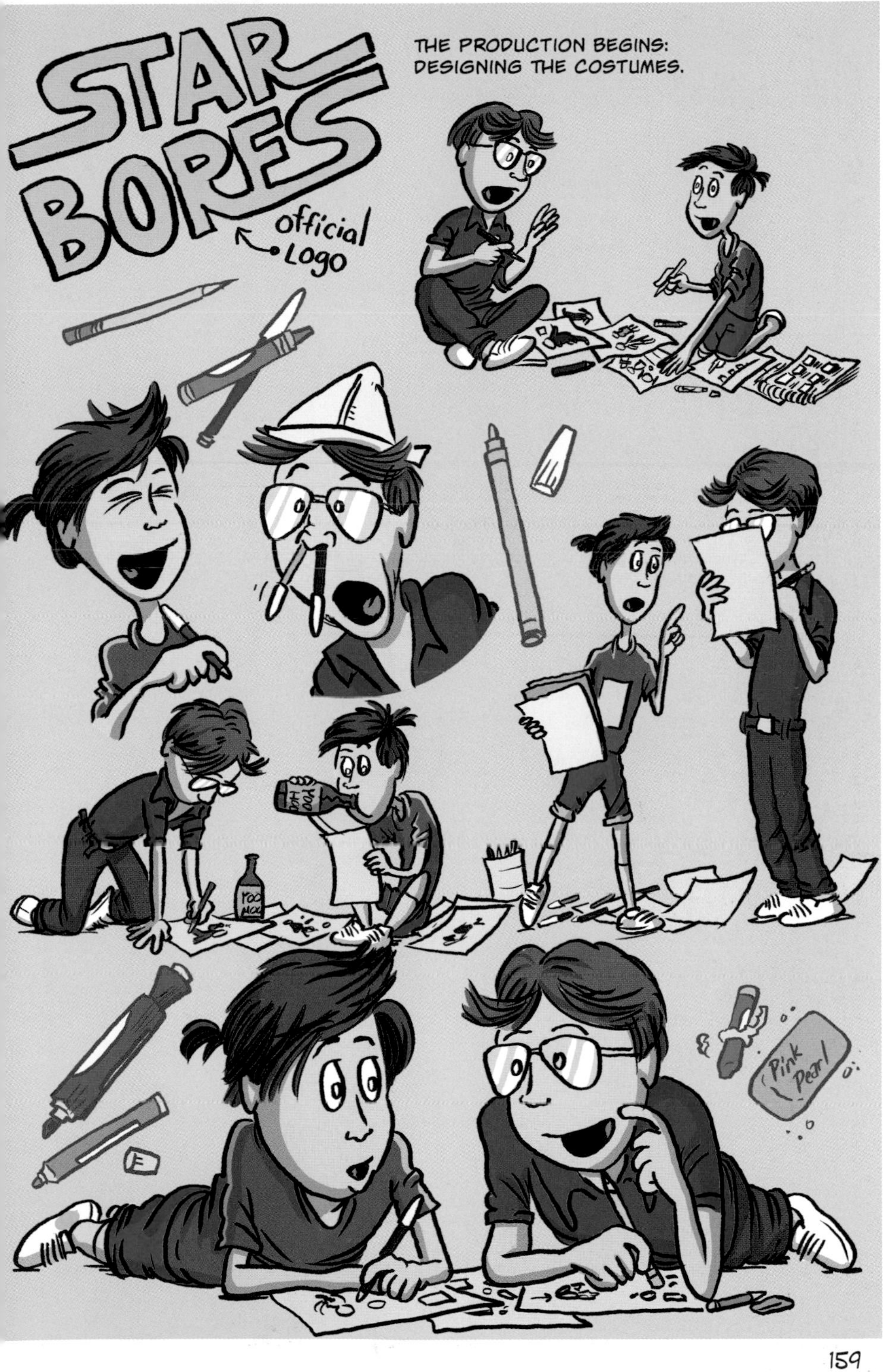

STAR BORES
official Logo
THE PRODUCTION BEGINS: DESIGNING THE COSTUMES.
Pink Pearl

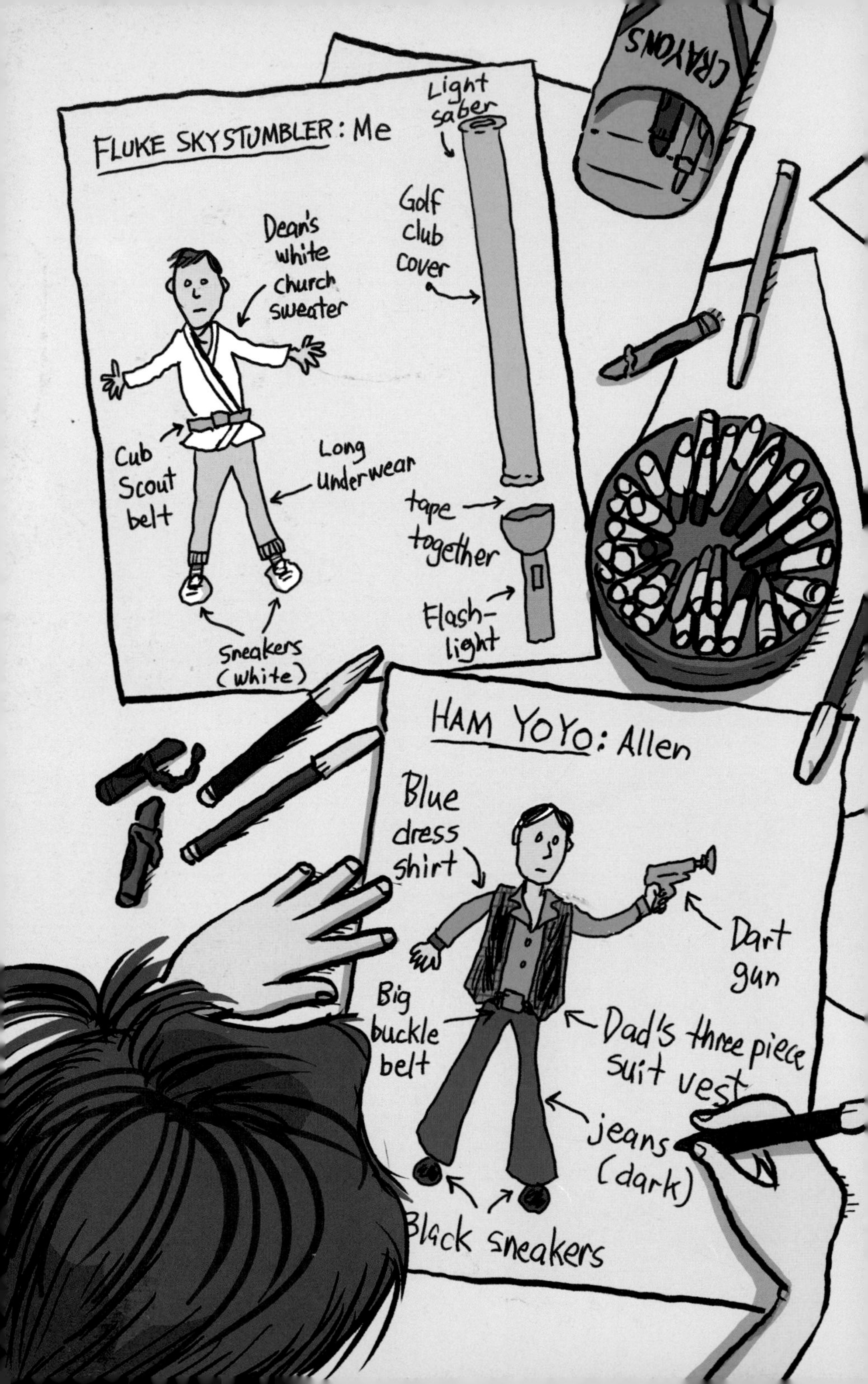
CRAYONS
FLUKE SKYSTUMBLER: Me
Light saber
Golf club cover
Dean's white church sweater
Cub Scout belt
Long underwear
tape together
Flash-light
Sneakers (white)
HAM YOYO: Allen
Blue dress shirt
Dart gun
Big buckle belt
Dad's three piece suit vest
jeans (dark)
Black sneakers

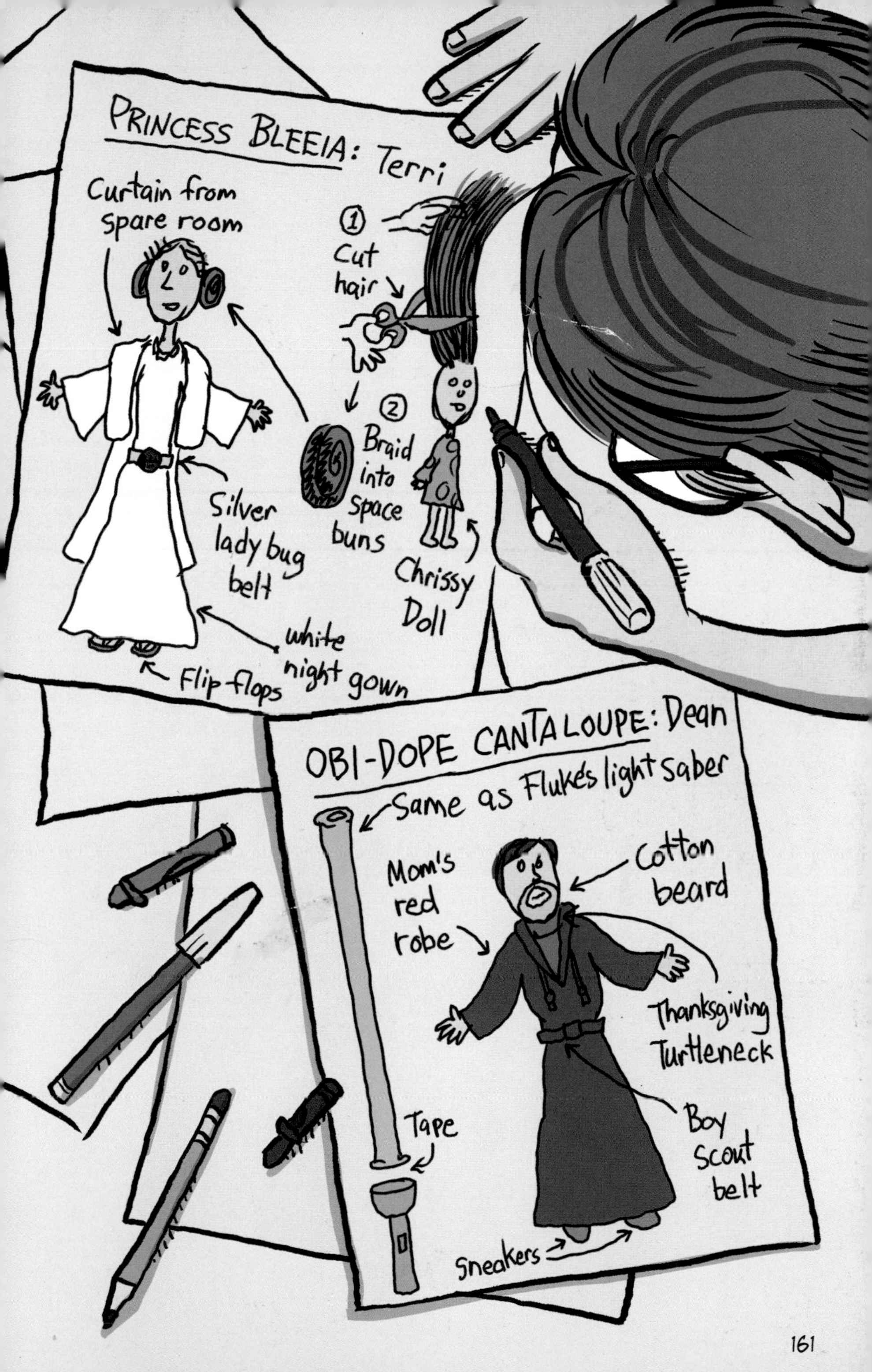
PRINCESS BLEEIA: Terri
Curtain from spare room
① Cut hair
② Braid into space buns
Silver lady bug belt
Chrissy Doll
white night gown
Flip-flops
OBI-DOPE CANTALOUPE: Dean
Same as Fluke's light saber
Mom's red robe
Cotton beard
Thanksgiving Turtleneck
Boy Scout belt
Tape
Sneakers

HOW'RE YOU GOING TO MAKE THIS BIG, FURRY THING?

THAT PART NEEDS THE TALLEST KID WE KNOW...

HEY, ALLEN.

FAMOUS MONSTERS STAR WARS SPECTACULAR

...AND THAT'S JOHN!

HE'S THE "WONKIE CHOMPBACCO," AND I'VE GOT THE PERFECT THING!

I PLAY CHEWIE?

"CHOMPIE."

AND LOOK! MY MOM'S OLD FURRY BLANKET!

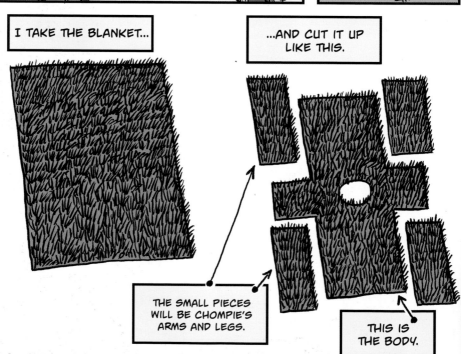

I TAKE THE BLANKET...

...AND CUT IT UP LIKE THIS.

THE SMALL PIECES WILL BE CHOMPIE'S ARMS AND LEGS.

THIS IS THE BODY.

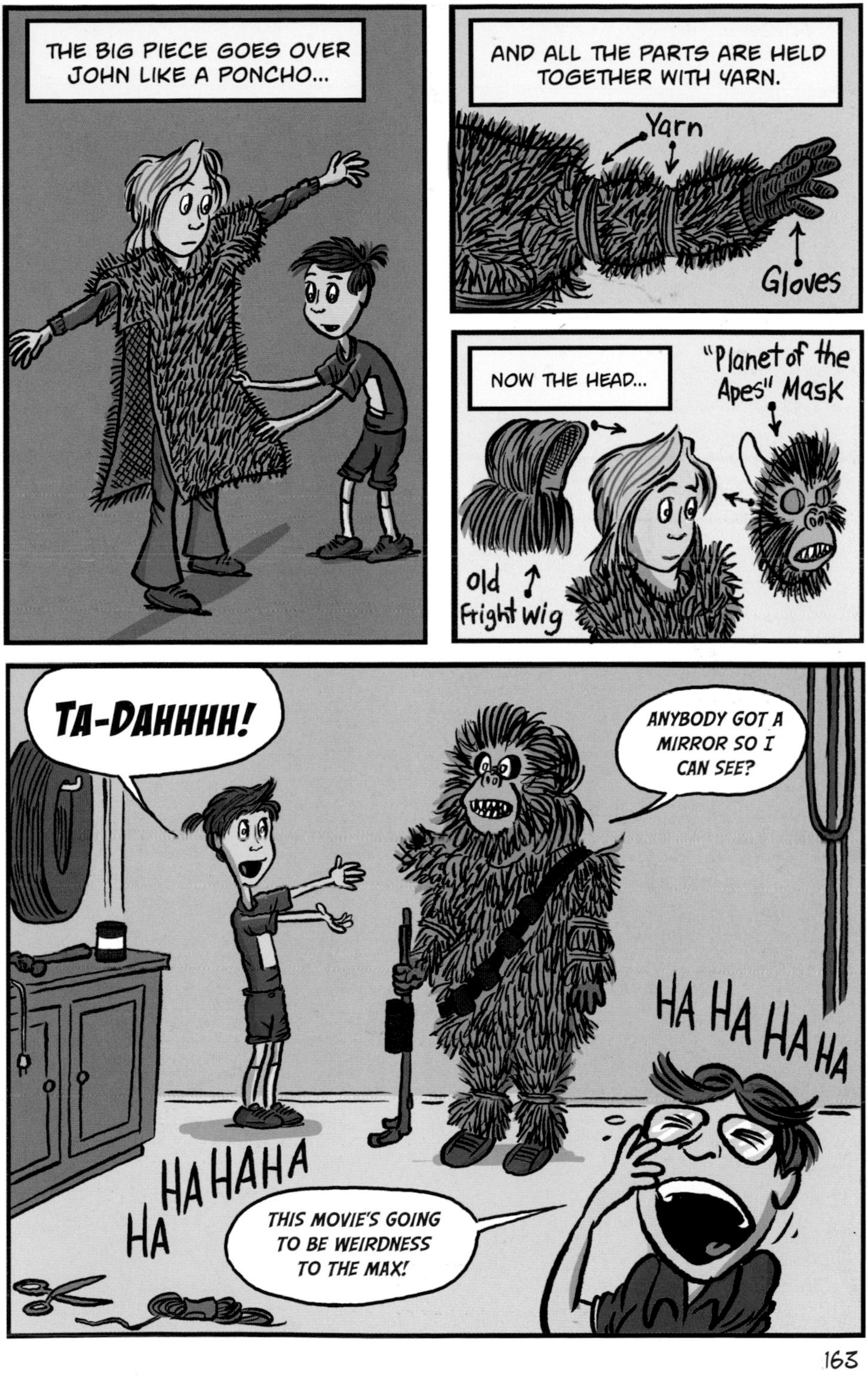
THE BIG PIECE GOES OVER JOHN LIKE A PONCHO...
AND ALL THE PARTS ARE HELD TOGETHER WITH YARN.
Yarn
Gloves
NOW THE HEAD...
"Planet of the Apes" Mask
Old Fright wig
TA-DAHHHH!
ANYBODY GOT A MIRROR SO I CAN SEE?
HA HA HA HA HA
HA HA HAHA HA
THIS MOVIE'S GOING TO BE WEIRDNESS TO THE MAX!

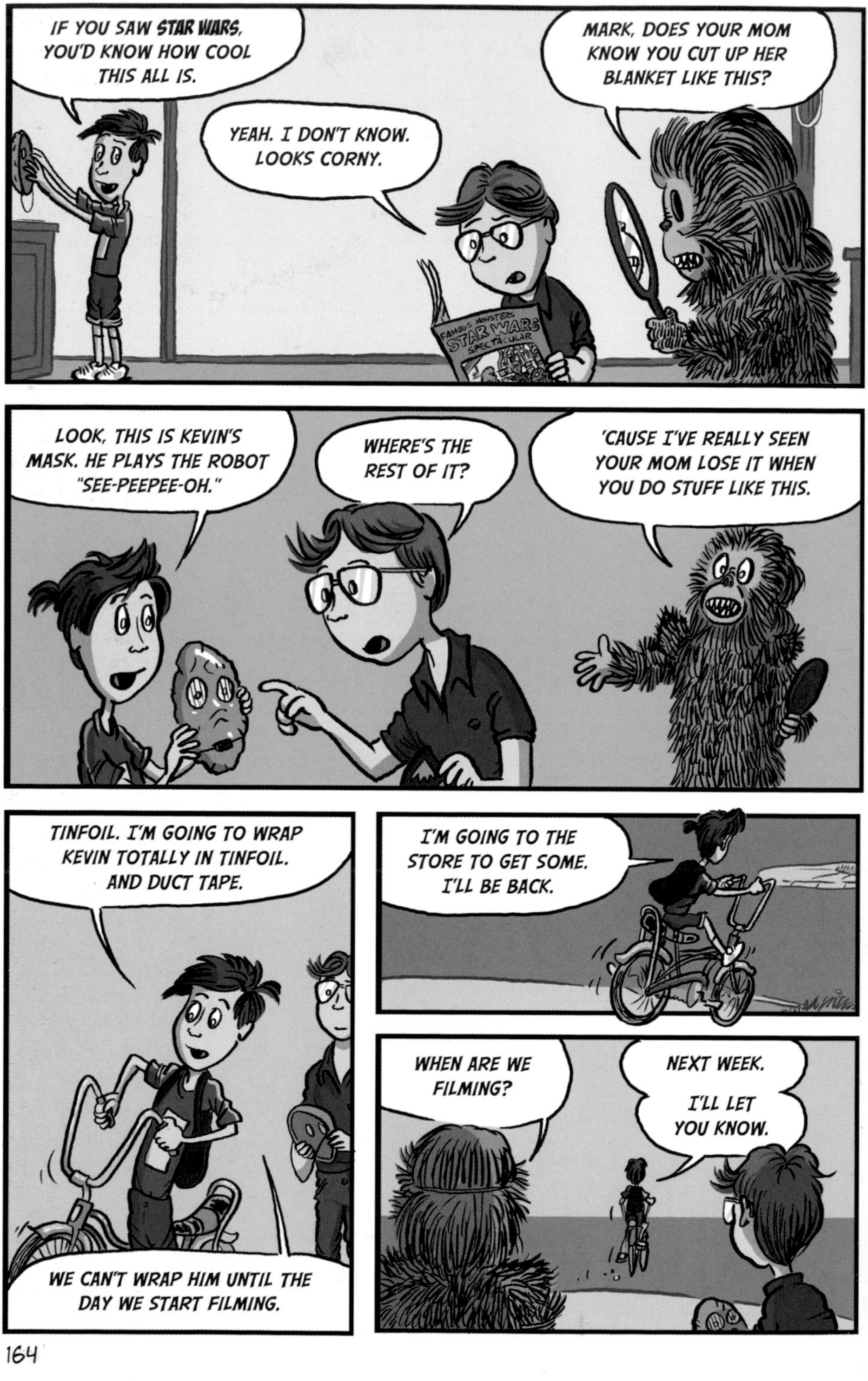
IF YOU SAW STAR WARS, YOU'D KNOW HOW COOL THIS ALL IS.
YEAH. I DON'T KNOW. LOOKS CORNY.
MARK, DOES YOUR MOM KNOW YOU CUT UP HER BLANKET LIKE THIS?
FAMOUS MONSTERS STAR WARS SPECTACULAR
LOOK, THIS IS KEVIN'S MASK. HE PLAYS THE ROBOT "SEE-PEEPEE-OH."
WHERE'S THE REST OF IT?
'CAUSE I'VE REALLY SEEN YOUR MOM LOSE IT WHEN YOU DO STUFF LIKE THIS.
TINFOIL. I'M GOING TO WRAP KEVIN TOTALLY IN TINFOIL. AND DUCT TAPE.
WE CAN'T WRAP HIM UNTIL THE DAY WE START FILMING.
I'M GOING TO THE STORE TO GET SOME. I'LL BE BACK.
WHEN ARE WE FILMING?
NEXT WEEK.
I'LL LET YOU KNOW.

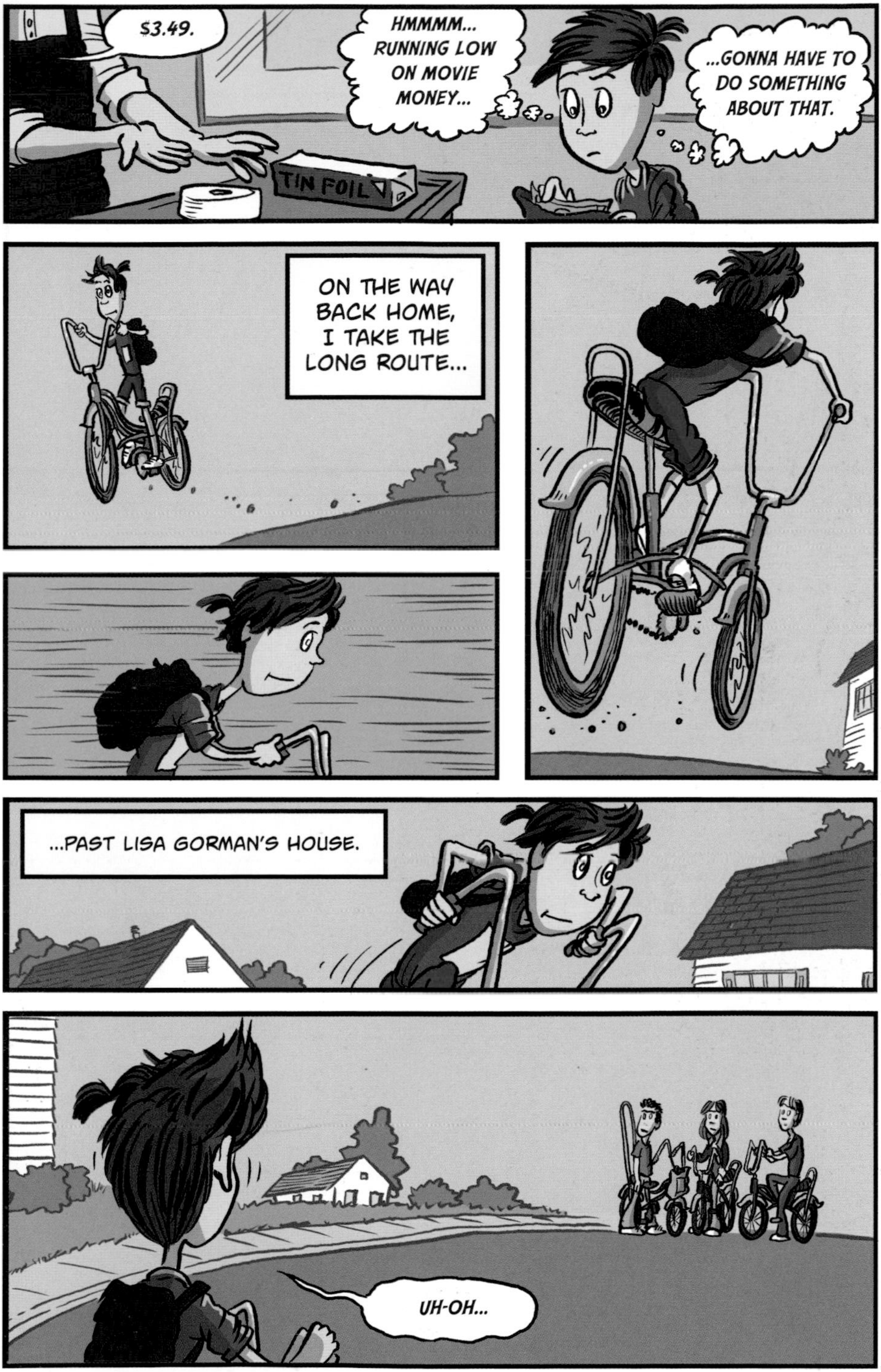
$3.49.
HMMMM... RUNNING LOW ON MOVIE MONEY...
...GONNA HAVE TO DO SOMETHING ABOUT THAT.
TIN FOIL
ON THE WAY BACK HOME, I TAKE THE LONG ROUTE...
...PAST LISA GORMAN'S HOUSE.
UH-OH...

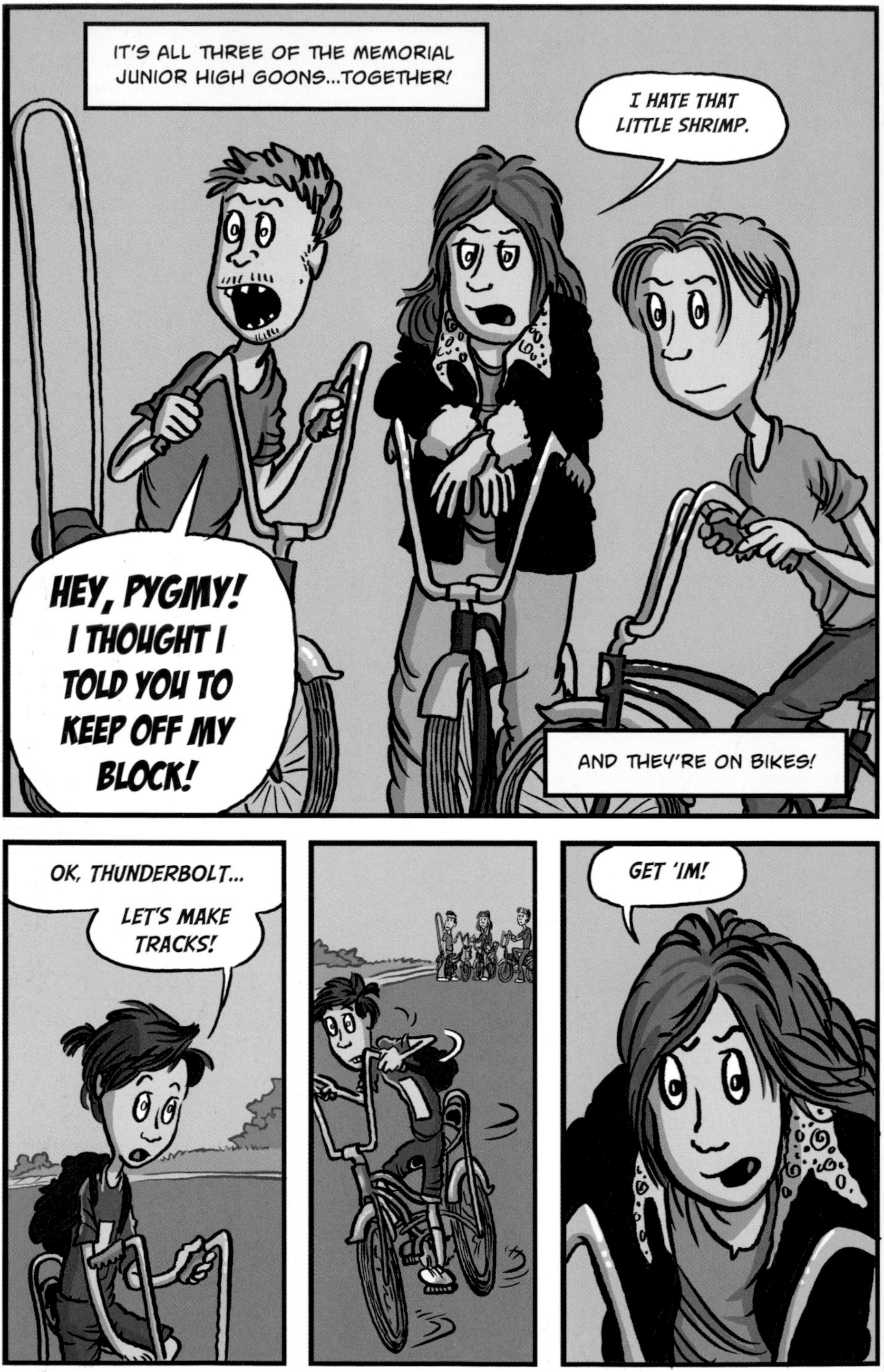
IT'S ALL THREE OF THE MEMORIAL JUNIOR HIGH GOONS...TOGETHER!
I HATE THAT LITTLE SHRIMP.
HEY, PYGMY! I THOUGHT I TOLD YOU TO KEEP OFF MY BLOCK!
AND THEY'RE ON BIKES!
OK, THUNDERBOLT...
LET'S MAKE TRACKS!
GET 'IM!

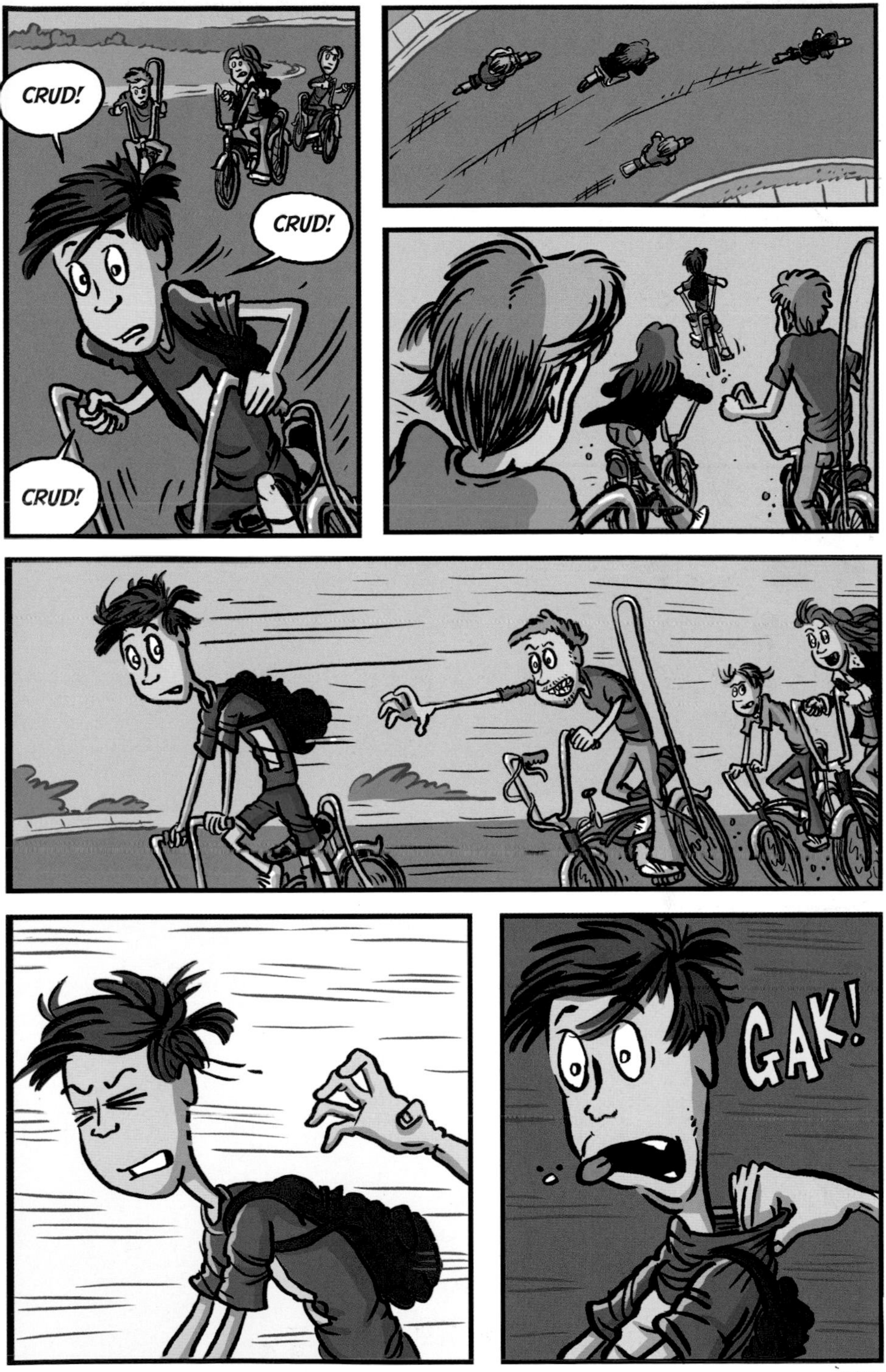
CRUD!
CRUD!
CRUD!
GAK!

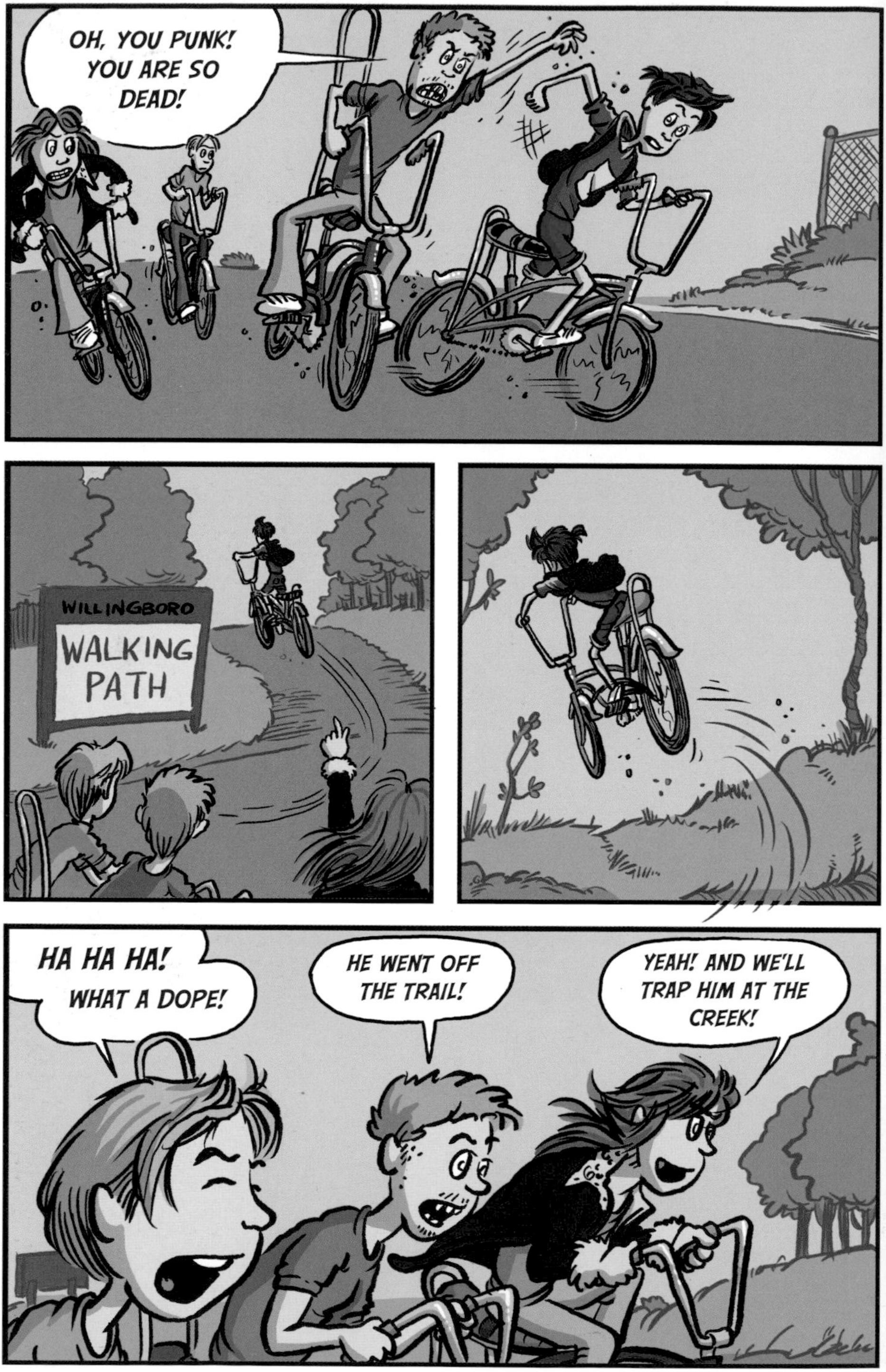
OH, YOU PUNK! YOU ARE SO DEAD!
WILLINGBORO
WALKING PATH
HA HA HA! WHAT A DOPE!
HE WENT OFF THE TRAIL!
YEAH! AND WE'LL TRAP HIM AT THE CREEK!

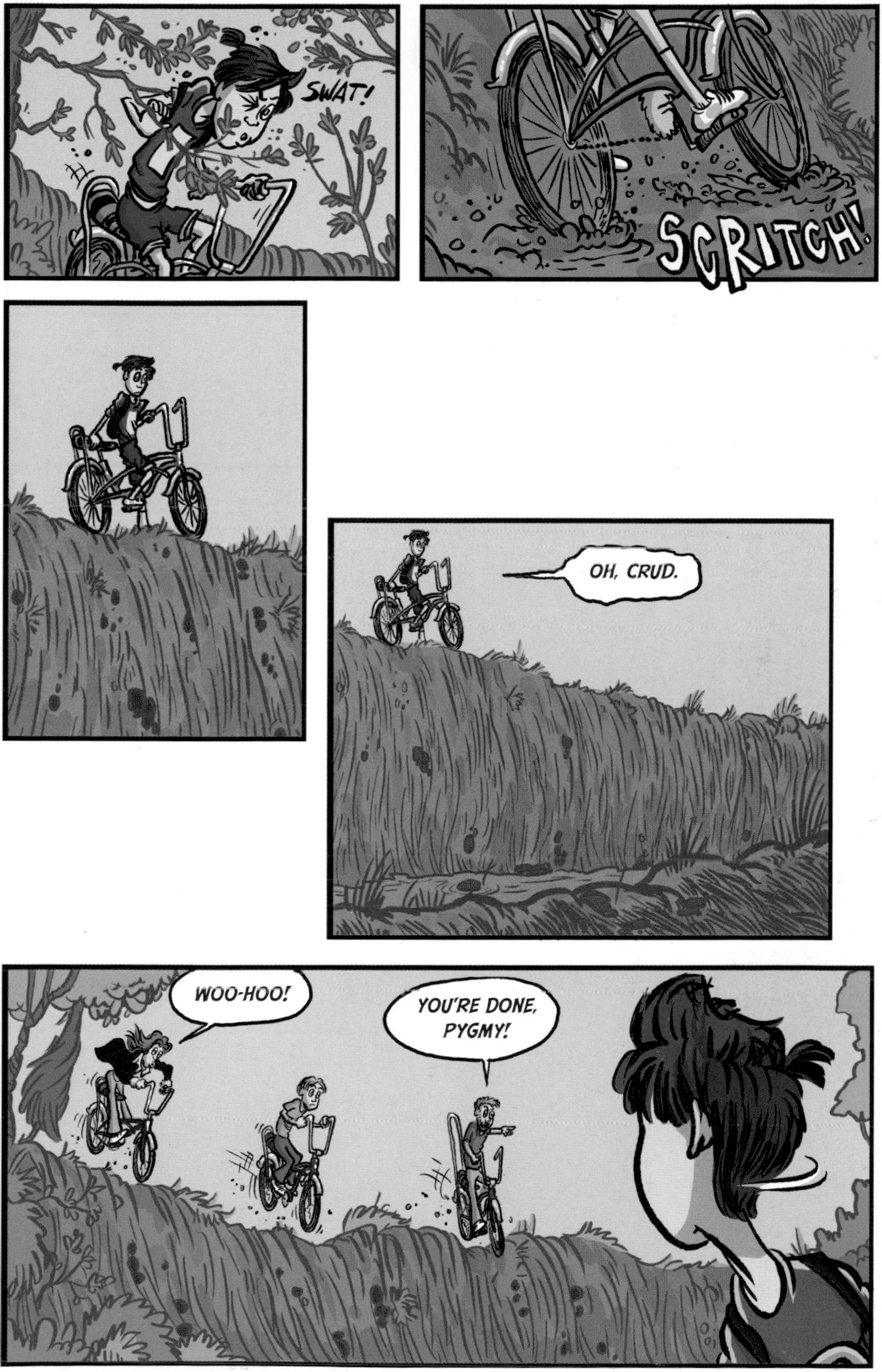
SWAT!
SCRITCH!
OH, CRUD.
WOO-HOO!
YOU'RE DONE, PYGMY!

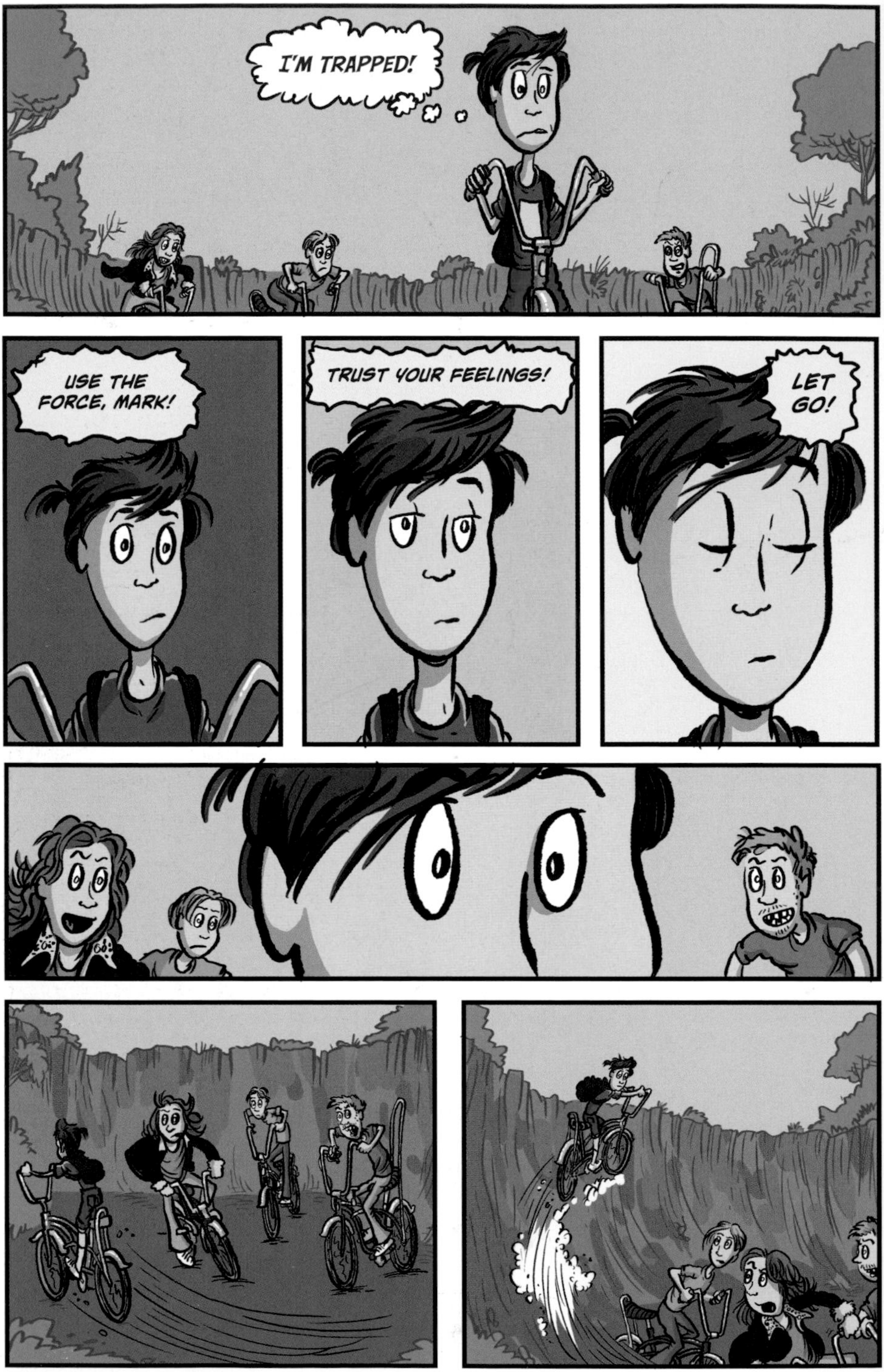
I'M TRAPPED!
USE THE FORCE, MARK!
TRUST YOUR FEELINGS!
LET GO!

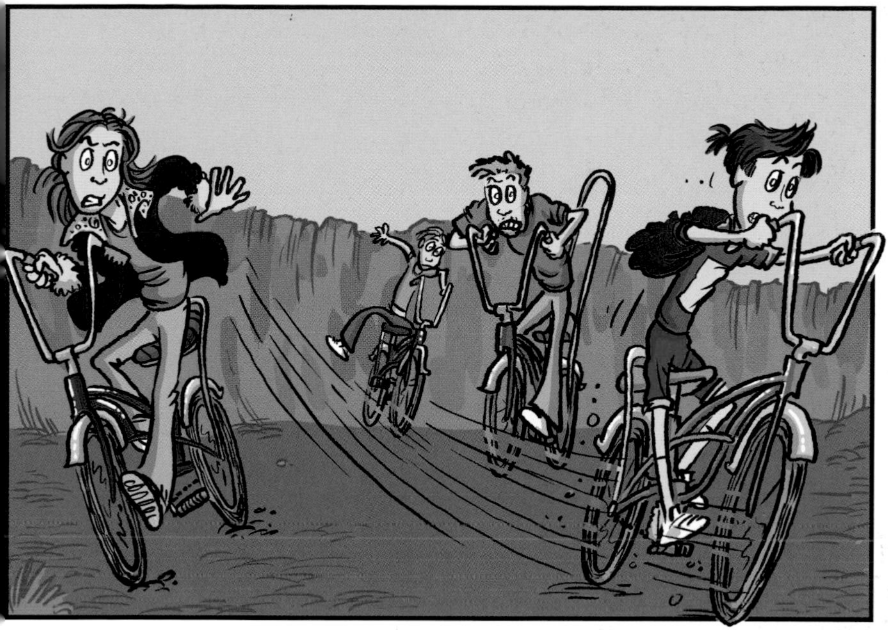

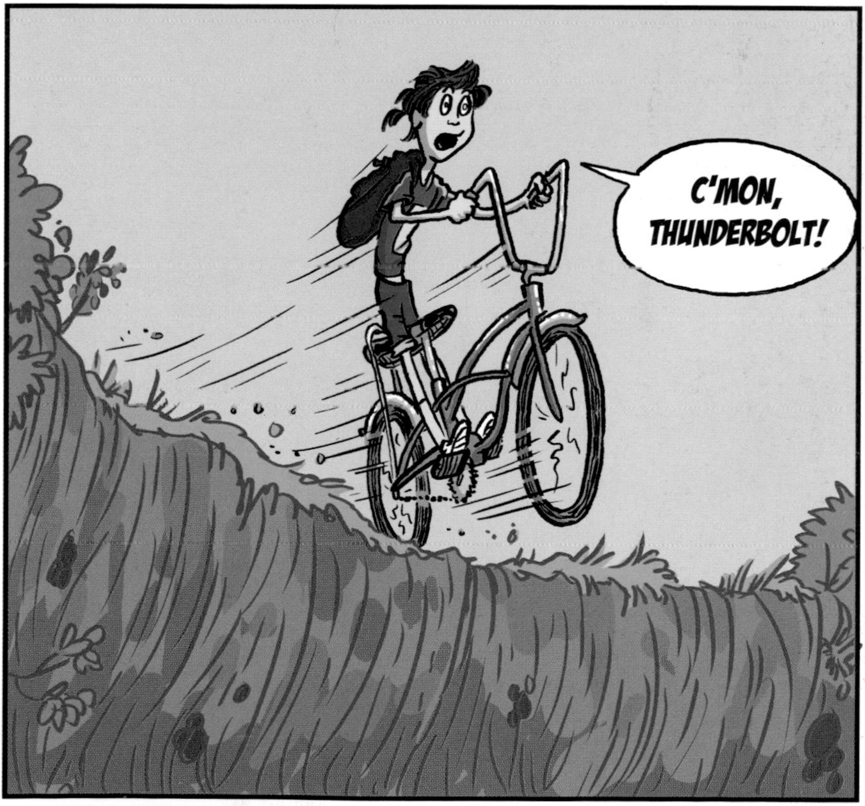
C'MON, THUNDERBOLT!

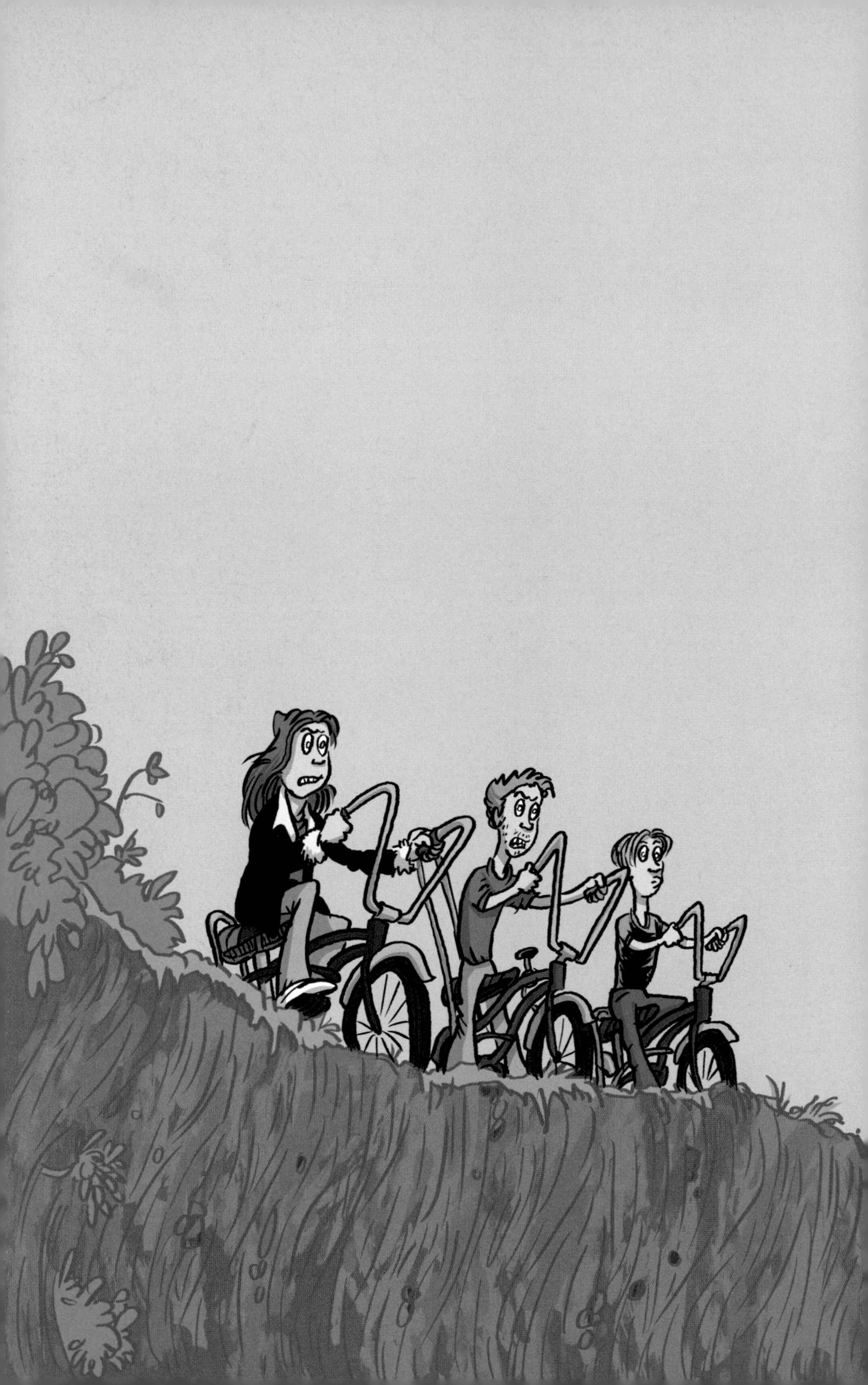

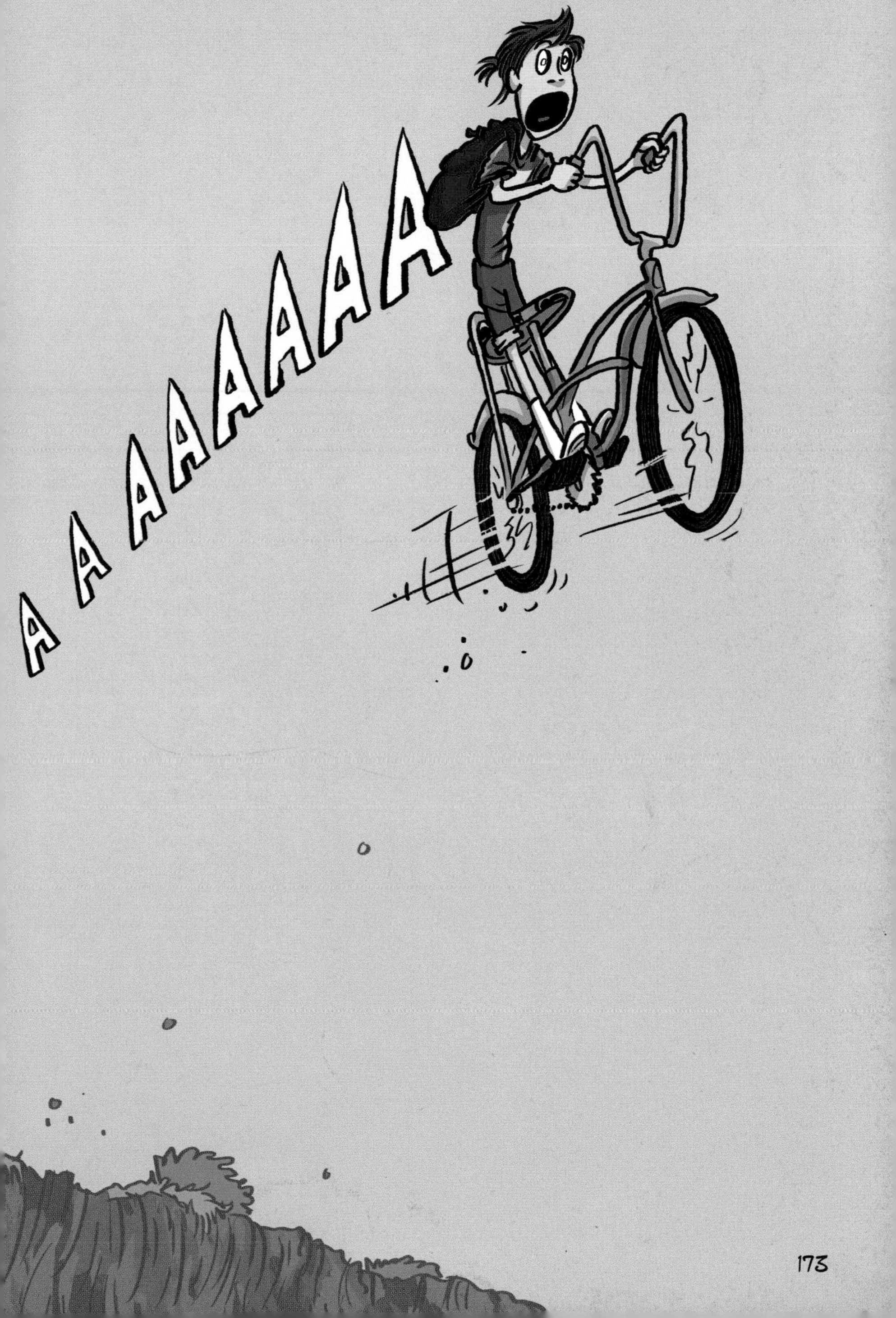
A A AAAAAAA

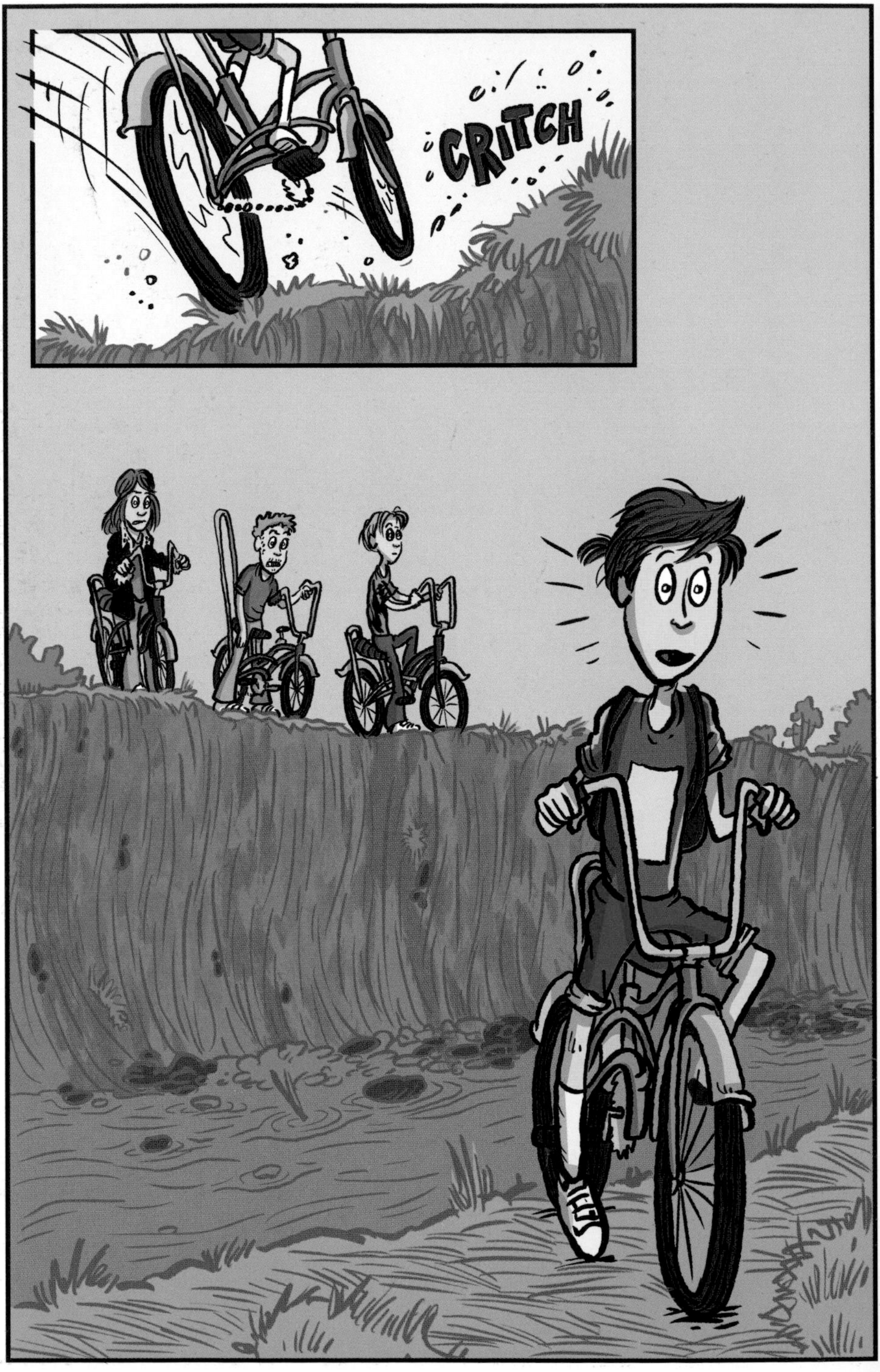
CRITCH

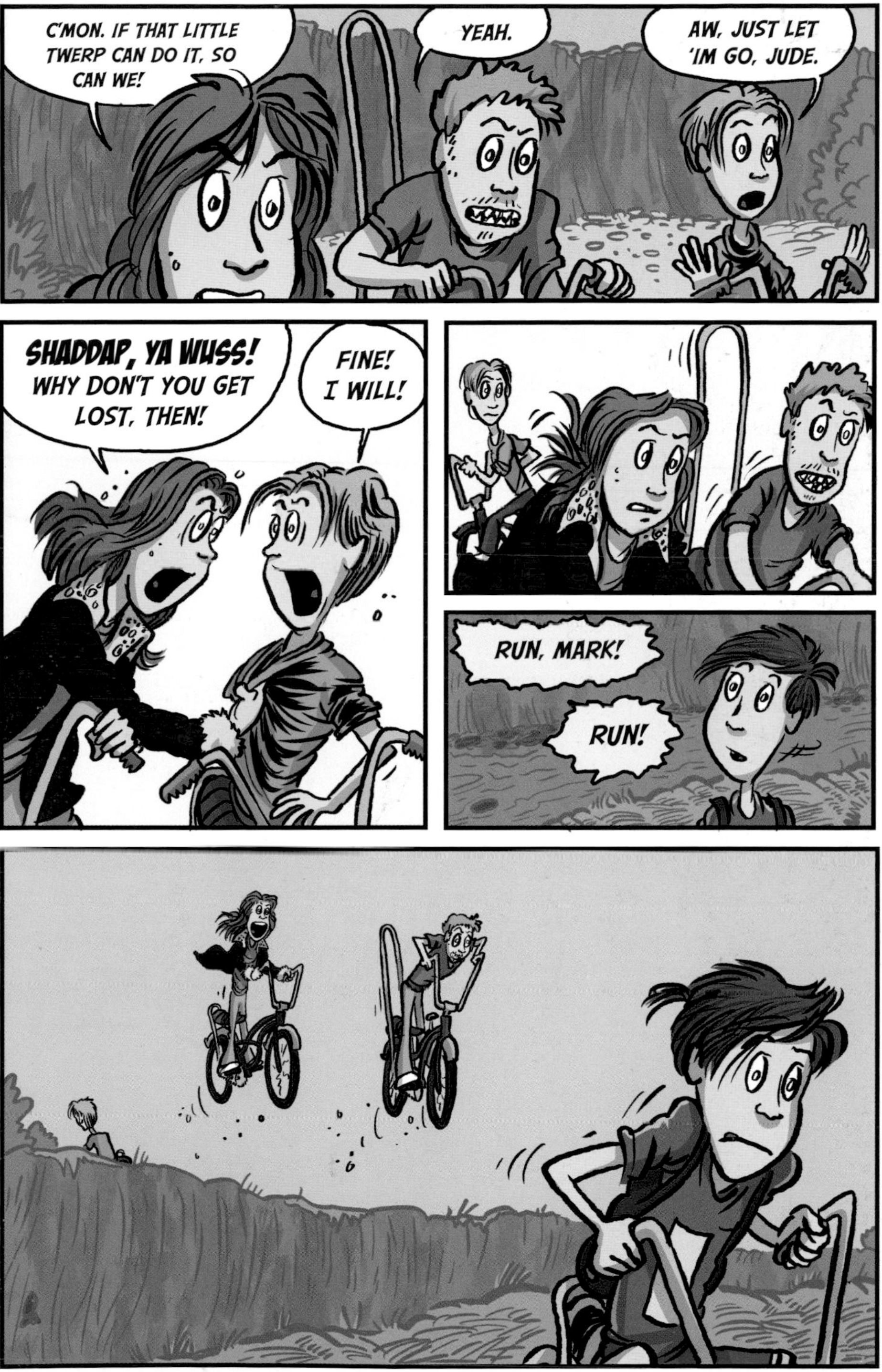
C'MON. IF THAT LITTLE TWERP CAN DO IT, SO CAN WE!
YEAH.
AW, JUST LET 'IM GO, JUDE.
SHADDAP, YA WUSS! WHY DON'T YOU GET LOST, THEN!
FINE! I WILL!
RUN, MARK!
RUN!

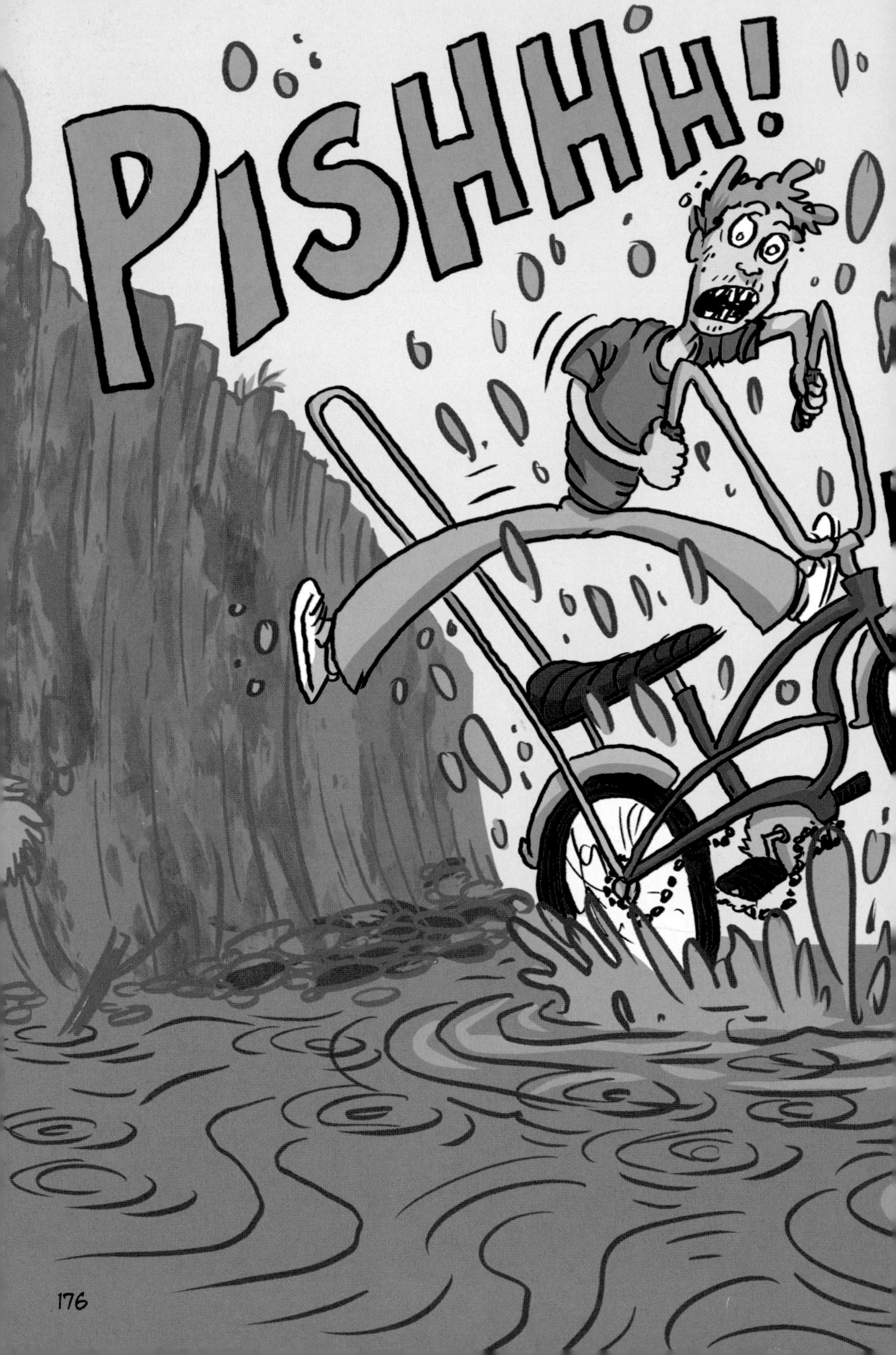
PISHHH!

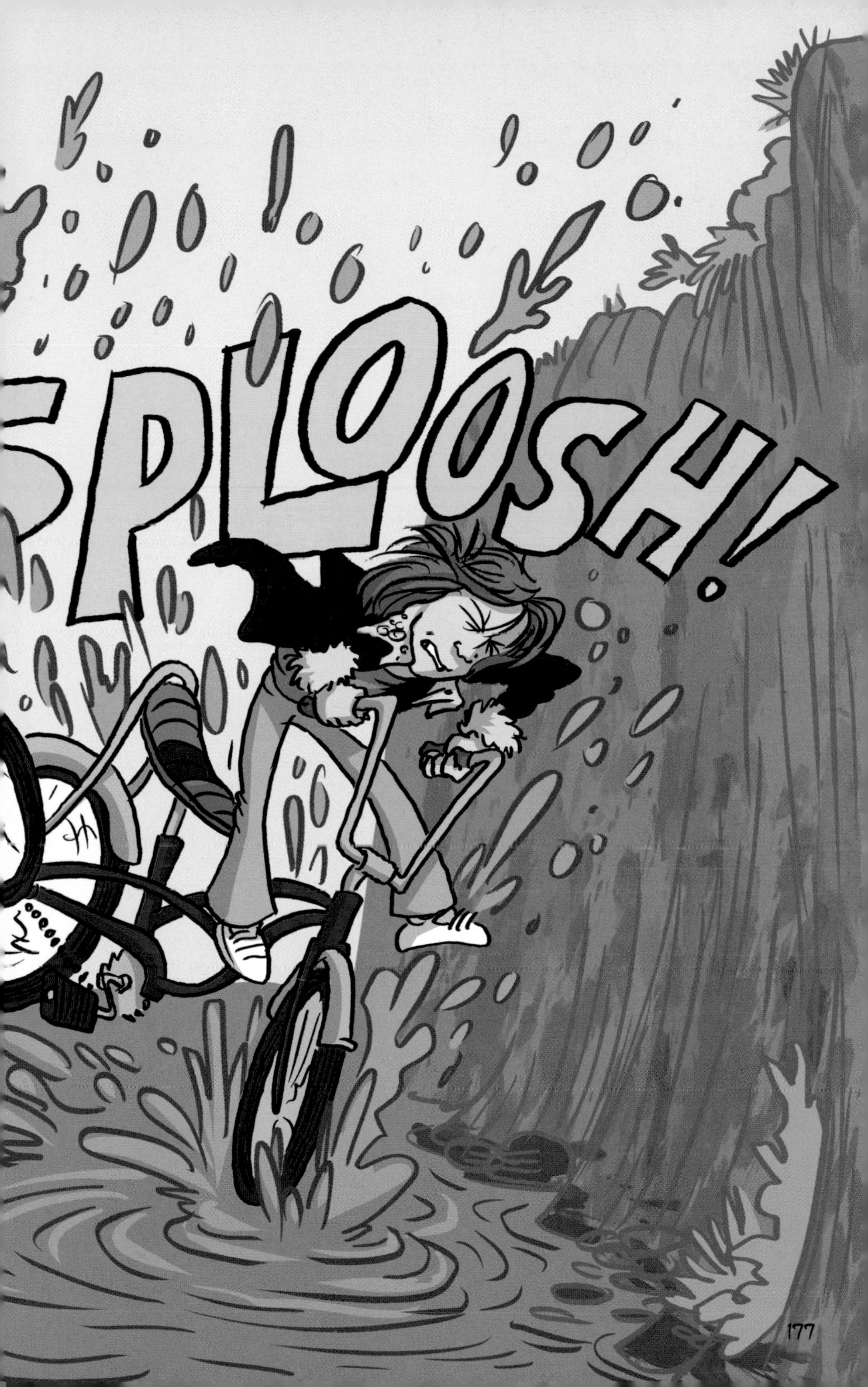
SPLOOSH!

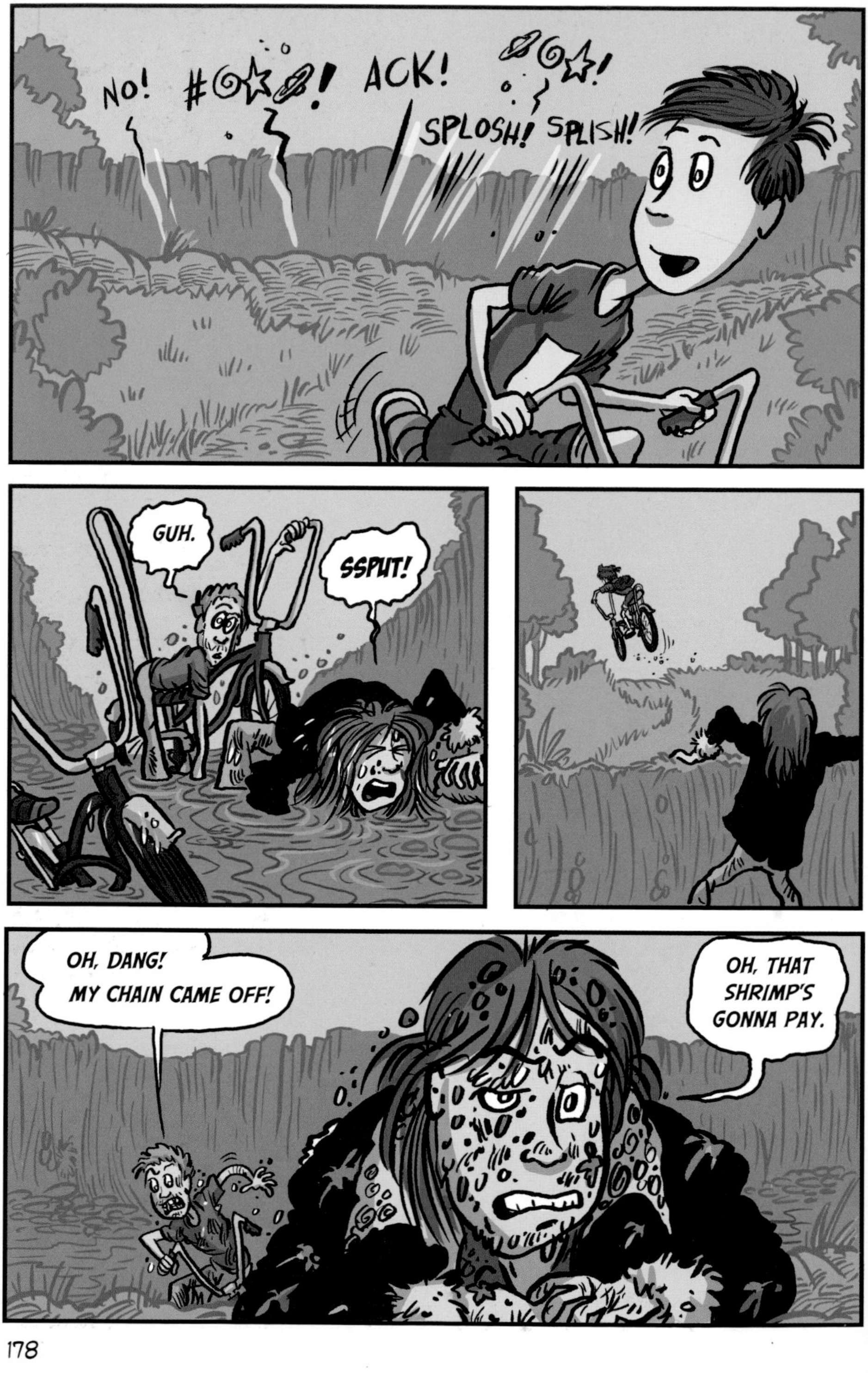
NO!
#@☆@!
ACK!
@@☆!
SPLOSH! SPLISH!
GUH.
SSPUT!
OH, DANG!
MY CHAIN CAME OFF!
OH, THAT SHRIMP'S GONNA PAY.

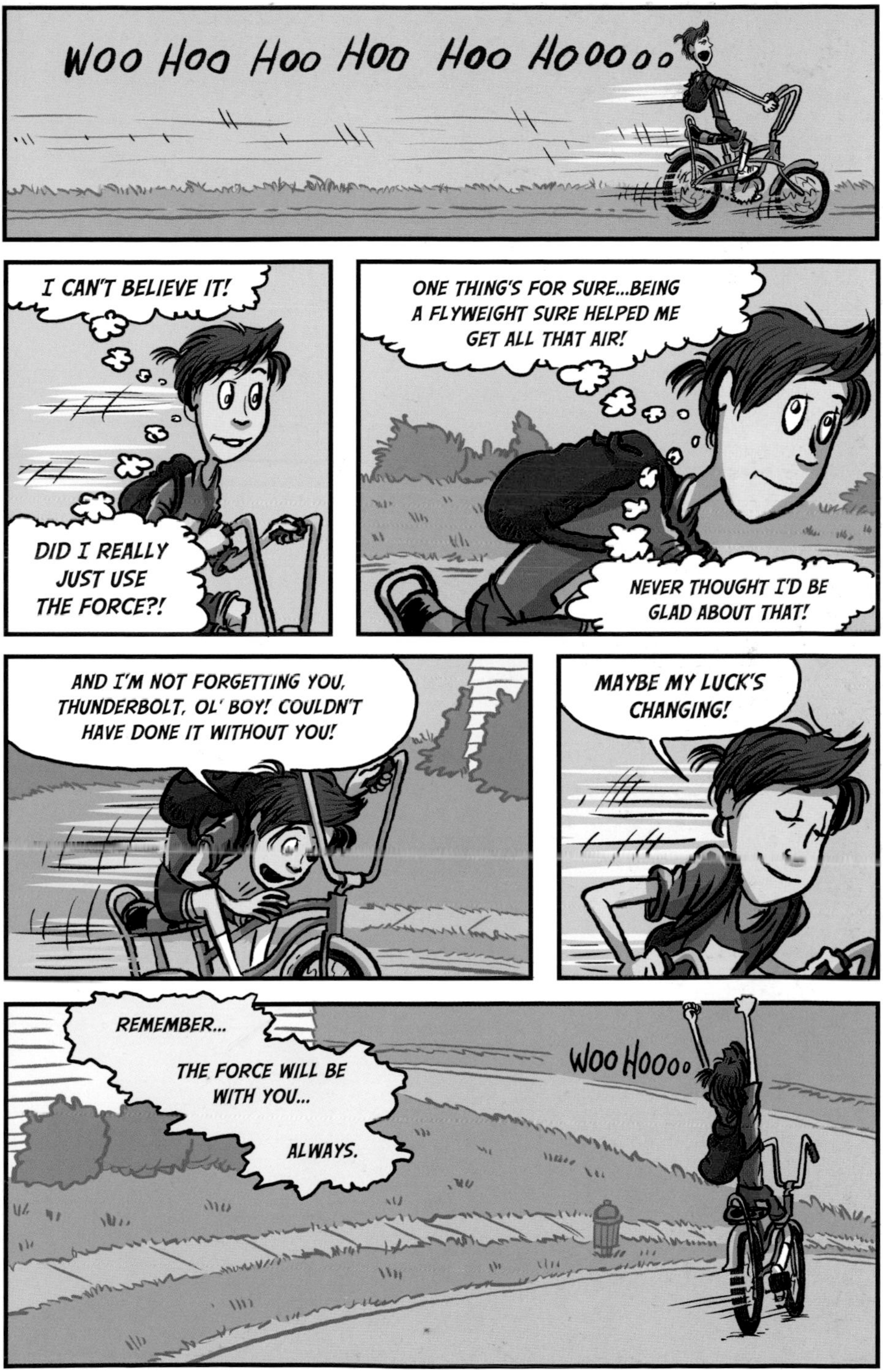
WOO HOO HOO HOO HOO HOOOOO
I CAN'T BELIEVE IT!
DID I REALLY JUST USE THE FORCE?!
ONE THING'S FOR SURE...BEING A FLYWEIGHT SURE HELPED ME GET ALL THAT AIR!
NEVER THOUGHT I'D BE GLAD ABOUT THAT!
AND I'M NOT FORGETTING YOU, THUNDERBOLT, OL' BOY! COULDN'T HAVE DONE IT WITHOUT YOU!
MAYBE MY LUCK'S CHANGING!
REMEMBER...
THE FORCE WILL BE WITH YOU...
ALWAYS.
WOO HOOOO

CHAPTER 11

CUT!
AND I COULD SURE USE SOME OF THAT FORCE NOW THAT WE STARTED FILMING "STAR BORES"!
TIN FOIL

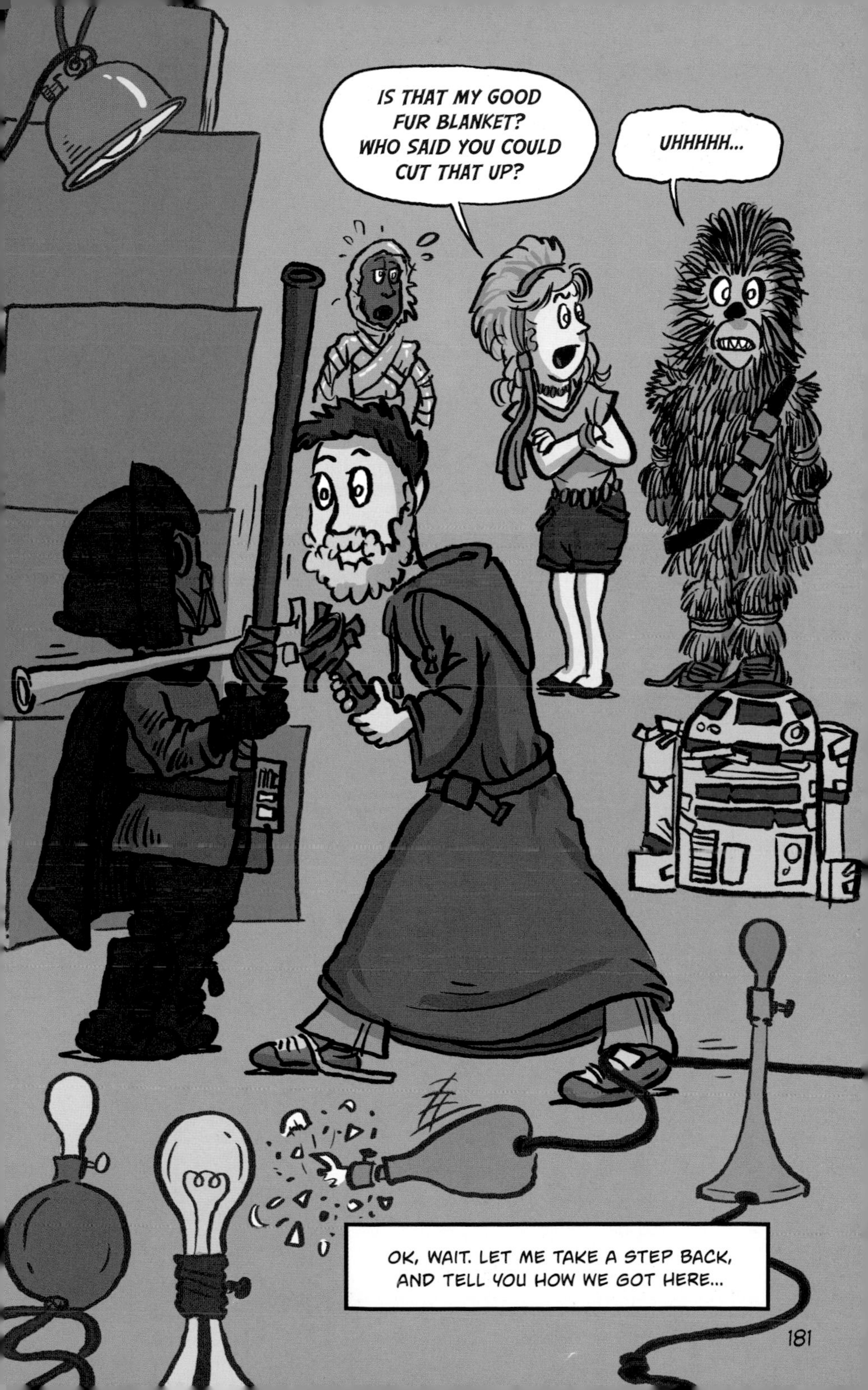
IS THAT MY GOOD FUR BLANKET? WHO SAID YOU COULD CUT THAT UP?
UHHHHH...
OK, WAIT. LET ME TAKE A STEP BACK, AND TELL YOU HOW WE GOT HERE...

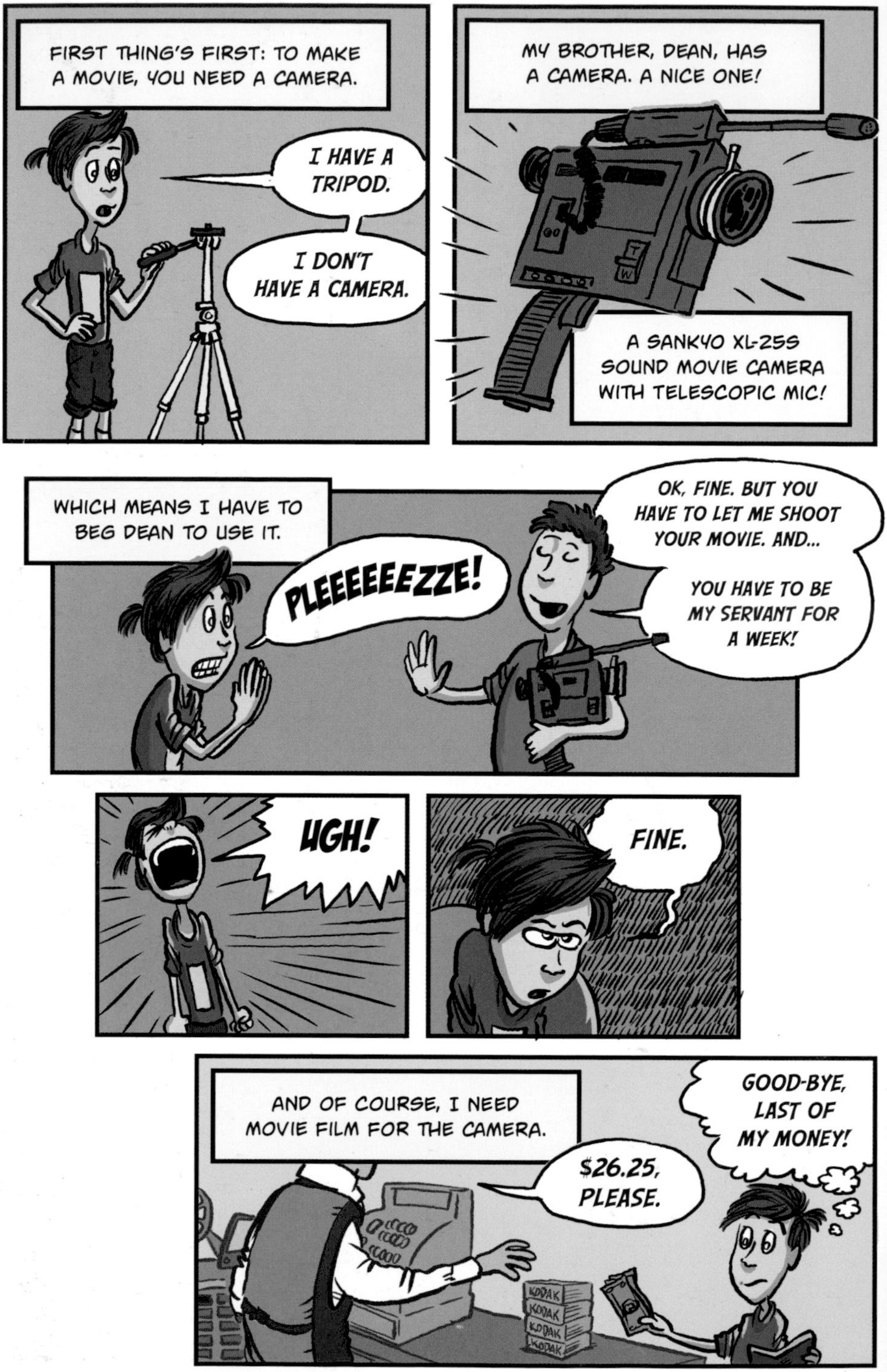
FIRST THING'S FIRST: TO MAKE A MOVIE, YOU NEED A CAMERA.
I HAVE A TRIPOD.
I DON'T HAVE A CAMERA.
MY BROTHER, DEAN, HAS A CAMERA. A NICE ONE!
A SANKYO XL-25S SOUND MOVIE CAMERA WITH TELESCOPIC MIC!
WHICH MEANS I HAVE TO BEG DEAN TO USE IT.
PLEEEEEEZZE!
OK, FINE. BUT YOU HAVE TO LET ME SHOOT YOUR MOVIE. AND...
YOU HAVE TO BE MY SERVANT FOR A WEEK!
UGH!
FINE.
AND OF COURSE, I NEED MOVIE FILM FOR THE CAMERA.
$26.25, PLEASE.
GOOD-BYE, LAST OF MY MONEY!
KODAK
KODAK
KODAK
KODAK

AND THEN, THE SETS...

HOW AM I GOING TO MAKE ALL THESE SETS?

INSIDE THE DEATH STAR, THE SPACESHIPS...

BOXES!

UH... OKAAY?

MY DAD HAS WORKED ON LOTS OF TV COMMERCIALS, SO I LISTEN TO HIS IDEA...

LOOK, I CAN GET YOU A BUNCH OF SQUARE MOVING BOXES...

THEN STACK THE BOXES TO MAKE THE BACKGROUND!

yellow

Gray

Blue

PAINT EACH SIDE A DIFFERENT COLOR.

Camera

Actors

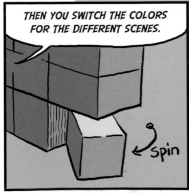

THEN YOU SWITCH THE COLORS FOR THE DIFFERENT SCENES.

Spin

IN A MOVIE LIKE THIS, PEOPLE AREN'T LOOKING AT THE BACKGROUND SO MUCH. THEY'RE WATCHING THE ACTORS!

HMMMMM...

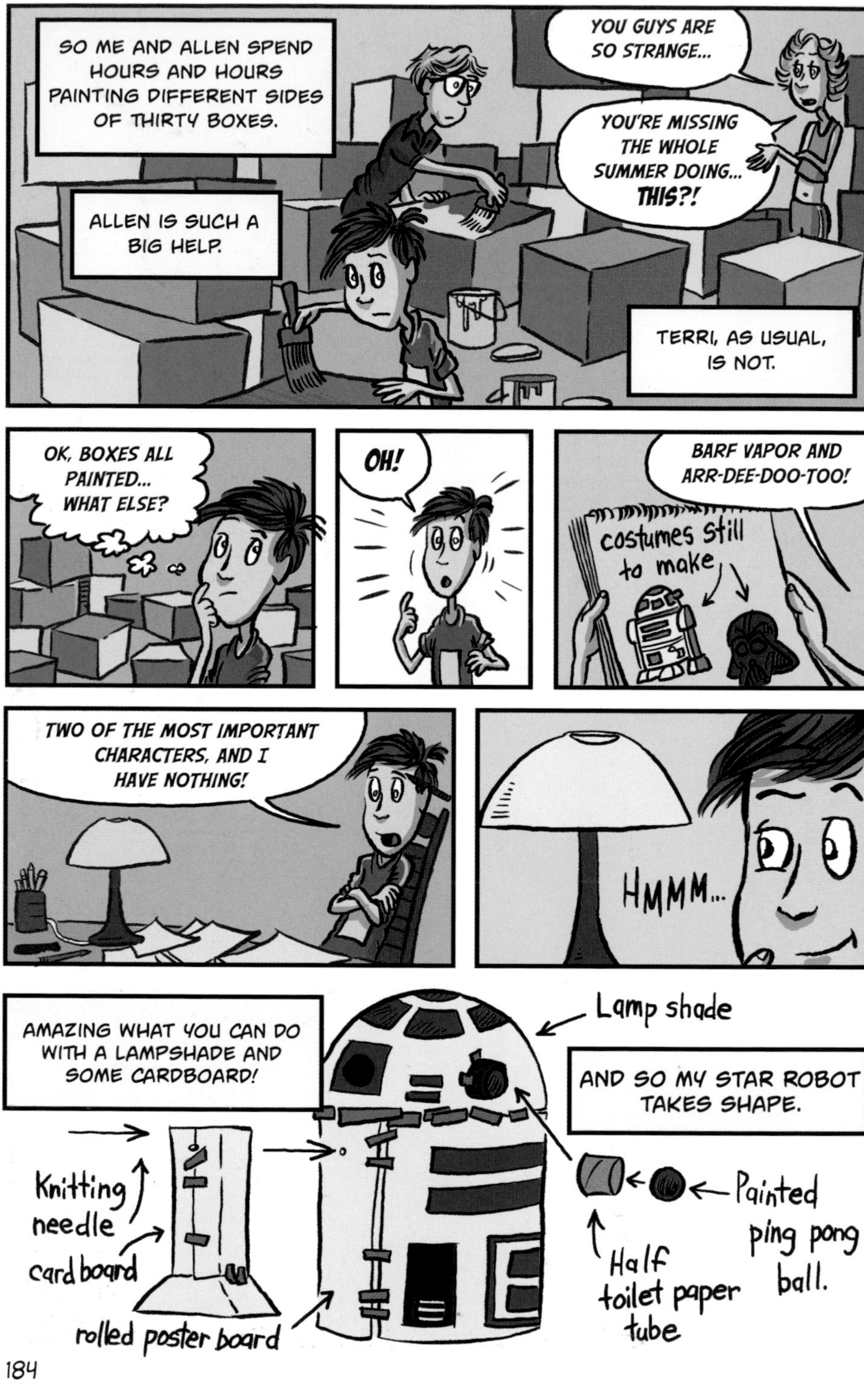

SO ME AND ALLEN SPEND HOURS AND HOURS PAINTING DIFFERENT SIDES OF THIRTY BOXES.
YOU GUYS ARE SO STRANGE...
YOU'RE MISSING THE WHOLE SUMMER DOING... THIS?!
ALLEN IS SUCH A BIG HELP.
TERRI, AS USUAL, IS NOT.
OK, BOXES ALL PAINTED... WHAT ELSE?
OH!
BARF VAPOR AND ARR-DEE-DOO-TOO!
costumes still to make
TWO OF THE MOST IMPORTANT CHARACTERS, AND I HAVE NOTHING!
HMMM...
AMAZING WHAT YOU CAN DO WITH A LAMPSHADE AND SOME CARDBOARD!
Lamp shade
AND SO MY STAR ROBOT TAKES SHAPE.
Knitting needle
card board
rolled poster board
Half toilet paper tube
Painted ping pong ball.

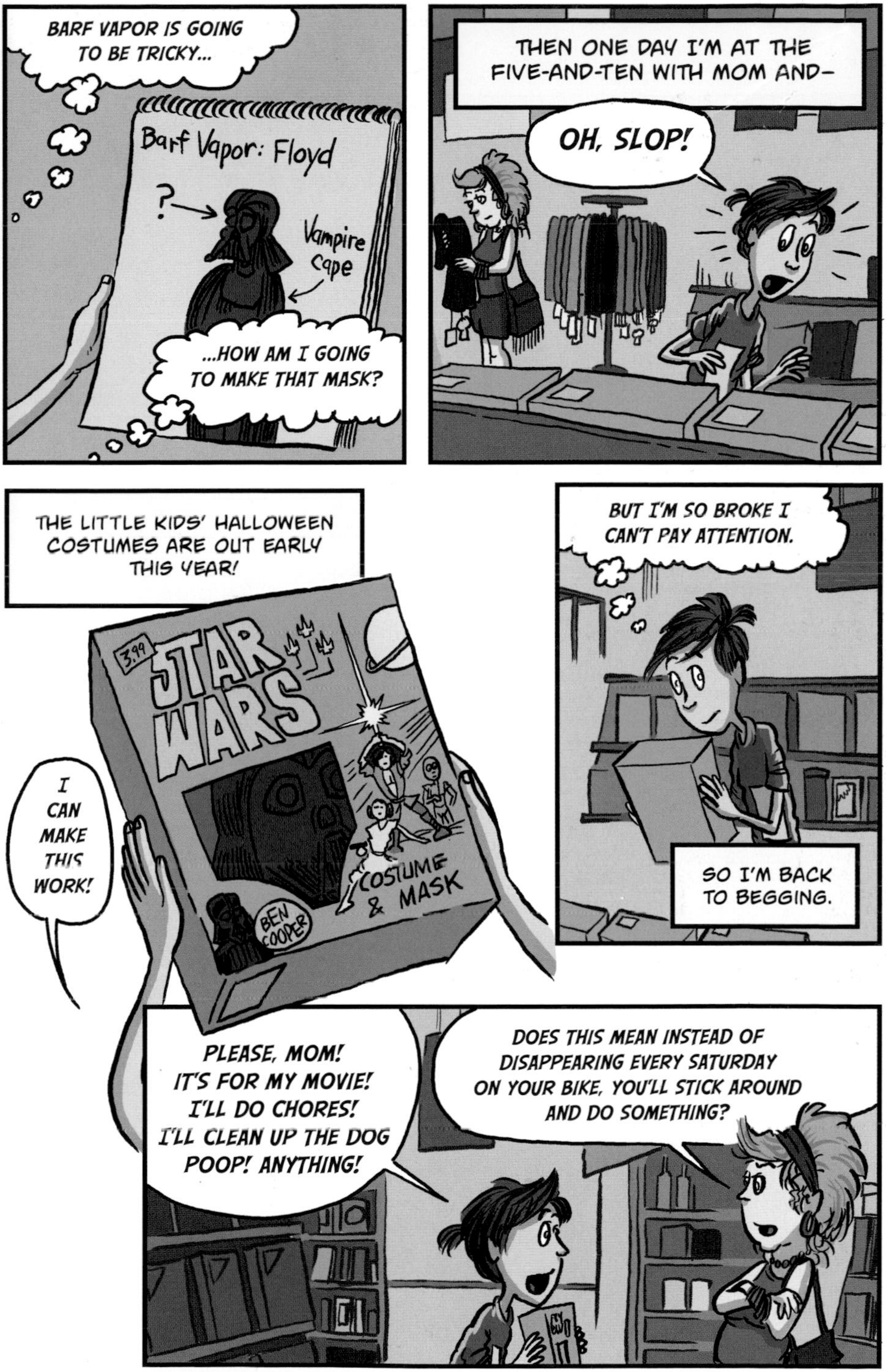
BARF VAPOR IS GOING TO BE TRICKY...
Barf Vapor: Floyd
?
Vampire Cape
...HOW AM I GOING TO MAKE THAT MASK?
THEN ONE DAY I'M AT THE FIVE-AND-TEN WITH MOM AND—
OH, SLOP!
THE LITTLE KIDS' HALLOWEEN COSTUMES ARE OUT EARLY THIS YEAR!
3.99
STAR WARS
COSTUME & MASK
BEN COOPER
I CAN MAKE THIS WORK!
BUT I'M SO BROKE I CAN'T PAY ATTENTION.
SO I'M BACK TO BEGGING.
PLEASE, MOM! IT'S FOR MY MOVIE! I'LL DO CHORES! I'LL CLEAN UP THE DOG POOP! ANYTHING!
DOES THIS MEAN INSTEAD OF DISAPPEARING EVERY SATURDAY ON YOUR BIKE, YOU'LL STICK AROUND AND DO SOMETHING?

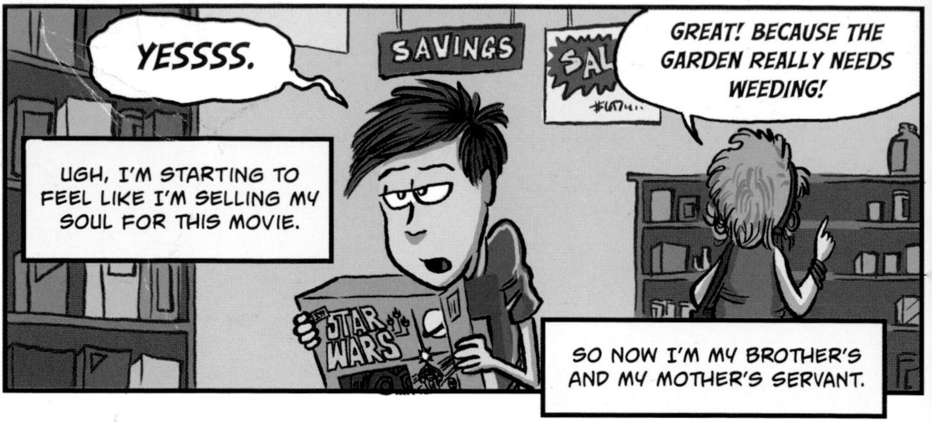
YESSSS.
SAVINGS
GREAT! BECAUSE THE GARDEN REALLY NEEDS WEEDING!
UGH, I'M STARTING TO FEEL LIKE I'M SELLING MY SOUL FOR THIS MOVIE.
STAR WARS
SO NOW I'M MY BROTHER'S AND MY MOTHER'S SERVANT.

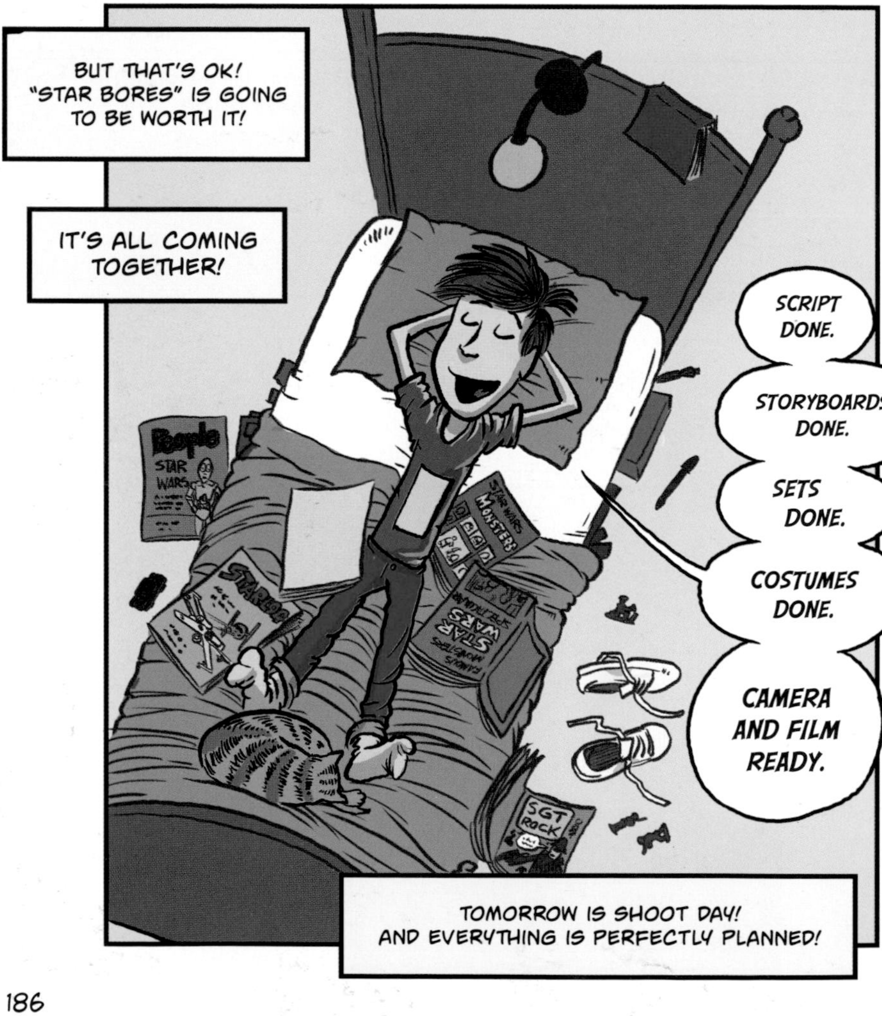
BUT THAT'S OK! "STAR BORES" IS GOING TO BE WORTH IT!
IT'S ALL COMING TOGETHER!
SCRIPT DONE.
STORYBOARDS DONE.
SETS DONE.
COSTUMES DONE.
CAMERA AND FILM READY.
People
STAR WARS
SGT ROCK
TOMORROW IS SHOOT DAY! AND EVERYTHING IS PERFECTLY PLANNED!

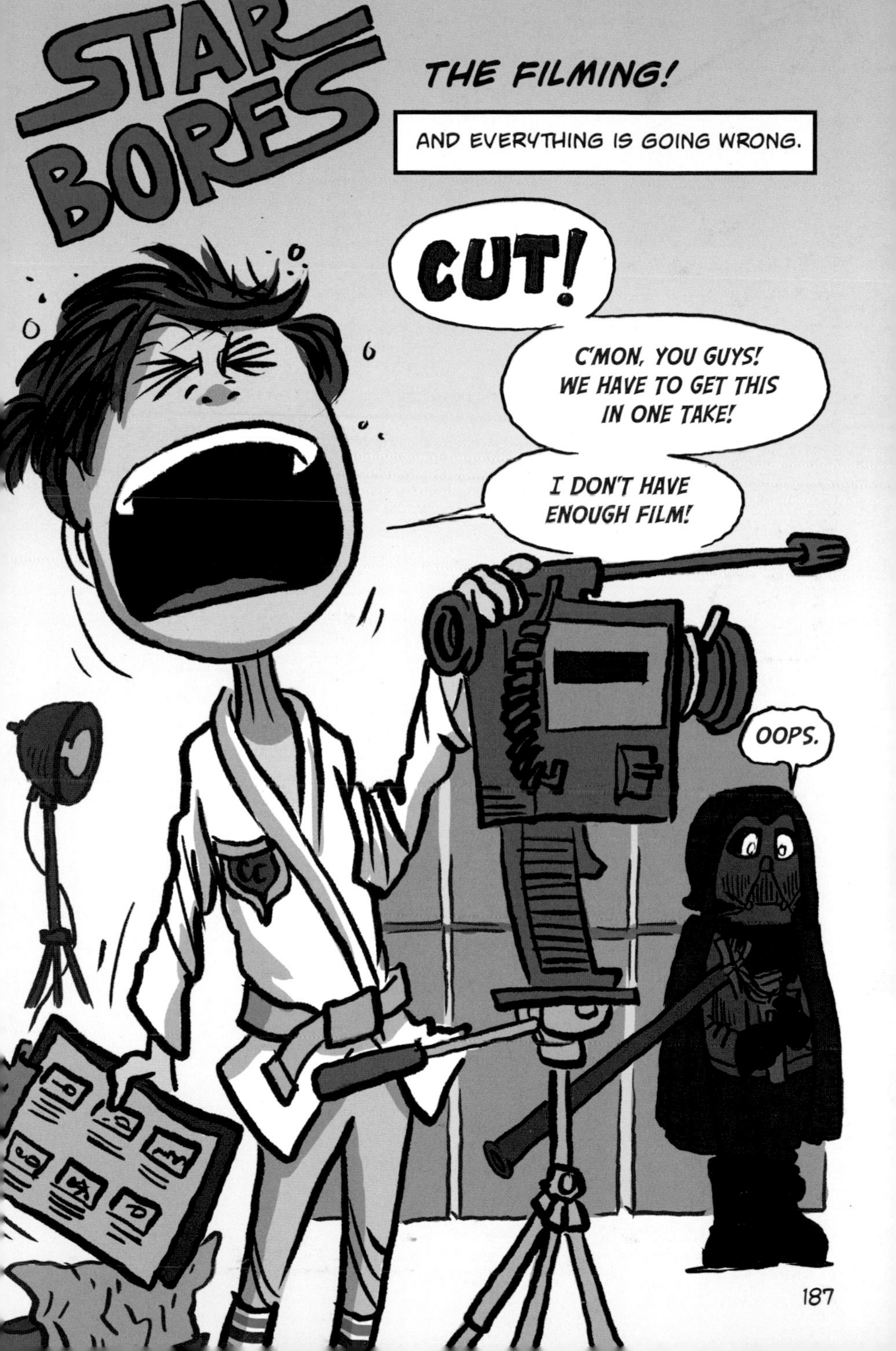
STAR BORES
THE FILMING!
AND EVERYTHING IS GOING WRONG.
CUT!
C'MON, YOU GUYS! WE HAVE TO GET THIS IN ONE TAKE!
I DON'T HAVE ENOUGH FILM!
OOPS.

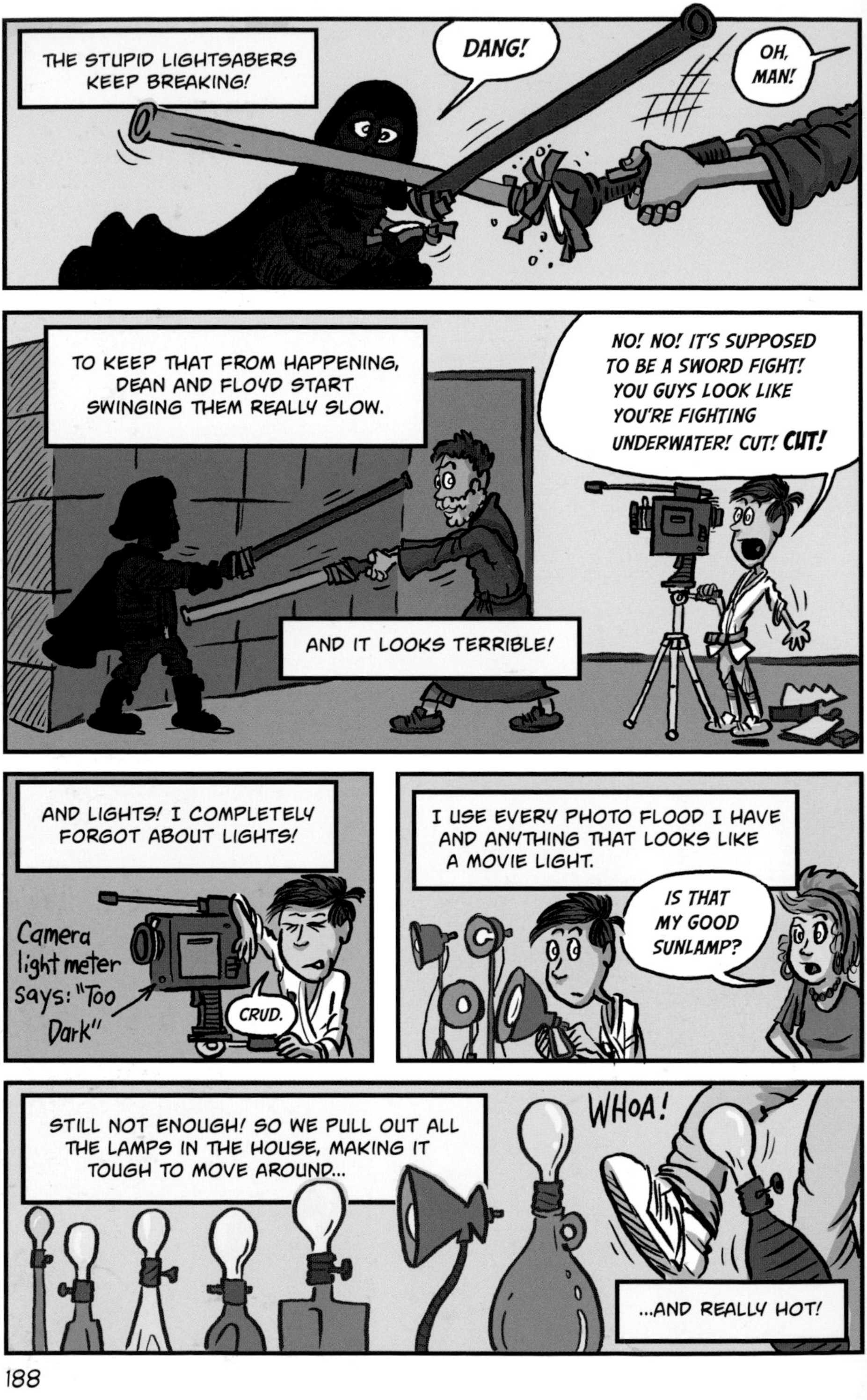
THE STUPID LIGHTSABERS KEEP BREAKING!
DANG!
OH, MAN!
TO KEEP THAT FROM HAPPENING, DEAN AND FLOYD START SWINGING THEM REALLY SLOW.
NO! NO! IT'S SUPPOSED TO BE A SWORD FIGHT! YOU GUYS LOOK LIKE YOU'RE FIGHTING UNDERWATER! CUT! CUT!
AND IT LOOKS TERRIBLE!
AND LIGHTS! I COMPLETELY FORGOT ABOUT LIGHTS!
Camera light meter says: "Too Dark"
CRUD.
I USE EVERY PHOTO FLOOD I HAVE AND ANYTHING THAT LOOKS LIKE A MOVIE LIGHT.
IS THAT MY GOOD SUNLAMP?
STILL NOT ENOUGH! SO WE PULL OUT ALL THE LAMPS IN THE HOUSE, MAKING IT TOUGH TO MOVE AROUND...
WHOA!
...AND REALLY HOT!

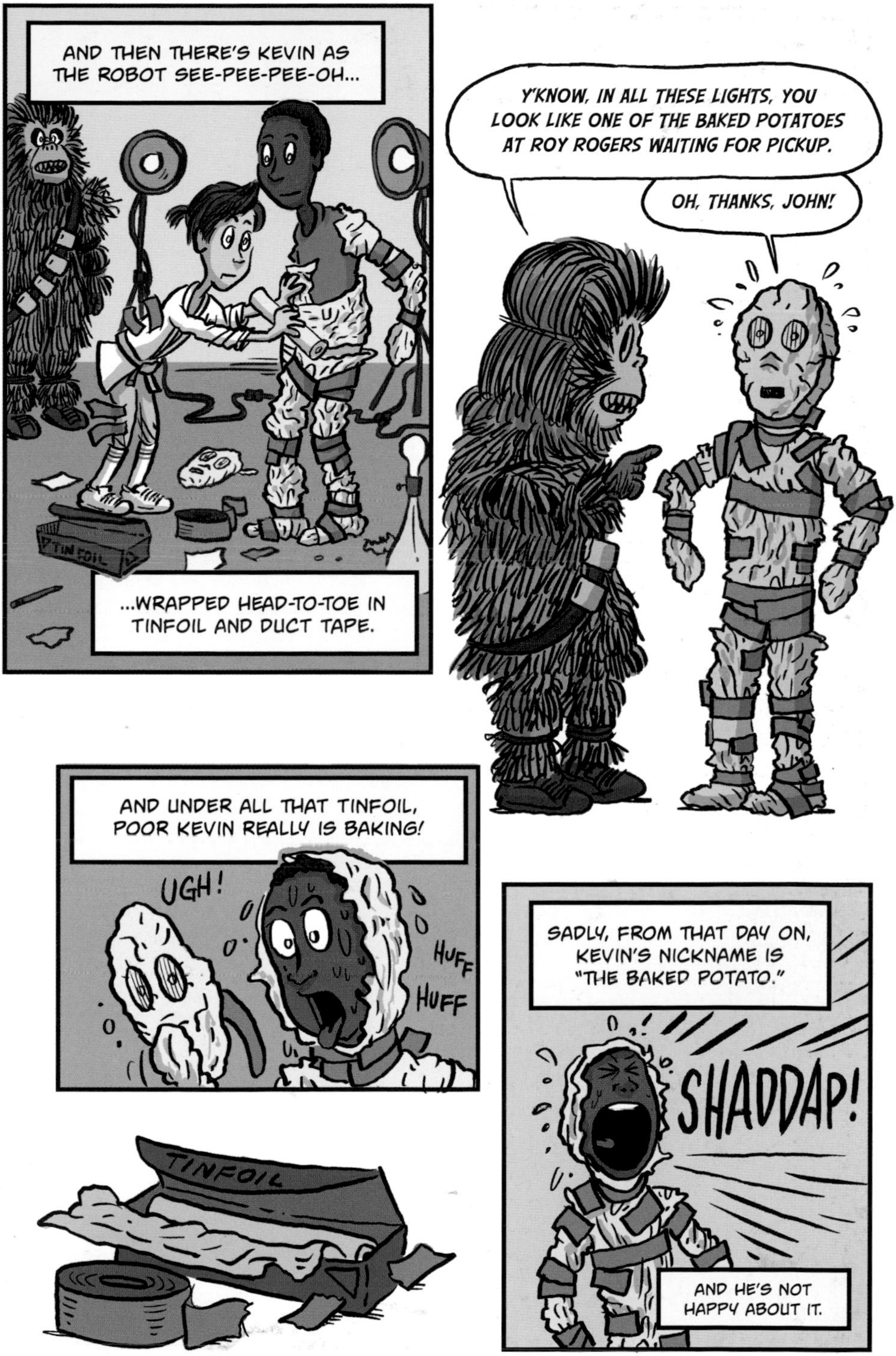

AND THEN THERE'S KEVIN AS THE ROBOT SEE-PEE-PEE-OH...
TINFOIL
...WRAPPED HEAD-TO-TOE IN TINFOIL AND DUCT TAPE.
Y'KNOW, IN ALL THESE LIGHTS, YOU LOOK LIKE ONE OF THE BAKED POTATOES AT ROY ROGERS WAITING FOR PICKUP.
OH, THANKS, JOHN!
AND UNDER ALL THAT TINFOIL, POOR KEVIN REALLY IS BAKING!
UGH!
HUFF
HUFF
TINFOIL
SADLY, FROM THAT DAY ON, KEVIN'S NICKNAME IS "THE BAKED POTATO."
SHADDAP!
AND HE'S NOT HAPPY ABOUT IT.

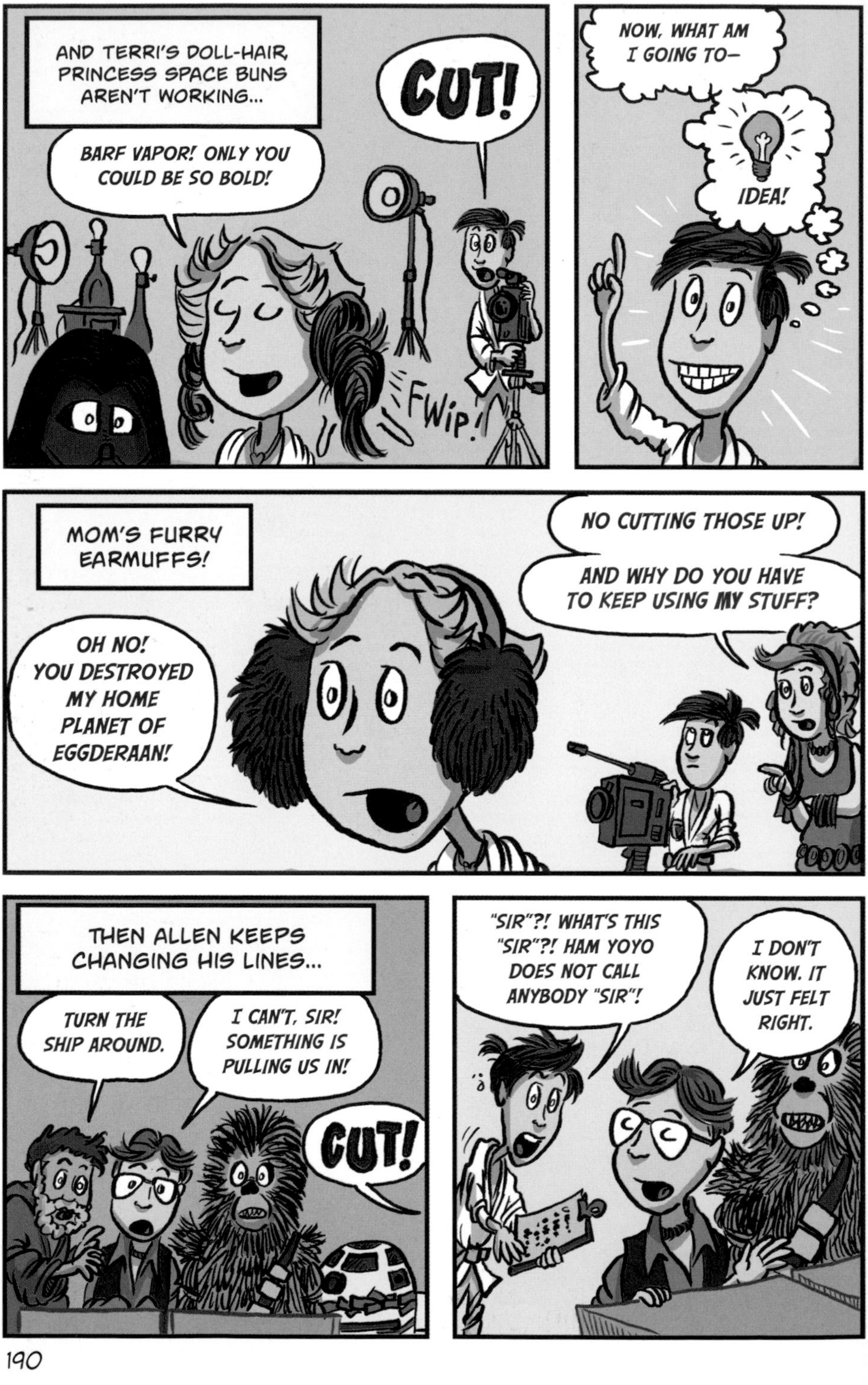
AND TERRI'S DOLL-HAIR PRINCESS SPACE BUNS AREN'T WORKING...
BARF VAPOR! ONLY YOU COULD BE SO BOLD!
CUT!
FWIP!
NOW, WHAT AM I GOING TO—
IDEA!
MOM'S FURRY EARMUFFS!
OH NO! YOU DESTROYED MY HOME PLANET OF EGGDERAAN!
NO CUTTING THOSE UP!
AND WHY DO YOU HAVE TO KEEP USING MY STUFF?
THEN ALLEN KEEPS CHANGING HIS LINES...
TURN THE SHIP AROUND.
I CAN'T, SIR! SOMETHING IS PULLING US IN!
CUT!
"SIR"?! WHAT'S THIS "SIR"?! HAM YOYO DOES NOT CALL ANYBODY "SIR"!
I DON'T KNOW. IT JUST FELT RIGHT.

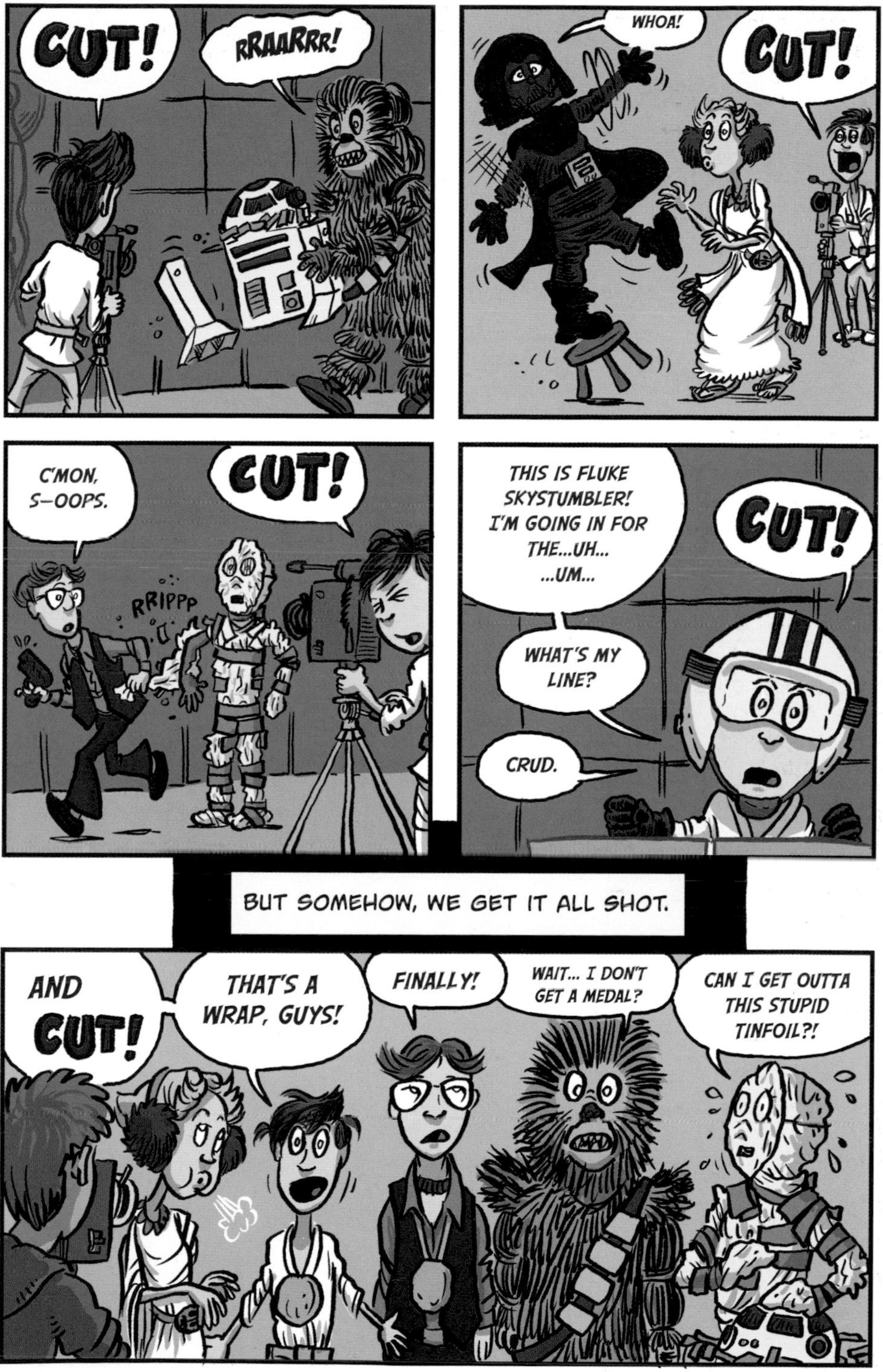
CUT!
RRAARRR!
WHOA!
CUT!
C'MON, S—OOPS.
CUT!
RRIPPP
THIS IS FLUKE SKYSTUMBLER! I'M GOING IN FOR THE...UH... ...UM...
CUT!
WHAT'S MY LINE?
CRUD.
BUT SOMEHOW, WE GET IT ALL SHOT.
AND CUT!
THAT'S A WRAP, GUYS!
FINALLY!
WAIT... I DON'T GET A MEDAL?
CAN I GET OUTTA THIS STUPID TINFOIL?!

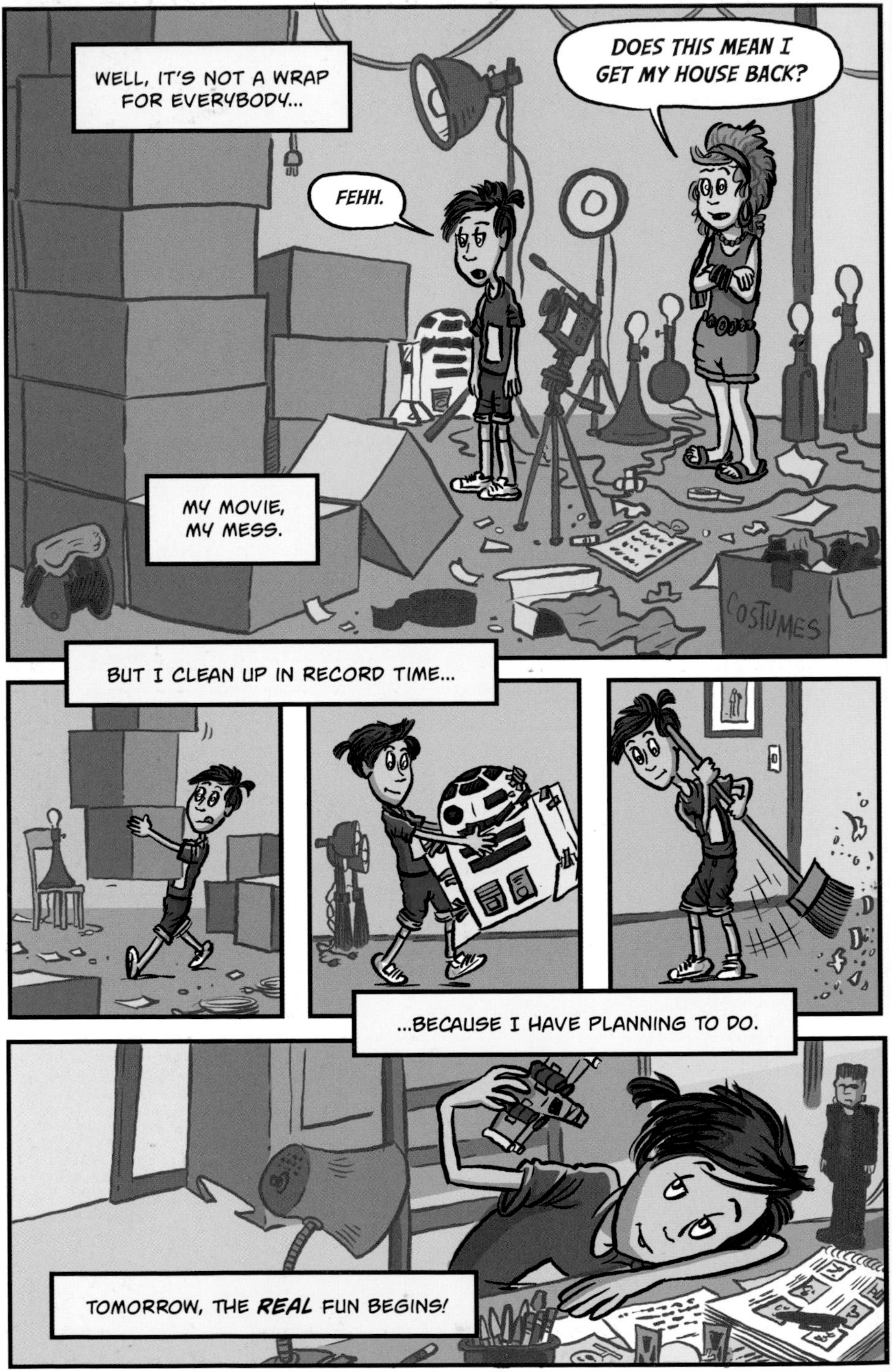
WELL, IT'S NOT A WRAP FOR EVERYBODY...
DOES THIS MEAN I GET MY HOUSE BACK?
FEHH.
MY MOVIE, MY MESS.
COSTUMES
BUT I CLEAN UP IN RECORD TIME...
...BECAUSE I HAVE PLANNING TO DO.
TOMORROW, THE ***REAL*** FUN BEGINS!

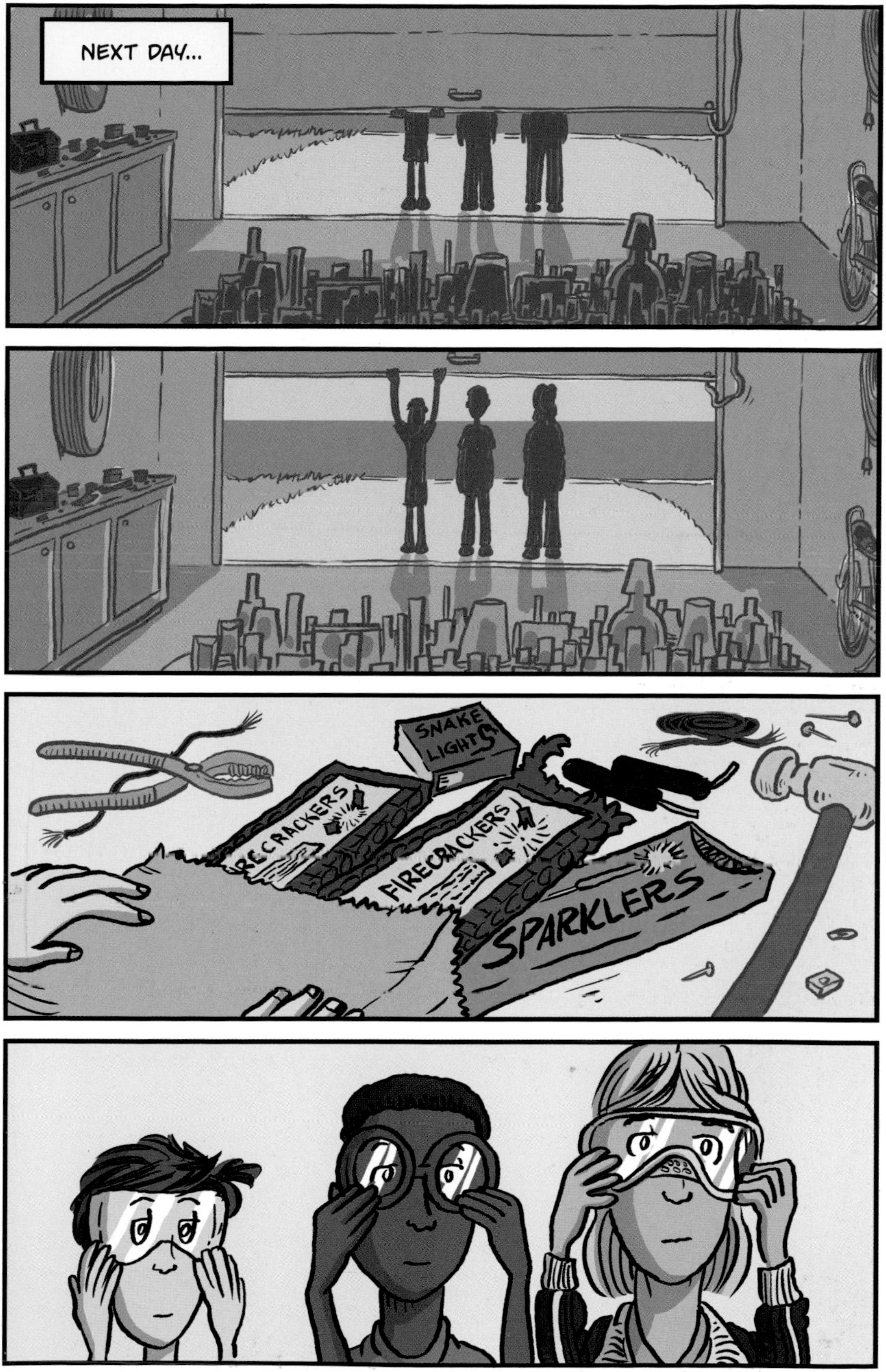
NEXT DAY...
SNAKE LIGHTS
RECRACKERS
FIRECRACKERS
SPARKLERS

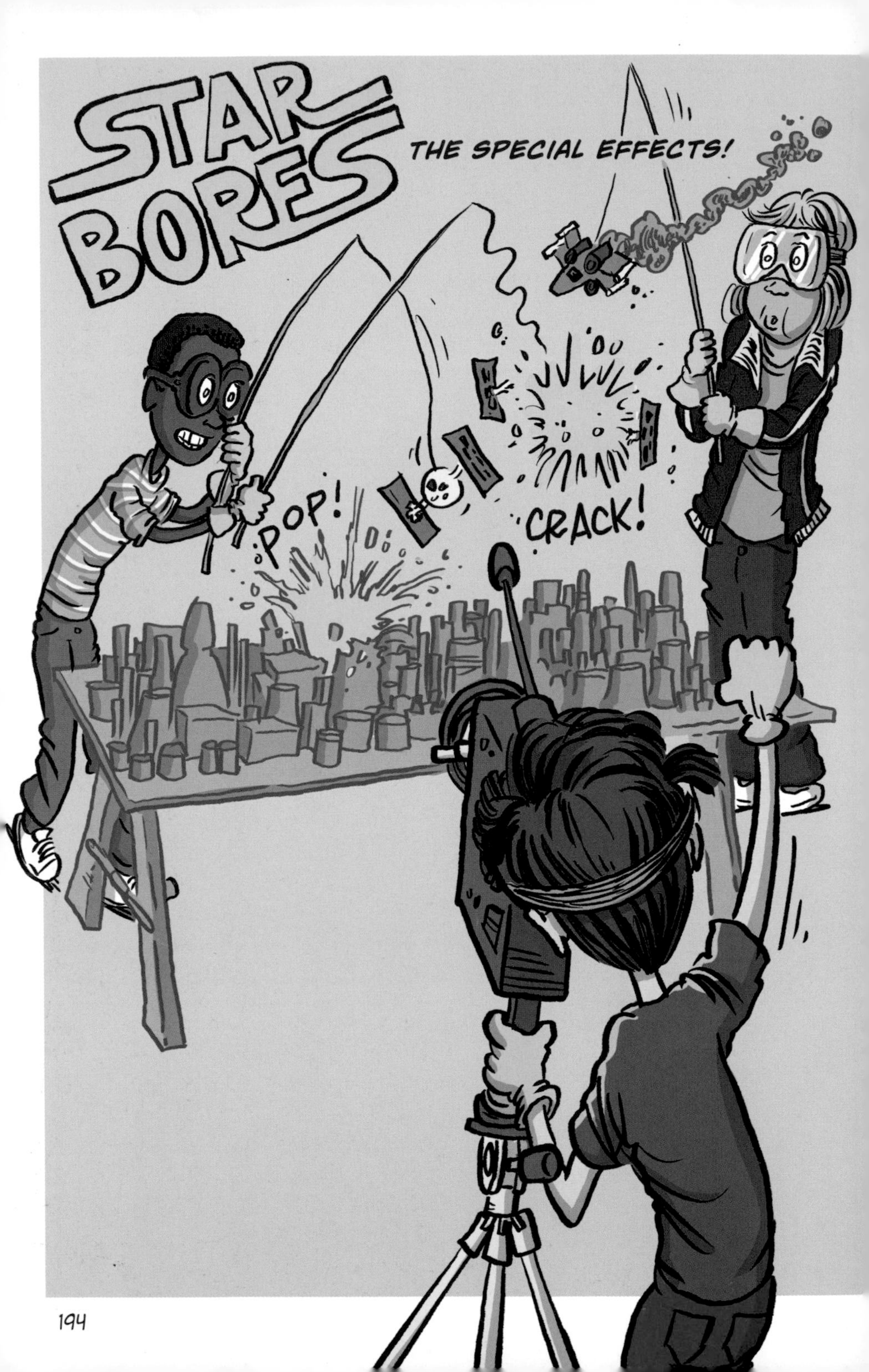
STAR BORES
THE SPECIAL EFFECTS!
POP!
CRACK!

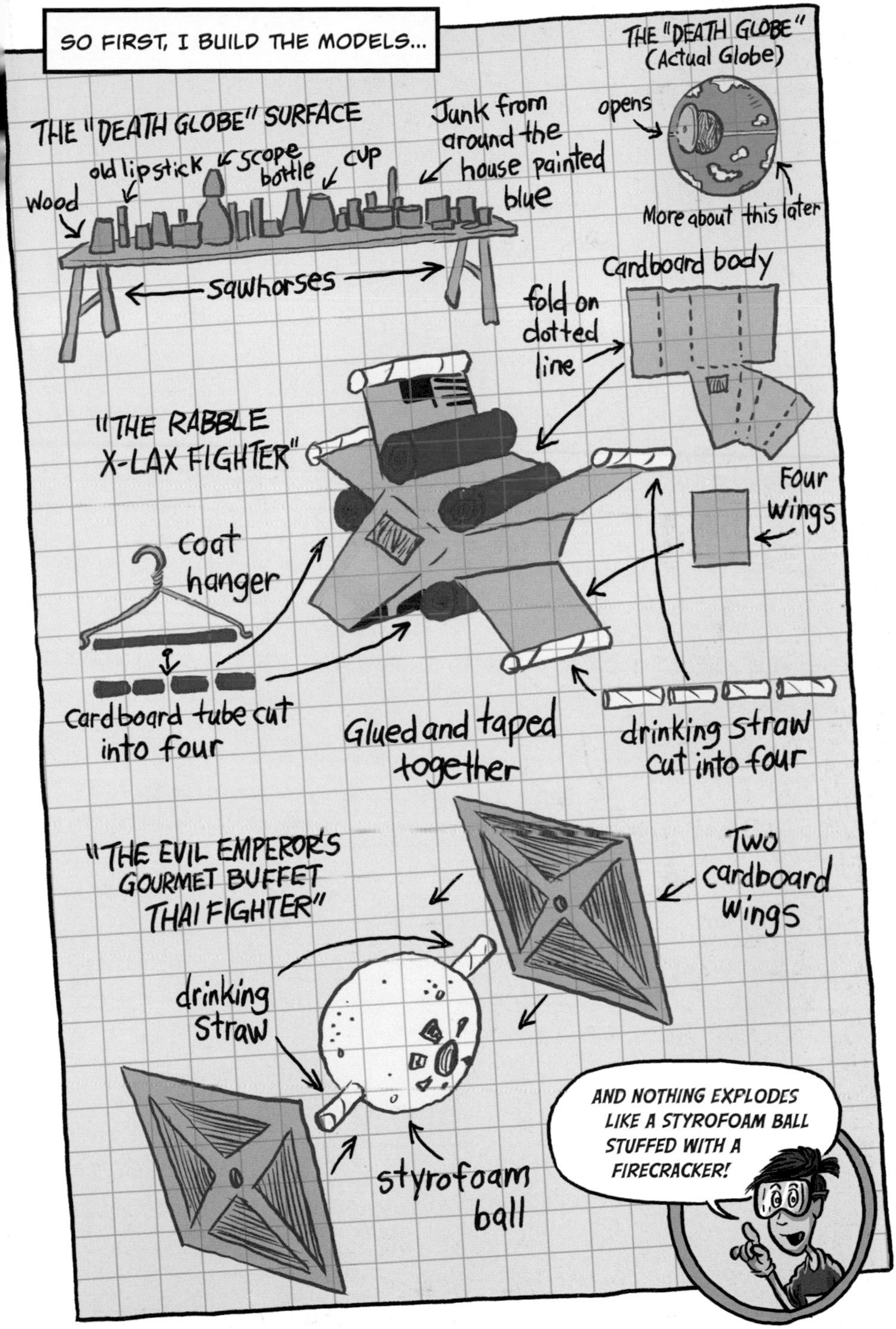
SO FIRST, I BUILD THE MODELS...
THE "DEATH GLOBE" SURFACE
wood
old lipstick
scope bottle
cup
Junk from around the house painted blue
sawhorses
THE "DEATH GLOBE" (Actual Globe)
opens
More about this later
Cardboard body
fold on dotted line
"THE RABBLE X-LAX FIGHTER"
Four wings
coat hanger
Cardboard tube cut into four
Glued and taped together
drinking straw cut into four
"THE EVIL EMPEROR'S GOURMET BUFFET THAI FIGHTER"
Two cardboard wings
drinking straw
styrofoam ball
AND NOTHING EXPLODES LIKE A STYROFOAM BALL STUFFED WITH A FIRECRACKER!

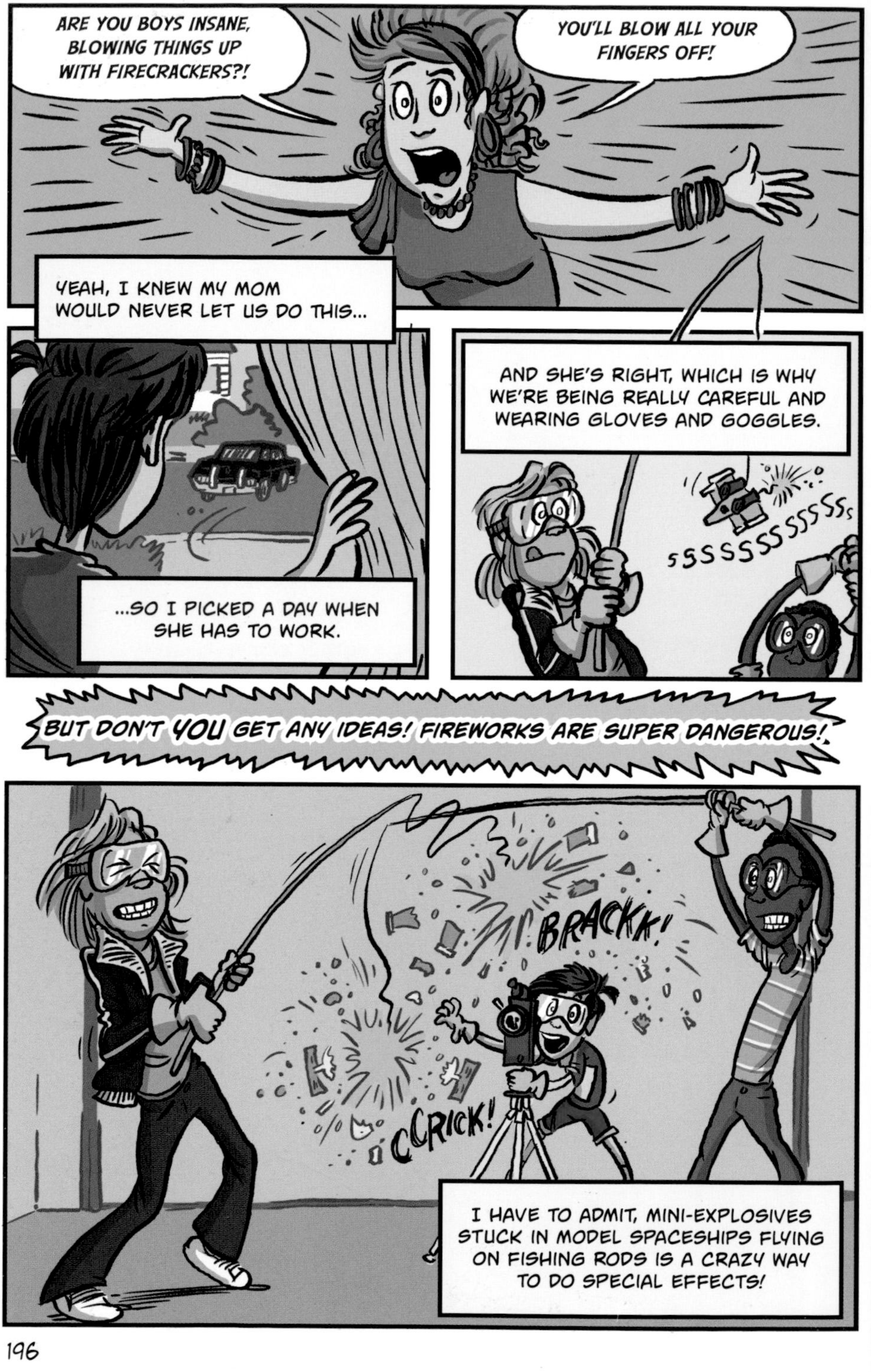
ARE YOU BOYS INSANE, BLOWING THINGS UP WITH FIRECRACKERS?!
YOU'LL BLOW ALL YOUR FINGERS OFF!
YEAH, I KNEW MY MOM WOULD NEVER LET US DO THIS...
...SO I PICKED A DAY WHEN SHE HAS TO WORK.
AND SHE'S RIGHT, WHICH IS WHY WE'RE BEING REALLY CAREFUL AND WEARING GLOVES AND GOGGLES.
SSSSSSSSSSSSSs
BUT DON'T YOU GET ANY IDEAS! FIREWORKS ARE SUPER DANGEROUS!
BRACKK!
CCRICK!
I HAVE TO ADMIT, MINI-EXPLOSIVES STUCK IN MODEL SPACESHIPS FLYING ON FISHING RODS IS A CRAZY WAY TO DO SPECIAL EFFECTS!

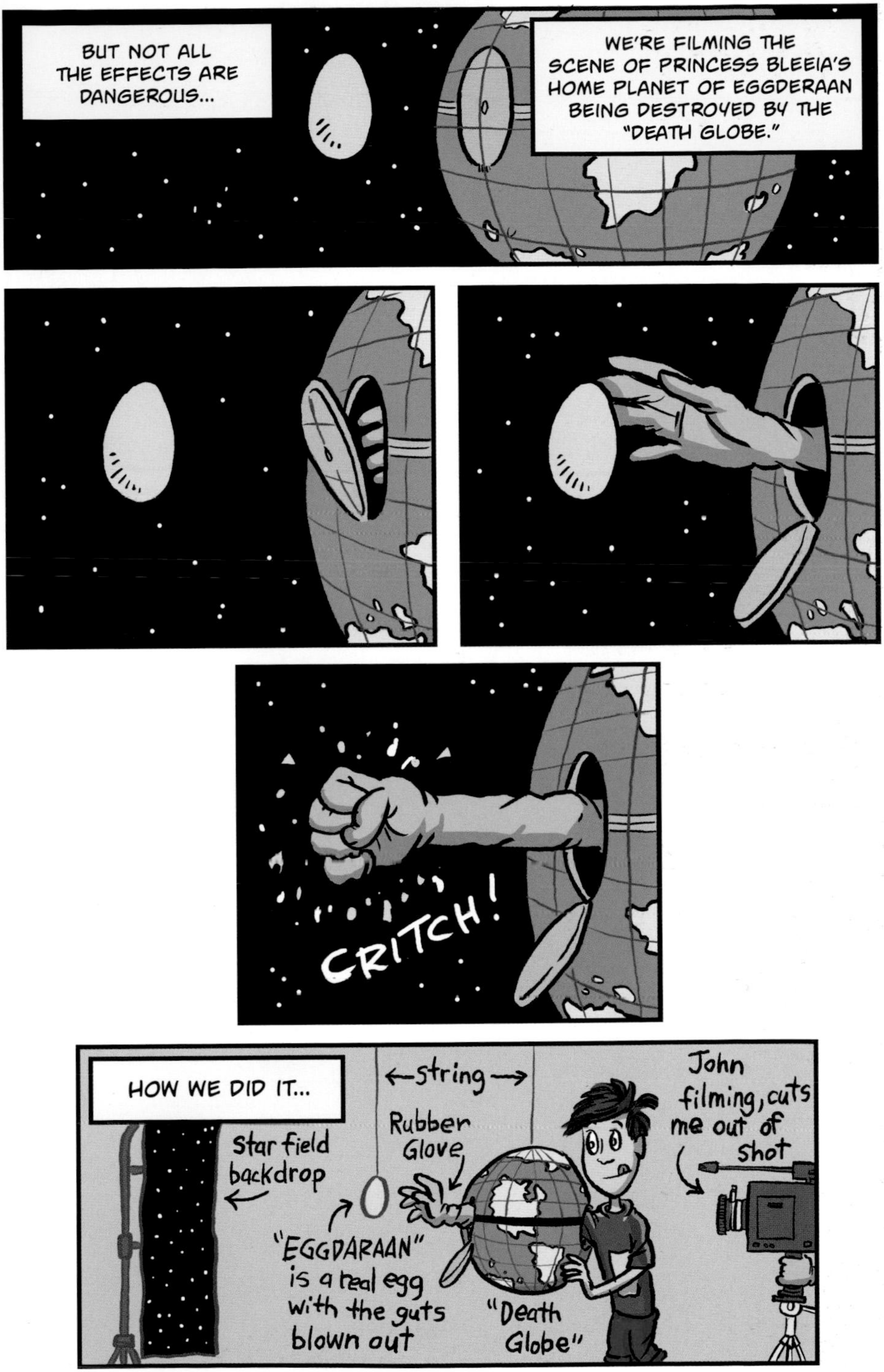
BUT NOT ALL THE EFFECTS ARE DANGEROUS...
WE'RE FILMING THE SCENE OF PRINCESS BLEEIA'S HOME PLANET OF EGGDERAAN BEING DESTROYED BY THE "DEATH GLOBE."
CRITCH!
HOW WE DID IT...
←string→
John filming, cuts me out of shot
Rubber Glove
Star field backdrop
"EGGDARAAN" is a real egg with the guts blown out
"Death Globe"

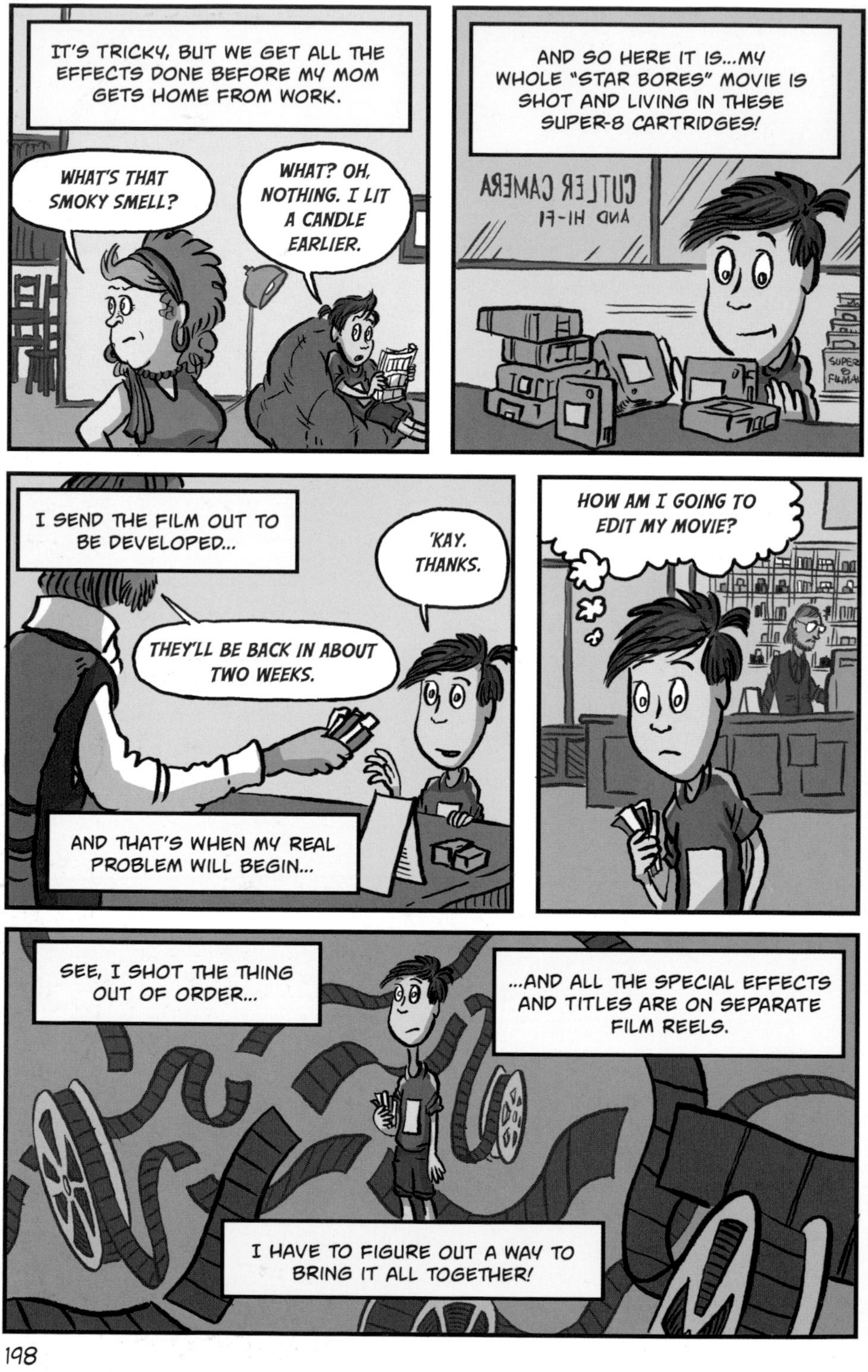
IT'S TRICKY, BUT WE GET ALL THE EFFECTS DONE BEFORE MY MOM GETS HOME FROM WORK.
WHAT'S THAT SMOKY SMELL?
WHAT? OH, NOTHING. I LIT A CANDLE EARLIER.
AND SO HERE IT IS...MY WHOLE "STAR BORES" MOVIE IS SHOT AND LIVING IN THESE SUPER-8 CARTRIDGES!
CUTLER CAMERA
AND HI-FI
I SEND THE FILM OUT TO BE DEVELOPED...
THEY'LL BE BACK IN ABOUT TWO WEEKS.
'KAY. THANKS.
AND THAT'S WHEN MY REAL PROBLEM WILL BEGIN...
HOW AM I GOING TO EDIT MY MOVIE?
SEE, I SHOT THE THING OUT OF ORDER...
...AND ALL THE SPECIAL EFFECTS AND TITLES ARE ON SEPARATE FILM REELS.
I HAVE TO FIGURE OUT A WAY TO BRING IT ALL TOGETHER!

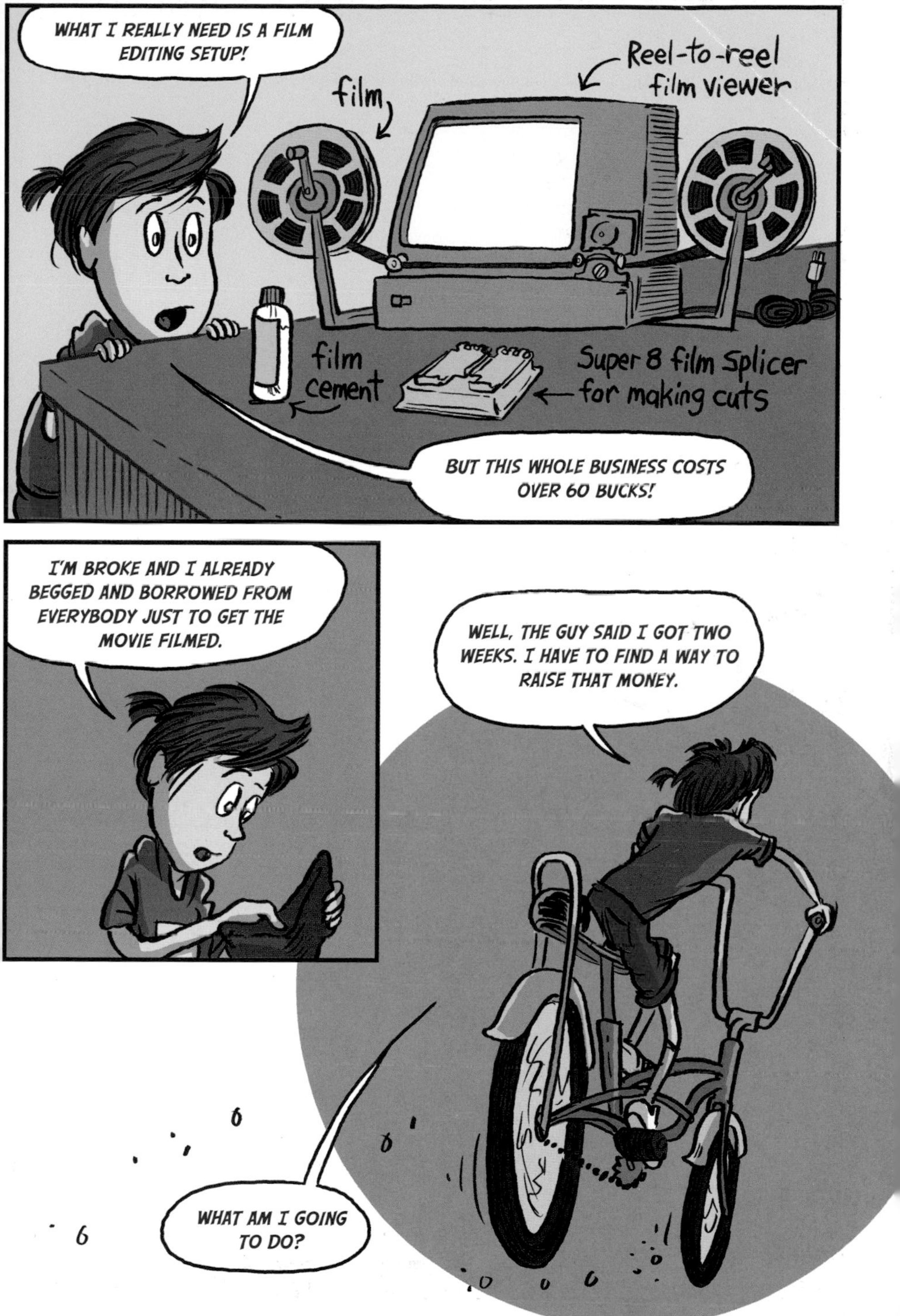
WHAT I REALLY NEED IS A FILM EDITING SETUP!
Reel-to-reel film viewer
film
film cement
Super 8 film Splicer for making cuts
BUT THIS WHOLE BUSINESS COSTS OVER 60 BUCKS!
I'M BROKE AND I ALREADY BEGGED AND BORROWED FROM EVERYBODY JUST TO GET THE MOVIE FILMED.
WELL, THE GUY SAID I GOT TWO WEEKS. I HAVE TO FIND A WAY TO RAISE THAT MONEY.
WHAT AM I GOING TO DO?

CHAPTER 12

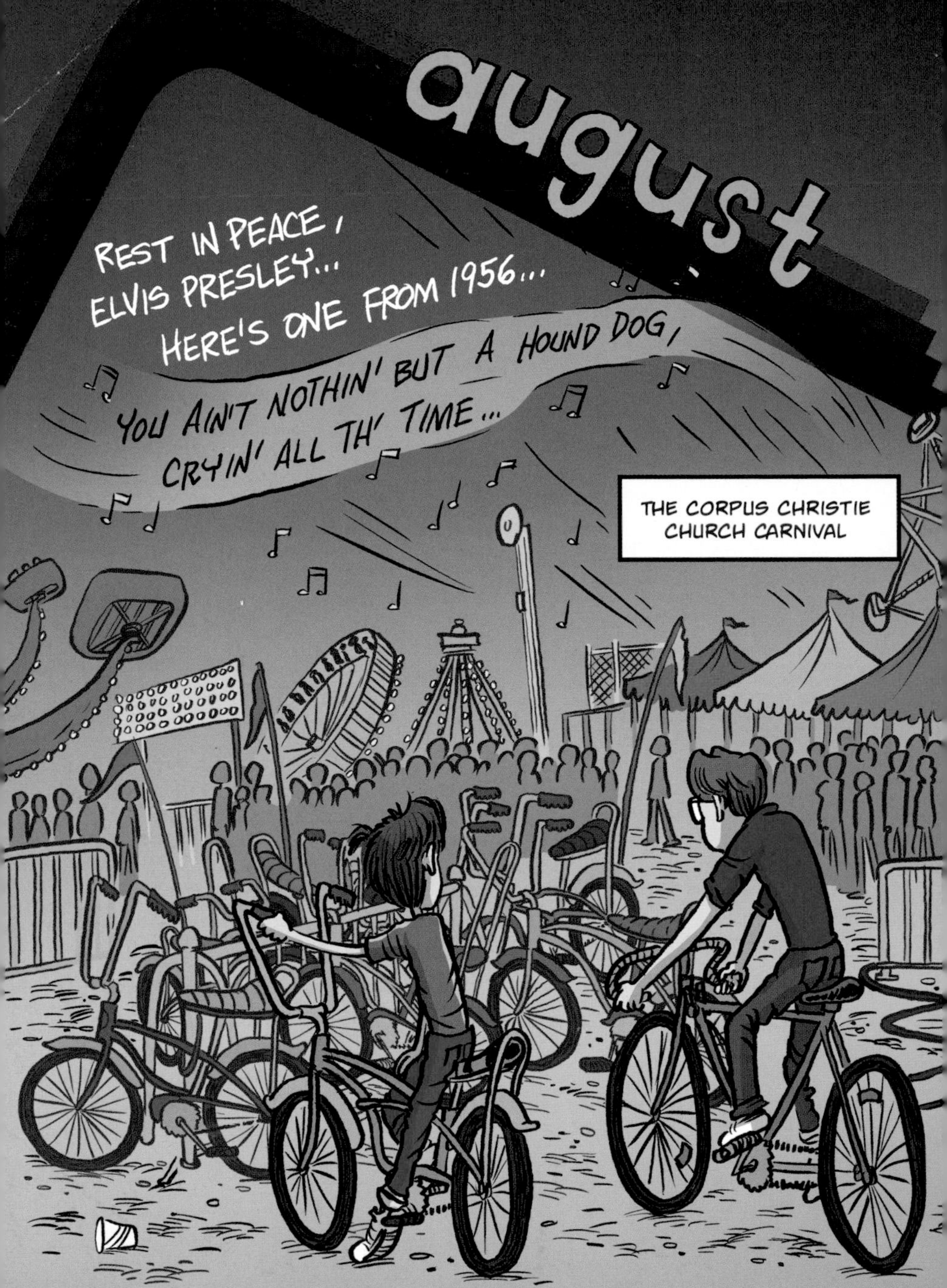
august
REST IN PEACE, ELVIS PRESLEY... HERE'S ONE FROM 1956...
YOU AIN'T NOTHIN' BUT A HOUND DOG, CRYIN' ALL TH' TIME...
THE CORPUS CHRISTIE CHURCH CARNIVAL

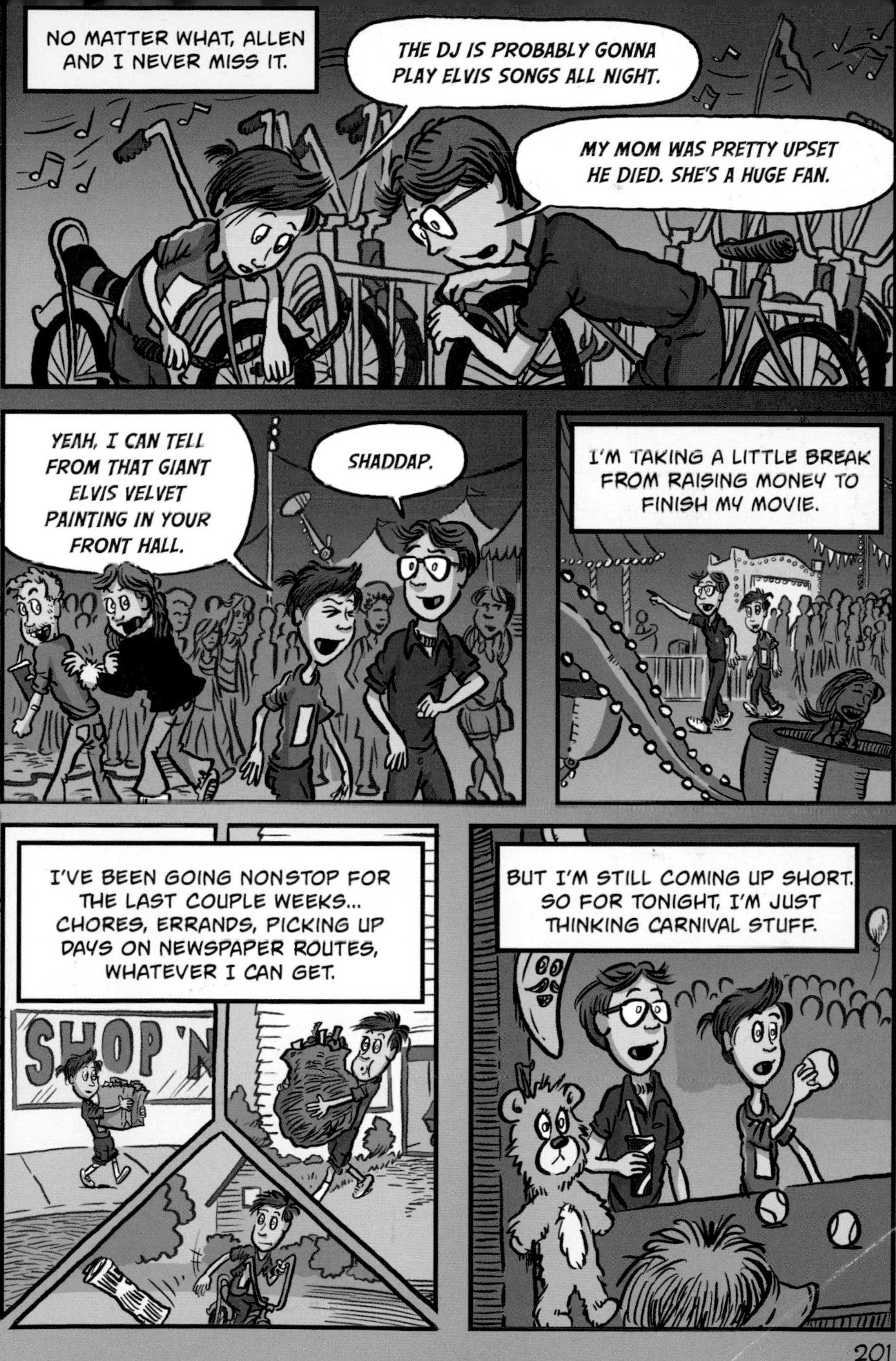

NO MATTER WHAT, ALLEN AND I NEVER MISS IT.
THE DJ IS PROBABLY GONNA PLAY ELVIS SONGS ALL NIGHT.
MY MOM WAS PRETTY UPSET HE DIED. SHE'S A HUGE FAN.
YEAH, I CAN TELL FROM THAT GIANT ELVIS VELVET PAINTING IN YOUR FRONT HALL.
SHADDAP.
I'M TAKING A LITTLE BREAK FROM RAISING MONEY TO FINISH MY MOVIE.
I'VE BEEN GOING NONSTOP FOR THE LAST COUPLE WEEKS... CHORES, ERRANDS, PICKING UP DAYS ON NEWSPAPER ROUTES, WHATEVER I CAN GET.
SHOP 'N
BUT I'M STILL COMING UP SHORT. SO FOR TONIGHT, I'M JUST THINKING CARNIVAL STUFF.

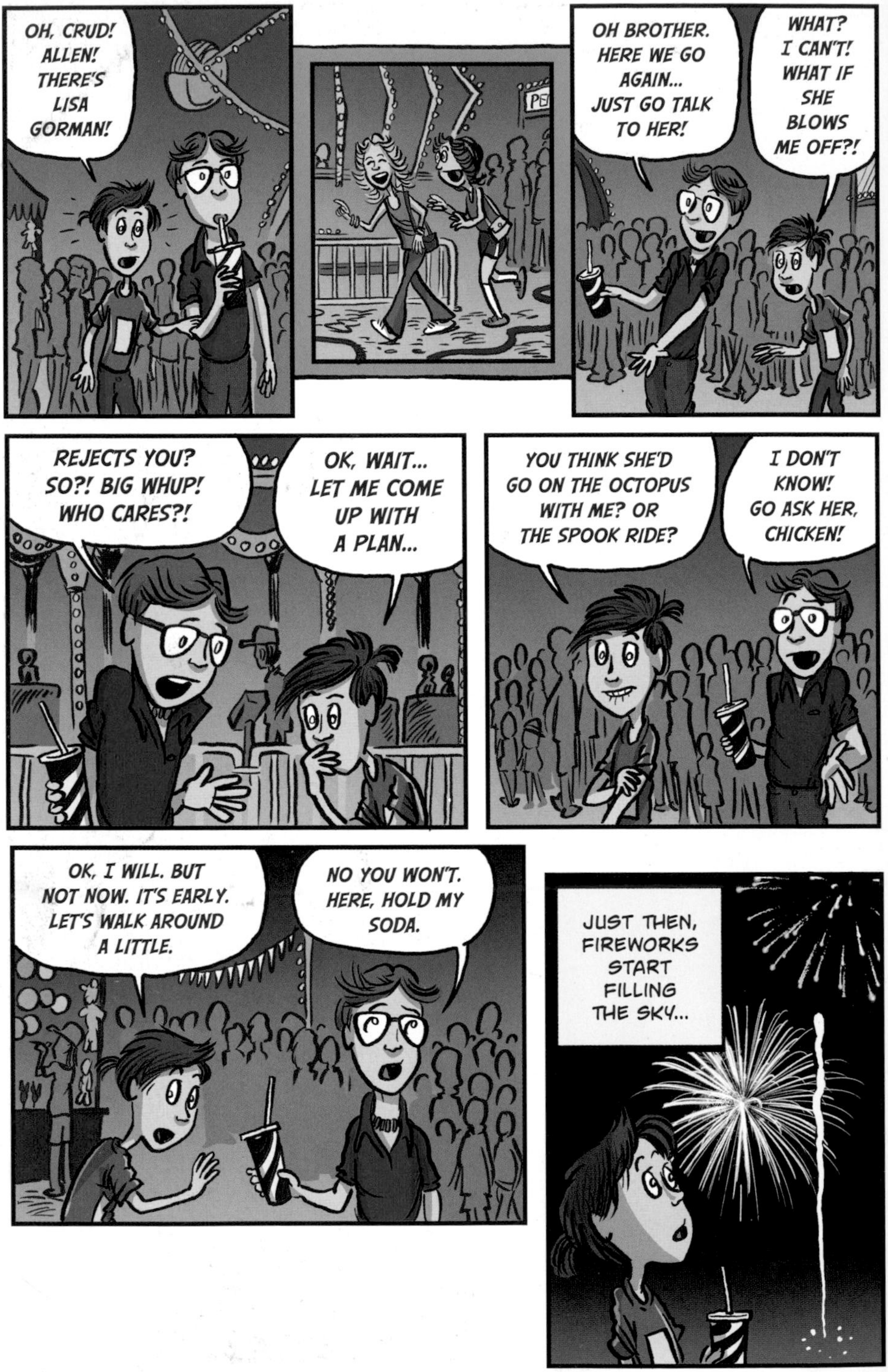
OH, CRUD! ALLEN! THERE'S LISA GORMAN!
OH BROTHER. HERE WE GO AGAIN... JUST GO TALK TO HER!
WHAT? I CAN'T! WHAT IF SHE BLOWS ME OFF?!
REJECTS YOU? SO?! BIG WHUP! WHO CARES?!
OK, WAIT... LET ME COME UP WITH A PLAN...
YOU THINK SHE'D GO ON THE OCTOPUS WITH ME? OR THE SPOOK RIDE?
I DON'T KNOW! GO ASK HER, CHICKEN!
OK, I WILL. BUT NOT NOW. IT'S EARLY. LET'S WALK AROUND A LITTLE.
NO YOU WON'T. HERE, HOLD MY SODA.
JUST THEN, FIREWORKS START FILLING THE SKY...

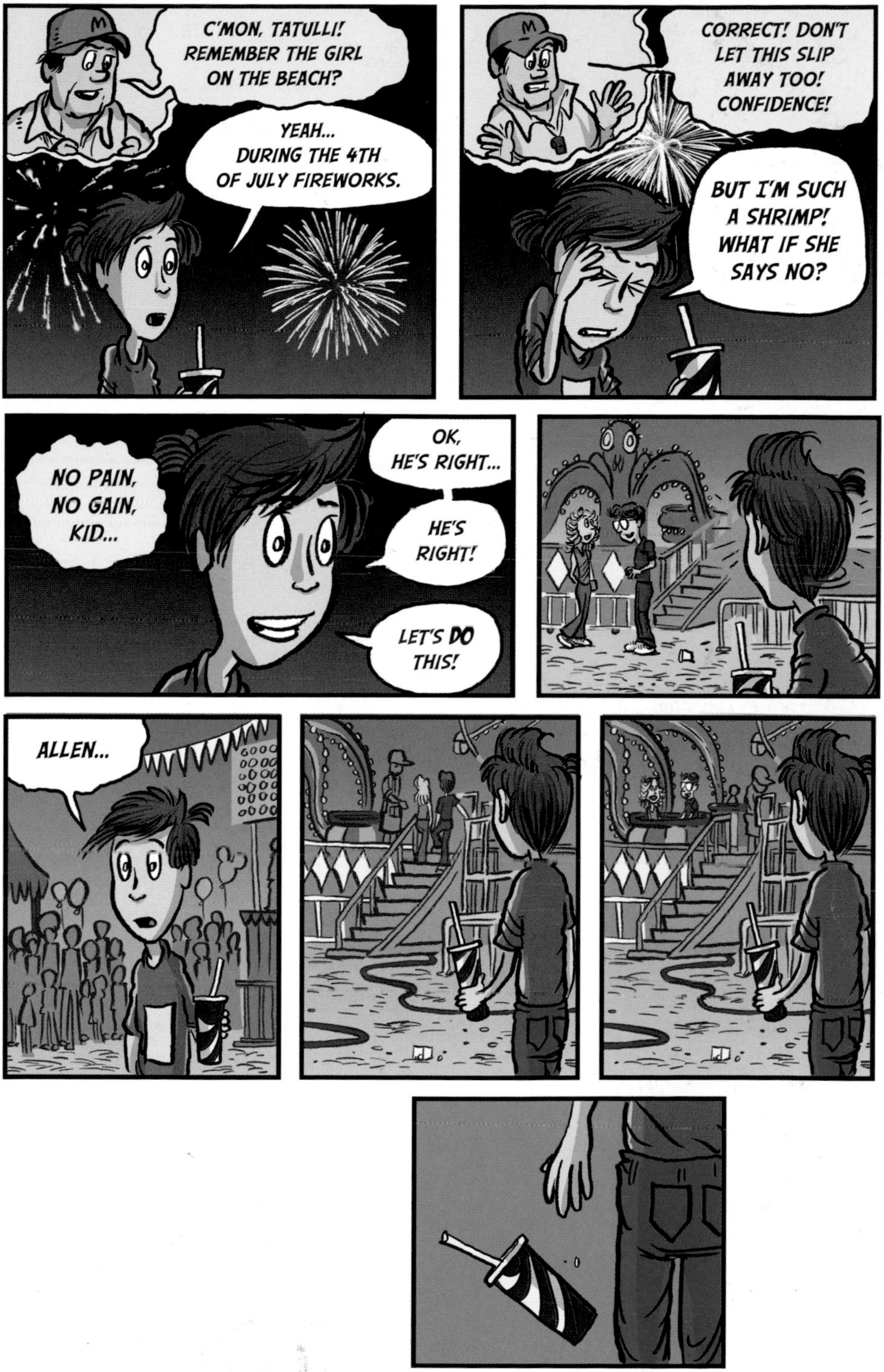
C'MON, TATULLI! REMEMBER THE GIRL ON THE BEACH?
YEAH... DURING THE 4TH OF JULY FIREWORKS.
CORRECT! DON'T LET THIS SLIP AWAY TOO! CONFIDENCE!
BUT I'M SUCH A SHRIMP! WHAT IF SHE SAYS NO?
NO PAIN, NO GAIN, KID...
OK, HE'S RIGHT...
HE'S RIGHT!
LET'S DO THIS!
ALLEN...

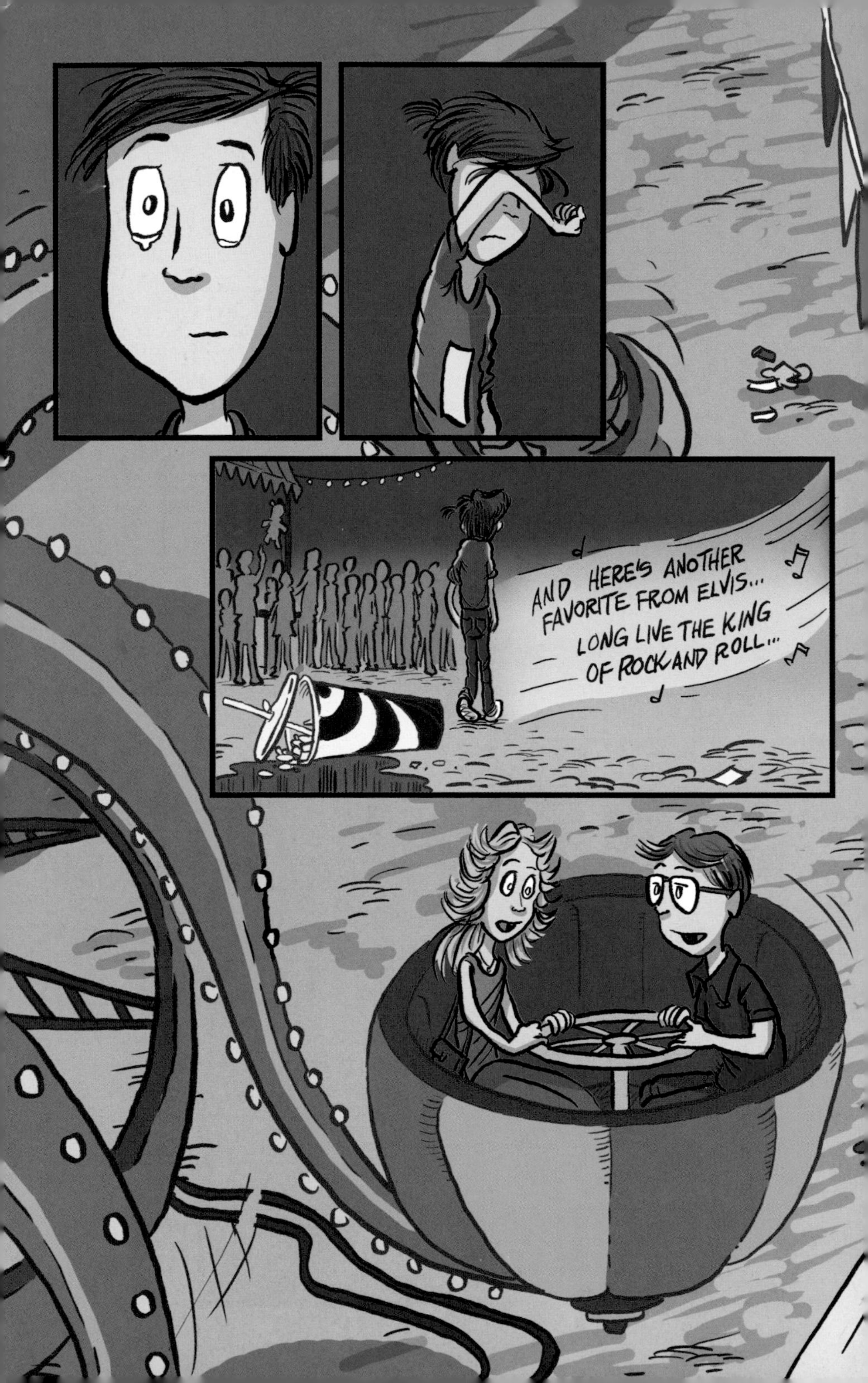
AND HERE'S ANOTHER FAVORITE FROM ELVIS...
LONG LIVE THE KING OF ROCK AND ROLL...

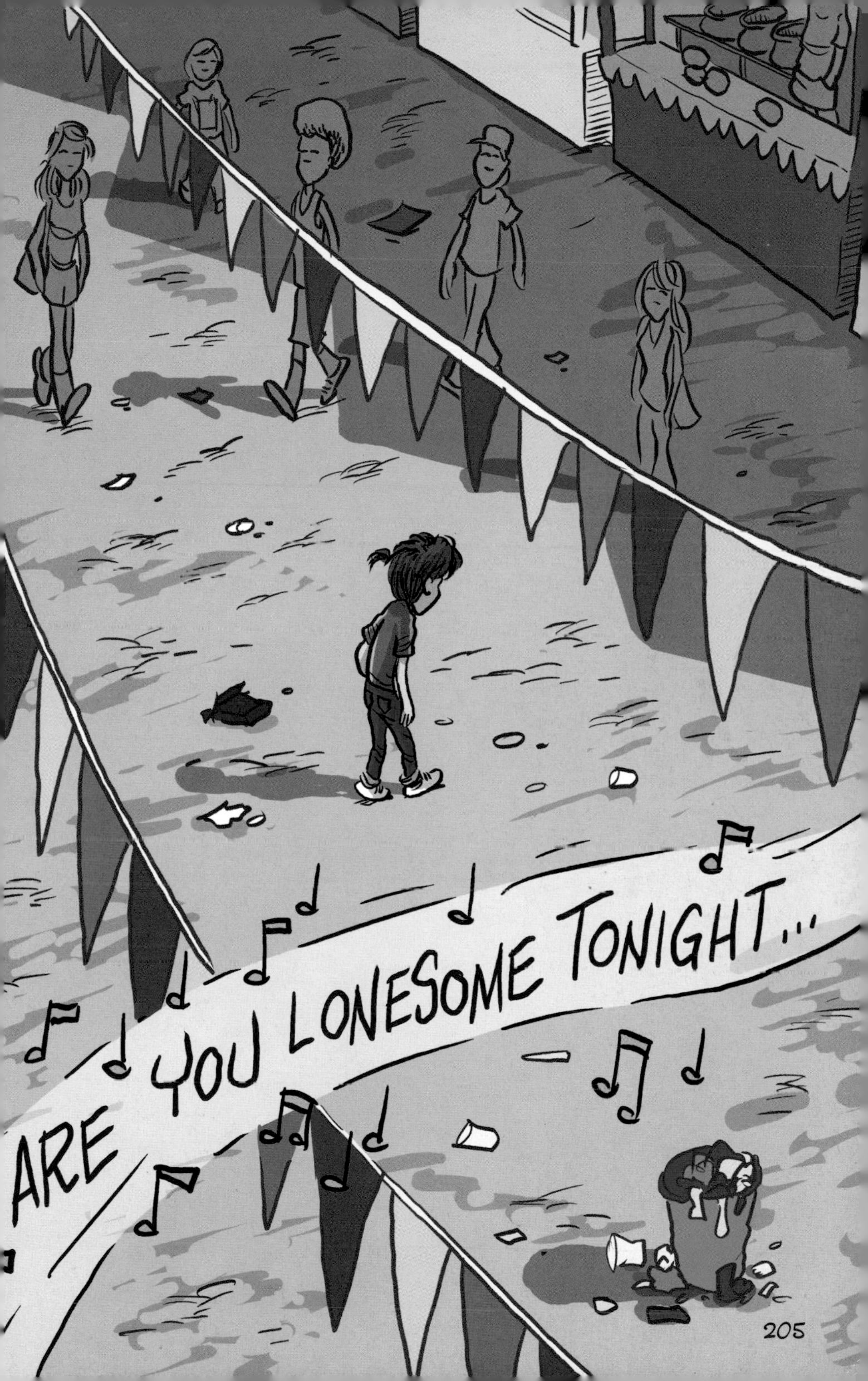
ARE YOU LONESOME TONIGHT...

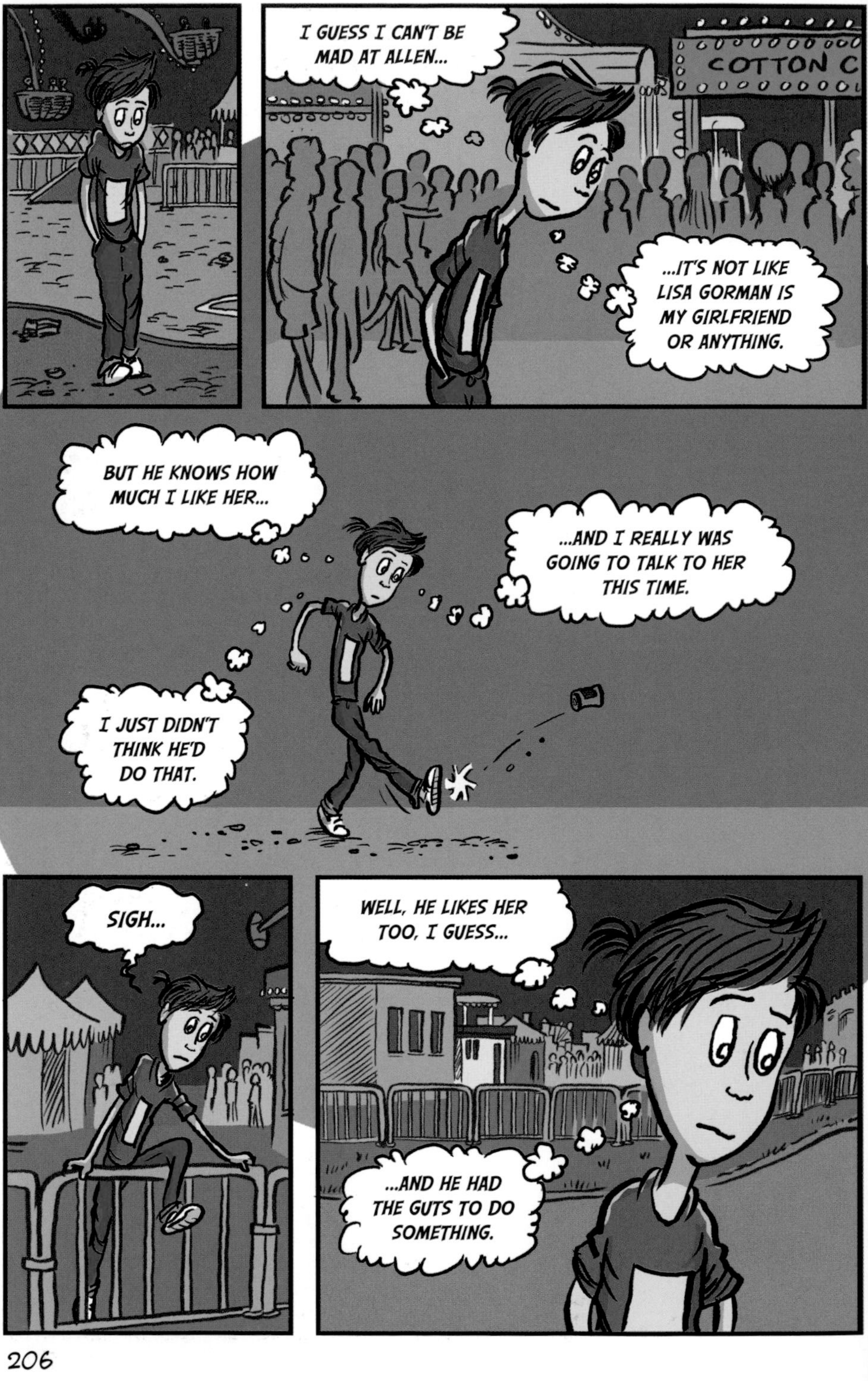
I GUESS I CAN'T BE MAD AT ALLEN...
COTTON C
...IT'S NOT LIKE LISA GORMAN IS MY GIRLFRIEND OR ANYTHING.
BUT HE KNOWS HOW MUCH I LIKE HER...
...AND I REALLY WAS GOING TO TALK TO HER THIS TIME.
I JUST DIDN'T THINK HE'D DO THAT.
SIGH...
WELL, HE LIKES HER TOO, I GUESS...
...AND HE HAD THE GUTS TO DO SOMETHING.

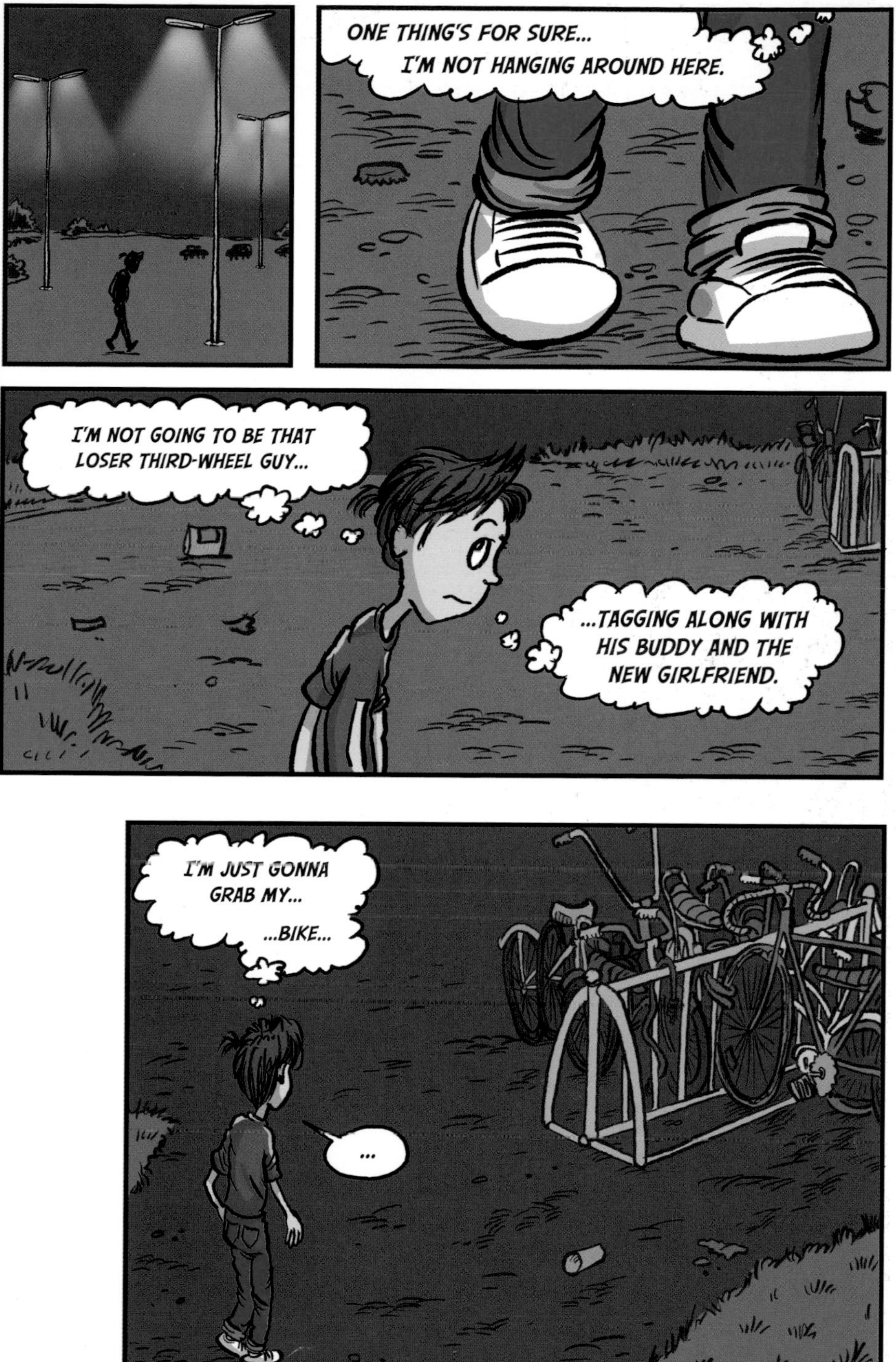
ONE THING'S FOR SURE... I'M NOT HANGING AROUND HERE.
I'M NOT GOING TO BE THAT LOSER THIRD-WHEEL GUY...
...TAGGING ALONG WITH HIS BUDDY AND THE NEW GIRLFRIEND.
I'M JUST GONNA GRAB MY... ...BIKE...
...

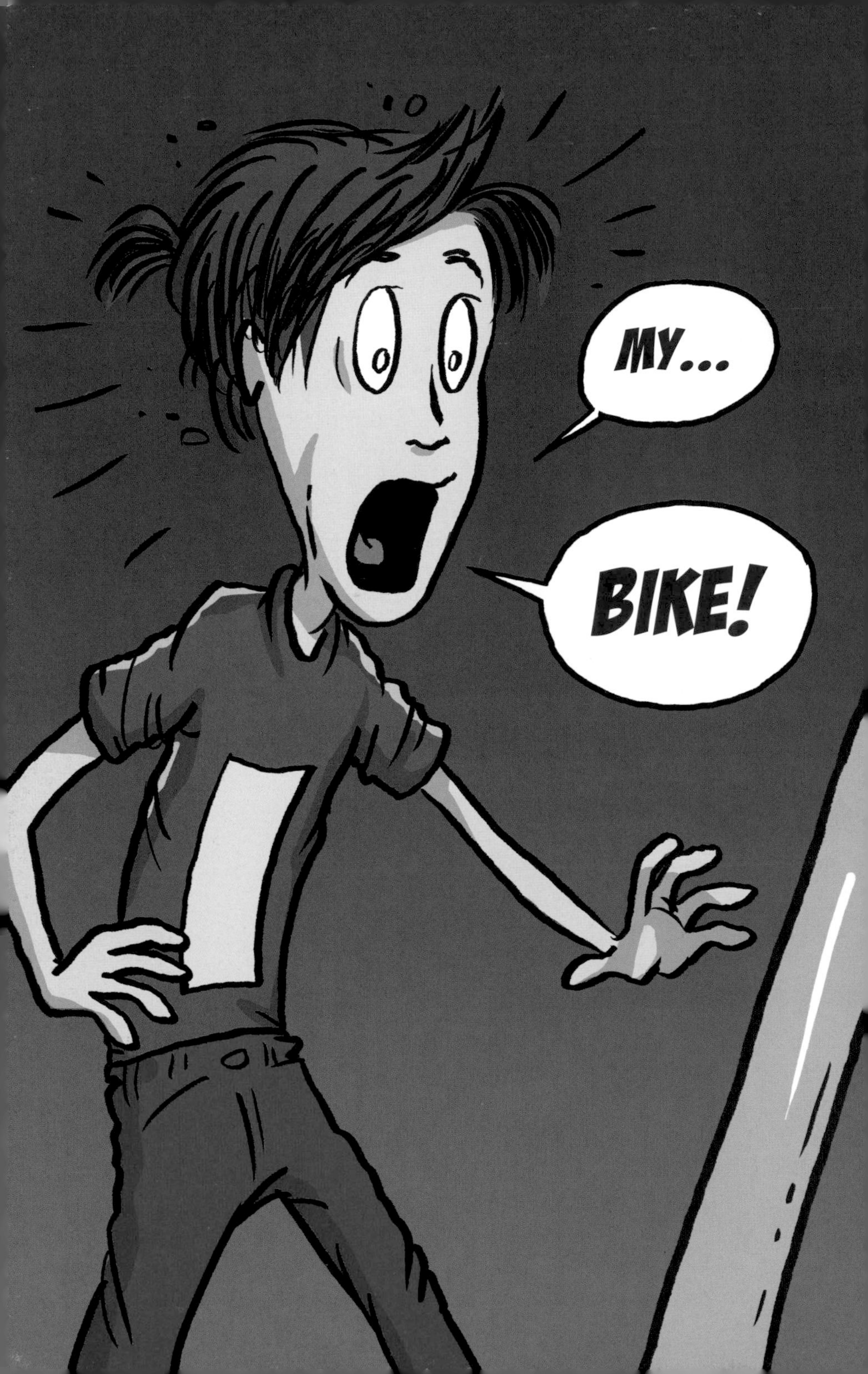
MY...
BIKE!

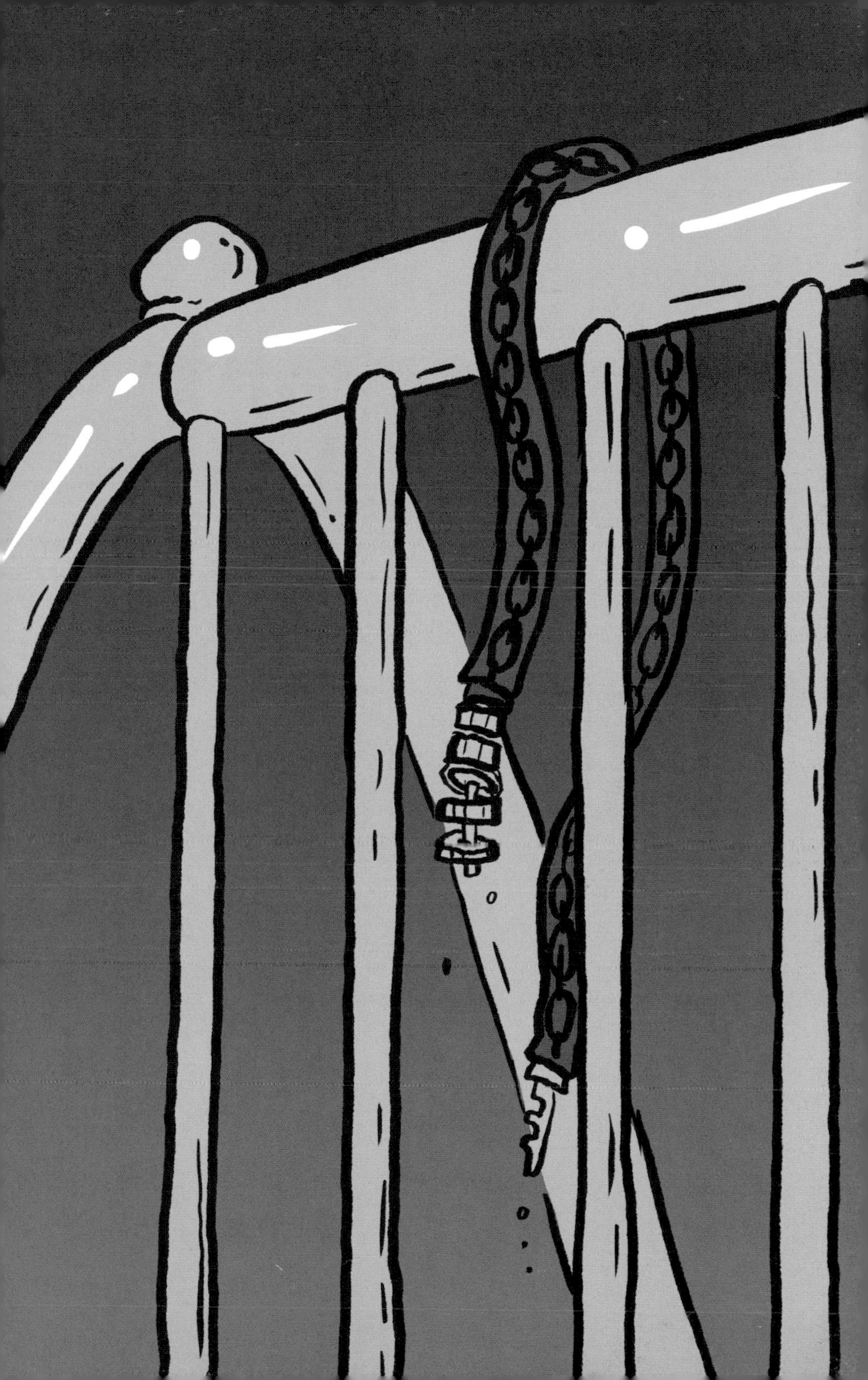

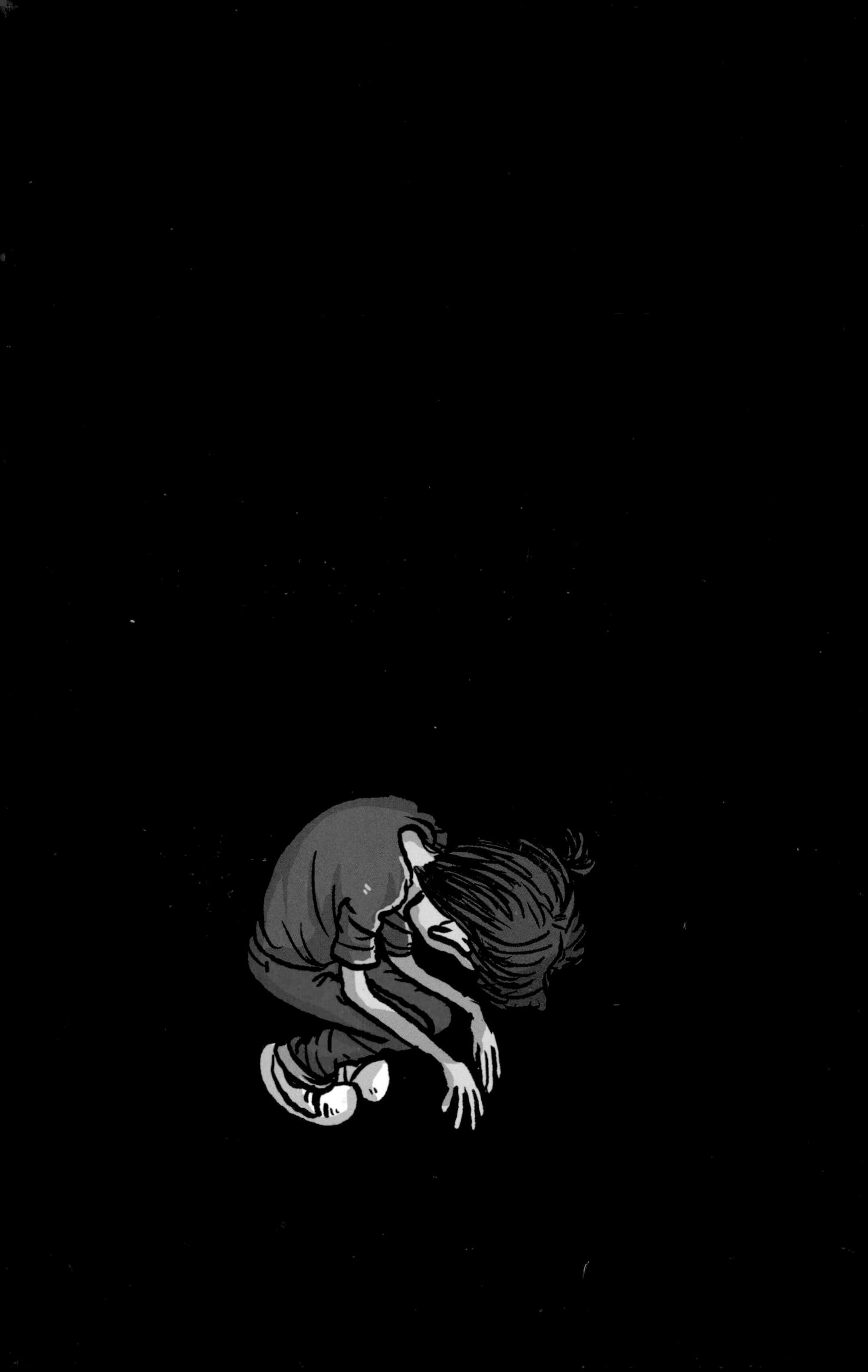

MY BIKE.

GONE.

THUNDERBOLT.

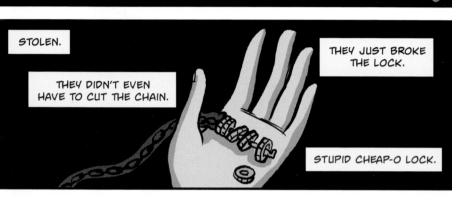

STOLEN.

THEY DIDN'T EVEN HAVE TO CUT THE CHAIN.

THEY JUST BROKE THE LOCK.

STUPID CHEAP-O LOCK.

I LOOK EVERYWHERE.

MAYBE THEY JUST DITCHED IT.

BUT I CAN GUESS WHO TOOK IT.

SHOULD HAVE JUST LET THEM KICK MY BUTT THAT DAY AT THE CREEK.

IT'S A LONG WALK HOME.

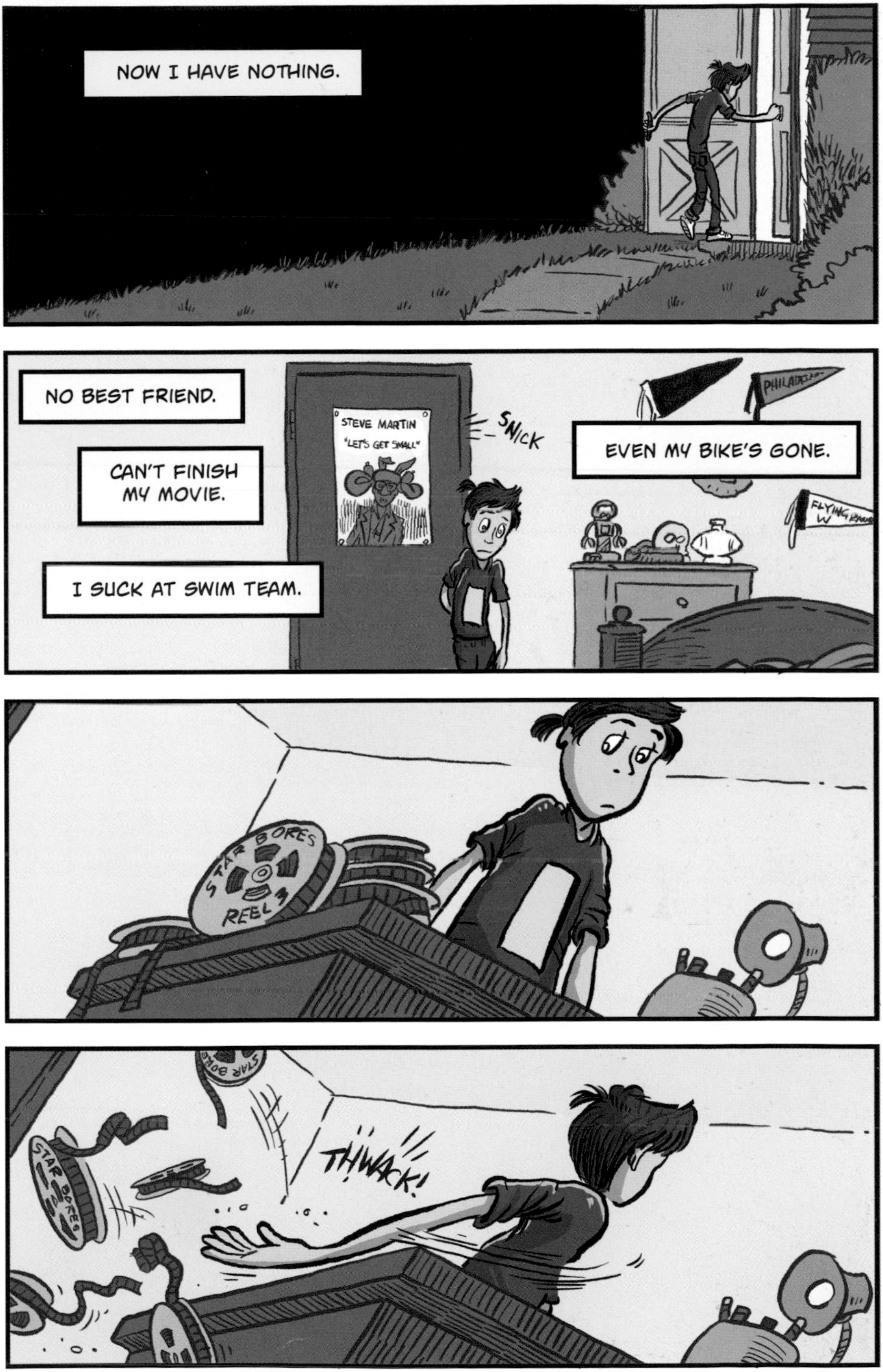
NOW I HAVE NOTHING.
NO BEST FRIEND.
CAN'T FINISH MY MOVIE.
I SUCK AT SWIM TEAM.
STEVE MARTIN "LET'S GET SMALL"
SNICK
EVEN MY BIKE'S GONE.
PHILADELPHIA
FLYING W
STAR BORES REEL 3
STAR BORES
THWACK!

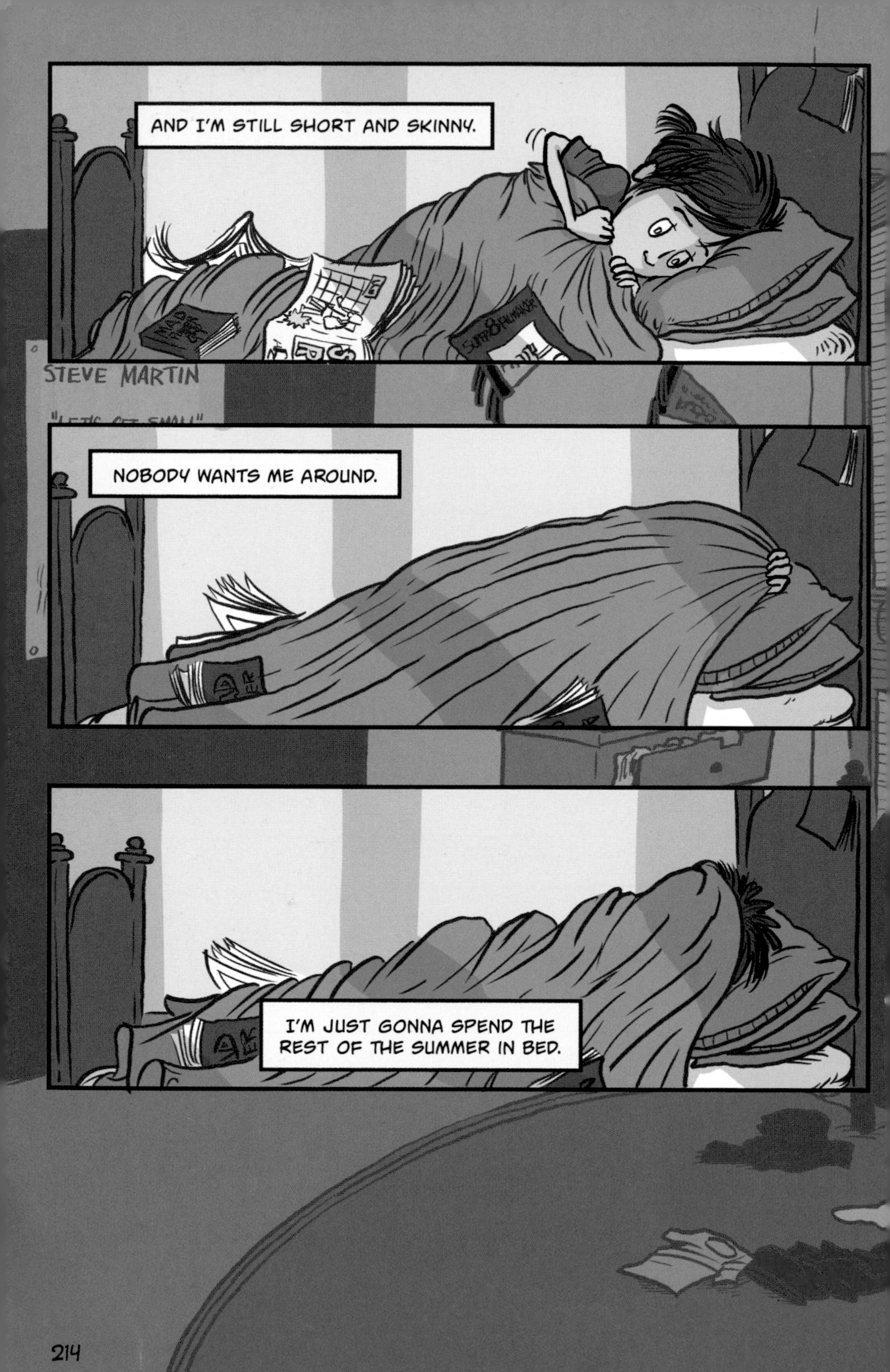
AND I'M STILL SHORT AND SKINNY.
STEVE MARTIN
NOBODY WANTS ME AROUND.
I'M JUST GONNA SPEND THE REST OF THE SUMMER IN BED.

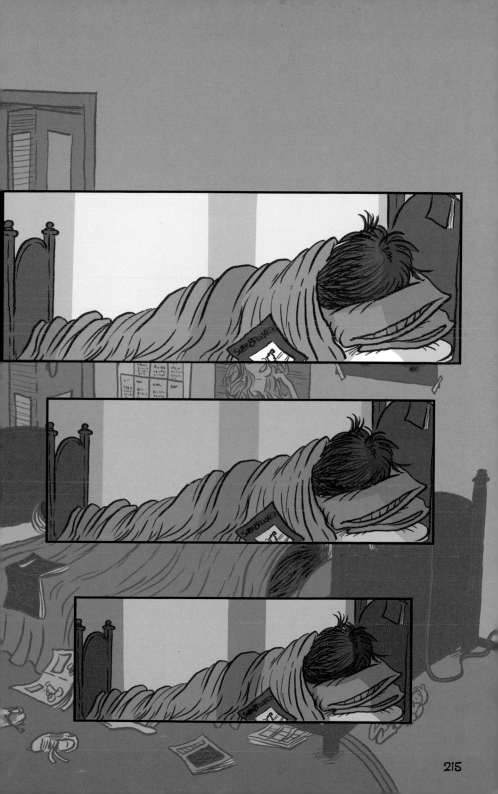

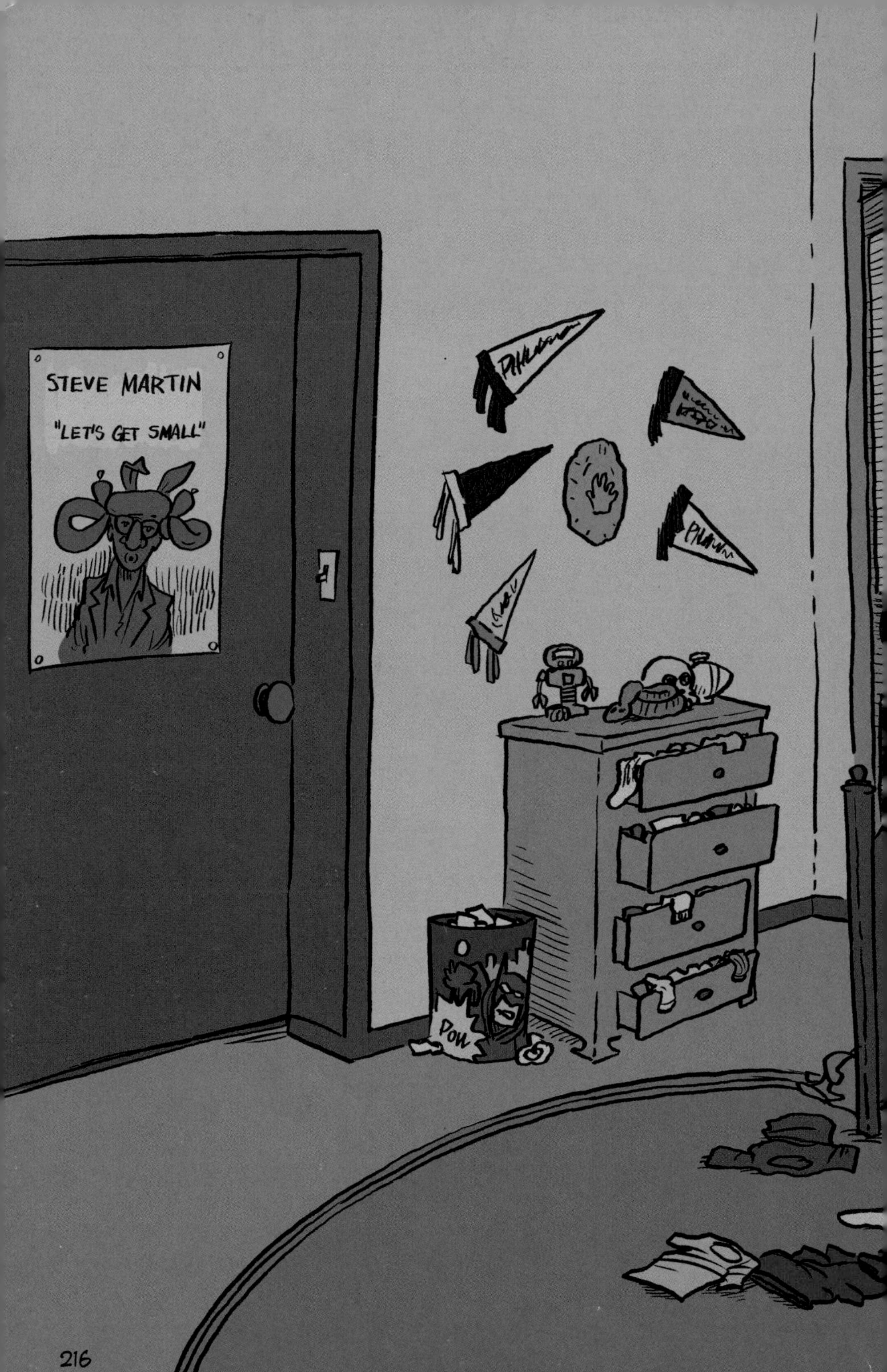
STEVE MARTIN
"LET'S GET SMALL"
POW

CHAPTER 13

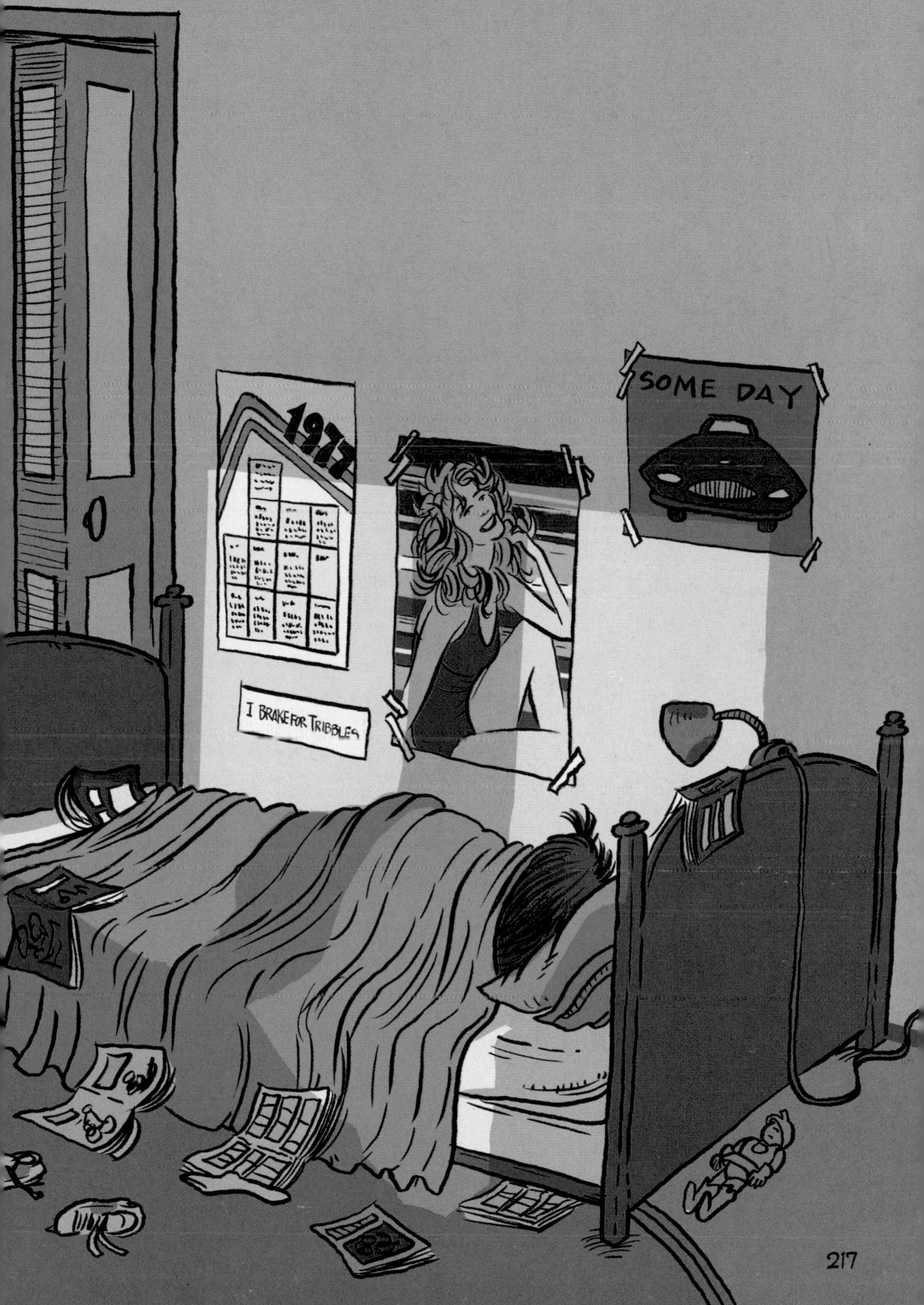
1977
SOME DAY
I BRAKE FOR TRIBBLES

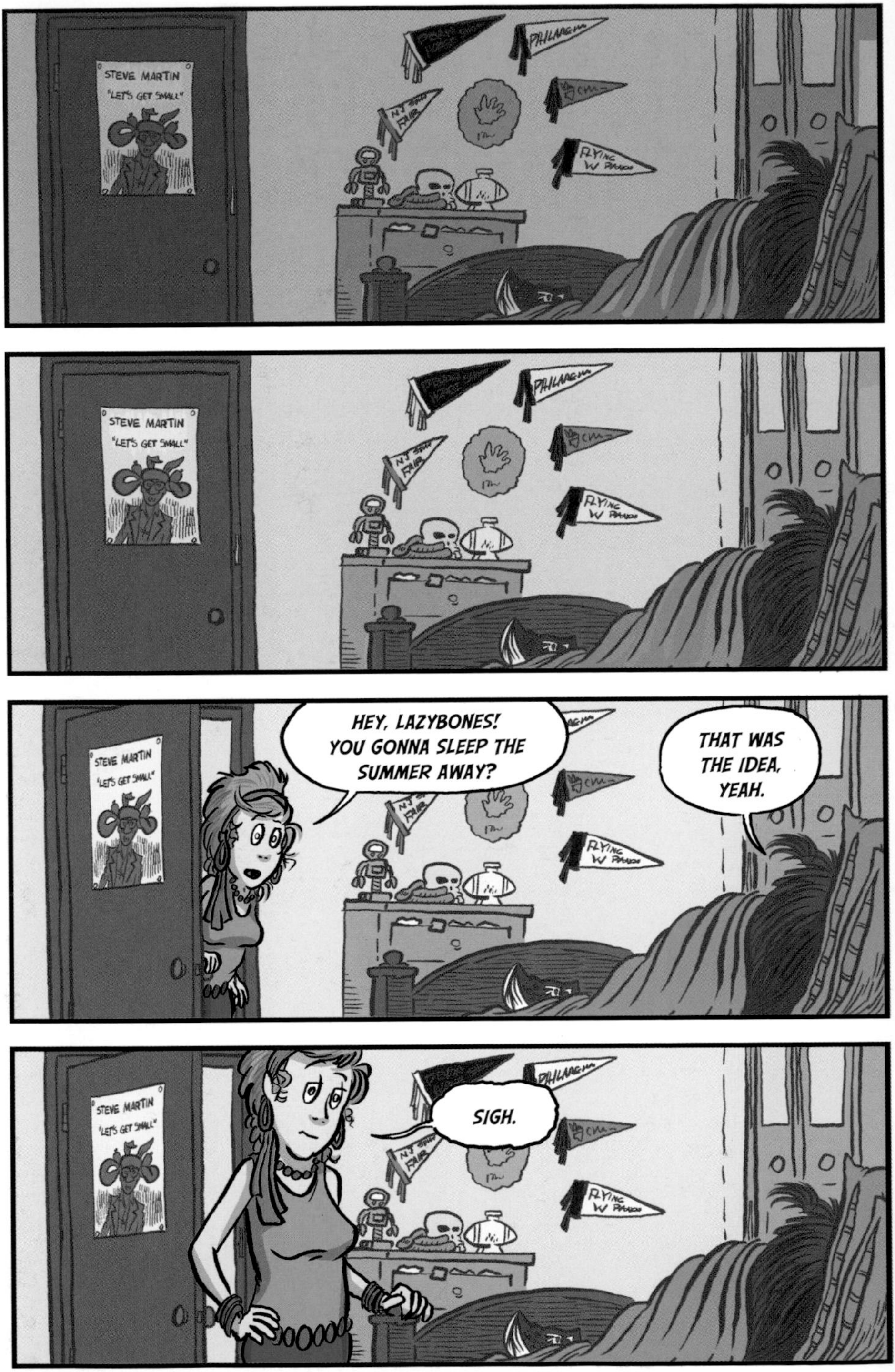
STEVE MARTIN
"LET'S GET SMALL"
HEY, LAZYBONES! YOU GONNA SLEEP THE SUMMER AWAY?
THAT WAS THE IDEA, YEAH.
SIGH.

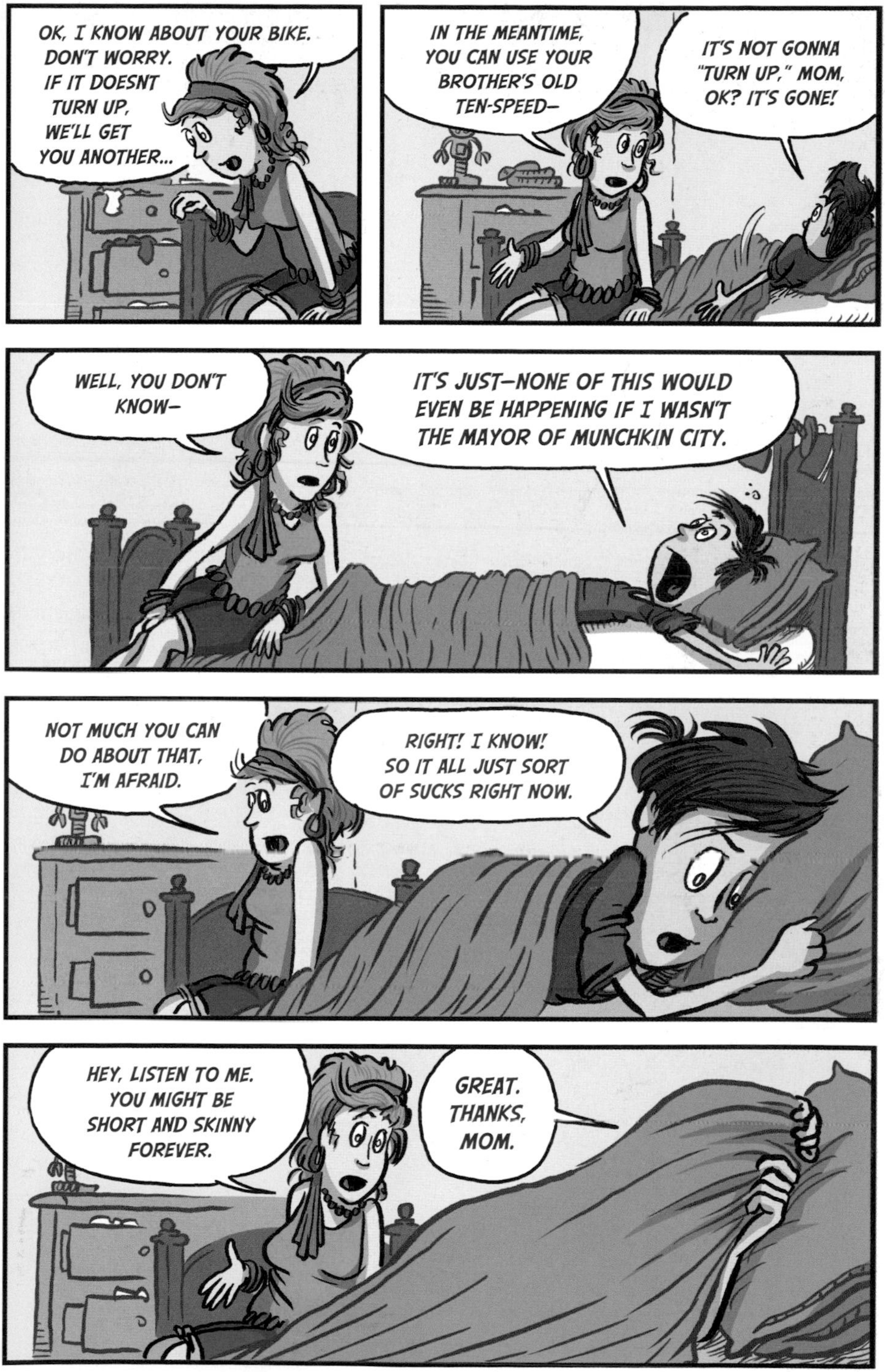
OK, I KNOW ABOUT YOUR BIKE. DON'T WORRY. IF IT DOESNT TURN UP, WE'LL GET YOU ANOTHER...
IN THE MEANTIME, YOU CAN USE YOUR BROTHER'S OLD TEN-SPEED—
IT'S NOT GONNA "TURN UP," MOM, OK? IT'S GONE!
WELL, YOU DON'T KNOW—
IT'S JUST—NONE OF THIS WOULD EVEN BE HAPPENING IF I WASN'T THE MAYOR OF MUNCHKIN CITY.
NOT MUCH YOU CAN DO ABOUT THAT, I'M AFRAID.
RIGHT! I KNOW! SO IT ALL JUST SORT OF SUCKS RIGHT NOW.
HEY, LISTEN TO ME. YOU MIGHT BE SHORT AND SKINNY FOREVER.
GREAT. THANKS, MOM.

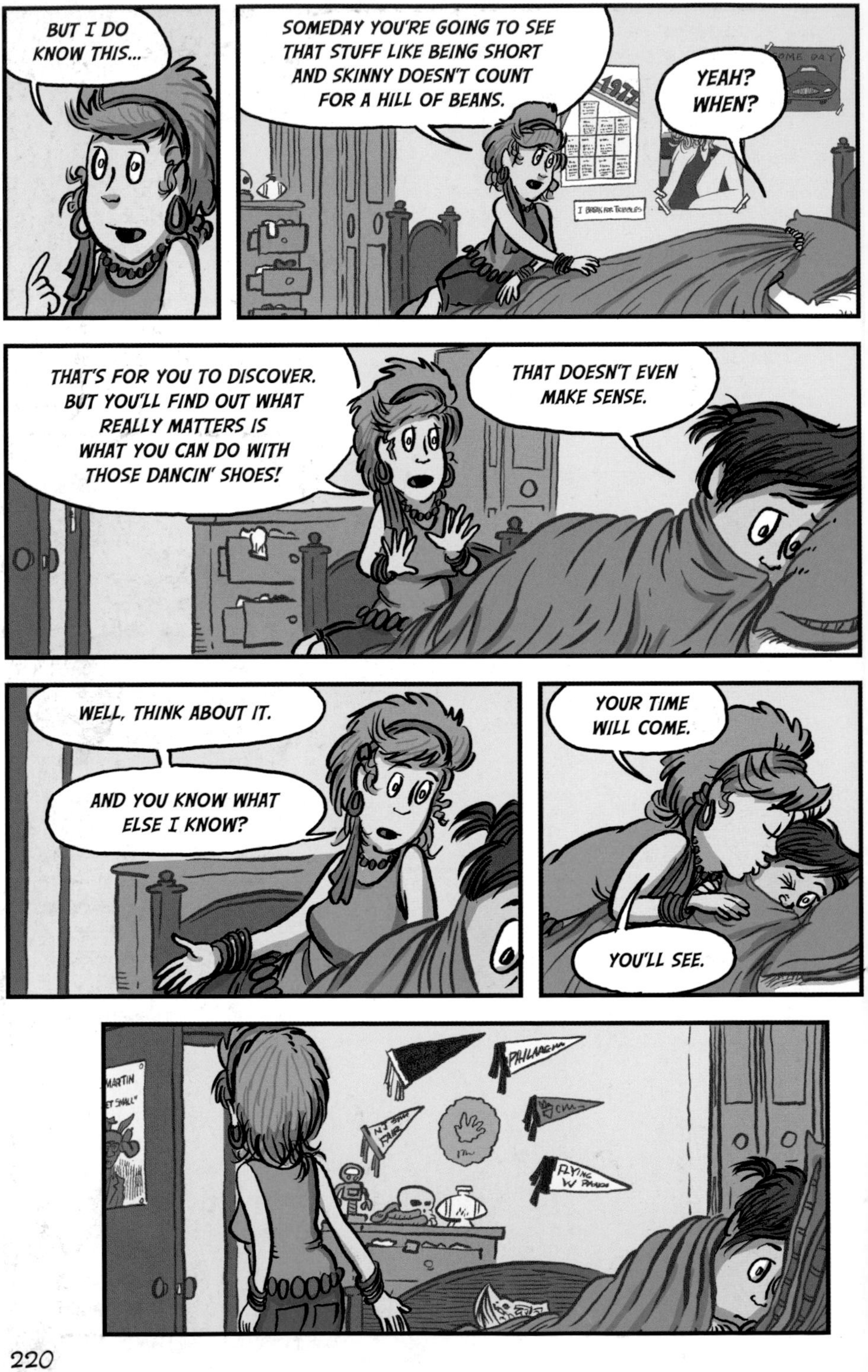
BUT I DO KNOW THIS...
SOMEDAY YOU'RE GOING TO SEE THAT STUFF LIKE BEING SHORT AND SKINNY DOESN'T COUNT FOR A HILL OF BEANS.
YEAH? WHEN?
1977
I BRAKE FOR TRIBBLES
THAT'S FOR YOU TO DISCOVER. BUT YOU'LL FIND OUT WHAT REALLY MATTERS IS WHAT YOU CAN DO WITH THOSE DANCIN' SHOES!
THAT DOESN'T EVEN MAKE SENSE.
WELL, THINK ABOUT IT.
AND YOU KNOW WHAT ELSE I KNOW?
YOUR TIME WILL COME.
YOU'LL SEE.
MARTIN
FLYING W

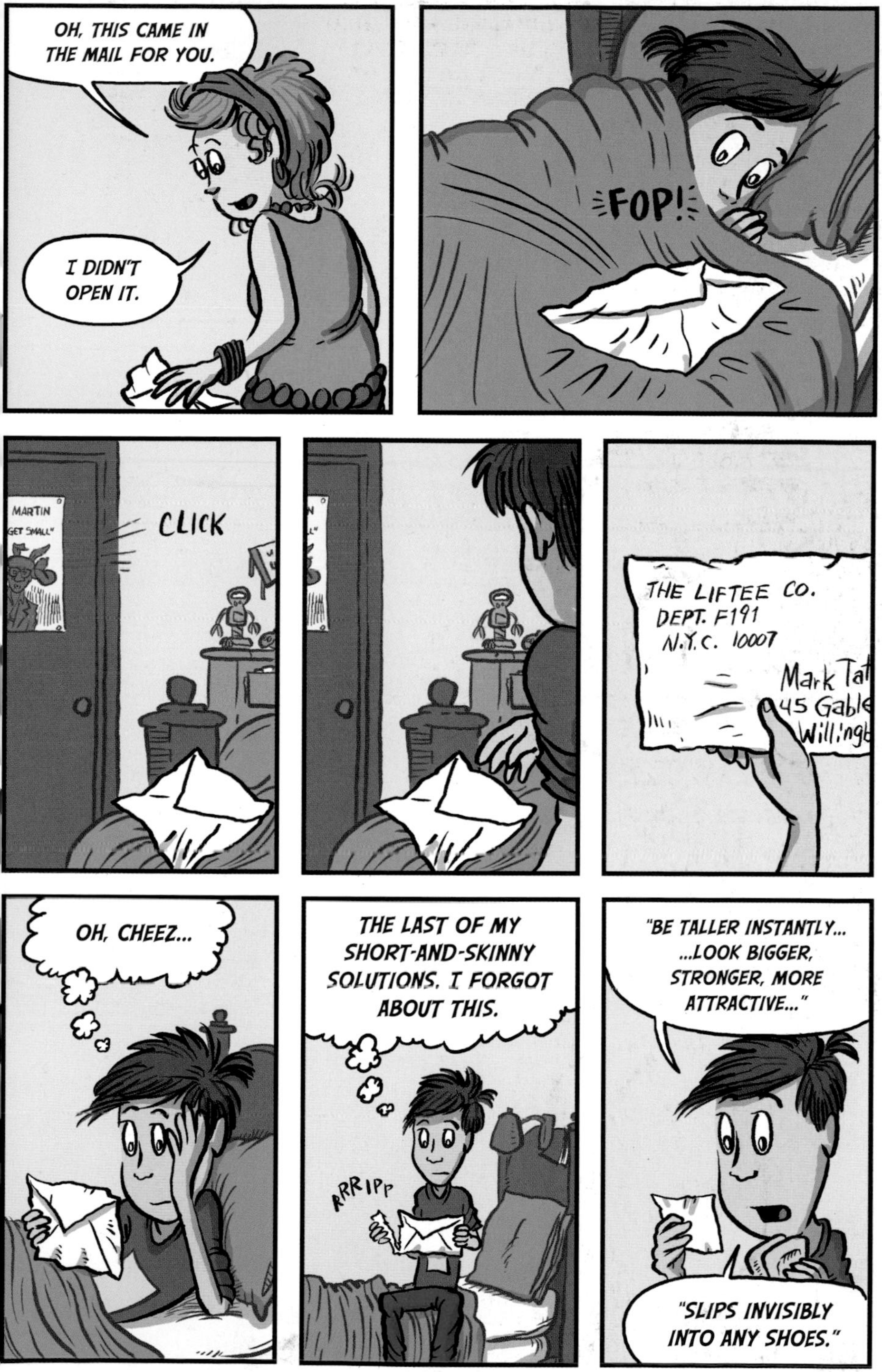
OH, THIS CAME IN THE MAIL FOR YOU.
I DIDN'T OPEN IT.
FOP!
MARTIN
"GET SMALL"
CLICK
THE LIFTEE CO.
DEPT. F191
N.Y.C. 10007
Mark Tat
45 Gable
Willingb
OH, CHEEZ...
THE LAST OF MY SHORT-AND-SKINNY SOLUTIONS. I FORGOT ABOUT THIS.
RRRIPP
"BE TALLER INSTANTLY... ...LOOK BIGGER, STRONGER, MORE ATTRACTIVE..."
"SLIPS INVISIBLY INTO ANY SHOES."

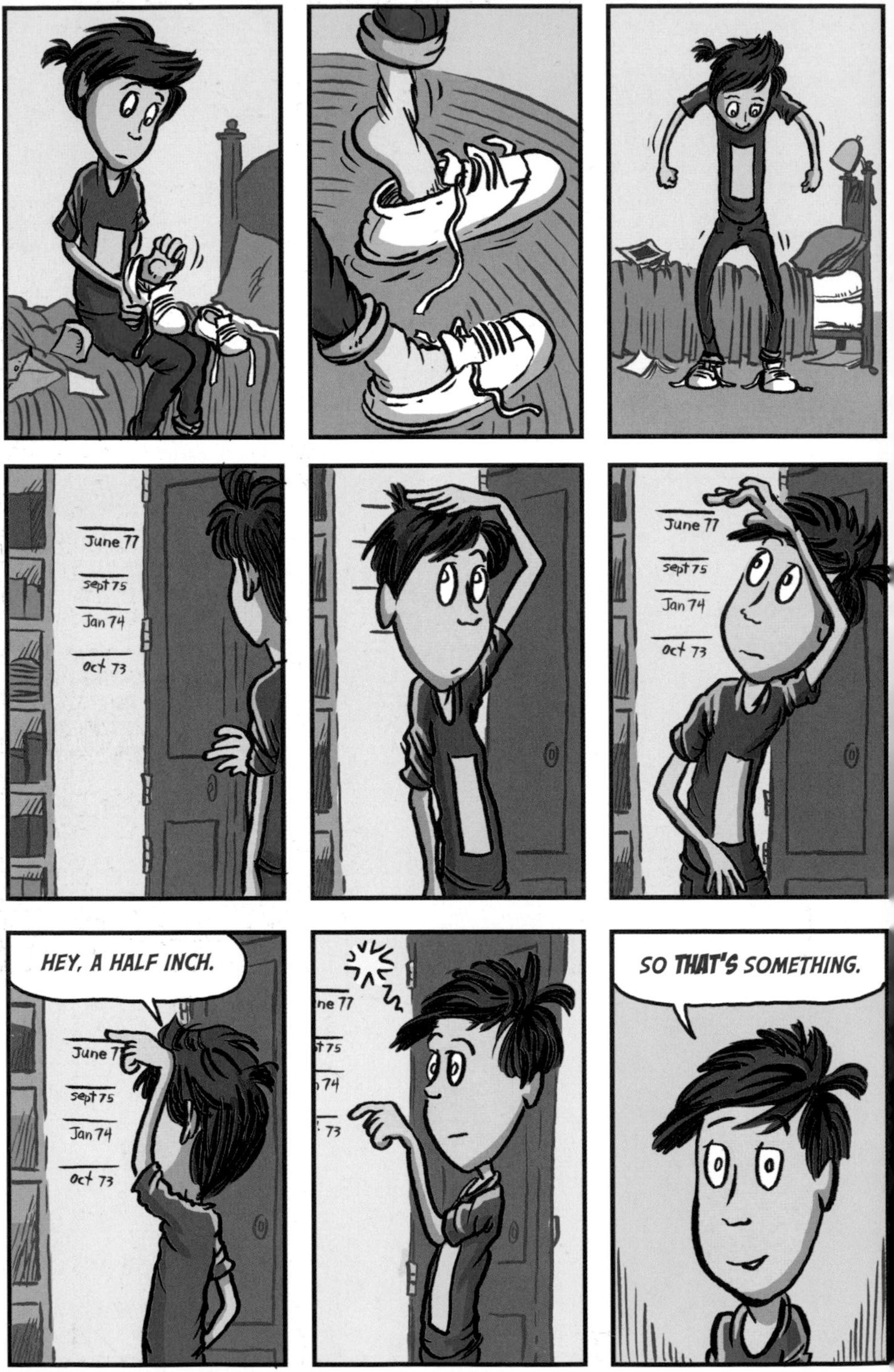
June 77
sept 75
Jan 74
Oct 73
June 77
sept 75
Jan 74
Oct 73
HEY, A HALF INCH.
sept 75
Jan 74
Oct 73
SO **THAT'S** SOMETHING.

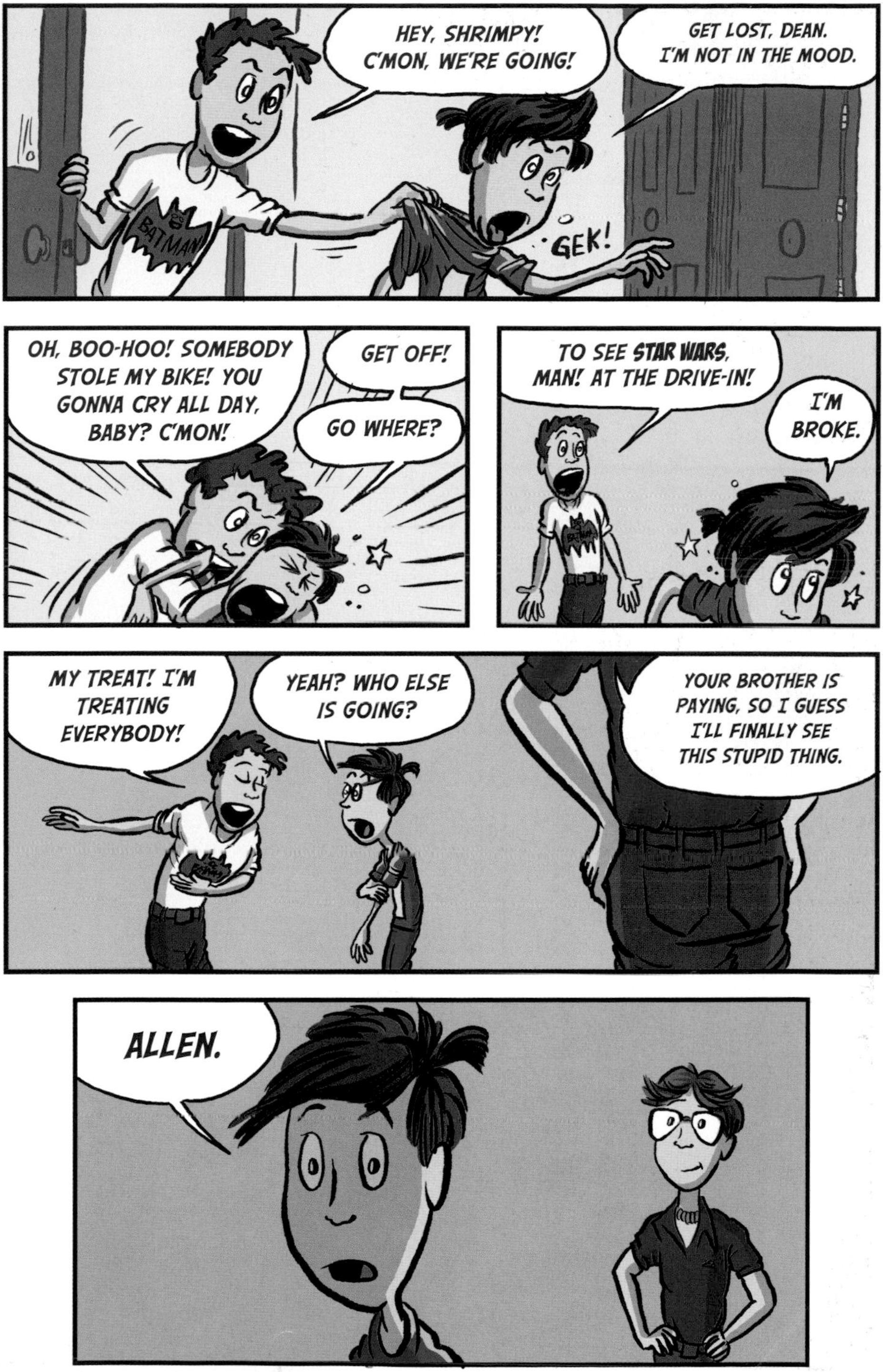
HEY, SHRIMPY! C'MON, WE'RE GOING!
GET LOST, DEAN. I'M NOT IN THE MOOD.
GEK!
OH, BOO-HOO! SOMEBODY STOLE MY BIKE! YOU GONNA CRY ALL DAY, BABY? C'MON!
GET OFF!
GO WHERE?
TO SEE STAR WARS, MAN! AT THE DRIVE-IN!
I'M BROKE.
MY TREAT! I'M TREATING EVERYBODY!
YEAH? WHO ELSE IS GOING?
YOUR BROTHER IS PAYING, SO I GUESS I'LL FINALLY SEE THIS STUPID THING.
ALLEN.

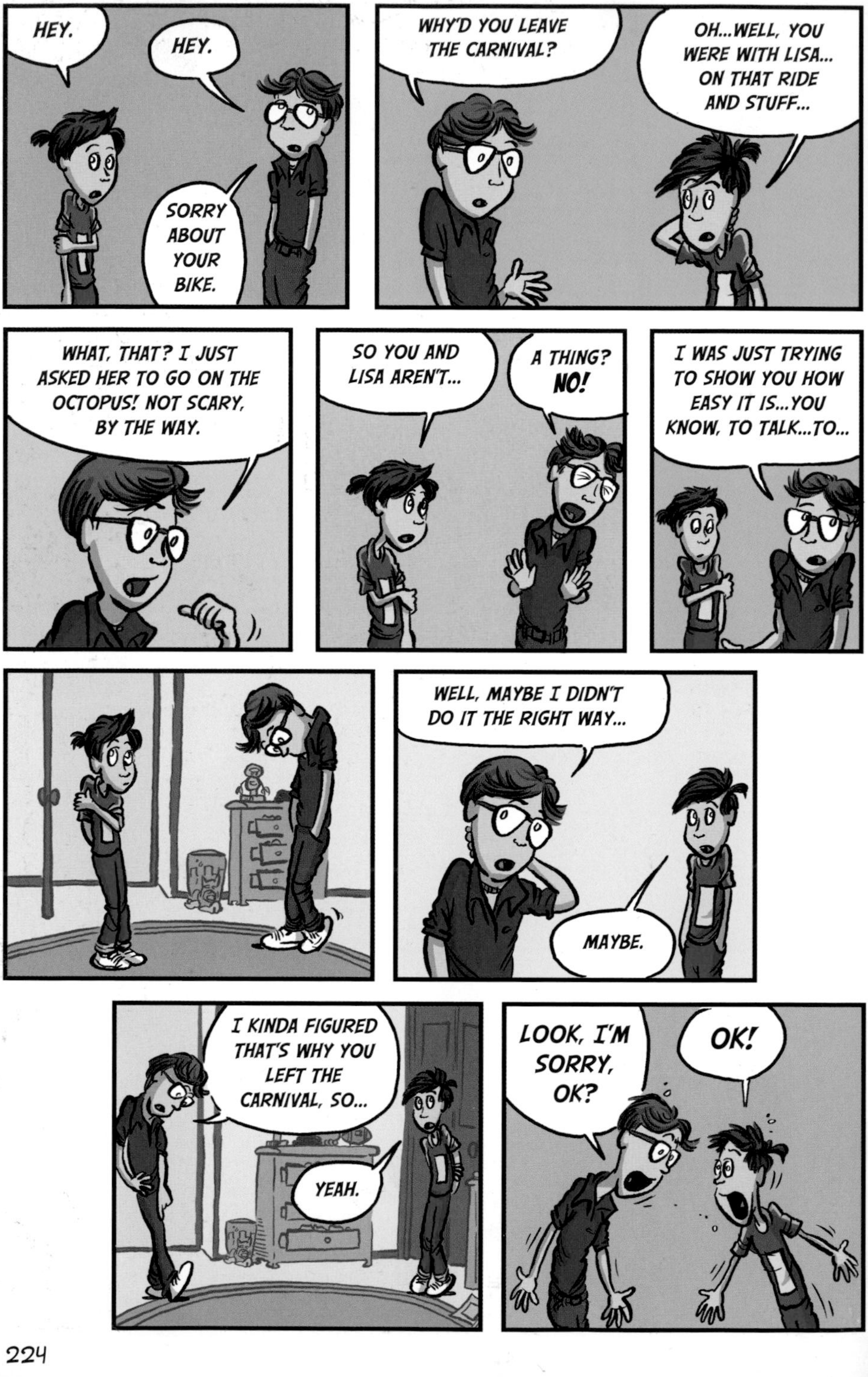

HEY.
HEY.
SORRY ABOUT YOUR BIKE.
WHY'D YOU LEAVE THE CARNIVAL?
OH...WELL, YOU WERE WITH LISA... ON THAT RIDE AND STUFF...
WHAT, THAT? I JUST ASKED HER TO GO ON THE OCTOPUS! NOT SCARY, BY THE WAY.
SO YOU AND LISA AREN'T...
A THING? NO!
I WAS JUST TRYING TO SHOW YOU HOW EASY IT IS...YOU KNOW, TO TALK...TO...
WELL, MAYBE I DIDN'T DO IT THE RIGHT WAY...
MAYBE.
I KINDA FIGURED THAT'S WHY YOU LEFT THE CARNIVAL, SO...
YEAH.
LOOK, I'M SORRY, OK?
OK!

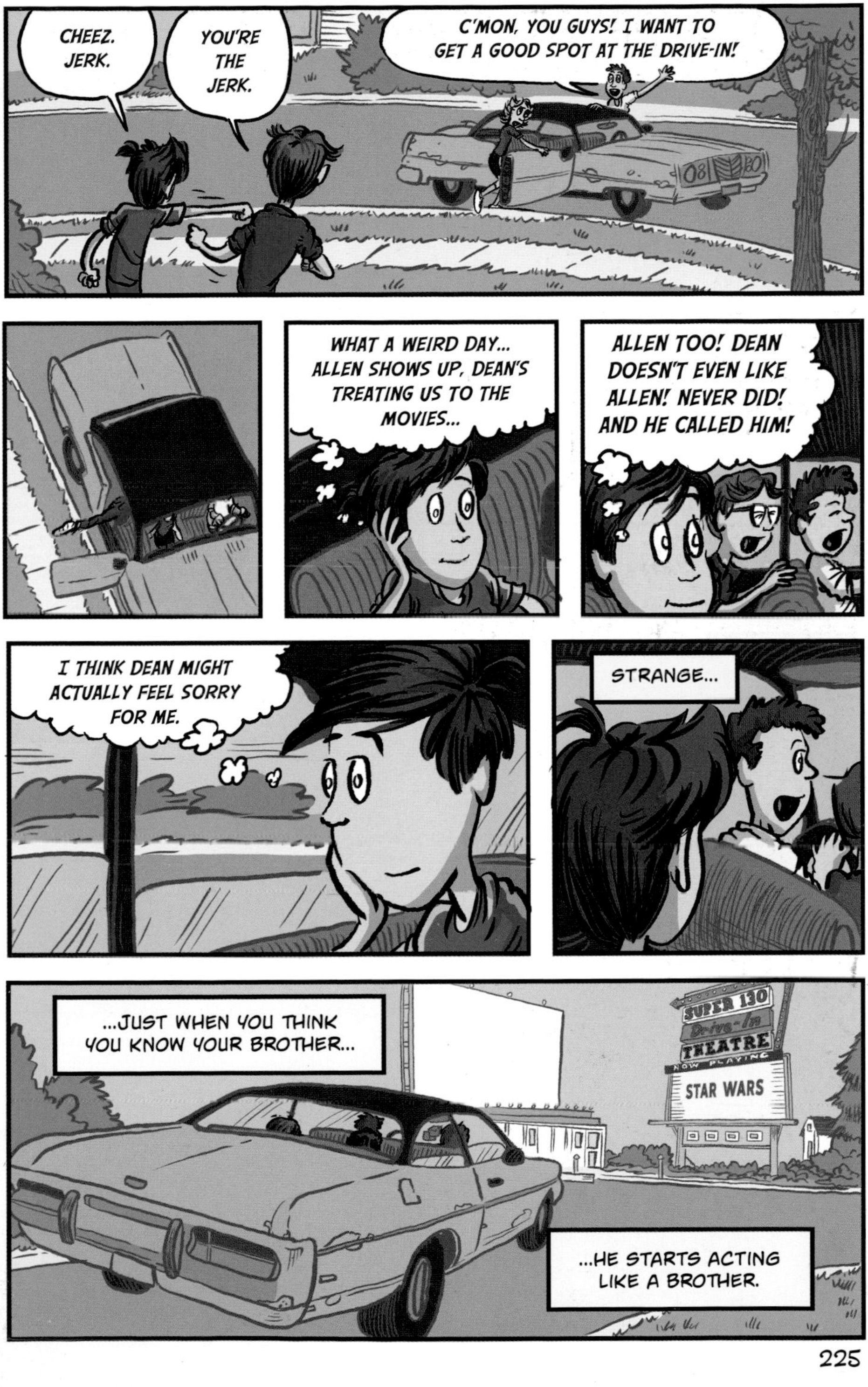
CHEEZ. JERK.
YOU'RE THE JERK.
C'MON, YOU GUYS! I WANT TO GET A GOOD SPOT AT THE DRIVE-IN!
WHAT A WEIRD DAY... ALLEN SHOWS UP, DEAN'S TREATING US TO THE MOVIES...
ALLEN TOO! DEAN DOESN'T EVEN LIKE ALLEN! NEVER DID! AND HE CALLED HIM!
I THINK DEAN MIGHT ACTUALLY FEEL SORRY FOR ME.
STRANGE...
...JUST WHEN YOU THINK YOU KNOW YOUR BROTHER...
SUPER 130 Drive-In THEATRE
NOW PLAYING
STAR WARS
...HE STARTS ACTING LIKE A BROTHER.

CHAPTER 14

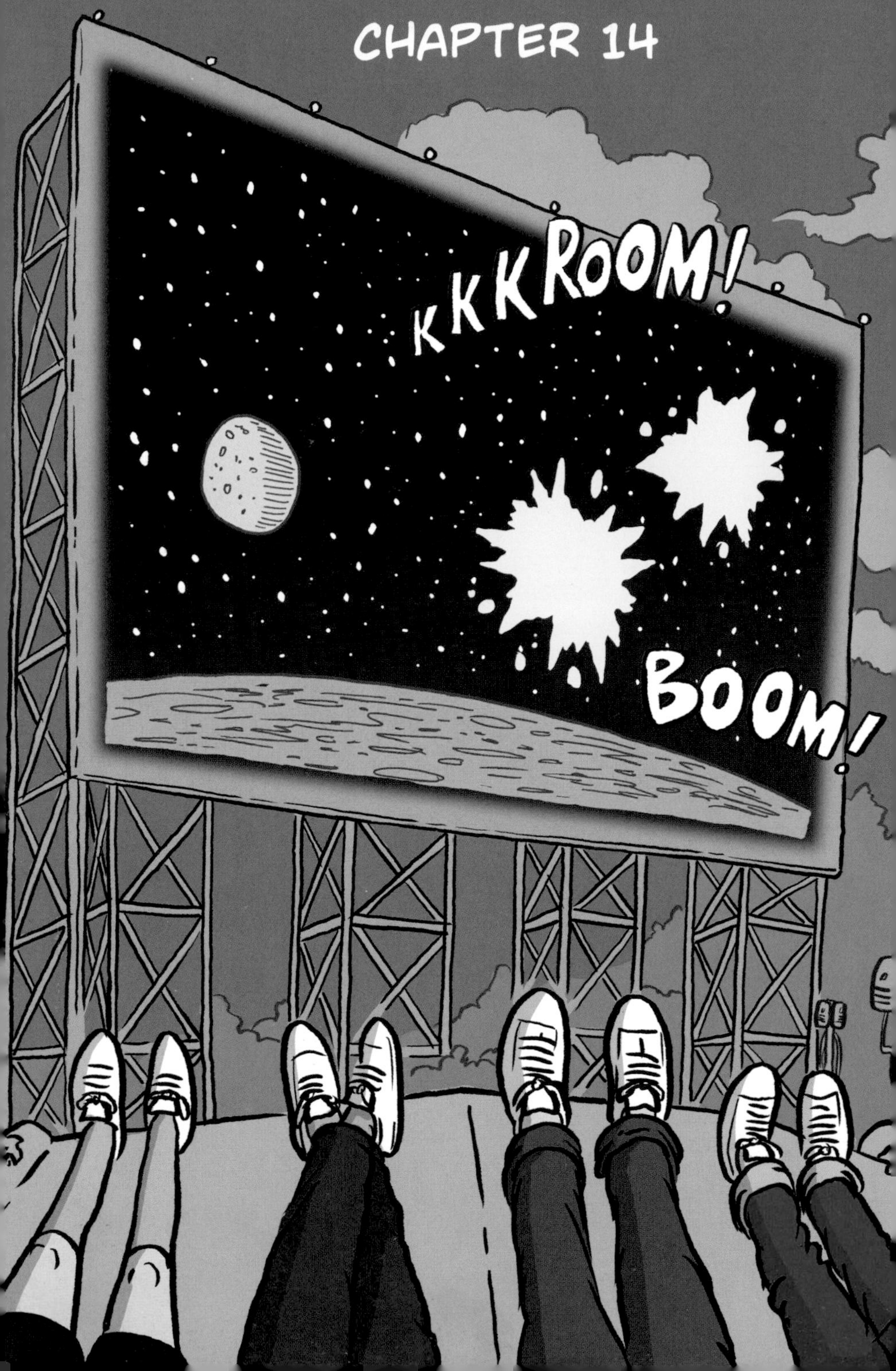
KKKROOM!
BOOM!

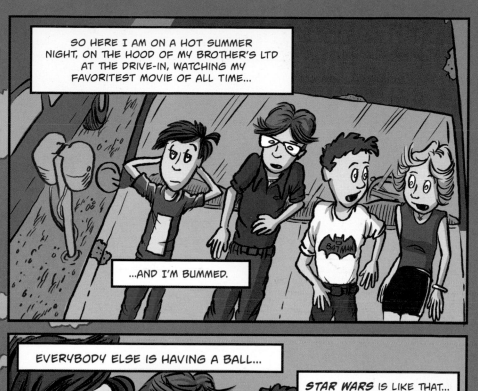

SO HERE I AM ON A HOT SUMMER NIGHT, ON THE HOOD OF MY BROTHER'S LTD AT THE DRIVE-IN, WATCHING MY FAVORITEST MOVIE OF ALL TIME...

...AND I'M BUMMED.

EVERYBODY ELSE IS HAVING A BALL...

STAR WARS IS LIKE THAT...

...IT MAKES EVERYBODY PALS.

WE SHOULD PUT ALL THE LEADERS OF THE WORLD IN A ROOM AND MAKE THEM WATCH IT TOGETHER...

...PROBABLY ALL THE FIGHTING WOULD STOP!

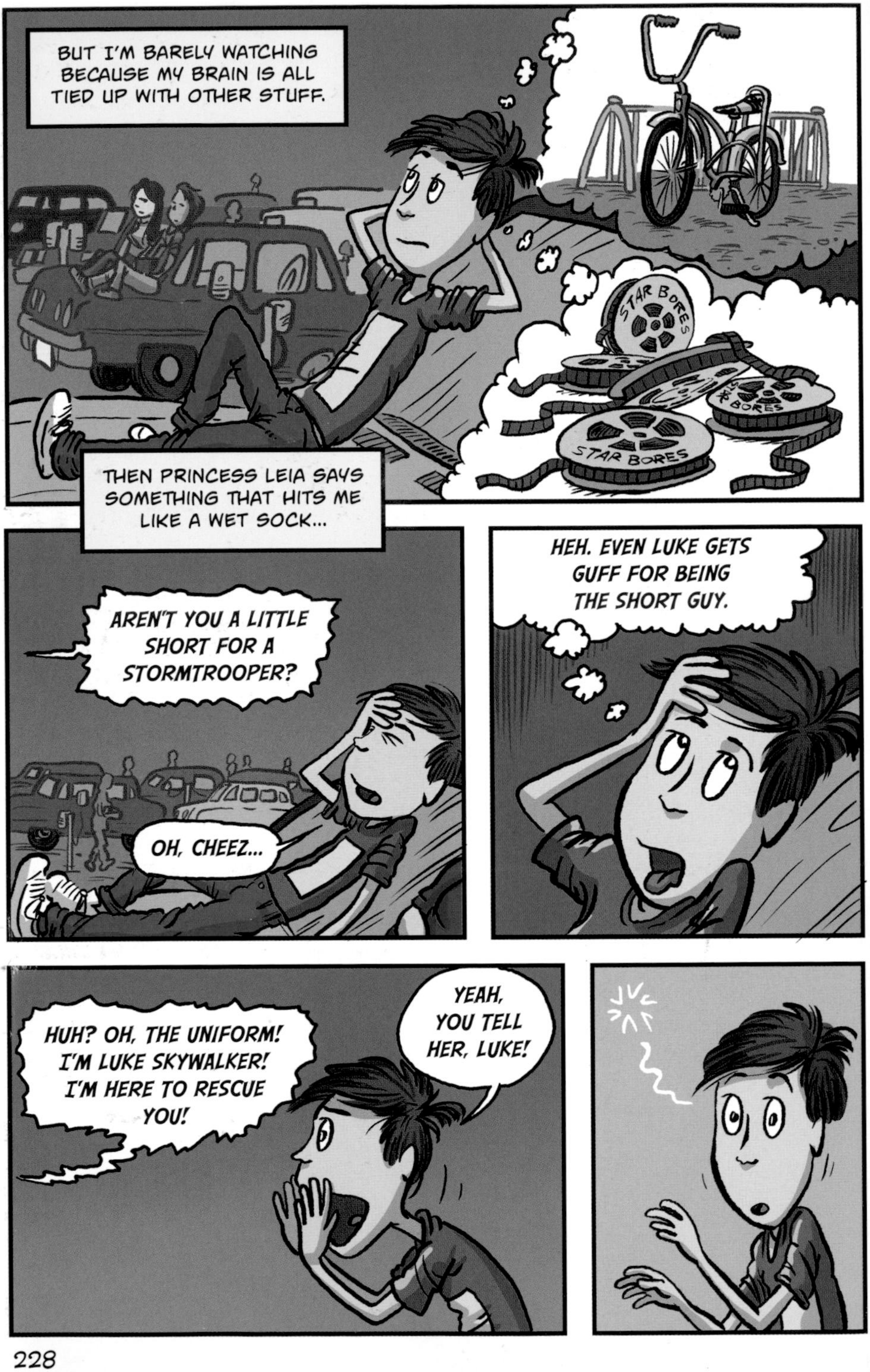
BUT I'M BARELY WATCHING BECAUSE MY BRAIN IS ALL TIED UP WITH OTHER STUFF.
STAR BORES
STAR BORES
STAR BORES
THEN PRINCESS LEIA SAYS SOMETHING THAT HITS ME LIKE A WET SOCK...
AREN'T YOU A LITTLE SHORT FOR A STORMTROOPER?
OH, CHEEZ...
HEH. EVEN LUKE GETS GUFF FOR BEING THE SHORT GUY.
HUH? OH, THE UNIFORM! I'M LUKE SKYWALKER! I'M HERE TO RESCUE YOU!
YEAH, YOU TELL HER, LUKE!

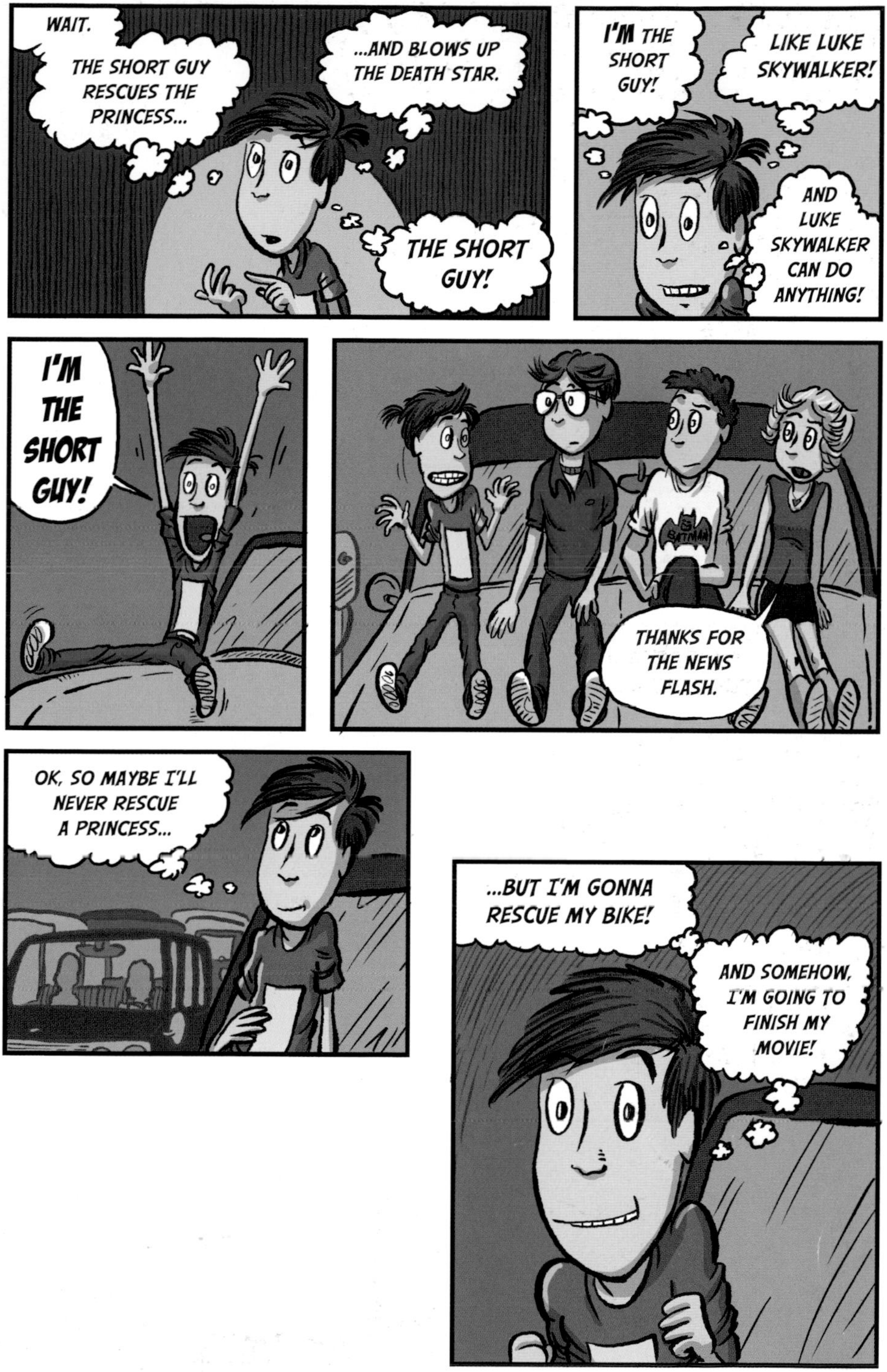
WAIT.
THE SHORT GUY RESCUES THE PRINCESS...
...AND BLOWS UP THE DEATH STAR.
THE SHORT GUY!
I'M THE SHORT GUY!
LIKE LUKE SKYWALKER!
AND LUKE SKYWALKER CAN DO ANYTHING!
I'M THE SHORT GUY!
THANKS FOR THE NEWS FLASH.
OK, SO MAYBE I'LL NEVER RESCUE A PRINCESS...
...BUT I'M GONNA RESCUE MY BIKE!
AND SOMEHOW, I'M GOING TO FINISH MY MOVIE!

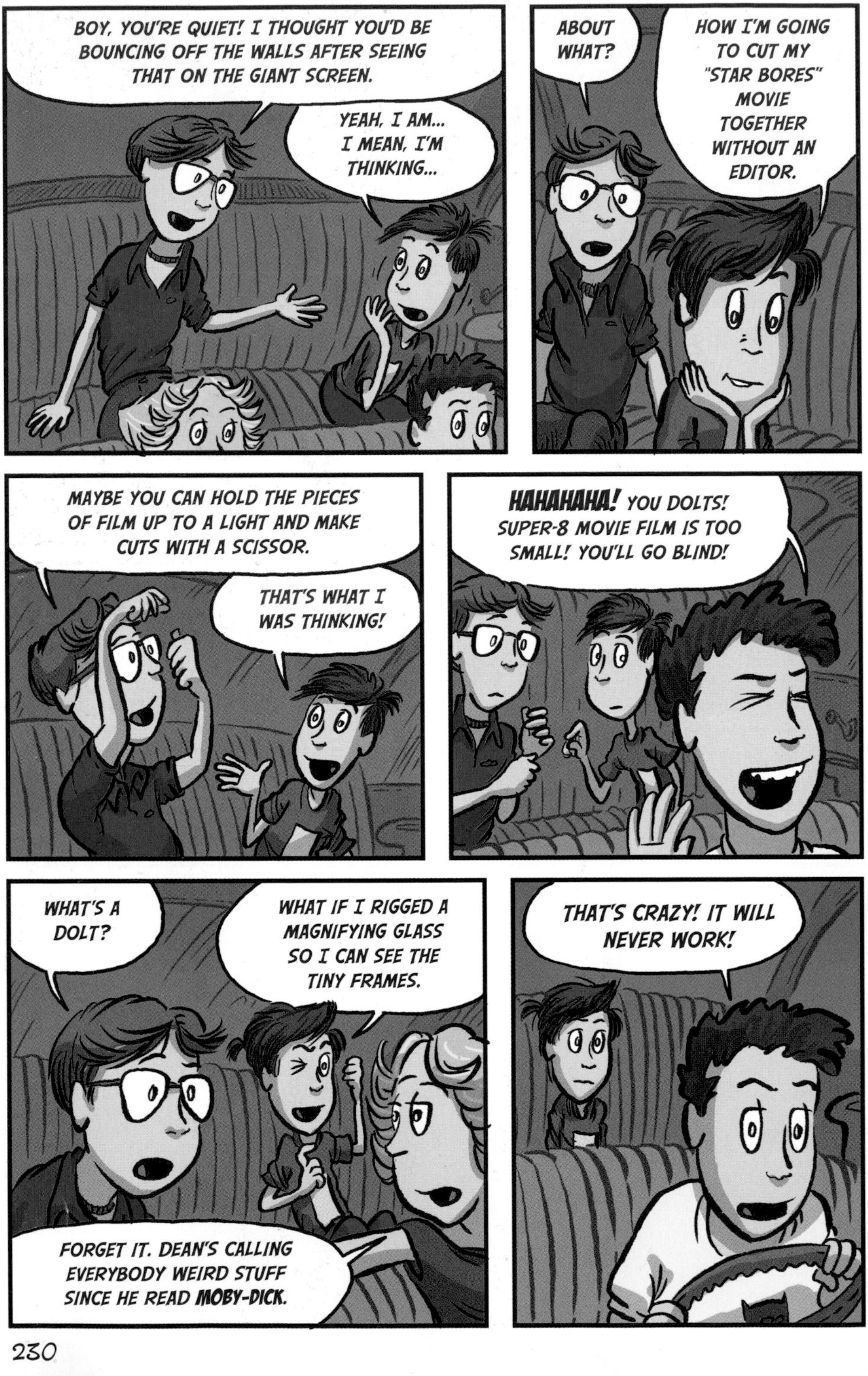

BOY, YOU'RE QUIET! I THOUGHT YOU'D BE BOUNCING OFF THE WALLS AFTER SEEING THAT ON THE GIANT SCREEN.
YEAH, I AM... I MEAN, I'M THINKING...
ABOUT WHAT?
HOW I'M GOING TO CUT MY "STAR BORES" MOVIE TOGETHER WITHOUT AN EDITOR.
MAYBE YOU CAN HOLD THE PIECES OF FILM UP TO A LIGHT AND MAKE CUTS WITH A SCISSOR.
THAT'S WHAT I WAS THINKING!
HAHAHAHA! YOU DOLTS! SUPER-8 MOVIE FILM IS TOO SMALL! YOU'LL GO BLIND!
WHAT'S A DOLT?
WHAT IF I RIGGED A MAGNIFYING GLASS SO I CAN SEE THE TINY FRAMES.
FORGET IT. DEAN'S CALLING EVERYBODY WEIRD STUFF SINCE HE READ MOBY-DICK.
THAT'S CRAZY! IT WILL NEVER WORK!

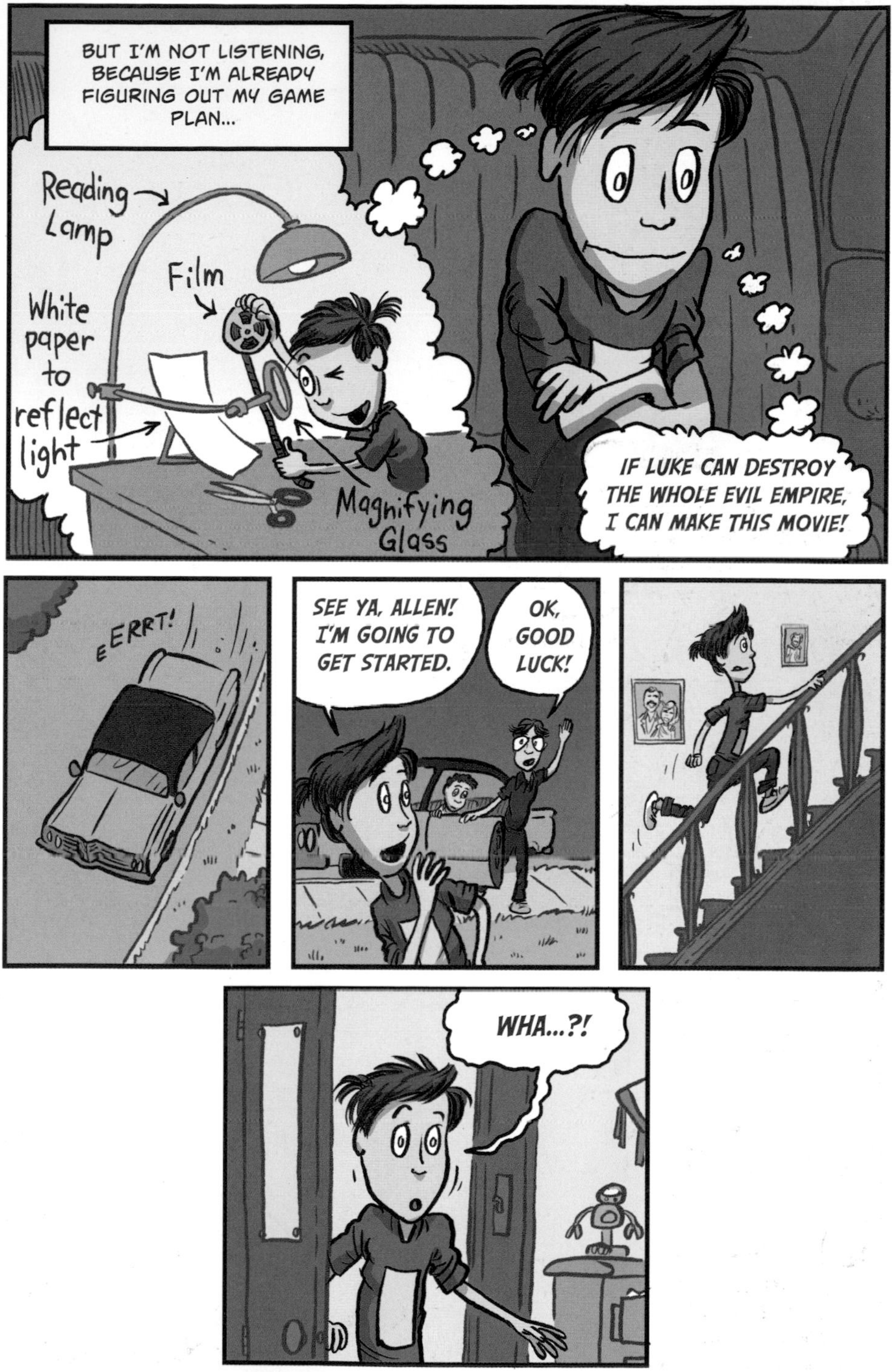
BUT I'M NOT LISTENING, BECAUSE I'M ALREADY FIGURING OUT MY GAME PLAN...
Reading Lamp
Film
White paper to reflect light
Magnifying Glass
IF LUKE CAN DESTROY THE WHOLE EVIL EMPIRE, I CAN MAKE THIS MOVIE!
EERRT!
SEE YA, ALLEN! I'M GOING TO GET STARTED.
OK, GOOD LUCK!
WHA...?!

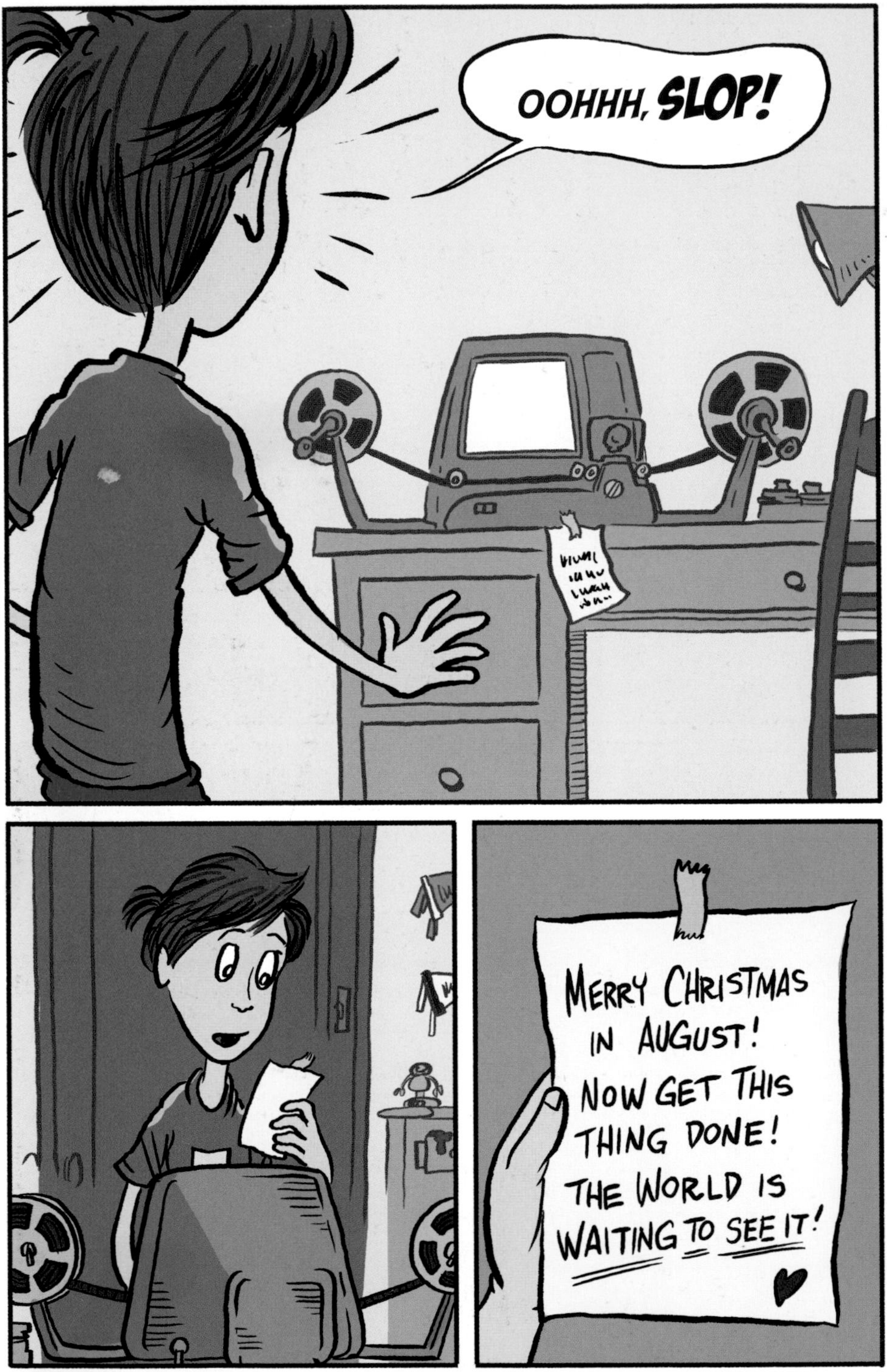
OOHHH, SLOP!
MERRY CHRISTMAS IN AUGUST! NOW GET THIS THING DONE! THE WORLD IS WAITING TO SEE IT!

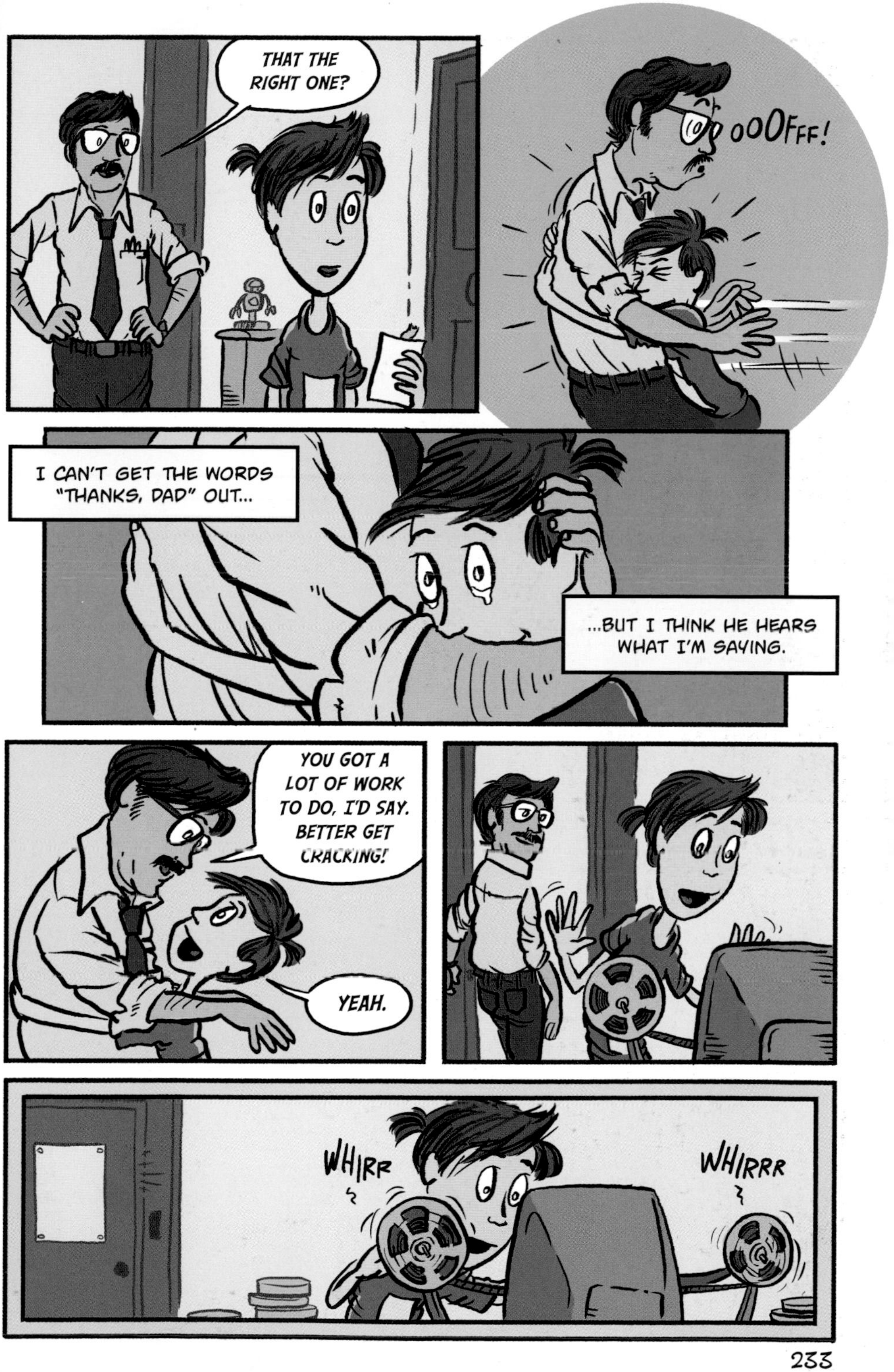
THAT THE RIGHT ONE?
OOOFFF!
I CAN'T GET THE WORDS "THANKS, DAD" OUT...
...BUT I THINK HE HEARS WHAT I'M SAYING.
YOU GOT A LOT OF WORK TO DO, I'D SAY. BETTER GET CRACKING!
YEAH.
WHIRR
WHIRRR

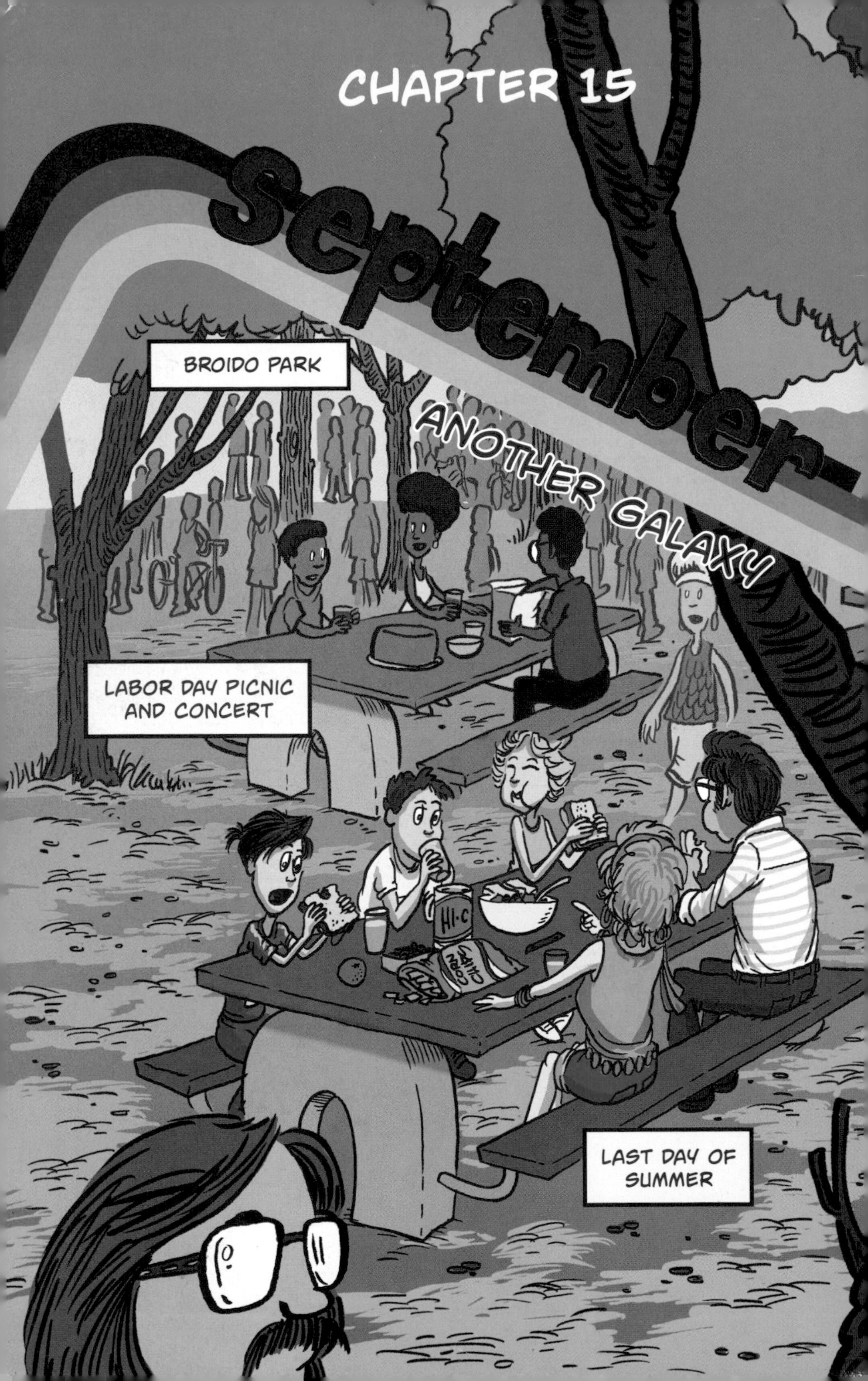
CHAPTER 15
September–
ANOTHER GALAXY
BROIDO PARK
LABOR DAY PICNIC AND CONCERT
LAST DAY OF SUMMER
HI-C
CORN CHIPS

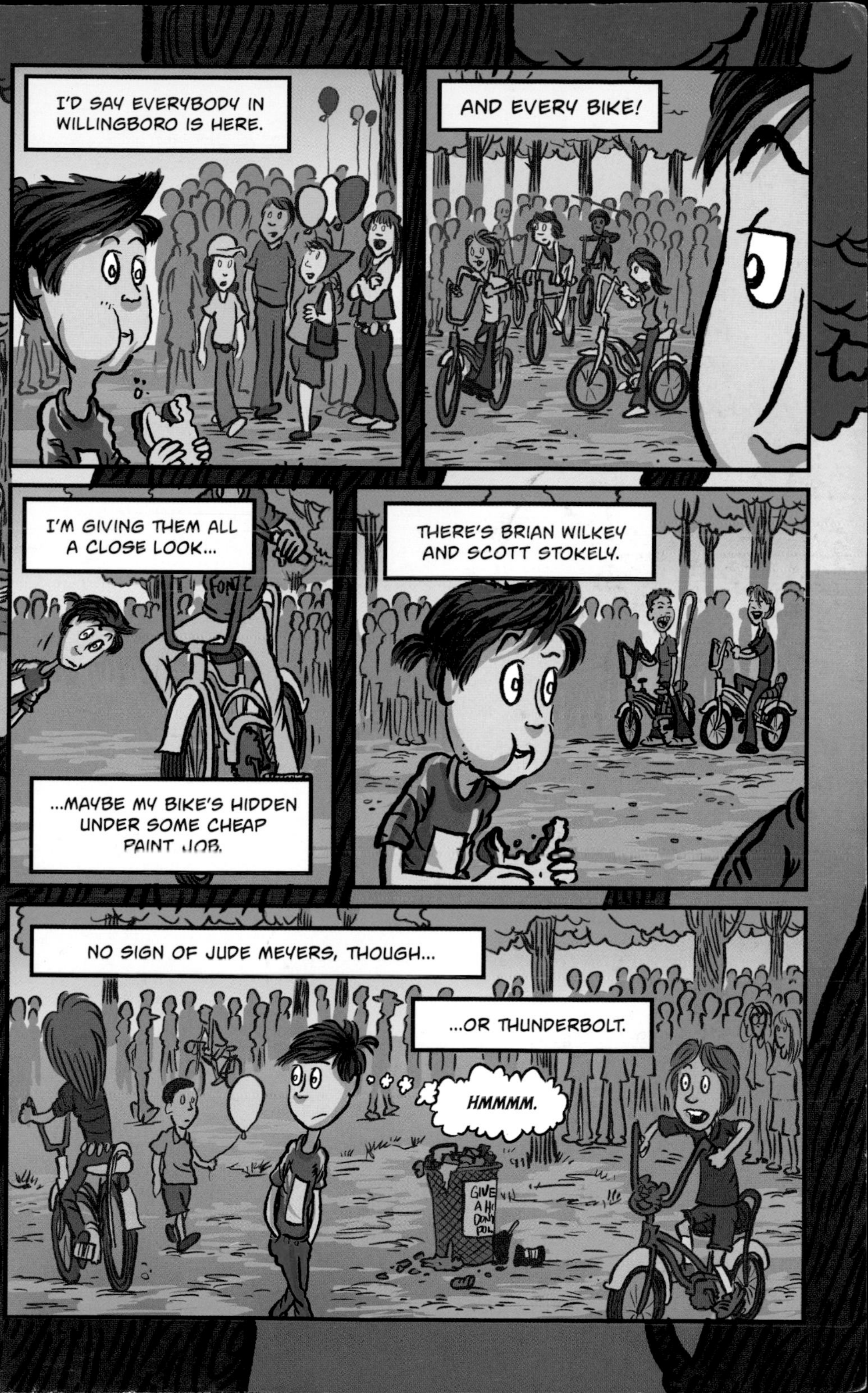
I'D SAY EVERYBODY IN WILLINGBORO IS HERE.
AND EVERY BIKE!
I'M GIVING THEM ALL A CLOSE LOOK...
...MAYBE MY BIKE'S HIDDEN UNDER SOME CHEAP PAINT JOB.
THERE'S BRIAN WILKEY AND SCOTT STOKELY.
NO SIGN OF JUDE MEYERS, THOUGH...
...OR THUNDERBOLT.
HMMMM.

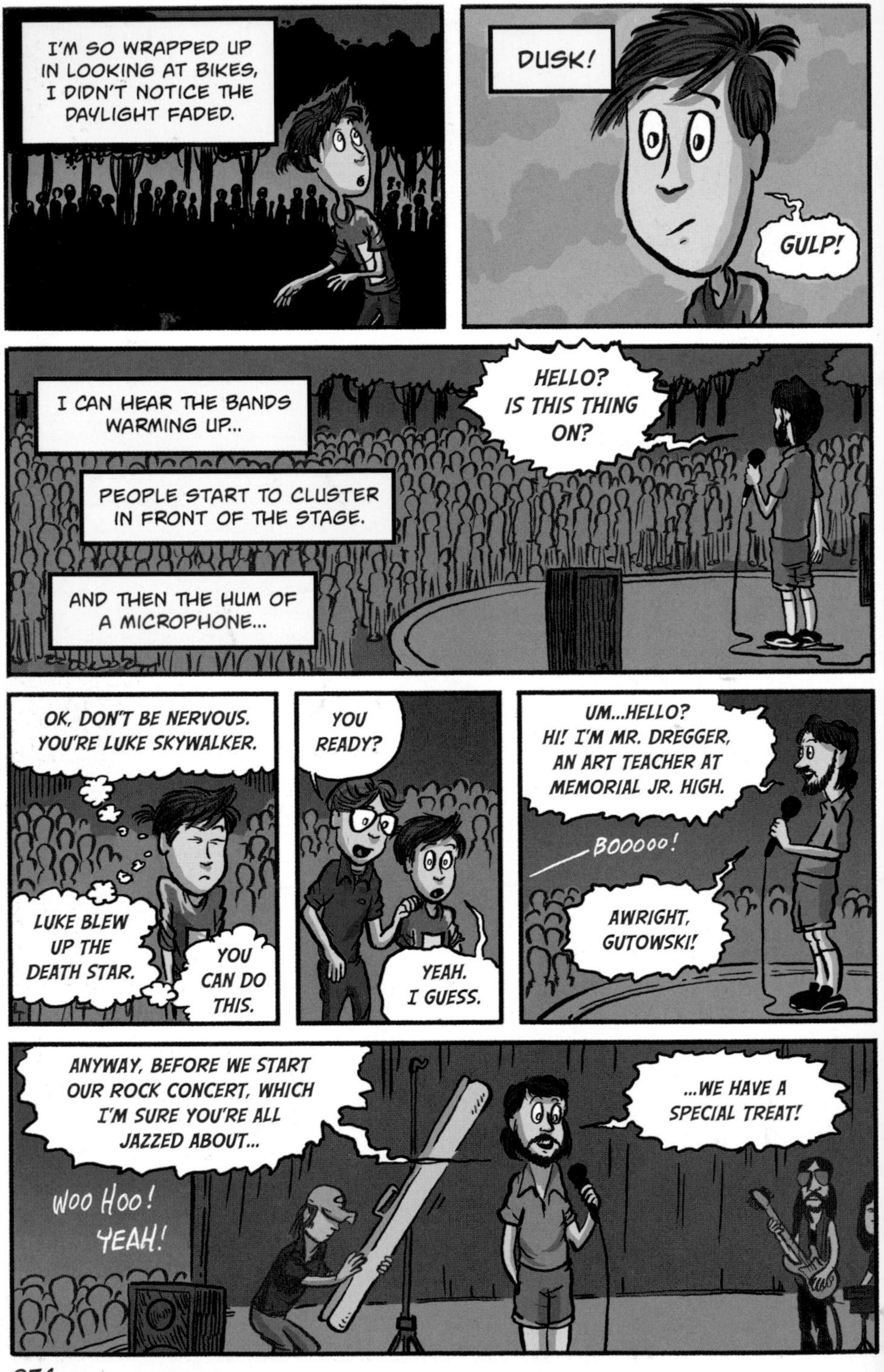
I'M SO WRAPPED UP IN LOOKING AT BIKES, I DIDN'T NOTICE THE DAYLIGHT FADED.
DUSK!
GULP!
I CAN HEAR THE BANDS WARMING UP...
PEOPLE START TO CLUSTER IN FRONT OF THE STAGE.
AND THEN THE HUM OF A MICROPHONE...
HELLO? IS THIS THING ON?
OK, DON'T BE NERVOUS. YOU'RE LUKE SKYWALKER.
LUKE BLEW UP THE DEATH STAR.
YOU CAN DO THIS.
YOU READY?
YEAH. I GUESS.
UM...HELLO? HI! I'M MR. DREGGER, AN ART TEACHER AT MEMORIAL JR. HIGH.
BOOOOO!
AWRIGHT, GUTOWSKI!
ANYWAY, BEFORE WE START OUR ROCK CONCERT, WHICH I'M SURE YOU'RE ALL JAZZED ABOUT...
...WE HAVE A SPECIAL TREAT!
WOO HOO!
YEAH!

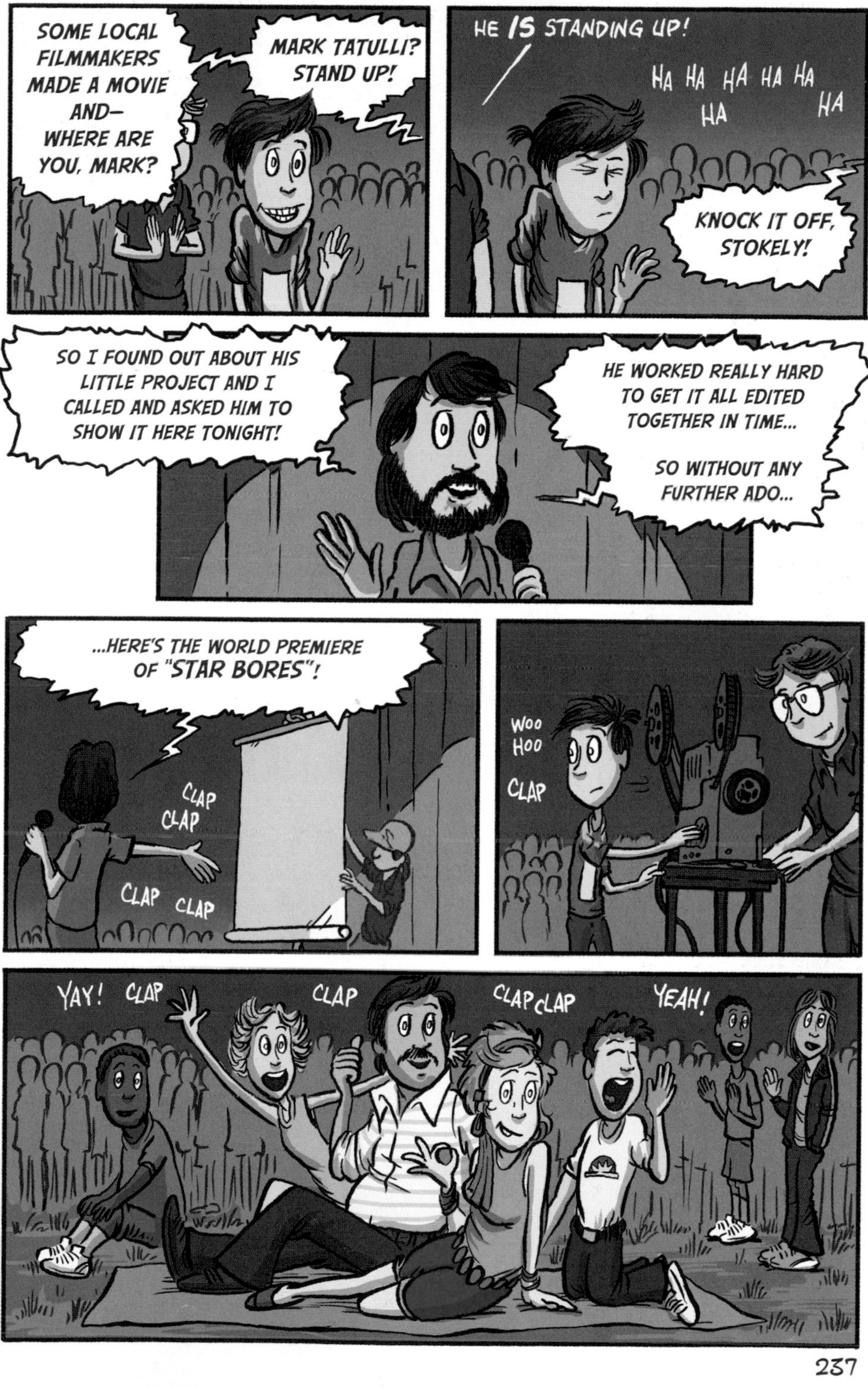

SOME LOCAL FILMMAKERS MADE A MOVIE AND— WHERE ARE YOU, MARK?
MARK TATULLI? STAND UP!
HE IS STANDING UP!
HA HA HA HA HA HA HA
KNOCK IT OFF, STOKELY!
SO I FOUND OUT ABOUT HIS LITTLE PROJECT AND I CALLED AND ASKED HIM TO SHOW IT HERE TONIGHT!
HE WORKED REALLY HARD TO GET IT ALL EDITED TOGETHER IN TIME...
SO WITHOUT ANY FURTHER ADO...
...HERE'S THE WORLD PREMIERE OF "STAR BORES"!
CLAP CLAP
CLAP CLAP
WOO HOO
CLAP
YAY! CLAP
CLAP
CLAP CLAP
YEAH!

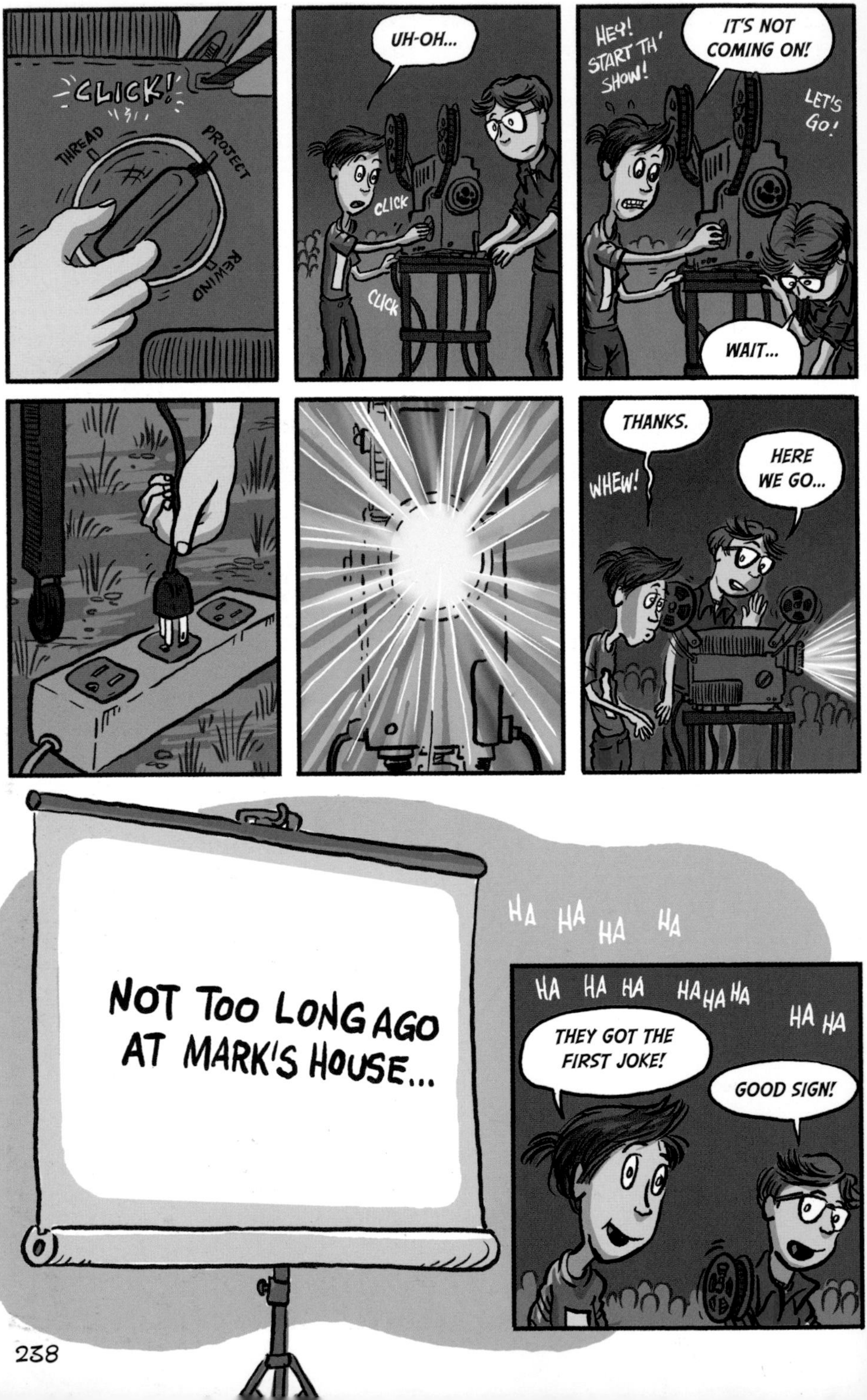
CLICK!
THREAD
PROJECT
REWIND
UH-OH...
CLICK
CLICK
HEY! START TH' SHOW!
IT'S NOT COMING ON!
LET'S GO!
WAIT...
THANKS.
WHEW!
HERE WE GO...
NOT TOO LONG AGO AT MARK'S HOUSE...
HA HA HA HA
HA HA HA HA HA HA
HA HA
THEY GOT THE FIRST JOKE!
GOOD SIGN!

AND THEN THE FAMILIAR STAR WARS MUSIC BLASTS OUT OF THE BIG SPEAKERS AND THE TITLE COMES UP...
AND THE PEOPLE START CHEERING!
FOR MY MOVIE!
STAR BORES
WELL, OK, MAYBE THEY'RE CHEERING MORE FOR THE MUSIC, BUT THAT'S MY MOVIE ON THE SORT-OF-BIG-SCREEN!
AND I'M LAUNCHED INTO ANOTHER GALAXY!

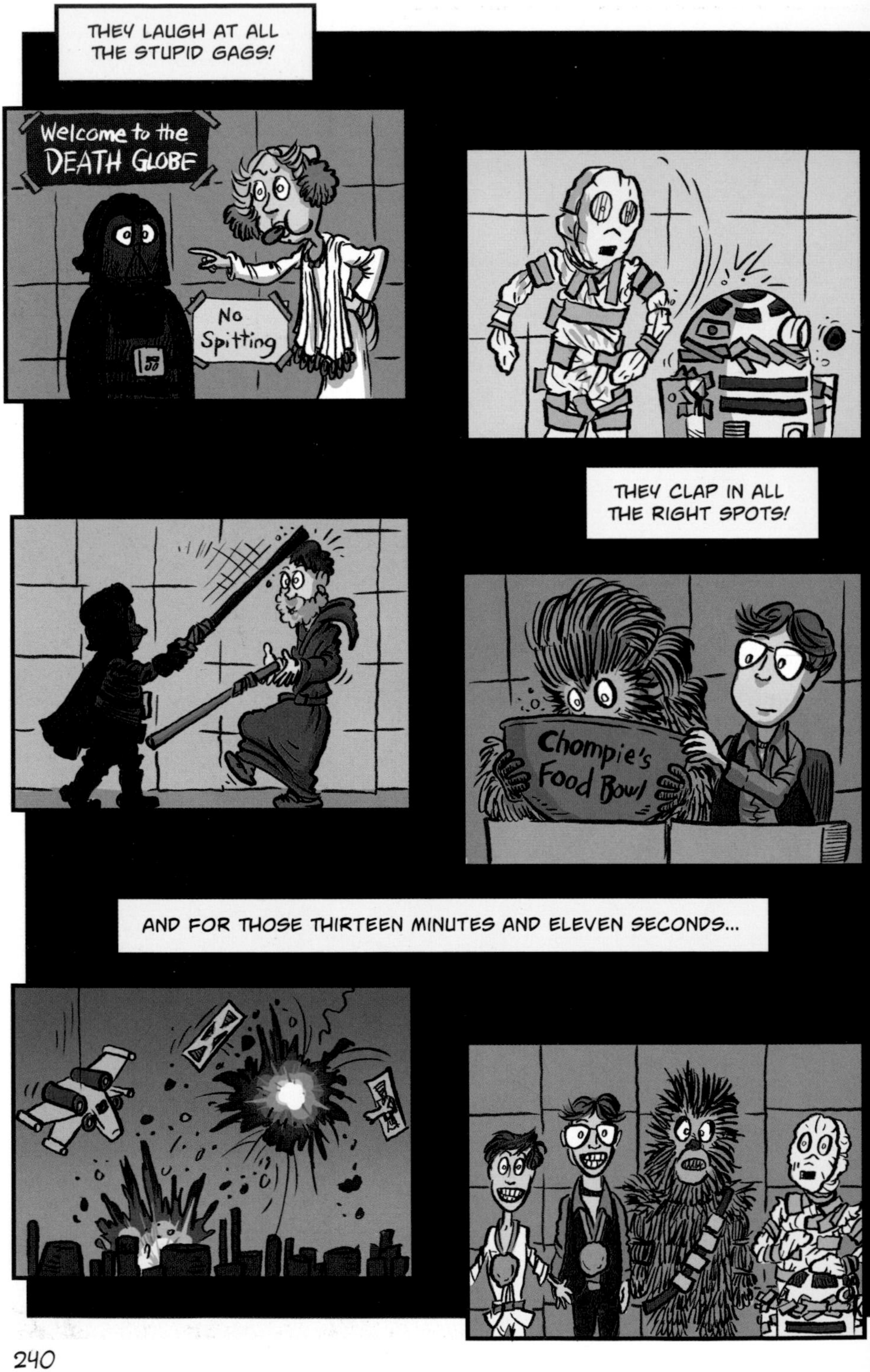
THEY LAUGH AT ALL THE STUPID GAGS!
Welcome to the DEATH GLOBE
No Spitting
THEY CLAP IN ALL THE RIGHT SPOTS!
Chompie's Food Bowl
AND FOR THOSE THIRTEEN MINUTES AND ELEVEN SECONDS...

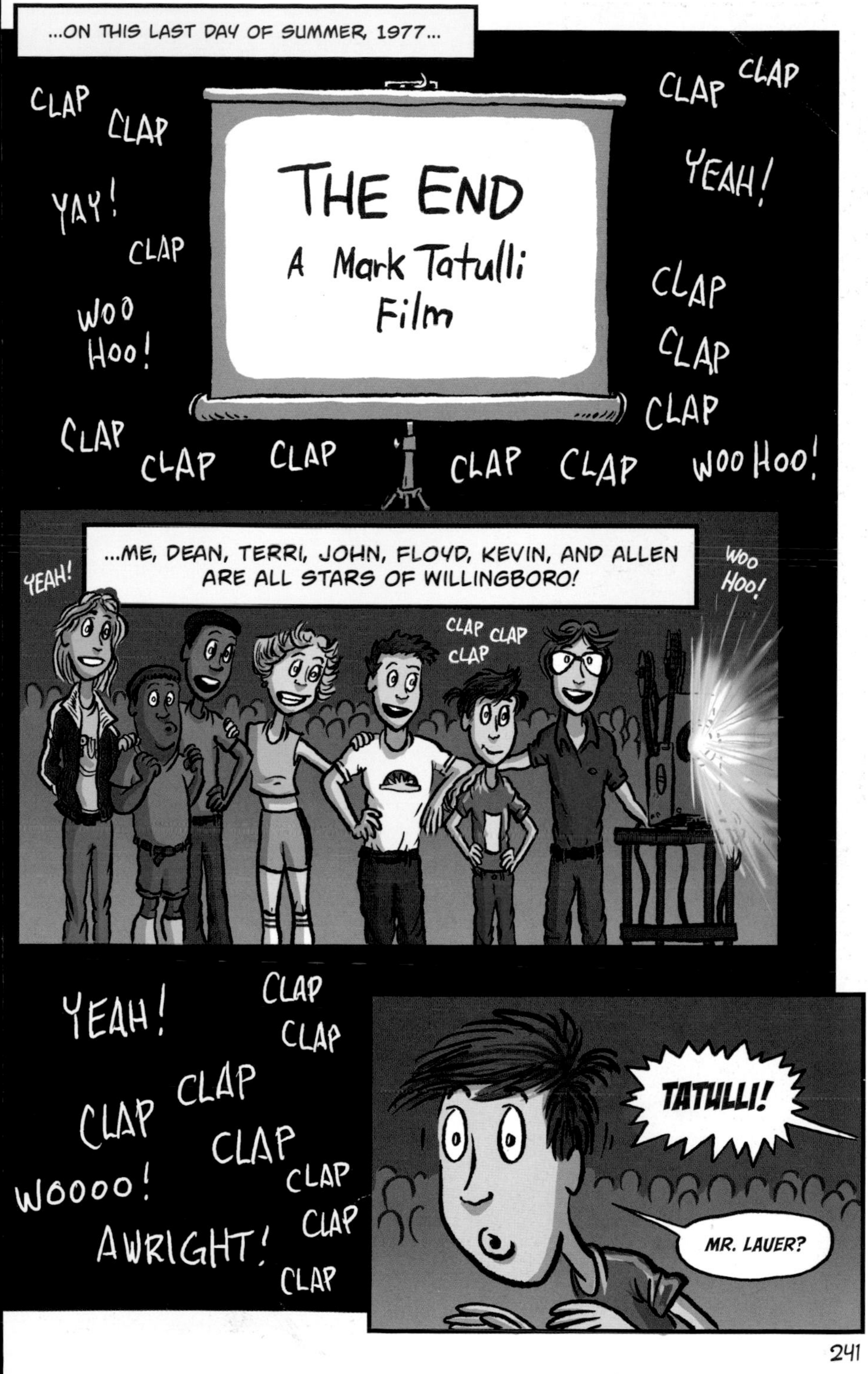
...ON THIS LAST DAY OF SUMMER, 1977...
CLAP
CLAP
YAY!
CLAP
WOO HOO!
THE END
A Mark Tatulli Film
CLAP
CLAP
YEAH!
CLAP
CLAP
CLAP
CLAP
CLAP
CLAP
CLAP
CLAP
WOO HOO!
...ME, DEAN, TERRI, JOHN, FLOYD, KEVIN, AND ALLEN ARE ALL STARS OF WILLINGBORO!
YEAH!
WOO HOO!
CLAP CLAP CLAP
YEAH!
CLAP
CLAP
CLAP
CLAP
CLAP
WOOOO!
CLAP
AWRIGHT!
CLAP
CLAP
TATULLI!
MR. LAUER?

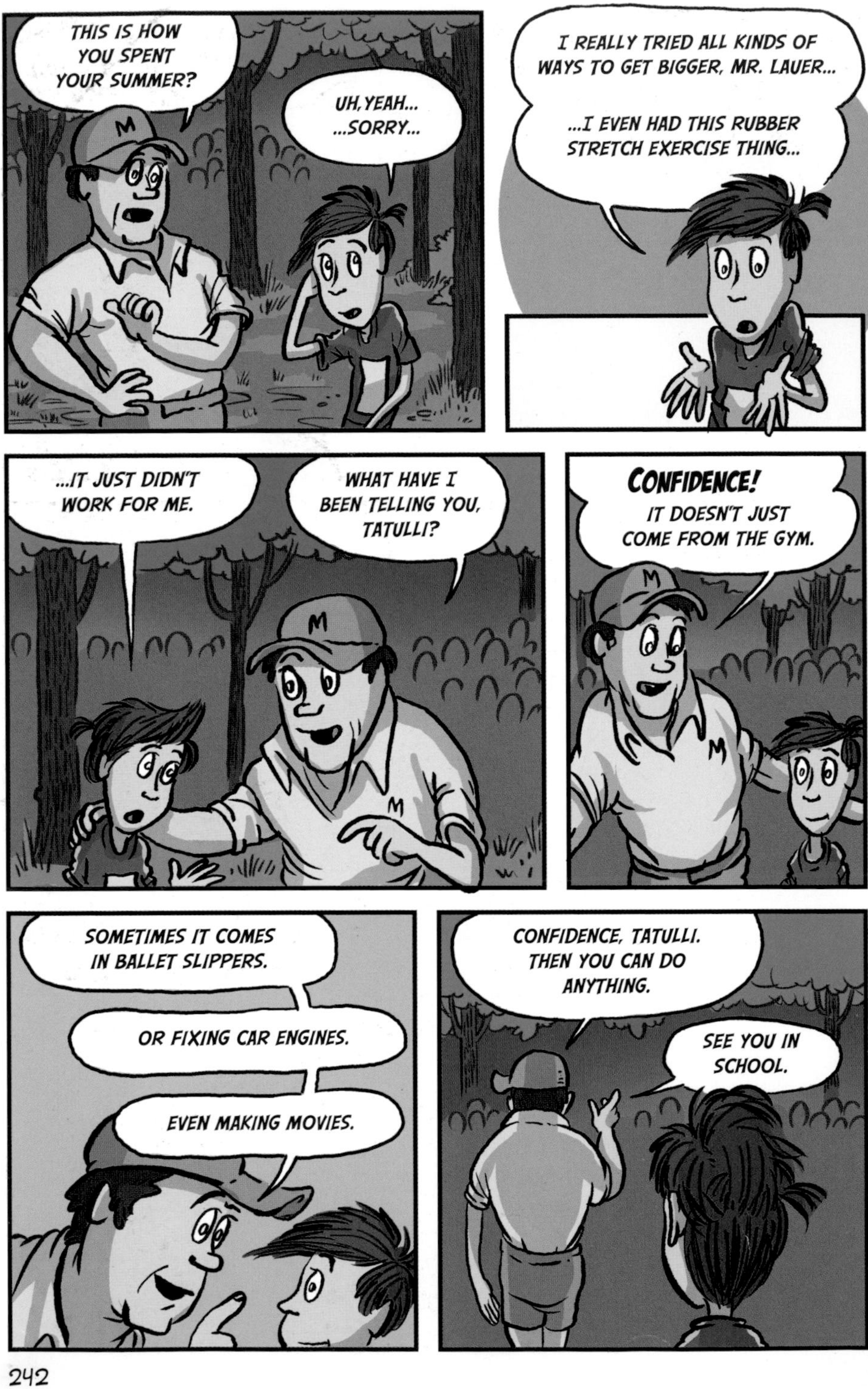
THIS IS HOW YOU SPENT YOUR SUMMER?
UH, YEAH... ...SORRY...
I REALLY TRIED ALL KINDS OF WAYS TO GET BIGGER, MR. LAUER...
...I EVEN HAD THIS RUBBER STRETCH EXERCISE THING...
...IT JUST DIDN'T WORK FOR ME.
WHAT HAVE I BEEN TELLING YOU, TATULLI?
CONFIDENCE! IT DOESN'T JUST COME FROM THE GYM.
SOMETIMES IT COMES IN BALLET SLIPPERS.
OR FIXING CAR ENGINES.
EVEN MAKING MOVIES.
CONFIDENCE, TATULLI. THEN YOU CAN DO ANYTHING.
SEE YOU IN SCHOOL.

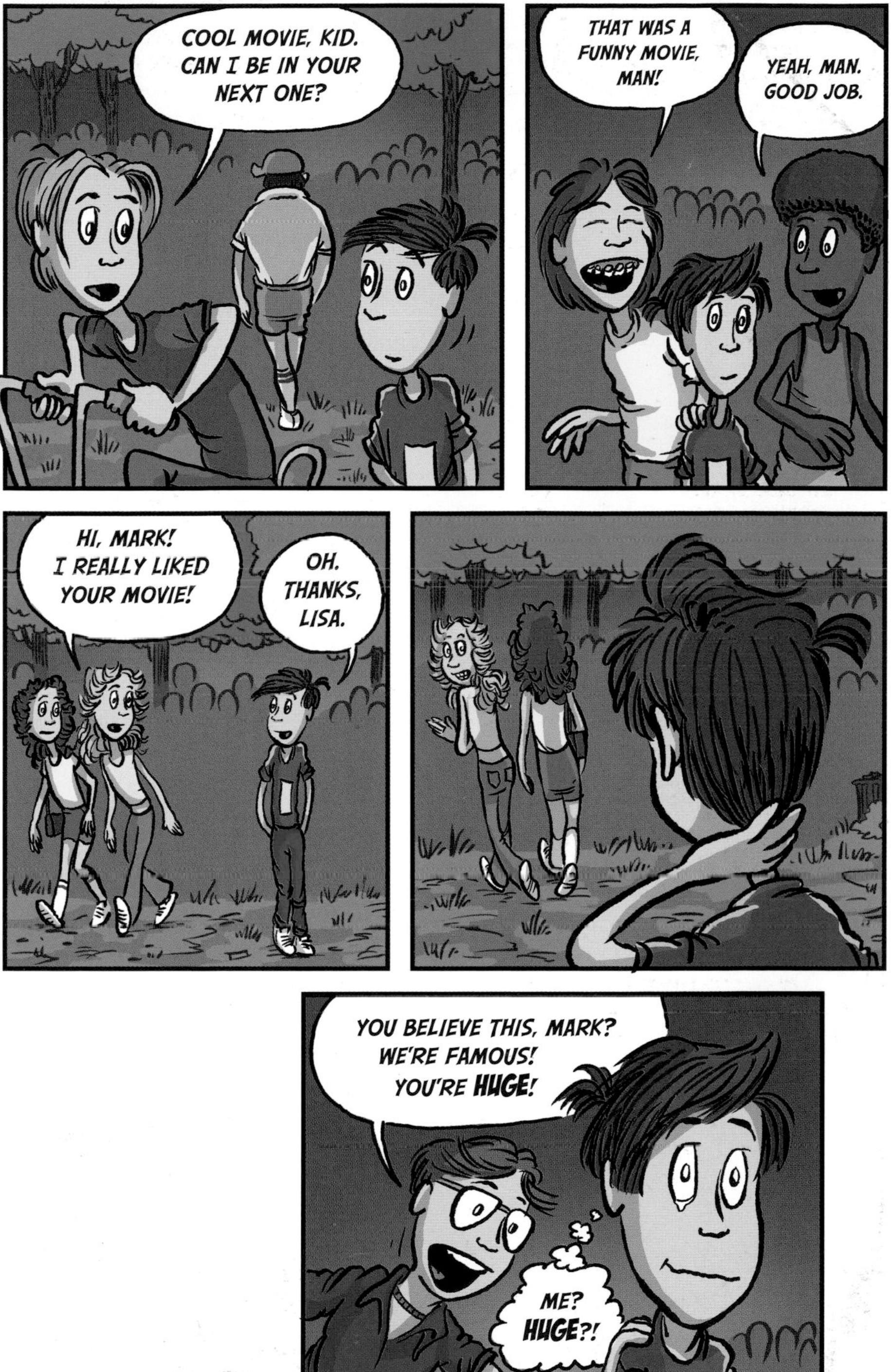
COOL MOVIE, KID. CAN I BE IN YOUR NEXT ONE?
THAT WAS A FUNNY MOVIE, MAN!
YEAH, MAN. GOOD JOB.
HI, MARK! I REALLY LIKED YOUR MOVIE!
OH. THANKS, LISA.
YOU BELIEVE THIS, MARK? WE'RE FAMOUS! YOU'RE HUGE!
ME? HUGE?!

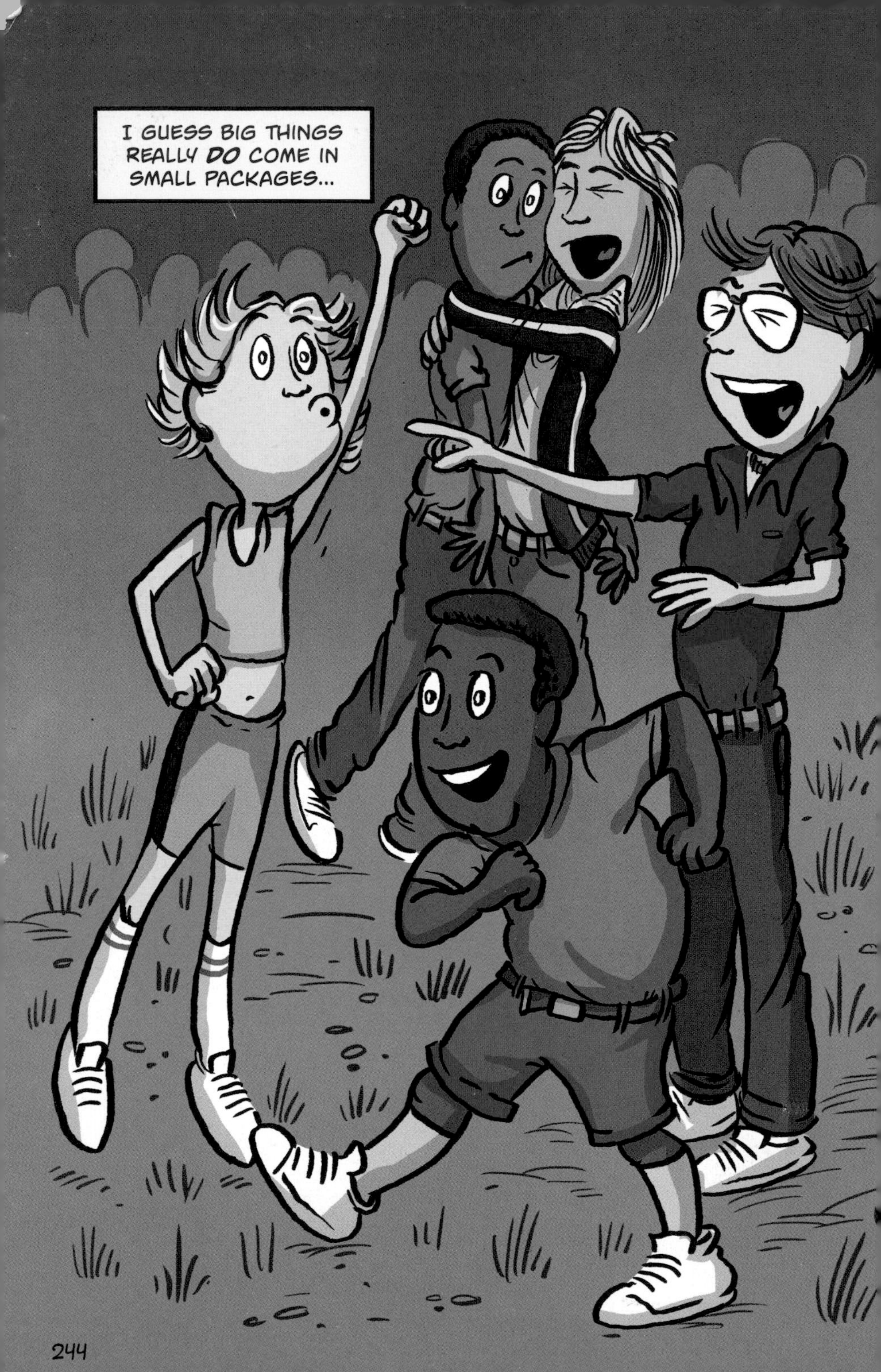
I GUESS BIG THINGS REALLY DO COME IN SMALL PACKAGES...

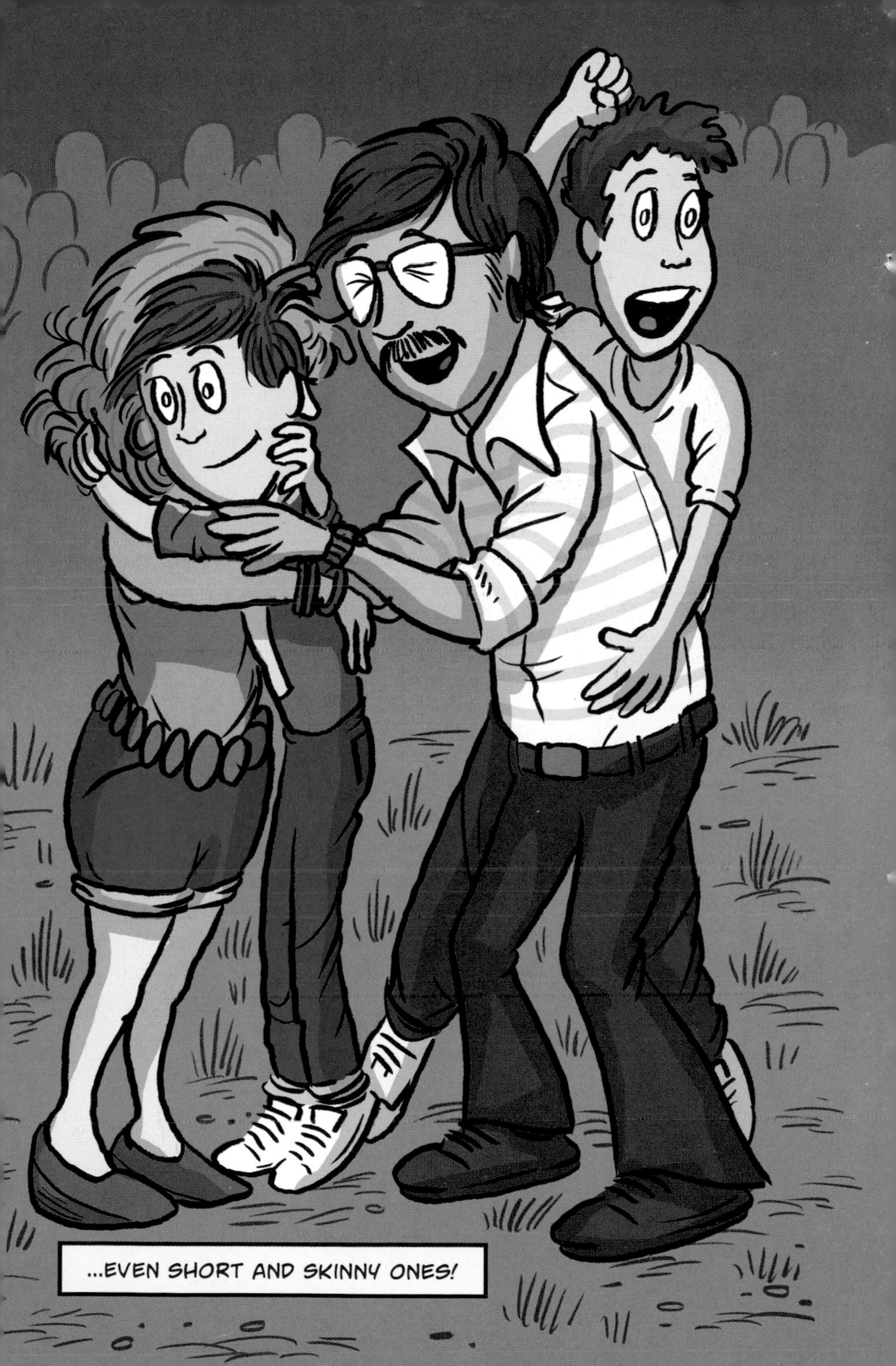
...EVEN SHORT AND SKINNY ONES!

ALLEN, KEVIN, FLOYD, AND I ALL STAYED FRIENDS THROUGH JR. HIGH AND HIGH SCHOOL. BUT THEN THEY WENT OFF TO COLLEGE AND WE LOST TOUCH. I RECENTLY RECONNECTED WITH ALLEN. HE WORKS IN COMPUTER TECHNOLOGY.

JOHN AND I REMAINED FRIENDS AND ENDED UP WORKING IN THE VIDEO/FILM BUSINESS TOGETHER (WE DIDN'T GO TO COLLEGE). HE WAS THE BEST MAN AT MY WEDDING AND NOW OWNS AND OPERATES HIS OWN VIDEO/STAGING BUSINESS.

TERRI STOPPED SWIMMING COMPETITIVELY WHEN SHE HAD SHOULDER SURGERY AFTER ALL THE YEARS OF HER AWARD-WINNING BUTTERFLY STROKE. SHE NOW LIVES QUIETLY IN THE SUBURBS NEAR WILLINGBORO AND HAS A SON WHO'S STUDYING CARTOON ANIMATION. AND SHE STILL HAS ALL HER RIBBONS!

SADLY, BOTH MY BROTHER, DEAN, AND FATHER HAVE PASSED AWAY...

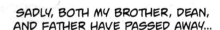

DEAN LOST HIS BATTLE WITH CANCER AT AGE 23, HIS LAST YEAR OF COLLEGE. I'LL NEVER FORGET HOW HE TRIED TO LIFT MY SPIRITS WHEN I WAS DOWN, BUT ALWAYS IN HIS ANNOYING BROTHER WAY—WITH A PUNCH AND A HEADLOCK!

246

AFTER "STAR BORES," MY DAD CONTINUED TO SUPPORT MY FILMS AND CREATIVE PROJECTS. HE BOUGHT ME MY FIRST SINGLE-FRAME ANIMATION CAMERA, WHICH LED TO MY LOVE OF STOP-MOTION AND MY FIRST JOB IN THE FILM BUSINESS!

HE PASSED AWAY IN 2013.

MY MOM STILL LIVES IN WILLINGBORO WITH A BUNCH OF CATS! MY SISTER, TERRI, SEES HER MORE THAN I DO, BUT SHE ALWAYS SUPPORTS MY CARTOONS AND WRITING WHENEVER WE TALK.

AND SHE STILL CALLS ME SPARK FAT.

AND ME...

I MADE A CAREER IN FILM AND TELEVISION, WHERE I WORKED FOR THIRTY YEARS! AND THOUGH I NEVER DID WIN ANY SWIMMING RIBBONS, I WON THREE EMMY AWARDS FOR MY TELEVISION ANIMATION.

NOW I DRAW AND WRITE TWO SYNDICATED COMIC STRIPS, AND ALL KINDS OF KIDS' BOOKS.

AND I'M STILL SHORT BUT NOT QUITE SO SKINNY...

AND I DON'T CARE!

BY THE WAY, I NEVER DID STOP LOOKING FOR MY BIKE THUNDERBOLT...

...I KEEP THINKING HE'S JUST SITTING SOMEWHERE WAITING TO BE RESCUED...

...BUT THAT'S ANOTHER STORY.